KINGS OF THE GARDEN

The New York Knicks and Their City

ADAM J. CRIBLEZ

AN IMPRINT OF CORNELL UNIVERSITY PRESS

ITHACA AND LONDON

First published 2024 by Cornell University Press

Printed in the United States of America

Library of Congress Cataloging-in-Publication Data

Names: Criblez, Adam, author.
Title: Kings of the Garden : the New York Knicks and their city / Adam J.
    Criblez.
Description: Ithaca : Three Hills, Cornell University Press, 2024. |
    Includes bibliographical references and index.
Identifiers: LCCN 2023034138 (print) | LCCN 2023034139 (ebook) |
    ISBN 9781501773938 (hardcover) | ISBN 9781501774461 (epub) |
    ISBN 9781501774478 (pdf)
Subjects: LCSH: New York Knickerbockers (Basketball team)—
    History—20th century. | Basketball—New York (State)—New York—
    History—20th century. | Basketball—Social aspects—New York
    (State)—New York. | Hip-hop—History—20th century. | New York
    (N.Y.)—History—1951-
Classification: LCC GV885.52.N4 C75 2024 (print) | LCC GV885.52.
    N4 (ebook) | DDC 796.323/64097471—dc23/eng/20231023
LC record available at https://lccn.loc.gov/2023034138
LC ebook record available at https://lccn.loc.gov/2023034139

CONTENTS

PREFACE

Ever since I was a young boy, I have connected professional basketball, the New York Knicks, and Black culture. It began sometime in 1992, when I played the video game Tecmo NBA Basketball, in which an unstoppable Patrick Ewing was paired with sharpshooting guard John Starks and imposing forwards Xavier McDaniel, Charles Oakley, and Anthony Mason. Around the same time, I first heard Dr. Dre's "Nuthin' but a 'G' Thang." For me, as a white middle-class suburbanite teenager, that song was incredibly cutting-edge. Soon after, a friend introduced me to the Beastie Boys' "So What'cha Want," with their music video featuring Mike D in an old school Knicks shirt, and a few years later the soundtrack for the film *Friday* became one of my favorite albums (thanks, Boof), and NBA Jam hit Super Nintendo. Not only was the Knicks trio of Ewing, Mason, and Starks—my favorite team—available to play in that game (lots of "Boomshakalaka" dunks), the Beastie Boys were secret playable characters too.

Then, for more than a decade, my basketball and hip-hop fandom waned. I went to college and graduate school, got married and started a family, and wrote a dissertation on a "real" history topic (nineteenth-century midwestern Independence Day celebrations). After that I won the academic lottery and landed a tenure-track position at Southeast Missouri State University teaching courses on the American Civil War and Missouri history. But when I started teaching a class to freshmen student-athletes who were far more engaged when we discussed sports in the context of history than politics or economics, I realized I could use sports to effectively contextualize American history. Within a few years, sport history became my primary academic focus.

While writing a book about the growth of the National Basketball Association during the 1970s, titled *Tall Tales and Short Shorts*, I stumbled across a 1979 column written by Peter Vecsey that used the term "N-----bocker" in reference to the 1979–80 Knicks, the league's first all-Black team. I was shocked. But I also knew I had found the seeds of the next story I wanted to tell.

As a teenager, my first exposure to Black culture came by way of Dr. Dre and the NBA. But after reading Vecsey's column and digging deeper into the history of rap, graffiti, and b-boying, I understood that this rise of intersecting Black culture—which included pro basketball and hip-hop—in New York City during the late seventies and early eighties was so important to the history of both sport and America.

ACKNOWLEDGMENTS

I have loved researching and writing about New York City and the Knicks. But without the support and encouragement of many, many people, this book would not exist. First, thanks to those I interviewed to better understand this era in Knicks' basketball: Harvey Araton, Butch Beard, Hubie Brown, Don Buse, Bill Cartwright, Jim Cleamons, Dave Cowens, Mel Davis, Len Elmore, Mike Glenn, John Hewig, Freddie Lewis, Mel Lowell, Rudy Macklin, Brendan Malone, Bob McAdoo, Bob Netolicky, Campy Russell, Rory Sparrow, Trent Tucker, Darrell Walker, Tom Werblin, and Harthorne Wingo. I can't tell you how much I appreciate the time each of you spent telling stories about your connections to the Knicks.

I would also like to thank my colleagues both at Southeast Missouri State University and those who attended the North American Society for Sport History conferences for their valuable input as the project developed. Similarly, thank you to the anonymous readers whose feedback helped me fine-tune the arguments and my writing. I would also like to thank Michael McGandy, Mahinder Kingra, and the team at Three Hills for shepherding this project through the laborious process of making a manuscript into a book. To Susan Welker—the queen of interlibrary loan—thank you for diligently tracking down obscure books, newspapers, and magazine articles.

To my parents, Roger and Anita Criblez, thank you for buying me Tecmo NBA Basketball and NBA Jam. You did some other cool stuff too. And finally, to my amazing wife Jennie and three daughters—Avery, Eliza, and Charlotte: my love and eternal thanks for supporting my obsession with a sport you aren't overly fond of.

KINGS OF THE GARDEN

Introduction

"Garden of Eden"

June 18, 1985—Madison Square Garden: Manhattan

"The New York Knicks, with the first pick," Commissioner David Stern began, a slight smile creasing the corners of his clean-shaven face, "select Patrick Ewing of Georgetown." Cameras cut away to a packed Felt Forum in Madison Square Garden for the 1985 National Basketball Association (NBA) draft, where Knicks fans cheered, pumped their fists, and broke into spontaneous chants of "Pa-trick! Pa-trick!"

Ewing, seated in the front row, unfolded his seven-foot-tall frame and walked to the stage, where he posed for photographs with Stern and Knicks executive Dave DeBusschere, holding a white number thirty-three jersey in front of his tailored gray suit. Over the next fifteen years, Ewing would lead the Knicks to a pair of NBA Finals appearances while carving out a career that ended in eleven All-Star appearances as well as a spot on the league's 50th Anniversary All-Time Team.

Looking back, for Knicks fans the Ewing Era would be a Silver Age: an almost dynasty.

May 5, 1973—The Forum: Inglewood, California

A dozen years before Ewing arrived on the scene, the Knicks were on top of the basketball world after winning their second NBA title in four seasons. Their victims in 1973, just as they had been three years earlier, were the flashy Los Angeles Lakers of Jerry West and Wilt Chamberlain. These Knicks, led by Willis Reed, Bill Bradley, Earl Monroe, Walt Frazier, and DeBusschere himself, who was then an all-star power forward, captivated New Yorkers with their unselfishness and moxie.

Madison Square Garden (a metaphorical Eden) was always full for home games, as fans incessantly chanted "De-fense! De-fense!" to urge on their hometown heroes. Dozens of books, headlined by Harvey Araton's *When the Garden Was Eden* (and Michael Rapaport's ESPN documentary of the same title), chronicle this period: the Golden Age of Knicks basketball.

In the decade or so between the end of the Golden Age and the beginning of the Silver Age, the Knicks struggled to maintain consistent on-court success. As Thomas Rogers wrote in the *New York Times*, "Madison Square Garden, which used to be a sort of Garden of Eden for the Knicks seems now to have turned into a torture chamber."[1] From 1973 to 1985, the franchise failed to return to the finals and missed the playoffs about as often as they made them. Player turnover hurt team chemistry while retirements of core Knicks players and replacements unable (or unwilling) to embrace the Knicks' style of play marked the end of a short-lived dynasty. And in the front office, the combined efforts of dozens of team executives failed to continue the success of the franchise as the league expanded from seventeen teams to twenty-three in the post-ABA-merger era. The Knicks were not alone in their ineptitude; many teams failed to adjust, and the era became largely remembered (if at all) for its lack of dynasties and star power, resulting in relative parity and fan apathy. Simply put, what had worked to build a dynasty in the early seventies did not work as free agency arrived mid-decade.

During this in-between era, no NBA team better epitomized the struggles of a developing Black culture in the United States than these Knicks. By the late seventies, most pro basketball players were African American; in 1979, the Knicks fielded the first all-Black team in NBA history. Locally, sportswriter Peter Vecsey quoted an unnamed source who called the team the "N-----bockers," an offensive term with which many white ethnic New Yorkers might have agreed; nationally, NBA owners debated the pros and cons of having so many dark-skinned players on their rosters while trying to appeal to their (mostly white) fan base as white backlash in opposition to measures like affirmative action propelled Ronald Reagan to the Oval Office. NBA attendance and TV ratings plummeted in this era, and no team witnessed a larger downturn than the Knicks. Free agency arrived, and the Knicks spent lavishly (and usually screwed up). Player salaries skyrocketed—again New York set the pace. Drug use among African Americans rose in the late seventies and early eighties, peaking with the crack epidemic of the mid-eighties, so it is fitting that two of the most high-profile drug users in the NBA, Spencer Haywood and Micheal Ray Richardson, developed cocaine habits in New York City as members of the Knicks.

This was a gritty period in the Knicks' hometown as well. Films like *Taxi Driver* and *Fort Apache: The Bronx* impart a sense of impending apocalypse in Gotham, particularly in the South Bronx, which came to symbolize "America's 'inner city' . . . an iconography of urban ruin in America."[2] The nation was facing a rising tide of conservatism, a drug epidemic, and a perceived urban crisis. In 1975, disgruntled cops handed out pamphlets that read "Welcome to Fear City," guidebooks for tourists hoping to escape Manhattan alive and unmugged.[3] Mayors Abe Beame and Ed Koch struggled through a crippling financial crisis while middle-class families continued their decades-old abandonment of the city for suburban safety. President Gerald Ford famously refused to bail out the near-bankrupt municipality, prompting the *Daily News* to print a headline proclaiming, "Ford to City: Drop Dead." An electrical blackout in July 1977 resulted in widespread looting, and arson that fall led to the apocryphal call that that the Bronx was burning. Crime, drugs, and white flight gutted the inner city while flashing neon signs advertising peep shows and X-rated movies lit up a lurid Times Square.

Still, not all was doom and gloom. Although disco music would later become a target of ridicule and scorn, it blossomed in downtown clubs like Studio 54 and reached its zenith with the 1977 hit movie *Saturday Night Fever*, set in Brooklyn. The influence of disco stretched far beyond wearing white polyester leisure suits and dancing the Hustle, however. It helped inspire a generation of impoverished young Black and Latin American men and women in the South Bronx to create a musical genre, later dubbed rap, within a new cultural phenomenon known as hip-hop. Deejays remixed disco records and competed against one another for turf, wiring their sound systems into the light poles of city parks so parties could last late into the night. Within a decade, this antiestablishment, countercultural musical style blending disco, funk, and R&B became the voice of a generation—much like rock 'n' roll or Motown in previous decades—exported globally and becoming as recognizably American as McDonald's and Michael Jordan.

By the early eighties, the two most forward-facing outlets of Black culture were professional basketball and hip-hop. Each was a potential avenue of advancement and recognition for young men of color.

On outdoor basketball courts, like Rucker Park in Harlem or The Cage in Greenwich Village, near the deejay stands where musical history was being made, another element of this evolving Black culture developed. There legendary basketball playground battles took place, sometimes featuring Knicks players in attendance or even lacing up sneakers to play. Knicks legend Earl Monroe was dubbed "The Pearl" by white media seeking an alliterative nickname, but on the playground, among Black fans and commentators, Monroe was known as "Black Magic."

Monroe was just one of the future Hall of Famers on the Knicks teams in the era after Eden. Although the franchise lacked consistent success, there were moments of transcendent individual brilliance. As a Knick, Monroe showcased his refined playground style, dipping, ducking, and spinning his way to more than seventeen thousand career points while Walt Frazier—the undisputed king of style in the league during the seventies—earned nearly a dozen All-NBA and All-Defensive team honors. Bob McAdoo was one of the greatest shooters in league history and, at six foot ten, was far ahead of his time as a "stretch center." When sober, Haywood was a nightly double-double threat, and Richardson became the first player in league history to lead the NBA in both assists and steals for a season. And then there was Christmas Day, 1984, when Bernard King dropped 60 points on the New Jersey Nets, setting a franchise record that would last for nearly three decades.

The cast of characters (Black and white) the Knicks employed during this era is almost unbelievable. Haywood told reporters he would save the Knicks when he arrived in '75; five years later, he was playing for the Lakers and, struggling with a cocaine addiction, arranged to have someone murder his head coach. Frazier and Monroe formed the celebrated Rolls-Royce backcourt, epitomizing style on and off the court. Bill Bradley would convey his popularity as a Knick who was supposed to be a white savior into a US Senate seat and a run for the presidency; his good friend Phil Jackson would win eleven championship rings coaching the Chicago Bulls and Los Angeles Lakers. King electrified New Yorkers with his near superhuman scoring skills but also faced allegations of alcoholism and sexual assault and, just three months after his prolific Christmas night scoring outburst, blew out his knee and played only six more games as a Knick. Richardson, nicknamed Sugar, struggled with a pronounced stutter and once told reporters, in response to a team losing streak, "the ship be sinking." When asked how low it could sink, he shrugged and said, "The sky's the limit." A few years later, Richardson would become one of the first players banned from the NBA for violating the league's substance abuse policy. He claimed his suspension was racially motivated to scare white players into quitting.

Team executives and coaches were no less colorful. Sonny Werblin managed the club on behalf of Gulf & Western for most of the decade after a career spent running a multimillion-dollar talent agency. He also once owned the American Football League's New York Jets and famously signed Joe Namath to an AFL contract in 1965. Werblin was energetic and blunt, firing one head coach for supposedly issuing him an ultimatum, and remained close friends with President Reagan during the ex-actor's time in the Oval Office.

Mike Burke, another team executive, led an almost unbelievable life; he tried out for the Philadelphia Eagles in 1941, served in the navy during World War II, married into the Ringling family (of circus fame), spied in Europe for the CIA during the Cold War, helped produce the film *Cloak and Dagger* based on his wartime experiences, battled Jimmy Hoffa's Teamsters on behalf of his family's circus, and bought and sold the

Yankees (to George Steinbrenner) before running both Madison Square Garden and the Knicks.[4]

Red Holzman was a Jewish man from Brooklyn who played pro basketball even before there was an NBA. Red had two stints as the Knicks' head coach before being replaced by Hubie Brown, now best known as an analyst but then a fiery, gravelly voiced coach who yelled and cursed unmercifully at his players.

I was fortunate enough to interview dozens of these Knicks players and executives, and their voices, augmented by extensive newspaper and magazine reports, provide an authentic, firsthand account of a team during a time of transformation in New York City.

Between 1973 and 1985, the Knicks fell from the top of the league to the bottom before slowly rising back into contention. They never attained the success of their championship squads as roster turnover, underperforming superstars, and a desire by the front office for short-term success trumped long-term franchise building. In some ways, their struggles mirrored those facing New York City over the same span. In the midseventies, as the Knicks lost more games than they won, the city was on the brink of bankruptcy thanks to short-sighted city officials, while street gangs and urban disinvestment created what *Ebony* magazine called "the crisis of the Black spirit."[5] By the end of the decade the budget was balanced, the Knicks were an all-Black squad, and rap music spilled out of the South Bronx and became the musical expression of the young, Black hip-hop generation. By the end of this era, the Knicks and the NBA began using hip-hop as integrationist music to appeal to both Black and white fans as the league emerged as a global enterprise. During the 1980s, Black men helped spur two global cultural phenomena, hip-hop and professional basketball, which became dominant elements of Black culture. In both, Black men provided creativity, maintained positions of leadership, and promoted commercialism around the world. The nexus of this story is the Knicks and New York City between the mid-seventies and mid-eighties.

But just as the Knicks' efforts at creating a new dynasty fell short, so too did this vision of unification through music and sports. People of color remained impoverished in the South Bronx; Mayor Koch's neoconservative politics targeted poor Black families; and the crack epidemic of the late eighties "turned Gotham into Gomorrah," even as Knicks players struggled through their own drug addictions.[6] And so, as both New York City and the Knicks struggled against many setbacks during the era after Eden, they came to collectively symbolize all that was right (and wrong) with the league, city, and nation.

1

"Then I'll Save"

1973–1975

In the Hall of Fame Lounge, up a short flight of stairs from the main lobby in Madison Square Garden, a dozen newspaper reporters held pens poised above notebooks, eagerly awaiting the arrival of the newest New York Knick. Seven years earlier, the team traded for Dave DeBusschere, who helped them win two NBA titles. Now, in October 1975, Knicks fans hoped another young veteran forward could revive the team's flagging fortunes.

Six-foot-eight Spencer Haywood certainly looked the part. He towered over the reporters, not to mention the team officials sent to introduce him to the press. Haywood was an Olympic hero and five-time All-Star at the peak of his physical prime. A year earlier, Muhammad Ali and Joe Frazier almost came to blows in the lounge before their January 1974 "Super Fight II." But on this day calm prevailed: journalists tossed Haywood a few easy questions, and he supplied the expected answers, declaring his intent to blend into the traditional Knick style." "I'm going to study the films of the Knick games and ask questions." Blah, blah, blah. Haywood even requested DeBusschere's uniform number twenty-two, explaining, "I want to do what [he] did for the Knicks." Team president Mike Burke ran his hands through his silver hair and chuckled, promising the reporters, "Spence can have anything he wants."[1]

What happened next has become part of Knicks legend. One of the reporters—maybe Sam Goldaper, covering the press conference for the *Times*, or perhaps Mike Lupica, representing the *Post*—asked Haywood what he thought about being the Knicks' savior. The All-Star forward grinned and said, "then I'll save."[2] Perhaps realizing he'd gone too far, Haywood quickly backtracked. "Being called a savior is a pretty heavy role. We're all saviors. My role," he reiterated, "will be to blend in with traditional Knick style."[3] Years later, Haywood reflected on his original statement. "One or two of the Knicks seemed to feel I came off a little too arrogant," he said. "If this team picked itself up and flew, [Walt Frazier] would be at least the co-savior and probably the senior savior."[4]

Why did New York need a savior in the fall of 1975? The Knicks ruled pro basketball earlier in the decade, winning two NBA titles powered by six Hall of Fame players and a Hall of Fame head coach, while Madison Square Garden was arguably the most iconic basketball court in the world. Movie stars like Dustin Hoffman, Woody Allen, and Robert Redford sat courtside for dramatic moments like Willis Reed gamely taking the floor before game seven of the 1970 NBA Finals despite a torn thigh muscle. Even rival players wanted to play in New York. Freddie Lewis, then a member of the American Basketball Association's Indiana Pacers, told me, "There were times that I wished I was on their team. They looked like they were living the greatest life that the NBA could offer."[5]

The 1970 Knicks rank among the most memorable NBA champions of all-time, with dozens of books written about their first league title. But the '73 team, which added future Hall of Famers Jerry Lucas and Earl "The Pearl" Monroe to the mix, was probably even better. "With this new infusion of talent," reserve forward Phil Jackson remembered, "we morphed into a more versatile team than we'd ever been before. We had more size and depth, a broader array of scoring options than the 1969–70 team, plus the perfect blend of individual skill and team consciousness."[6] Woody Allen watched many games from his usual seat just behind the scorer's table and believed that the '73 Knicks "were just such a perfect blend of art and science that they fulfilled every desire the most picayune fan could have."[7]

Picayune or not, Knicks fans worshipped the title winners long after the players retired. When DeBusschere rejoined the team as an executive in the eighties, he still answered to calls on the street of "Hey, Dave, De-fense!" with a smile and a wave. Archie Bunker, the quintessential New Yorker (as a fictional character hailing from Queens), was a huge Knicks fan and in one episode of *All in the Family* gave his wife Edith a pair of tickets for their twenty-fifth wedding anniversary. Edith was not impressed, but Spike Lee, then a teenage filmmaker, would have been. In his 1997 memoir, Spike explained the passion New Yorkers felt for their team. "We're hungry. We're loud. We boo. We shout. We are dyed-in-the-wool, unregenerate, no flip-flopping Knicks fans."[8] Spike would know—he snuck into the Garden many times to cheer on the Knicks during their title runs in the early seventies, including once while thirteen years old after blowing off his father's jazz concert to see Reed's remarkable game seven performance.[9]

But there was no bigger Knicks fan in the early seventies, at least as far as it helped his political aspirations, than New York City mayor John Lindsay. Lindsay was Gotham's answer to John F. Kennedy: young, good-looking, and ambitious. Sure, he was probably not as popular as DeBusschere, Reed, or the rest of the Knicks, but who was? And sure, he let the city spiral toward bankruptcy by expanding city services even as the local tax base eroded, but he still won re-election in 1969. In 1972, he ran for the presidency but abandoned the race during the primaries amid accusations of neglecting city business while traveling to solicit votes. There was no better way to rebuild community goodwill than by hitching his wagon to the "Garden of Eden" Knicks.

And so, on May 15, 1973, Lindsay hosted a celebration at City Hall Plaza, presenting the title-winning players and coaches with diamond jubilee medals commemorating the seventy-fifth anniversary of the formation of New York City. "What better symbol," the *Times* asked, "than the five-man-team-minded Knicks could there be to celebrate the anniversary of the five-borough consolidation."[10] Lindsay also earned a few laughs in his proclamation, citing his own unsuccessful presidential campaign as proof that "it's not so easy to win on the road."[11]

All in all, 1973 was a magical year for Knicks fans. Future Knick Mike Glenn dubbed them "America's team" because of "how they shared the ball [and] moved the ball."[12] Longtime fan George Lois said they brought a "romance to [the game], the pure love of an unusual team that basketball hadn't seen before," wistfully adding, "you didn't have to think too much about Richard fucking Nixon."[13] In fact, Watergate hearings started just two days after Lindsay's celebration, and Nixon would resign shortly after the 1973–74 NBA season.

In the spring of '73, there was no reason for fans to believe that they were nearing the end of the Knicks' Golden Age. Sure, some journalists joked that the team was made up of basketball's senior citizens, better suited for canes than championship rings. But with minimal roster turnover and continued good health, the Knicks should have remained the team to beat for at least a few more seasons.

Then DeBusschere dropped a bombshell.

In June, DeBusschere announced that the 1973–74 season would be his last and that, after retiring, he would run the American Basketball Association's New York Nets. The ABA, founded six years earlier, was emerging as a legitimate challenger to the NBA, and Nets forward Julius Erving, Dr. J., was a budding superstar making headlines in New York newspapers for his high-flying performances. Was this a conflict of interest? DeBusschere didn't think so. "The Knicks still will be my main job," he told reporters. "But I'll be concerned with the Nets the way most people are concerned about their investments in the stock market."[14] It was a bad comparison; at the time, the stock market was in one of the worst downturns since the Great Depression and, perhaps more importantly for Knicks fans, the team lacked replacement options for their All-Star forward.

The Knicks remained a talented bunch heading into the season. At guard, Monroe and Frazier (both twenty-eight) were entering their physical primes. Monroe was a Philadelphia playground legend nicknamed "Thomas Edison" (for his inventiveness) in addition to "Black Magic" and "Earl the Pearl." He had deked and spun his way to two All-Star appearances with the Baltimore Bullets—teammate Ray Scott proclaimed that "God couldn't go one-on-one against Earl Monroe"—before a shocking 1971 trade sent the Pearl to the Big Apple, where he gamely accepted a secondary role.[15] "It took a little while for Clyde and

I to click as a tandem," Monroe admitted later.[16] But by 1973 the Rolls-Royce backcourt was firing on all cylinders.

Forwards DeBusschere and Bill Bradley were a little older—thirty-three and thirty respectively—but both were named to the 1973 All-Star team. The Knicks knew DeBusschere was retiring, and Bradley's future was always up in the air; he played on a series of one-year contracts, and rumors of a congressional run made the rounds every off-season. Future Hall of Fame centers Jerry Lucas and Willis Reed had combined to average 21 points and 16 rebounds during the championship season, despite struggling with injuries, and rounded out the team's top six. The Knicks and their fans were hopeful they could put together another title run.

Patrolling from the sideline, fifty-three-year-old Red Holzman was one of the best coaches in the game. On defense, Red reminded his players to "see the ball," and on offense, to "find the open man." He had joined the Knicks as an assistant coach in 1958 and had 299 career wins as head coach going into the 1973–74 season. Red's low-key persona perfectly fit the veteran squad. Jack Ramsay, a fellow NBA coach, explained, "Red would come into your building, kick your ass, and tell the local media what a great job you were doing."[17] Or, as one journalist remembered, "someone once asked Holzman what he would consider a real disaster." Red thought for a second and said, in a nasally New York deadpan, "Coming home and finding we have run out of scotch."[18] The old Knicks also knew where not to drink on road trips. According to Bradley, Red had three rules: "See the ball, hit the open man, and if you guys want a drink, go someplace else—the hotel bar is mine."[19]

Holzman's Knicks were led by Reed, the team captain who won the 1970 MVP award, but by 1973 the captain was no longer the Knicks' best player. That honor belonged to Frazier. Nicknamed Clyde because of his affinity for a style of hat made famous by Warren Beatty in the 1967 film *Bonnie and Clyde*, Frazier was a powerful point guard—six foot four and nearly two hundred pounds—whose lockdown defensive skills and quick hands earned him seven straight All-Defense awards. "Clyde," teammate Bill Hosket joked, "is the only man who can strip a car while it's going forty miles an hour."[20]

Frazier also had style in spades. Decked out in a crushed velvet suit and platform shoes, he would "pat down his 'burns" and "mash down his 'stache" before making his grand entrance into a party.[21] Clyde rarely drank alcohol but loved hanging out at hip joints like Smalls Paradise and regularly closed them down at three or four in the morning.[22] Frazier, who was married for two years while in his early twenties, was one of New York City's most eligible bachelors for much of the seventies. In 1975, *Jet* magazine interviewed Clyde after he told reporters he admired Italian actress Sophia Loren; he promised readers, "I dig Black girls more."[23]

On the court, Clyde was just as cool. "The louder the Garden got," Spike Lee remembers, "the calmer—and quicker—Frazier became."[24] Clyde seemed to play at the same speed all game, picking his spots carefully. He would launch his turnaround jump shot a half-inch above an opponent's outstretched fingertips and steal the ball when the dribbler glanced away for a split second. Whether or not Clyde was the best guard in the NBA was debatable; that he was the best New York Knick was not.

The Knicks kicked off the '73–74 season with an opening-night win over the Detroit Pistons, giving Holzman 300 for his Knicks career. But the team struggled over the next several weeks, including an embarrassing 85–69 loss to the Chicago Bulls, their lowest point total since the NBA had introduced the shot clock twenty years earlier. Fans unfortunate enough to witness the event in person loudly booed.[25] At least those attending the game missed the latest news; Watergate's "Saturday Night Massacre" dominated broadcasts that evening, as both the attorney general and assistant attorney general resigned rather than follow Nixon's order to fire the Watergate special prosecutor.

A few days later, the boobirds were out again as the Knicks lost to the Capital (formerly Baltimore) Bullets, one of their biggest rivals. After the game, a frustrated Reed, who hobbled around for sixteen ineffectual minutes off the bench, was uncharacteristically blunt. "The talent is here," he said, "but you wonder what the hell is going on."[26] Knicks fans, rarely shy about expressing their emotions, were also curious about what was going on. "They're playing like they don't care," one fan complained.[27] Sure, the old Knicks never finished a season 82–0. But not seeing the ball on defense? Missing the open man on offense? That just wasn't the Knicks way.

Given the fans' pessimism, it sometimes seemed like the Knicks never won any games in the fall of 1973. But by the time the calendar turned over from 1973 to 1974, the team was 23–16. There was also some levity for Knicks fans over the holidays: during one December game "play was delayed briefly in the fourth quarter when a husky spectator in high spirits wandered onto the court, grabbed the ball and took a hook shot that missed. He spilled popcorn over the court while shooting and then fell down while chasing the ball."[28]

If any Knick was in high spirits that winter, it was DeBusschere, who was excited about playing in Detroit for the last time. He had been born and raised in a blue-collar household on the east side of the city and also been two-sport star at the University of Detroit. After college he signed with both the NBA's Pistons and Major League Baseball's Chicago White Sox, pitching professionally for three seasons before hanging up his cleats to focus full-time on hoops. In 1964, at the ripe old age of twenty-four, Detroit named DeBusschere their player-coach, making him the youngest head coach in NBA history. Four years later, the Pistons traded DeBusschere to the Knicks, but the Motor City remained home to him. When the Knicks visited the Pistons on February 1, 1974, more than eleven thousand fans packed Cobo Hall to see their hometown hero one last time. New York lost, but after the game DeBusschere received telegrams from dozens of well-wishers, including one from the White Sox scout who signed him to his first baseball contract more than a decade earlier.[29]

DeBusschere was also a huge star in New York City. Newly elected Abe Beame, who rose through the ranks of Tammany Hall to become the city's first Jewish mayor, proclaimed April 26, 1974, "Dave DeBusschere Day." "We express our admiration," Beame told DeBusschere during the ceremony, "for the skills you developed on the baseball court." The crowd laughed at the misstep, and the diminutive mayor quickly corrected himself: "the basketball court."[30]

The Knicks finished the 1973–74 season with the second-best record in the Eastern Conference and, for the sixth straight season, met the Bullets in the playoffs. The Knicks won, their fifth victory in that stretch, and earned the right to play another hated rival—the Boston Celtics—for a chance to go to the NBA Finals. To win the '73 title, New York had ruined the best regular season in Celtics history.[31] Now Boston wanted revenge.

CBS nationally televised the first game of the Eastern Conference Finals on Easter Sunday, April 14. The game was embarrassingly one-sided. John Havlicek scored 25 points and Dave Cowens chipped in 16 as the Celtics cruised to a 113–88 victory. Perhaps fearing another blowout, CBS executives decided to televise the Western Conference Finals on April 16 instead of the rematch between Boston and New York. They chose wisely; the Celtics won by a dozen.

Game three was an emotional roller coaster for Knicks fans. DeBusschere played gamely through a pulled abdominal muscle, and Frazier contributed another classic playoff performance, tallying 38 points, 10 rebounds, 4 assists, and 3 steals to help the Knicks to an important win. But after the game, Jerry Lucas announced his retirement. Once half of a feared two-headed center monster (with Reed), Lucas, a prodigious intellectual who claimed to have memorized the Manhattan phone book and aspired to be the "country's best known magician," contributed just 2 points and 0 rebounds in the Knicks victory.[32]

Game four followed an all-too-familiar pattern; New York kept the game close early, but Boston pulled away late. It would prove to be the last game DeBusschere, Lucas, or Reed would ever play in Madison Square Garden.

Headed to Boston for game five, the Celtics were clearly in control of the series. Leading 3–1, in a best-of-seven series, against a depleted Knicks team, Boston felt good about its chances to make the finals. Reed did not play (no last-minute heroics this time), Lucas did not score, and DeBusschere managed only one basket in sixteen minutes as Boston cruised to another double-digit win. Weeks later the Celtics won their twelfth NBA title after defeating Kareem Abdul-Jabbar and the Milwaukee Bucks.

After losing to the Celtics, New Yorkers uttered the common refrain: we'll get 'em next year. But in hindsight, the 1974 playoffs marked the end of the Golden Age. "We knew that was it," Frazier admitted later. "We'd had our run."[33] Decades after losing to Boston, Phil Jackson retained a strong emotional connection to that final series together. "I remember sitting in Logan Airport with my teammates after that loss," Jackson wrote, "and feeling as if our once-glorious dynasty had come to an end. Nothing was the same after that."[34]

Some Knicks fans bemoaned the end of an era, and others looked ahead to the next year, but many New Yorkers had more pressing concerns than basketball. In the 1950s, city planner Robert Moses proposed the Cross-Bronx Expressway, displacing thousands of residents to create an eight-mile-long thoroughfare.[35] The area bisected by the Cross-Bronx, and the surrounding neighborhoods, slumped into an economic depression as families were forcibly evicted or reduced to living in poverty. During the sixties, this area—much of it encompassing the South Bronx—gradually fell into disrepair. "It happened so slowly," one longtime resident remembered, "that I wasn't even aware of changes until one day I decided to take a walk around the block and discovered we had no block. Then I decided to take a walk around the neighborhood and found that we had no neighborhood."[36]

By the time the Knicks made their title runs in the early seventies, residents of the South Bronx earned half of what other New Yorkers made, suffered disproportionately from malnutrition and infant mortality, and witnessed a resurgence in gang activity that was, at least in part, race-based: Black gangs battled their Latinx counterparts for racial supremacy and street credibility.[37] In 1973, Moses admitted, "This Bronx slum and others in Brooklyn and Manhattan are unrepairable. They are beyond rebuilding, tinkering and restoring. They must be leveled to the ground."[38] Residents responded bitterly. As Luis Cedeño (better known as DJ Disco Wiz, the self-proclaimed first Latino hip-hop deejay) recalled, "the politicians treated the Bronx and the people in it as disposable."[39]

Gangs were a part of the fabric of life in the South Bronx and, for many young men and women, served as surrogate families, providing structure for runaways or children from broken homes.[40] As one member of the Savage Skulls explained, "We like to stay together . . . that's the only way we can survive out here, because if we all go our own ways, one by one, we're gone."[41] Violent turf wars erupted throughout South Bronx neighborhoods as the Savage Skulls battled the Savage Seven, Black Spades, and dozens of other factions for territory and social status. At their peak, more than three hundred gangs claiming over nineteen thousand members ruled the city streets.[42]

But even as gang activity increased, a new type of crew was emerging that marked territory in a less violent, if no less controversial, manner. In the summer of 1969, Apollo 11 astronauts Buzz Aldrin and Neil Armstrong walked on the moon; hippies invaded a sleepy town upstate for a music festival dubbed Woodstock; and in Washington Heights, a teenager named Demetrius with no gang affiliation was bored. Demetrius bought a few cans of spray paint and scrawled his nickname (Taki) and street number (183rd) on light poles and subway stations around town. Two years later, Demetrius was still at it, and the *Times* published an article about the "art" of "TAKI 183."[43]

Following TAKI 183's lead, groups of graffiti artists began staking out the best spots to paint their signatures ("tags") on open surfaces throughout the five boroughs. TAKI 183's simple, single-colored signature was superseded by elaborate scrawls, instantly recognizable to fellow artists. Soon graffiti marked nearly every subway car in the city, causing Mayor Lindsay to adopt an anti-graffiti bill in March 1973. Six months later, just before Beame replaced Lindsay in Gracie Mansion, the Metropolitan Transit Authority (MTA) completely repainted its 6,800-car fleet, even though clean cars provided would-be artists with a beautifully blank canvas.[44]

When budget cuts gutted city services in 1975, sanitation suffered. Striking workers allowed nearly sixty thousand tons of garbage to accumulate across the boroughs.[45] But graffiti was an even bigger eyesore to many administrators, who saw it as a stark reminder of the disorder plaguing their city. New York spent millions trying to cover up spray-painted buildings and subway cars, even as graffiti tags became increasingly artistic, and elaborate murals soon urged New Yorkers to reimagine what constituted art.[46] Some New Yorkers bemoaned the lawlessness and berated city officials for not policing the rampant vandalism.[47] But fans of graffiti saw beauty in a subway car painted by artists like PHASE 2 with his trademark bubble letters.

Little did they know it at the time, but artists like TAKI 183 and PHASE 2 were pioneering a new urban youth culture. New York City was divided by ethnicity and social class; graffiti art, transported by subway cars throughout all five boroughs, transcended traditional boundaries.

In the summer of 1974, many New Yorkers saw spray-painted subway cars as a nuisance and knew nothing of the musical sensation that would soon join graffiti art to create a new, Black aesthetic. What they did know, however, was that the Knicks might be in trouble.

DeBusschere and Lucas were gone, but the team hoped Reed could hobble through one more season. After working out all summer to coax his body into playing shape, however, the captain announced his retirement in September.[48]

In 1974, NBA free agency was still two years away, so the Knicks could not sign top players from other teams to replenish their suddenly depleted frontcourt. Instead, they hoped to find help through the NBA Draft. That June, the Knicks connected with the other seventeen NBA teams via conference call to choose top collegiate players. UCLA's seven-foot, red-headed, hippie center Bill Walton was everyone's consensus number one pick, landing in Portland to play for the Trail Blazers. Unhappy with the players available by the time their pick rolled around, the Knicks traded their top draft choice to the Chicago Bulls for Howard Porter, who would last just half a season in New York. In the sixth round, New York chose Terry Mikan, the son of legendary Minneapolis Lakers center George Mikan. Terry would never play an NBA game, but Holzman joked of the Knicks' pick, "You never pass up a chance to draft a Mikan."[49]

Entering training camp that fall, the Knicks hoped third-year center John Gianelli could replace at least one of the three lost frontcourt Hall of Famers. Gianelli had attended Pacific University and, with his "Shirley Temple-like curls and long sideburns," looked every bit the laid-back West Coast dude.[50] He tried lifting weights after college but told reporters, "The weights and I just didn't get along. It's hard work and boring."[51] Still, he pushed himself during the '74 offseason and looked good in camp. Holzman, at least, was thoroughly impressed. "We thought we had the next Bill Russell," he later said.[52] But when Gianelli told reporters "I don't expect basketball to be my lifetime career. It fills the void now," it was clear he was no Russell (or Reed, Lucas, or DeBusschere).[53]

With Gianelli manning the middle, Holzman's Knicks clung tenuously to third place in the Atlantic Division in late 1974, sporting a 19–15 record at the end of the year. Yet Holzman feared their modest success was unsustainable. He lengthened practice times and required players to watch hours of game film in a vain attempt to recapture the unselfish play that had been the hallmark of his championship-winning teams. Slowly, Red had to abandon the free-flowing offense emphasizing ball movement ("find the open man!") and relied more and more heavily on the individual creativity of the Rolls-Royce backcourt.

"We just aren't getting enough scoring out of our frontline," Frazier complained to reporters. "We got nothing up front. No rebounds. No points. No nothin'. There isn't anybody who can win with a guard offense."[54]

But if any backcourt player could carry his team, it was Clyde. On January 2, 1975, Frazier tallied 32 points, 7 rebounds, 6 assists, and 6 steals in a win over the Phoenix Suns. Two days later, the Cleveland Cavaliers traveled to New York and, with seven seconds left, led by one. Everyone in the Garden knew the ball was going to Frazier. It didn't matter. His twenty-foot jump shot swished through the net as time expired to give New York a thrilling 103–102 win.

In February, Clyde traded his Knicks orange and blue for a gaudy purple uniform to team up with a dozen fellow Eastern Conference players for the annual NBA All-Star Game. For the first time in league history, fans voted for All-Star starters, and Frazier finished second in overall votes, earning a spot on over ninety-one thousand ballots (a few thousand shy of high-scoring Buffalo Braves center Bob McAdoo).[55] Monroe started alongside Frazier and helped the East to a 108–102 victory, which earned Frazier, on the strength of his 30-point performance, All-Star MVP honors. There was no longer any doubt; Clyde was the best guard, and one of the best players, in the entire NBA.

Lost in the rise of Frazier to superstardom was a changing of the guard in the changing room. NBA locker rooms in the early days of the league were like clubhouses: players smoked, drank, and might as well have put up a sign reading "No girls allowed." But in January 1975, two female reporters were granted access to the locker rooms at the National Hockey League All-Star game. A month later, Jane Gross, a reporter for *Newsday*, entered the Knicks locker room for the first time. Some of the players were shy, or at least respectful, covering themselves with a towel. Others "didn't care," Knicks ball boy Keith Blauschild told me, "almost like they didn't want them there."[56]

Returning from the All-Star break and growing used to having female reporters in the locker room, teams began to settle into a pecking order in the Eastern Conference. The Bullets and Celtics led their respective divisions, Buffalo was hot on Boston's heels in the Atlantic, and the Knicks and the Houston Rockets won about as often as they lost. While playing .500 ball marked a step forward in Houston, where fourth-year players Rudy Tomjanovich and Calvin Murphy were just entering their primes, New Yorkers saw it as unacceptably mediocre. Hoping a roster shakeup might pull the team out of its rut (this would become a recurring theme), the Knicks traded reserve guard Henry Bibby to New Orleans for center Neal Walk and guard Jim Barnett.

Trading Bibby for Walk and Barnett dramatically transformed the Knicks' locker room; something like swapping out lite beer for moonshine.

Bibby, whose son Mike would go on to a fourteen-year NBA career, made the most of his athletic talent. Henry's toughness and headiness served him well in a long and successful playing, and later coaching, career.[57]

Barnett, nicknamed "Crazy Horse," could not have been more different. Sporting wavy hair, long sideburns, a bushy moustache, and a perpetually mischievous grin, Crazy Horse was like a grown-up Dennis the Menace who fully embraced his wild side. "Two years ago between playoff games," he told reporters, "I went 70 feet up an oak tree in the forest where we live, sawing off a limb with a chainsaw." He shrugged. "I like to live dangerously."[58] Tales of Barnett's exploits are Bunyanesque; he punted a football into the third tier at Oakland Coliseum, spent a road trip sleeping in the luggage rack of a bus, and once tossed around lit firecrackers during practice.[59] On the court, Barnett was just as reckless. "I'm just Jim Barnett and that's how I play," he explained, "I pick up fouls and don't always see the open man because my head is down. But I can't change."[60] Not quite the Knicks way.

Walk was another odd duck. In 1969, a coin flip between the Bucks and Suns sent Lew Alcindor (later Kareem Abdul-Jabbar) to Milwaukee and Walk to Phoenix. Despite the pressure of being the-guy-picked-after-Kareem, Walk flourished in the Arizona desert and peaked in his fourth season, averaging 20 points and 12 rebounds per game. Walk stood six foot ten, wore his hair in an unruly mop, kept a frizzy black beard, and might hold the unofficial league record for most body hair. Like Bill Walton, the NBA's newest sensation, Walk embraced vegetarianism and the freedom of the counterculture. "I liked being back here in New York City," Walk said later, "for two days. That's all I can take. Personally I enjoy being outdoors, seeing blue skies and tall mountains."[61] After one game, Holzman saw Walk getting dressed and noticed that he pulled on his blue jeans without putting anything on first. "No underwear, huh?" Red asked. Walk looked at him and said, "Nonfunctional, Red. Nonfunctional."[62] Unlike Barnett, Walk was not known for his fiery play. "He has become a latter-day flower child," Boston sportswriter Bob Ryan would mock in 1975, "whose competitiveness is in question."[63]

Reporters asked Holzman about his new players. The old coach shrugged and responded, in a thick New York accent, "What the hell, all trades are a gamble."[64]

Approval for the Bibby trade came from Holzman's boss, Knicks president Mike Burke, who had recently succeeded the legendary Ned Irish in the role. Irish founded the Knicks in 1946 and, as Harvey Araton explained, "was arguably more powerful than the league commissioner" in pro basketball.[65] But by the mid-seventies, Irish had served as team president for almost thirty years and was burnt out. "It's not fun anymore," he complained to reporters. "Lawyers . . . agents . . . players' associations . . . suits . . . countersuits . . . you get a little tired of it."[66] Irish stayed on as an honorary chairman until he passed away in 1982 but provided little input on player or personnel decisions after Burke arrived on the scene.

Irish was an institution in New York City, but if anyone could follow that act, it was Burke. Burke was a renaissance playboy who wore his silver hair long and favored plaid turtlenecks or dress shirts unbuttoned to the navel. Hey, it was the seventies.

Before coming to the Knicks, Burke had, among many other endeavors, run the New York Yankees with George Steinbrenner. Unsurprisingly, Burke's partnership with the notoriously difficult Steinbrenner was short-lived, and he joined the Knicks a few months after it dissolved. Initially Burke ran Madison Square Garden, giving him oversight of the main arena as well as a smaller five-thousand seat venue and a rotunda. Each year, hundreds of events took place on site; in one three-day span under Burke, the Garden hosted an Ali-Frazier fight, a Knicks-Celtics game, and a Bob Dylan concert. But Burke's top priority was stopping the Knicks' on-court free fall. "A championship team had disintegrated," Burke explained later, "its holdovers were in decline, and I knew even less about basketball than baseball." Maybe most problematically, at least for Burke, "the magic had fled the court at Madison Square Garden."[67]

The Madison Square Garden Burke inherited was the fourth building with that name. The first, located at the corner of Madison Avenue and Twenty-Sixth (Madison Square) was originally run by P. T. Barnum as the pompously named "Monster Classical and Geological Hippodrome" before the Vanderbilt family bought the property in 1879 and renamed it. A decade later, this Madison Square Garden was demolished and a new structure put in its place, featuring an eight-thousand-seat arena and the world's largest indoor swimming pool. By the 1920s, Manhattan needed an even larger venue to host boxing matches promoted by the legendary

Tex Rickard, and the Madison Square Garden name relocated north to the corner of Eighth Avenue and Forty-Ninth Street. In 1946, the Knicks played their first home game in that arena, a 78–68 loss to the Chicago Stags; twenty-two years later, they beat the Philadelphia 76ers in their final game at "Garden III" before the "New Garden" opened in February 1968.[68] The New Garden (also known as "Garden IV"—today just Madison Square Garden) opened about halfway between Madison Square and Garden III, above Penn Station between Seventh and Eighth Avenues and 33rd and 31st Streets, standing thirteen stories tall.[69] Fittingly, Walt Frazier scored the Knicks' first points in the New Garden, helping the team to a 114–102 win over the San Diego Clippers as the team embarked on its garden of Eden era.[70]

Trading for Walk and Barnett, Burke hoped, would help the team recapture the magic of these early days of the New Garden. But the trade did little to stop the Knicks' decline, and the team dropped five games in a row and eight of their next ten. By the end of February 1975, it was becoming increasingly clear that shuffling bench players was not enough of a shakeup to make a real difference. And so, in a move defined as "a separation of the two functions," Burke relieved Holzman of his personnel decision-making duties.[71] Red would stay on the bench to coach the players, but Buffalo Braves general manager Eddie Donovan, the architect of New York's Golden Age, Garden of Eden title-winning teams, would return to help Burke negotiate trades and make draft choices.[72]

In March 1975, the race for the final two playoff spots in the Eastern Conference was heating up. Despite their losing streak, the Knicks remained in the hunt; with five games remaining, New York, at 37–40, trailed Cleveland and Houston by a single game in the standings. The Knicks won their next two, setting up an important game against the Cavaliers. The game set an NBA attendance record as 20,239 fans packed into the Coliseum at Richfield, the Cavs' brand-new, state-of-the-art suburban arena. The Knicks led by four at halftime, but Cleveland guard Jim Cleamons scored 17 second-half points, hit a key free throw, and stole the ball from Monroe as time expired to secure a Cavs win, sending the Knicks to the brink of elimination from playoff contention.

With their loss to Cleveland, New York needed a miracle. Not only did they have to beat a very good Buffalo team, they also needed the mediocre

Kansas City–Omaha Kings to upset the surging Cavs. The first half of their own game was a disaster, but a 14–0 run in the third quarter gave the Knicks a lead they never relinquished. Their season now hinged on a single game that they had to helplessly watch play out on television.

Holzman tuned into the Kings-Cavs game on a small black-and-white television in his office, nervously smoking a stogie and knocking back scotch while wringing his hands and sweating through his blue Oxford shirt. Monroe entirely avoided watching or listening to the game and instead attended a showing of *The Wiz*, a new Broadway musical with an all-Black cast featuring Brooklynite Stephanie Mills in the role of Dorothy. Frazier, whose reputation as a man about town hid his natural introversion, hosted a rare party ("I'm a partygoer, not a partygiver") in his forty-fifth-floor apartment at the Excelsior, located on Fifty-Seventh Street at Second Avenue. Several Knicks brought wives or girlfriends to watch the game on Clyde's television set. Frazier was too nervous to sit, instead pacing around his bedroom, which featured shag carpeting, a huge circular bed with a custom-fit white mink blanket and matching round ceiling mirror (complete with "Clyde" sandblasted on one pane).[73]

In Frazier's living room, Knicks players watched helplessly as Cleveland had the ball, down by one point, with three seconds left. An eternity. The Cavs caught the inbounds pass, but Kings swingman Ron Behagen (born and raised in the Bronx) blocked their last-second shot attempt, sending the Knicks to the playoffs for the ninth straight season. Frazier and his teammates erupted in cheers, and the next day the host was still ecstatic. "This is the first party I've ever thrown," he said. "I guess I couldn't have picked a more perfect time."[74] But even the usually cool Clyde admitted, "I can't take many like that!"[75]

Sizing up the 1975 playoffs, two things were clear: the league's two top teams played in the Eastern Conference, and neither of them was the Knicks. At 60–22, the Celtics were defending NBA champions poised to repeat behind Cowens, Havlicek, and guard Jo Jo White. The renamed Washington Bullets finished with an identical regular-season record and boasted three All-Stars of their own: guard Phil Chenier and big men Elvin Hayes and Wes Unseld.

For the first time in league history, the playoffs included ten teams and featured a best-of-three first-round matchup between the lowest two seeds in each conference. In the West, the Seattle SuperSonics pulled out a 2–1 series win over the Pistons, while, in the East, the Rockets held home-court advantage for their short series against the Knicks.

Bettors installed Houston as 2.5-point favorites in game one, and the Rockets destroyed the spread, pulling away late to win by fourteen. Frazier, as usual, played superbly in the high-stakes playoff atmosphere, and after the game a reporter suggested that Clyde looked like the Lone Ranger on the court with performance in a losing effort (21 points, 8 rebounds, 11 assists, and 4 steals). Frazier ran his hand through his short Afro and said, "Yeah, and I thought Tonto had deserted."[76]

The Knicks won game two in the Garden behind Frazier's 26 points, but their season ended with a fizzle on April 12, when the Rockets mauled the Knicks 118–86 in front of a raucous Houston crowd. Weeks later, New Yorkers watched Rick Barry and the Golden State Warriors shock the basketball world, sweeping the heavily favored Bullets in the finals.

"The 1974–75 season was a crossroads for the Knicks," Holzman later wrote, "because our roster changed in dramatic ways."[77] Despite making the playoffs, the team's 40–42 record marked the first losing season in Holzman's tenure in New York. Also, not only had Reed, Lucas, and DeBusschere retired, Burke had replaced Irish as team president and Alan Cohen became the CEO of Madison Square Garden. Cohen "was more of a corporate man," Holzman wrote, "a bottom-line type of guy."[78] In fact, Mel Lowell, another team executive, told me they nicknamed him "Bottom Line Cohen" because when asked about potential trades or signings, Cohen's stock response was "What's the bottom line?"[79] Cohen must have hated the Knicks' lackluster performance in his first year on the job. For years, the Knicks regularly sold out the Garden; now they filled the building in less than half their games. Sure, they still led the league in attendance by a wide margin, attracting more than eighteen-thousand fans per game, but that was their lowest total in nearly a decade—and it was about to get much, much worse.[80]

For the Knicks, the summer of 1975 was shaping up to be another busy off-season. At least this year, they did not have to replace three future Hall of Famers; in fact, if rumors were true, the Knicks might add at least one future Hall of Famer to their roster.

In the mid-sixties, Lew Alcindor became a high school phenomenon at Manhattan's Power Memorial Academy. The "Tower from Power" led his school to a 71-game winning streak and three City Catholic titles.

Alcindor, now known as Kareem Abdul-Jabbar following his conversion to Islam, was a six-time All-Star and three-time NBA MVP asking for a trade away from the Milwaukee Bucks. "Milwaukee is middle America," Abdul-Jabbar told reporters, "and things that are for me and what I am have nothing to do with middle America."[81]

Kareem wanted to play in a big city, ideally New York, but how could the Knicks convince Milwaukee to give them the best player on the planet? Hoping to open negotiations in person, Donovan and Burke hopped on a plane (this too would become a recurring theme) and flew to Wisconsin. "We put $1 million on the table for openers and asked what more we could add to it in players and draft choices," said Burke later.[82] Even with a seven-figure check literally on the table (Bottom-Line Cohen must have been having fits), the Bucks remained noncommittal. In fact, they already had another deal in place, and, by the time Burke and Donovan returned to the Big Apple, the news broke that Abdul-Jabbar was going to Los Angeles.[83] The Knicks and their fans were stunned.

With Kareem headed to Hollywood, New York turned to the second name on their wish list: forward George McGinnis of the ABA's Indiana Pacers. McGinnis was built like a linebacker; in high school, in fact, he fielded two hundred football scholarship offers before committing to play basketball at Indiana University. He left Indiana early and was drafted by both the Philadelphia 76ers of the NBA and the Pacers of the ABA. He chose Indy and, in 1975, was coming off an amazing season in which he shared league MVP honors with Julius Erving after averaging a gaudy 30 points, 14 rebounds, and 6 assists per game. He was even better in the playoffs and in game seven of the ABA semifinals, McGinnis tallied 40 points, 23 rebounds, and 8 assists in the Pacers' victory. McGinnis was great in the finals too, although Indiana lost to the Kentucky Colonels and their fiery head coach Hubie Brown.

McGinnis was a stud. Unfortunately, Philadelphia thought the same and still held his draft rights. The Sixers tried to sign Big George but were told "he insists on playing in New York."[84] Less than twenty-four hours after the Pacers lost to the Colonels, McGinnis filed suit in US District Court challenging the legality of the NBA's collegiate draft, arguing that his selection by the 76ers restricted his right to negotiate with multiple teams.[85] Rather than wait on the court's decision, McGinnis quickly signed a contract with the Knicks. He was thrilled, saying, "Coming to

New York is a big step for me. It bothered me that no one knew much about me while I was playing in the ABA. The Knicks are the guys everybody watched on television."[86] Sure, he was a celebrity in Indianapolis, but McGinnis was relatively unknown outside the Hoosier State, and part of what sold McGinnis on the Knicks was the chance to be a household name on the level of Frazier, Joe Namath, and Mickey Mantle. The next summer, George Steinbrenner used a similar tactic to lure Reggie Jackson to the Big Apple. Could McGinnis be the straw that stirred the Knicks' drink? After signing with New York, McGinnis dropped his lawsuit against the league, allowing his fate to be decided by the NBA commissioner, who just happened to be on his first week on the job.

New commissioner Larry O'Brien was born to Irish immigrant parents in Springfield, Massachusetts, in 1917, just twenty-six years after James Naismith invented basketball at the YMCA down the street. Larry loved basketball as a boy, but any aspirations of a professional career were dashed long before he emerged as a prominent political figure in the state. O'Brien grew close to the Kennedy family, especially young John, in the early 1950s when the future president was still in the House of Representatives; he later joined Jackie Kennedy in Air Force One after his friend's assassination. The Kennedys often joked about O'Brien's love of "roundball" (they preferred football) and encouraged O'Brien to handle Bobby Kennedy's run for the presidency in 1968, which ended with another Kennedy assassination.[87]

In the early seventies, O'Brien rose to national prominence as the chair of the Democratic National Committee after burglars attempted to break into his office at the Watergate Hotel in Washington. "It was my phone that the Watergate burglars tapped and my personal files that they photographed," O'Brien wrote in his autobiography. "But I had long since come to regard the whole sordid affair as a national tragedy."[88] Nixon resigned the presidency following the scandal started in O'Brien's office, and less than a year later the NBA needed a new commissioner to replace outgoing Walter Kennedy. O'Brien was reluctant. "I had really no knowledge of the operation of the league office," he admitted.[89] He had season tickets for Knicks home games, but that hardly qualified him to be the new commissioner. Walter Kennedy spent months courting O'Brien until finally he agreed to give it a shot.[90]

Before the ink could dry on his new contract, Commissioner O'Brien faced a full slate of problems, including the pending Oscar Robertson lawsuit (which ultimately brought free agency to the NBA), a potential merger with the rival ABA, and the McGinnis situation.

Waiting on O'Brien's ruling about McGinnis and the legal entanglements posed by an NBA team trying to sign an ABA player already claimed by a different NBA team, Knicks execs prepared for the 1975 collegiate draft. Selecting ninth in the first round, they chose Jackson State forward Eugene Short, who would go on to play just thirty-four NBA games. New York's subsequent picks were even less inspiring. In the second round they chose Luther "Ticky" Burden, who later went to jail for bank robbery; third-rounder Larry Fogle had been kicked off his college team for disciplinary reasons; and fourth-rounder David Vaughan had dropped out of two colleges.[91]

A week after the draft, O'Brien handed down his decision on McGinnis, invalidating George's contract with New York. Not only did the Knicks lose McGinnis, they also lost their 1976 first-round draft pick as a penalty for the premature signing. Sixers general manager Pat Williams was relieved, adamant that the "other teams were just waiting for O'Brien to deal out major punishment for the Knicks, who thought they could do anything."[92] Five days later McGinnis became a Sixer.

In September 1975, ABC aired its newest sitcom, *Welcome Back, Kotter*, starring Gabe Kaplan in the title role. In *Welcome Back*, Kotter teaches a group of remedial students, collectively nicknamed the Sweathogs, at Brooklyn's fictional James Buchanan High School. In the second episode, Freddy "Boom Boom" Washington struts into the classroom proudly wearing a Buchanan basketball jersey, convinced he is on the fast track to a pro career. "I'm gonna be a star," Washington informs his classmates, "and stars ain't got to do nothin' but shoot baskets."[93] Vinnie Barbarino, played by John Travolta, offers to be Washington's manager. "I'll negotiate your college scholarship, and then after college we sign a fat contract with the New York Knicks," the coolest Sweathog promises. "Stick with me, and you'll be up to your 'fro in dough." By the time Mr. Kotter returns to the classroom, Boom Boom is perched behind the teacher's desk, practicing his commercial pitch. "Where you gonna play? Forward?" Kotter asks his student. Freddy responds, "No . . . star. I've got the moves of

Walt Frazier and the finesse of Kareem Abdul-Jabbar." "You've also got the modesty of Muhammad Ali," Kotter quips. Of course, by the end of the episode Washington realizes the importance of an education ("I don't have that contract with the Knicks sewn up yet").

With Abdul-Jabbar, McGinnis, and, apparently, Boom Boom Washington unavailable, Burke and Donovan were growing increasingly desperate to sign a star. So they called Wilt Chamberlain. After retiring from the Lakers in 1973, Wilt signed with the ABA's San Diego Conquistadors. But when a California court ruled him ineligible to play, Wilt became the team's unwilling, and mostly disinterested, coach. Now, nearly thirty months after his last on-court appearance, Chamberlain was again a hot commodity. Lakers owner Jack Kent Cooke told reporters, "Wilt could be the ingredient that makes the Knicks a success as they ought to be for the New York fans."[94] But the NBA's reserve clause, threatened by the pending Oscar Robertson suit, kept Chamberlain's rights with Cooke in L.A.; without free agency, Wilt could only play for the Lakers. If he wanted to sign elsewhere, the Lakers had to trade or release him. Cooke had the Knicks over a barrel and wanted to extract as much as he could for his retired superstar. New York hoped for a cash transaction, but Cooke wanted players—asking for some combination of Monroe, Jackson, and a high draft choice.[95] "I'm not interested in money," the multimillionaire owner declared, "I can't play money."[96]

This time, O'Brien ruled in the Knicks' favor. Chamberlain had to report to Los Angeles, and the Lakers could either employ him at his previous salary, trade him, or release him. Chamberlain, vacationing in Hawaii at the time, had no interest in flying home to fulfill O'Brien's decision, and, further complicating matters, ABA commissioner Dave DeBusschere sent telegrams reminding both the Knicks and Lakers that Chamberlain's contract with the Conquistadors ran through 1976.

As opening night neared, Wilt remained unsigned, Knicks season ticket sales were down by nearly two thousand, and without a box-office draw like Chamberlain (or McGinnis or Abdul-Jabbar or, hell, Boom Boom Washington), even fewer fans might venture to the Garden.[97] "Without Wilt Chamberlain," one journalist wrote, "the Knicks might be the highest paid last-place team in history. With him, the Knicks might still be the highest-paid, last-place team in history. But at least there will be more people in the stands watching them lose."[98]

With Wilt scheduled to return from his Hawaiian vacation in mid-October, Burke and Donovan flew to L.A. hoping to meet with Chamberlain. Everyone expected Wilt to sign with New York; the Knicks even packed a jersey with the number thirteen and Chamberlain's name stitched on the back.[99] But when Burke and Donovan arrived, Wilt was nowhere to be found, and a few days later they learned he was still in Hawaii. Wilt blamed the Knicks for the miscommunication. "I'd like to play for the Knicks," Chamberlain told reporters, but he joked that he would be happier if they "sent out two fine New York women and a corned beef sandwich with a little mustard."[100] Burke and Donovan were livid. Although Wilt briefly flirted with a comeback in the eighties, he never played another game of professional basketball.

Despite striking out on Chamberlain, Burke and Donovan's trip to L.A. ultimately netted them an even bigger prize than Chamberlain. While waiting on Wilt, the Knicks received a call from Seattle SuperSonics owner Sam Schulman. He was in town and wanted to discuss Seattle's All-Star power forward Spencer Haywood, who was at odds with coach Bill Russell. Over a few cups of coffee, the men discussed a possible Haywood trade. When the meeting with Wilt fell through, Burke called Schulman back, packed up Chamberlain's never-to-be-worn Knicks jersey, and boarded a flight back to New York.

Why were the Knicks so hell-bent on luring a superstar to New York? Sure, they needed frontcourt help; Gianelli, Walk, and Jackson could never replace DeBusschere, Lucas, and Reed on the court. But it was more than that. As Spike Lee later wrote, "I'm a Knicks fan. I'm looking for The Answer—to recapture the championship seasons of 1969–70 and 1972–73."[101] Like Spike, the Knicks front office wanted another run at the top. Luckily, it looked like "The Answer" was dropping like manna from heaven (or at least from Seattle) in the form of Haywood.

Unbeknown to Spike or other rabid Knicks fans like real estate magnate Donald Trump—a new season ticket holder—Burke worked tirelessly to close the Haywood deal.[102] Having already lost out at acquiring McGinnis, Abdul-Jabbar, and Chamberlain that summer, Burke was not about to let Haywood slip away. He kept Schulman on the telephone and, in the middle of the night, finalized the deal. New York would send cash and Eugene Short, the Knicks top draft choice a few months earlier, to Seattle for Haywood.

Figure 1. Knicks forward Spencer Haywood goes for a layup, watched by teammate Bob McAdoo and Dwight Jones and Kevin Kunnert of the Houston Rockets. © Larry Berman—BermanSports.com. Used by permission.

While Burke and Donovan were in California trying to buy a savior, the Big Apple faced a crippling financial crisis. During Lindsay's tenure as mayor, and continuing when Beame took office in 1974, New York City officials annually outspent city income to realize their goal of "socialism in one city."[103] Meanwhile, federal funding cuts, deindustrialization, and white flight shrunk the city's tax base while health care costs, employee pensions, welfare, and subsidizing the City College of New York increased expenditures. Each fiscal year, city administrators sold bonds to cover annual expenses, hiding shortfalls through creative accounting practices even as interest on their loans crept higher and higher.

When he served as city comptroller in the sixties, Beame recommended using bridge loans to plug the gap between income and expenses. Now banks refused to market any more New York City bonds, and eventually even Beame, as mayor, had to admit defeat. In the summer of '75, Beame laid off nearly fifty thousand municipal employees, including 20 percent of the police force and elementary school teachers.[104]

It wasn't nearly enough.

"Fear City" became the label of the day. Angry off-duty cops papered the city with "Welcome to Fear City" pamphlets, which, a forty-year-retrospective piece in the British *Guardian* said in 2015, "read like one more piece of the dystopia porn filling American cinemas . . . Taxi Driver, The French Connection, Marathon Man, Escape from New York, Death Wish, and The Warriors." The pamphlets infuriated Beame with their lurid description of the dangers of city life and urging visitors to "stay away from New York City . . . until things change." Some municipal workers demonstrated downtown, and others picketed on major roadways during rush hour. Garbage collectors staged a walkout, chanting "This isn't Fear City, it's Stink City!," and out-of-work teachers marched with signs reading "Fear City, Stink City and now, Stupid City."[105]

By October 1975, New York City stood on the edge of civil war and the brink of bankruptcy. "We needed to figure out which services were essential, and which weren't," Beame's press secretary said. "Teachers weren't life-or-death. Hospital services and keeping the highways open were essential."[106] On October 17, New York was less than an hour from defaulting on its loans, and a car idled outside City Hall containing documents officially declaring the bankruptcy of the largest city in the United States. An eleventh-hour reprieve provided by borrowed teacher pension funds was the only reason the city remained solvent.[107] In desperation, local leaders asked President Gerald Ford for a bailout. From the podium of the National Press Club in Washington, Ford issued his response. "I can tell you, and tell you now, that I am prepared to veto any bill that has as its purpose a federal bailout of New York City to prevent a default. . . . Why should other Americans," he continued, "support advantages in New York that they have not been able to afford for their own communities?"[108]

The next day, New York's *Daily News* paraphrased his opposition with the sensationalist headline, in 144-point type, reading: "Ford to City: Drop Dead."[109] Ultimately, the headline doomed Ford and became a rallying cry for New Yorkers. But in 1975, all hope seemed lost. Maybe Haywood could save the Knicks after all. With Ford unwilling to bail out a city on the brink of bankruptcy, graffiti artists tagging subway cars, and street violence in the South Bronx at its peak, surely something had to go right for Gotham.

1973–74 Knicks
Record: 49–33
Playoffs: Lost Eastern Conference finals to Boston Celtics
Coach: Red Holzman
Average Home Attendance: 19,133
Points Per Game: (101.3—15th of 17)
Points Allowed Per Game: (98.5—1st of 17)
Team Leaders:

> Points: Walt Frazier (20.5 per game)
> Rebounds: Dave DeBusschere (10.7 per game)
> Assists: Walt Frazier (6.9 per game)
> Steals: Walt Frazier (2.0 per game)
> Blocked Shots: Willis Reed (1.1 per game)

All-Stars: Dave DeBusschere and Walt Frazier
Notable Transaction: Traded a 1974 first-round draft pick to the Chicago Bulls for Howard Porter

1974–75 Knicks
Record: 40–42
Playoffs: Lost Eastern Conference First Round to Houston Rockets

Coach: Red Holzman
Average Home Attendance: 18,556
Points per Game: (100.4—14th of 18)
Points Allowed per Game: (101.7—8th of 18)
Team Leaders:

  Points: Walt Frazier (21.5 per game)
  Rebounds: John Gianelli (8.6 per game)
  Assists: Walt Frazier (6.1 per game)
  Steals: Walt Frazier (2.4 per game)
  Blocked Shots: John Gianelli (1.5 per game)

All-Stars: Earl Monroe and Walt Frazier
Notable Transaction: Traded Henry Bibby and a 1975 first-round draft
  pick to the New Orleans Jazz for Jim Barnett and Neal Walk

2

"You Don't Get to Rebuild If You Are the New York Knicks"

1975–1977

Spencer Haywood's move to the Knicks was a big deal. But it paled in comparison to another arrival in the New York City sporting world in 1975. That summer, the New York Cosmos, of the North American Soccer League (NASL), added the most famous soccer player on the planet, Pelé. In June, the thirty-four-year-old Brazilian forward signed a multimillion-dollar contract and immediately reinvigorated the struggling NASL. In three years, he would lead the Cosmos to one league title and help generate interest in the league to the point that thousands had to regularly be turned away from Cosmos home games at the 22,000-seat Downing Stadium at Randall's Island. By 1977, the Cosmos were the toast of the town. They outgrew Downing and had to play home games at Giants Stadium in New Jersey. "We transcended everything, every culture, every socio-economic boundary," goalkeeper Shep Messing recalled in 2005. "We were international, we were European, we were cool, we were Americans from the Bronx. We were everything to everybody."[1]

Pelé turned around the fortunes of his team and league almost overnight. New York's newest hoops star knew turning around the Knicks would be a challenge. But nothing in Haywood's life had ever been easy. He grew up on a cotton farm in Mississippi and, like many Black southerners in the sixties, faced terrible discrimination. At fifteen, his mother sent him to live with foster families in Detroit where he developed, in his own words, into a six-foot-six teenager with "the physical maturity and coordination of an adult."[2]

After graduating from high school, Haywood signed with the University of Tennessee to become the first Black basketball player in the history of the Southeastern Conference. "Somebody had to integrate college basketball in the South," said Haywood later, "and Mama always told me I was special. Who better to take on this mission?"[3]

But when Haywood failed Tennessee's entrance exams, he ended up at tiny Trinidad State Junior College in Colorado. After an exceptional freshman season in which he averaged better than 28 points and 22 rebounds per game, officials invited him to try out for the 1968 Olympic team.

In the United States, the 1968 Summer Olympic Games are best remembered for the black-gloved salutes raised by American sprinters John Carlos and Tommie Smith. But just as Carlos and Smith represented a stand for civil rights in the Games, so too did the absence of many high-profile college basketball players like the future Kareem Abdul-Jabbar. "It was too difficult for me," Abdul-Jabbar wrote in his autobiography, "to get enthusiastic about representing a country that refused to represent me or others of my color."[4] With less fanfare, other Black college stars pulled out of the Games, leaving Haywood, the only junior college player and youngest basketball Olympian in US history, to carry a heavy load. "The Black players on our team were looked at as Uncle Toms for going to the Olympics," Haywood later recalled. "We were sellouts."[5] Still, he put on a show, and by the end of the Games the precocious nineteen-year-old was a celebrated gold-medal winner.[6] "In three years' time," he remembered later, "I had gone from picking and chopping cotton as a slave to being a hero for the United States."[7]

Eight years after Mexico City, news of the Haywood trade energized Knicks players and fans alike. Season ticket sales soared, and Bill Bradley was stoked; "when we talk about winning, we can talk about it right now," the future US senator gushed.[8] But not all Haywood's new teammates were excited. Harthorne Wingo was devastated. Wingo was a playground legend who first came to the attention of the Allentown Jets of the Eastern League thanks to his play in a Greenwich Village pickup game.⁹ Wingo worked his way up through basketball's minor leagues and sat at the end of the Knicks bench for two seasons before finally getting his shot. "I really felt I was coming into my own at that time," Wingo told me. "But then . . . they went out and got Spencer Haywood from Seattle, which made me realize that I was pretty much through in New York."¹⁰ Less than a year later, Wingo was out of the NBA, trying to scratch out a living playing overseas.

With Haywood in the fold, the Knicks expected to drastically improve on their 40–42 record. A lineup featuring a healthy Rolls-Royce backcourt, forwards Bradley and Haywood, and steady center play from a Neal Walk and John Gianelli that could at least be competitive in the Eastern Conference. Maybe 1975 would kickstart the next great Knicks dynasty.

Optimistic New Yorkers packed Madison Square Garden for Haywood's Knicks debut. Spencer put together a solid game, tallying 8 points and 8 rebounds, and Frazier and Monroe combined for 52 points to steamroll the Cavaliers. A week later, the Sixers came to town; George McGinnis sat out with an injury, and the Knicks won by a dozen to even their season record at 3–3. Against Philly, the Knicks fired on all cylinders. Frazier led the team with 25 points and 10 assists, Haywood scored 23 and pulled down 17 rebounds, Monroe and Bradley each chipped in 19 points, and the center duo of Walk and Gianelli combined for 16 points and 18 rebounds.

In late October 1975, one week before Haywood's Knicks debut, WNBC-TV aired the second episode of *NBC's Saturday Night* (later *Saturday Night Live*). That night, Simon and Garfunkel performed half a dozen songs, and Chevy Chase took his first on-screen pratfall. Most memorable, though, was the one-on-one game between five-foot-three Paul Simon and six-foot-eight Connie Hawkins, a New York City playground legend now winding down his career with the Los Angeles Lakers. Simon, dressed in a white jersey with red and blue trim (just like the Knicks), pulled the miraculous upset as the crowd laughed. It would be a rare feel-good moment for New York basketball fans that fall.

For years, the Knicks had relied on a patterned offense designed by Coach Holzman emphasizing ball movement and unselfishness. Holzman was born in 1920 on the Lower East Side and grew up in Brooklyn, the son of a Jewish tailor.[11] Friends and family described him as "a cultural Jew" who fasted on Yom Kippur and celebrated Hannukah but rarely attended synagogue.[12] During World War II, Red—who earned the nickname because of his head of then-flaming orange hair—enlisted in the navy and attended the City College of New York, where he played basketball for legendary coach Nat Holman.[13] After a short pro career, Red, at age thirty-three, became the head coach of the Milwaukee Hawks and followed the franchise south when they moved to St. Louis. In 1958, Knicks head coach Fuzzy Levane, an old friend, convinced Red to join him in New York as a scout. Levane lasted only one more season, but Red stayed with the franchise for the next thirty, replacing Dick McGuire as the team's head coach in 1967.[14]

Holzman won two titles in New York with a group of veterans who played with an uncanny ability to anticipate the actions of one other on the court. But in 1975–76 that continuity was gone. "What was wrong?" Haywood later wrote, "Make a list. Red Holzman . . . had us running the same offensive patterns his teams had been running for fifty years . . . and then there was this crazy thing called chemistry."[15] The old Knicks had it, the new Knicks did not.

Holzman blamed a lack of effort, particularly on the defensive end. After years as one of the league's top defensive teams, New York finished as one of the worst in 1975–76.[16] A frustrated Red told reporters, "You want to win in this league, you get yourself a big mobile center and a lot of defense. Every team," he continued, "has players who can score, so the emphasis has to be on stopping the other fellow."[17]

On March 30, 1976, with six games left on the schedule, the Knicks were mathematically eliminated from the playoffs, their first missed postseason in a decade. "It hurts not being in the playoffs," reserve forward Phil Jackson admitted, "but I learned more about basketball this season than any other. . . . I know why a good bunch of individuals does not necessarily make a good team."[18]

Although neither Jackson nor Holzman mentioned Haywood by name, he was an obvious scapegoat for the team's failures. Haywood "was supposed to be the new Dave DeBusschere," Sam Goldaper wrote in the *Times*.

"He was supposed to fit into the offense, score points, grab rebounds, get picks, and insure a playoff berth for the Knicks." Instead, Haywood was "basically a one-on-one shooter not noted for his defense [and did] not fit into the Knicks 'helping' type of team offense and defense."[19] For the season, Haywood managed just 92 assists, barely more than 1 per game. Sure, Frazier and Monroe did the lion's share of the shot-creating in New York, but all frustrated Knicks fans saw in Haywood was a ball hog.

Even before the silver-maned Mike Burke introduced Haywood as the newest Knick in his October 1975 press conference, the team knew he had some baggage. Yes, he had won Olympic gold, but he also had attended three different colleges, pioneered the practice of leaving school early for professional basketball, sued the NBA for violating antitrust laws, played for six different coaches in his first six professional seasons, and published his first autobiography before he turned twenty-six.[20]

Still, Haywood seemed to cope well with the pressure of playing in New York, especially as music became an increasingly important outlet to him. "Jazz," Haywood recalled, "was my refuge, my church."[21] On Saturday afternoons, Haywood spun records on WRVR 106.7 FM.[22] "New York is definitely the capital," he told reporters. "I've seen and heard more jazz here in just one summer than in six years any place else."[23] Spencer filled his apartment, located above the Liberation Bookstore in Harlem, with thousands of records.[24] He also embraced religion, taking meals at the Nation of Islam, on 125th Street, and studying the Quran after a long spiritual conversation with Kareem Abdul-Jabbar. In private, some friends even called him Abdullah.[25] Soon a budding romantic relationship would create an even tighter bond between Haywood and the city.

Haywood met Zara Mohamed Abdulmajid, nicknamed Iman, at Cleo's, a trendy restaurant on Broadway and Sixty-Third featuring hip jazz music and a cool vibe.[26] Haywood and Iman hit it off immediately; she had recently broken up with actor Warren Beatty (the "Clyde" in *Bonnie and Clyde*, source of Walt Frazier's nickname) and had moved to New York for a modeling career. "I didn't have nobody," Haywood wrote, "and she didn't have nobody so we just clung to each other." Even better, she was not an NBA fan—as Haywood explained, "she didn't know basketball for shit."[27] Instead, the two talked about much bigger plans for themselves.

"Our dream," Haywood later remembered, "was that we could unite the Blacks of Africa . . . with the Blacks of America." Iman and Haywood quickly became A-listers in New York City and even appeared together on *Good Morning America*, where they shared their hope to unite people of color from around the world. By then, the couple was the toast of the town; he was one of the highest-profile Knicks, and she scored the cover of *Vogue*. Iman began sitting courtside to cheer on her boyfriend, and, five months after they began dating the couple was pregnant. Haywood explained, "We decided to get married and let love grow."[28]

Haywood managed to cobble together a solid, if unspectacular, first season in New York, finishing second on the team in scoring at 19.9 points per game, and first in rebounds with 11.3. But clearly a 38–44 record was unacceptable in a city not known for its patience. "You don't get to rebuild," Frazier explained, "If you are the New York Knicks."[29]

With the 1975–76 season in the books, Knicks players scattered across the country. Backup guard Butch Beard flew home to Louisville; Jim Barnett went to the West Coast (probably to juggle chainsaws); Walk vacationed in New England; Jackson took a road trip back to Montana, his home state; Haywood and reserve forward Mel "Killer" Davis started summer classes at New York University; and Monroe kept regular hours at the Tiffany Entertainment Corporation he created, where he teamed with record producer Dick Scott (who later managed New Edition and the New Kids on the Block) to represent and manage recording artists like the BB&Q (Brooklyn, Bronx, and Queens) Band and Curtis Hairston.[30]

That summer, NBA executives, led by rookie commissioner O'Brien, redoubled their efforts to end the long-running feud with the ABA. Officials from both leagues met to renew merger talks despite numerous sticking points, including the right of player free agency. But one of the most pressing concerns was the situation between the Knicks and the ABA's New York Nets. Unsurprisingly, the Knicks refused to allow the Nets to remain in New York, even though the Nets played home games at the Nassau Veterans Memorial Coliseum in Uniondale rather than in Manhattan. Besides understandable concerns about territorial rights, Knicks execs had to be at least a little scared about the Nets stealing local fans. After all, the Nets won the ABA title in 1976, with the most electrifying player in the world, twenty-six-year-old Julius Erving.

In August, the two leagues finally came to an agreement, and the NBA added four former ABA teams: the Nets, Denver Nuggets, Indiana Pacers, and San Antonio Spurs. Each of the four had to pay a multimillion-dollar admission fee and forego several years of television revenue while the Nets also owed the Knicks $3 million in territorial rights. To pay the steep fee, the Nets sold Erving to the 76ers, decimating the "other" New York team while further strengthening one of the Knicks' most bitter rivals.[31]

League-wide, the most important change was the arrival of free agency to pro basketball. And while this free agency was restricted, requiring compensation to be sent to teams in return for lost players, within a year there was a nearly 40 percent turnover on NBA rosters.[32] Some fans and curmudgeonly owners cried foul at a lack of team loyalty, but proponents of free agency celebrated the ability for franchises to quickly rebuild by buying up talented players. Clearly the Knicks would use their financial power to their advantage. Right?

While basketball bigwigs met on Cape Cod to iron out merger details, residents of the South Bronx were witnessing the birth of a worldwide cultural phenomenon. They just didn't know it yet.

Beyond the economic devastation and crippling poverty of the era, the early seventies witnessed a decline in the Black Power movement and in Puerto Rican nationalism across the country. Coupled with deindustrialization and the increasing power of gangs, a Black youth subculture emerged.[33] In the mid-seventies, New York City lost 340,000 jobs, and teenage unemployment skyrocketed. By 1976, 70 percent of Black teens and 80 percent of Hispanic teens lacked jobs.[34] "The Bronx was the epicenter of poverty," DJ Charlie Chase of the Cold Crush Brothers recalls, "the epicenter for kids who were full of energy, who didn't know what to do with it, didn't have a lot of activities, didn't have role models."[35]

Many residents of the South Bronx moved there out of necessity, either because they could not afford to live elsewhere in New York or because they were freshly arrived from Latin America and the Caribbean. This immigration helped repopulate areas affected by white flight and profoundly changed the cultural makeup of the area.

Life for these newcomers, as well as for families who lived there for generations, was hard, as Mr. Wiggles, a B-boy dancer, later recalled. "We didn't call nothing hip-hop," he said. "We didn't look at anything as culture. It was just something to do to keep our minds off the bullshit that we had to deal with on a regular basis. And those parts of the Bronx," he continued, "are the reason why hip-hop was so important—it was the one gift that God was able to give us to help us to get past all that BS."[36]

One man who dealt well with "that BS" was a Jamaican immigrant named Clive Campbell, who ran with a graffiti crew called the Ex-Vandals, where his nickname was "Clyde as Kool," in homage to Walt Frazier.[37] Before joining the Ex-Vandals, Campbell was a member of the Five Percenters, a Bronx gang who gained his loyalty after a few of them rescued young Clive from a fight started during a pickup basketball game. "I hung out with them and started picking up the slang," Campbell remembers. "Pretty soon I was Americanized."[38] His musical tastes also became Americanized after his dad got him hooked on James Brown. Campbell loved the repetitive beats and driving rhythms that were signatures of the Godfather of Soul. He was not alone.

As graffiti crews began to replace traditional gang culture, Campbell spent less time tagging and more time jamming to James Brown. Friends stopped calling him Clive because, as he explained, they "couldn't recall my name Clive . . . they'd be like 'you mean like 'Clyde' Frazier'?" After using the nickname "Clyde as Kool" for a while, Campbell began referring to himself as Kool Herc—"Herc" being a shortened version of "Hercules" and a nod to his rough play on the basketball court.[39] In the summer of 1973, just weeks after Frazier and the Knicks won their second NBA title, Kool Herc threw a birthday party for his sister in the community room of his apartment complex at 1520 Sedgwick Avenue. At the party, he revealed a new technique he called the Merry-Go-Round, switching back and forth between two records to extend the break—the part of a song when the singer steps aside and the drumbeat carries the rhythm. Kids throughout the neighborhood heard about the party, and his next one drew a bigger crowd, many of them high schoolers too young to hit the downtown clubs.[40] "With the music outside, you went to a jam," MC Debbie D recalls. "There's a thousand kids standing there. We ain't got nothing else to do."[41]

By the fall, Herc had to relocate to a bigger space, eventually landing at Cedar Park, where he wired his speakers and record players into light poles. "When Kool Herc hit the scene he started to get the buzz that something was different," DJ Disco Wiz recalls. "The funk he threw on the turntables and the soul that came across with African beats, was something I could relate to. I could feel it." Kool Herc dubbed his close associates the Herculoids and his speaker system the Herculord.[42] "We heard the music *way* down the block," Spice Nice remembered. "The closer we got, the louder the bass got."[43]

DJ Kool Herc is rightfully celebrated as the godfather of hip-hop. But others improved on the Merry-Go-Round, introducing exciting new elements. Grandmaster Flash brought a new quick-mixing technique, while his protégé, Grand Wizzard Theodore, developed scratching and needle-dropping with pinpoint precision. And in the fall of 1976, Afrika Bambaataa, another hip-hop pioneer, threw his first official party as a deejay at the Bronx River Community Center.[44] Little is known about Bambaataa's early life, but by the 1980s his influence spread from the Bronx to lower Manhattan, breaking down barriers between the predominately Black neighborhood he grew up in and the "white art-crowd and punk-rock clubs" located downtown. As a young man, Bambaataa was heavily influenced by the 1964 film *Zulu*, and he adopted the film's pan-Africanist message to cross New York City turf boundaries and form bonds with rival gangs. He transformed his own street gang—the Black Spades—into a music crew, renamed them the Universal Zulu Nation, and helped forge a truce between rival crews throughout the city.[45]

Thanks to the efforts of Bambaataa and others with similar goals, street gangs slowly faded into the background of the Bronx, replaced by hip-hop crews that carved out their own space in the city and jealously guarded their turf. Now, instead of guns, knives, and fists, groups mostly battled with toasts, dance-offs, and deejay contests (though sometimes gang members acting as bouncers did get a little violent).[46] "We had the support of the whole community," remembers Jazzy Jay. "It's like, we'd rather see them doing that, doing something constructive, than to be down the block beating each other upside the head like they used to do in the gang days."[47]

Battles between rival deejays and B-boy crews required large open spaces capable of hosting several hundred spectators if the crews were well-known. High school gymnasiums were ideal, but they cost money to rent and in the summer months were closed. When the weather cooperated, crews preferred the flat concrete surfaces found at the parks that

also played host to pick-up basketball games.[48] Asphalt courts across the
city provided space for crews to practice and hosted many battles between
rival dancers and deejays as playground basketball continued around
them.[49] "You had different levels of people at the jams," DJ Disco Wiz
explained. "There were b-boys and b-girls mixing it up on the dance floor,
stick-up kids looking for prey, dudes looking to hook up with girls, and
gangbangers looking really out of place because by this time the street
gangs had been all but shut down in the city."[50] In fact, when the blackout
of 1977 hit, Wiz was playing at a park on 183rd and Valentine and was
afraid his sound system, illegally plugged into the streetlight, had blown
out the electricity in the neighborhood.[51]

When Herc hosted his first party on Sedgwick Avenue, the Knicks were
the reigning NBA champions. Although just ten miles separated Herc's
neighborhood from Madison Square Garden, these were two completely
different worlds. But within a few years, hip-hop and basketball would be
all but inseparable.

On October 21, 1976, the Knicks retired Willis Reed's number nineteen,
the first jersey to hang from the rafters in Madison Square Garden. It was
opening night, and the Los Angeles Lakers were in town, poised for a
breakout season behind reigning NBA MVP Kareem Abdul-Jabbar. The
Knicks pulled out a five-point win thanks to six players in double figures,
led by Monroe, but only drew an abysmal 13,675 fans, the lowest opening night total ever at the New Garden. And that was the paid attendance;
as the *Times* noted, "many didn't show up."[52] The Knicks sold just 7,250
season tickets that year, down from over 12,000 in 1976 and far below the
16,000 they regularly sold when the Garden was Eden.

Despite fan lack of interest, New York won their first three games of
the season, posting wins over the Lakers, Spurs, and Braves. But they
crashed back to earth with four straight losses, and in November injuries began to pile up. By Thanksgiving, Monroe, Haywood, and Bradley
watched from the sidelines. Frazier, who managed to stay healthy, was
growing frustrated with the team's effort. After a misstep cost the Knicks
a game in late November, Frazier's post-game comment was simply, "bad
pass, lost the game."[53] The cool, collected cat who held New York City
in the palm of his hand as Clyde in the early seventies was slowly being
replaced by the naturally quiet, shy, and introverted Walt.

Figure 2. Members of 1976–77 New York Knicks on the sideline. *Left to right*: Lonnie Shelton, Jim McMillian, Bill Bradley, Walt Frazier, coach Red Holzman, and trainer Dan Whelan. © Larry Berman—BermanSports.com. Used by permission.

Formerly there was a clear hierarchy among players. Now, as the team struggled, there was locker room tension regarding playing time. Luther "Ticky" Burden joined the Knicks after the NBA merger with the ABA, where he had starred as a member of the Virginia Squires and earned first-team All-Rookie honors. Now he was unhappily sitting on the bench and not shy about sharing his discontent with reporters. "I'm the fifth guard on this team and to think I'm behind Mo Layton and (Butch) Beard," Burden told the *New York Amsterdam News*, "I think it's a joke." Burden even asked management for a trade, insistent that he should be in the starting lineup—if not on the Knicks, then somewhere else in the NBA.[54] Little did he know at the time, but Burden was about to slide even further down the pecking order.

On Tuesday, December 7, Americans commemorated the thirty-fifth anniversary of the attack on Pearl Harbor; in New York, residents read headlines warning of potential transit system cuts; in Madison Square Garden, the Knicks dropped to 10–13 after a seventeen-point loss to Portland; and sportswriters across the country reported that the Braves' all-star center Bob McAdoo was on the trading block.[55]

In late October, McAdoo and his agent began meeting with the Braves about a contract extension. Coming off his second straight All-NBA team and third consecutive scoring title, McAdoo was clearly one of the best players in the NBA. And he expected to be paid like it. More specifically, McAdoo wanted Julius Erving–level money after news broke that Dr. J had signed a six-year, $3.2 million deal with the Sixers. Braves co-owner Paul Snyder balked at McAdoo's demands and insisted they already had a handshake deal in place. "He had agreed to sign," Snyder said, "but . . . his lawyer would not accept the deal. He wanted some other things, and I told him to go to hell." As negotiations broke down, Snyder decided to trade McAdoo, sending him and backup center Tom McMillen to New York for John Gianelli and cash (reportedly $3 million).[56] McMillen, like Bradley a former Rhodes Scholar at Oxford and future US congressman, was in the checkout line at the supermarket when he heard about the trade; McAdoo was Christmas shopping in Toronto with teammate Randy Smith when Mrs. McAdoo called to tell him they were headed to the Big Apple, giving the Knicks their next "store-bought Messiah."[57]

McAdoo was born and raised in Greensboro, North Carolina, during the height of the civil rights movement—he was nine years old when Black college students sat-in at a Woolworth lunch counter two miles from his elementary school.[58] In high school, McAdoo chose to enroll at Smith High instead of all-Black Dudley, while Greensboro residents heatedly debated school integration and busing. At Smith, McAdoo played the saxophone in the marching band and excelled athletically, setting the state high school high jump record by leaping 6 feet, 7 inches his senior year. Poor college entrance exam scores kept McAdoo from playing Division I basketball after high school, so he attended Vincennes Junior College in Indiana for two years. In 1971, he enrolled at the University of North Carolina, becoming the only junior college transfer legendary UNC coach Dean Smith recruited in his thirty-six years in Chapel Hill. He immediately led the Tar Heels to the Final Four before declaring for the NBA Draft—also becoming the first player Smith lost early to the pros. "I was ten years ahead of [Michael] Jordan and [James] Worthy doing it," McAdoo said, "I guess I helped clear the way for those guys because I caught hell for leaving."[59] Then-commissioner Walter Kennedy advised teams to pass on McAdoo in the 1972 draft because of rumors about a possible secret contract with the ABA's Virginia Squires, so, Portland selected LaRue Martin, one of the greatest busts in draft history, before the Braves ignored Kennedy's advice and selected the precocious Tar Heel with the second overall pick.

As a rookie, the Braves played McAdoo out of position at small forward, starting him alongside second-year center Elmore Smith and burly All-Star power forward Bob Kauffman. McAdoo still finished second on the team in scoring (18 points per game) and earned Rookie of the Year honors. That offseason, Kauffman and Smith left the Braves, allowing McAdoo to move to center, his natural position. All McAdoo did as a sophomore was lead the NBA in scoring (30.6 points per game) and field goal percentage (54.7%). Paired with dynamic rookie point guard Ernie DiGregorio and electrifying wing players Randy Smith and Jim McMillian, McAdoo thrived in the up-tempo, high-scoring offense head coach Jack Ramsay created in Buffalo.

What set McAdoo apart from other NBA centers was his ability to shoot accurately from long distance. In the 1970s, teams expected their centers to set up near the basket, grapple for position inside, and try to navigate the painted area for easy baskets or rebounds. A handful of centers—Reed, Dave Cowens, and Jerry Lucas, for example—could step out for a 15-foot jump shot, but McAdoo was comfortable past the modern three-point line. As legendary center Bill Russell said of McAdoo, "he's the best shooting player at *any* position I've ever seen." "You try to get him out of range," Russell continued, "but he never is."[60] Cowens, who guarded McAdoo for half a dozen years, agreed. "My whole thing was protect the rim, protect the basket," Cowens told me. "And now all of a sudden you're out on the perimeter . . . you're like 'wait, it's not supposed to be this way!' He wore my ass out."[61] In 1974–75, McAdoo was named league MVP after scoring 2,831 points. At the time, it was the most ever recorded in a season by anyone other than Wilt Chamberlain, and it still ranks as the eighth-highest single-season point total in NBA history.

Despite his on-court success, McAdoo grew increasingly unhappy in Buffalo. Teammates and friends accepted that some of it was just his personality (he could be moody), but it was more than just that.[62] McAdoo felt underappreciated. "I don't think anyone pays much attention to what I do," McAdoo told a reporter.[63] Playing in a small market also limited McAdoo's exposure. Nationally televised games were rare and usually featured big-market teams. Buffalo was the twenty-eighth largest city in the United States and the second smallest with an NBA team (ahead of only Portland). And, even in Buffalo, McAdoo was second to Bills running back O. J. Simpson in terms of media visibility.

New Yorkers were excited about the newest Knick, although even McAdoo's attorney admitted that adding another star player to the roster meant that "they're short about four basketballs there."[64] Fans packed the box office to buy tickets after the trade was announced. As one police officer said, "we get [large crowds] when tickets go on sale for a rock show, but not for the Knicks."[65] Veteran Knicks also recognized the difference. "The Garden was a ghost town," Frazier admitted later. "There were no lines outside. No people. No ticket requests." With McAdoo in the fold, that changed overnight. "Now the beautiful people are trying to get their tickets back," Frazier said; "the Garden is the place to be seen again."[66] Not all Knicks players were convinced the trade would prove beneficial. "He can help the team," Burden admitted, "but I think some of the veterans will slack up and not carry their weight."[67] Still, McAdoo remained humble at his introductory press conference. "I'll just try and blend in with the rest of the fellows," McAdoo told reporters, "and bring a banner back to New York."[68]

Maybe more than McAdoo's other new teammates, the thirty-three-year-old Bradley was excited about the potential for one more NBA title. Bradley was a throwback. He was a six-foot-five Rhodes Scholar who made the most of limited natural athleticism. "His shoulders slope, his muscles are unimpressive, he is a poor jumper, and he is not an unusually fast runner," Pete Axthelm wrote in *The City Game*. But Bradley "forced the other Knicks to keep in motion, virtually assuring the perennial presences of that nightly Knicks hero, the open man."[69] Despite being dubbed a "Great White Hope" in leading the Princeton Tigers to the 1965 NCAA Final Four, Bradley resisted the label and became, according to Frazier, "the least prejudiced player I've ever met."[70] Like other brilliant minds, he could also be somewhat flighty. Bradley met his wife, Ernestine Schlant, a comparative literature professor, in his apartment building. "There were times when he was without a telephone or electricity," she later wrote, "because he had forgotten to open the mail and pay the bills." The two married during the 1974 All-Star break so Bradley would not miss any games; it was a small ceremony, and they kept it secret so no one would make a fuss.[71] It was classic Bradley. On the title-winning teams, Bradley quietly did all the little things; he would score about a dozen points, secure three or four rebounds, and drive his opponent crazy with his physical defense. Holzman almost never called a play for Bradley but knew he would always be in the right place at the right time.

Even as Bradley's role on the Knicks became more marginal, expectations soared. Haywood, replaced by McAdoo as the team's star attraction, raved about his new teammate. "We're getting the ball out and playing my kind of game now," Haywood told reporters after McAdoo's second week with the team. "McAdoo has opened things up for us and I can go inside more." Frazier, asked to dial back his role on offense, said, "The pack is back," and he told reporters, "So far there are no egos on this team."[72] The Knicks won six of their first seven with McAdoo in the lineup; their only loss was a one-point, Christmas Day heartbreaker against the Sixers witnessed by a capacity crowd of 19,694 in which scalpers were getting as much as $50 for $12 Garden seats.[73] Mel "Killer" Davis was blunt when reminding me, years later, "There was a lot of talent out there."[74]

The honeymoon between the Knicks and McAdoo was short-lived, however. New York went 4–10 in January, and McAdoo complained that Frazier and Monroe walked the ball up the court rather than pushing the pace.[75] Sometimes during timeouts, taking a break from chomping on a towel, McAdoo would encourage teammates to pass him the ball more. "I haven't had a shot in three times down the floor," he would tell guards like Butch Beard, who tried to spread the ball around to keep everyone happy.[76] "It's not Red's fault," Frazier said when asked about Holzman's struggles to adapt. "He's coaching the talent he has. This team is more of a one-on-one team than a team that runs plays like we were then. Red still relates to the players, he's still in control of the situation. He's the same coach. He's a great coach." Despite Frazier's support, the Knicks named Holzman's eventual successor in the middle of the season, announcing that Willis Reed, captain of the legendary Garden of Eden squads, would one day replace his old mentor.[77]

As the Knicks remade themselves with new frontcourt players McAdoo and Haywood, the cultural phenomenon known as hip-hop was slowly spreading beyond the boundaries of the South Bronx.

Kool Herc might have created record-mixing, but he was not a song-writer and was not recording new music. Instead, he repurposed older or obscure tracks like James Brown's "Give It Up Turn It Loose," "The Mexican" by Babe Ruth (the English rock band), and a rare piece called "Apache," covered by the Incredible Bongo Band. Eddie Luna, the founder of the Dynamic Rockers dance crew, still got excited decades later about Apache. "Apache?" he said, "forget it! I can't listen to Apache. I just—I start sweating, you know! And I get angry! And it's like, I wanna hit the floor!"[78] Soon, wannabe Hercs were trolling local record stores in search of rare singles to one-up the master.[79] Downtown Records, located in the Forty-Second Street and Sixth Avenue subway station, fielded tele-phone calls from kids throughout the South Bronx looking for copies of obscure cuts like Dennis Coffy's "Son of Scorpio," Jeannie Reynolds's "Fruit Song," or, as Grandmaster Flash put it, "crazy beats from the Phil-ippines and India with sounds I didn't know a human being could make."[80] Many of these hip-hop pioneers used disco music for their tracks. "If you listen to early rap," DMC (of Run-DMC) argues, "everybody would use disco. People minds is blown away how connected disco's presentation was, just a hybrid form or cousin of hip-hop."[81]

Herc and other deejays following in his footsteps used the extended breaks created by the Merry-Go-Round to give kids more time to show off their best moves on the dance floor.[82] Dancers called themselves B-boys or B-girls—the B stood for break or beat or Bronx, depending on who you asked—but the media dubbed them break dancers (a name authentic B-girls and B-boys despised).[83] Twins Kevin and Kieth Smith became two of the first top-shelf B-boys after showing up to early Kool Herc parties. Kevin was only twelve years old at the time, but the duo tore up the dance floor with their moves, including pioneering the practice of taking their dancing to the floor, mixing in the toprock and, later, the downrock.[84] Herc dubbed them the "Nigga Twins," and they soon joined the Herculoids.[85]

Breaking was physically demanding and mimicked violent action; every movement from entering the dance floor through the performer's exit was deliberate, if unscripted. Certain songs became clearly identi-fied with dance battles. "The Mexican," for example, was "more for fighting," explains one B-boy. "That's the type of song you just wanna uprock. Like when you doing 'Mexican,' man, you always wanna go out there and just fight. Like battling."[86] B-girls and B-boys drew inspiration from old-fashioned dances like the Charleston and Lindy as well as recent phenomena like kung-fu (which was popular at the time) and capoeira, the acrobatic Afro-Brazilian martial art.[87] At least they looked like they borrowed from capoeira. "We didn't know what the fuck no capoeira was, man," remembers Crazy Legs. "We were in the ghetto!"[88] Bambaataa's crew, the Zulu Kings, integrated increasingly difficult moves into their repertoire, working in "ass spins, spider walks, footwork, and mime similar to the electric boogie."[89] Just like playground basketball players, breakers, according to Trac 2 of the Star Child la Rock Crew, competed for "ghetto celebrity status."[90] To be known as a highly skilled baller or a nasty downrocker with sick footwork? That was ghetto celebrity.

Hoping to shake the Knicks out of their funk, the team's biggest ghetto celebrity, Clyde Frazier, stepped down as team captain, a position he had inherited a few years earlier from Reed. "The captaincy is not my bag," Frazier told the *Times*. "I'm not a verbal guy. I'm not a leader. If the players want to follow me, let them follow my leadership on the court."[91] At the same time, management was also growing unhappy with his on-court performance. Frazier was still solid defensively but was no longer elite and had lost a little quickness. Tellingly, he was left off the All-Star team for the first time in the seventies and some fans questioned his motivation after signing a $450,000 per year contract.[92] On February 1, Holzman left Frazier out of the starting lineup and, for the first time since 1969, brought him into the game as a reserve.

While Frazier faltered, the new captain, Monroe, regained some of his old swagger. In November 1976, the team traveled to Philadelphia where Earl the Pearl, born and raised in South Philly, met up with old friends after the game. "I get them all tickets for that first game with the Sixers," he said, "and I found out that they'd all become Sixers fans. Damn."[93] Perhaps motivated by his buddies, Monroe looked like the "Black Magic" of old, spinning on a dime and using his backside to pin defenders on his hip. When Monroe was at his best, trying to guard him was—in the words of David Halberstam—like facing a "ghost."[94]

In the 1960s, Monroe was a playground hero whose legend was only surpassed by the real thing. He was "Black Jesus" and "Magic." But now, in the late seventies, Monroe struggled with creaky knees and bone spurs, reminders of hours spent pounding up and down hot asphalt courts. Still, he was one of Woody Allen's favorite Knicks (alongside Frazier), and a young Spike Lee called Monroe "the Miles Davis of hoop" for his improvisational brilliance.[95]

When Earl the Pearl reemerged in the middle of the 1976–77 season, sportswriter Mike Lupica compared him to "a retired magician who has taken his full box of tricks from deep in the closet, dusted it off, and said to a new audience every night, 'This is the way it used to be.' The Magic Show."[96] That winter, Earvin Johnson was just a seventeen-year-old kid attending high school in Lansing, Michigan; in basketball, there was only one Magic—and his name was Earl Monroe.

After a rough January, February brought a few bright spots for New York and the Knicks. The rock band Kiss made their Madison Square Garden debut, filling the arena for their show, Monroe made the All-Star team for the fourth (and final) time, and rookie Lonnie Shelton was looking like the blue-collar forward the team lacked since DeBusschere retired.

Then Pistol Pete happened.

On February 22, the Knicks hosted the New Orleans Jazz and won 119–102, limiting NBA scoring leader Pistol Pete Maravich to 28 points. Three days later, the teams met again, this time in New Orleans. Maravich came out firing, and on the Jazz's first possession he connected on a baseline layup, converting the three-point play when officials called a foul on Tom McMillen. Maravich kept scoring, and the Knicks had no answer. They started Frazier against him, but turned to Monroe, Beard, Burden, and even Dean Meminger in a futile attempt to slow down Maravich.

Nothing worked.

By the time Maravich fouled out with two minutes left in the game, he had tallied 68 points, the most ever for a guard at that point in NBA history. Only Elgin Baylor (who was coincidentally coaching Maravich and the Jazz that night) and Wilt Chamberlain had ever scored more in a single game. For the entire fourth quarter the New Orleans crowd stood, cheering every time Maravich touched the ball. Monroe was spellbound. "There was no way we could stop him," he admitted afterward. "The Pistol was hot tonight, he was really going off. The thing that came to mind was that he was hitting shots from everywhere. Unconscionable shots."[97] Holzman was also impressed. "It was a beautiful thing to watch for the fans here," said Red. "We didn't play well, but he was phenomenal."[98]

After losing in New Orleans, and five of their next eight, Holzman dropped a bombshell, announcing his retirement at the end of the season. "Red was done," Haywood wrote later. "He didn't want to coach no more."[99] According to Holzman, he was basically fired by Alan "Bottom Line" Cohen. And to keep Reed, named coach-in-waiting two months earlier, from interviewing for other coaching vacancies, the Knicks felt they had to pull the trigger mid-season.[100]

The Knicks went 10–7 after Holzman's announcement, but their 40–42 season record earned them a third-place finish in the Atlantic (behind Boston and Philly) and another spring spent watching the playoffs from home and seeing Bill Walton lead the Trail Blazers to their first NBA title.

Arriving back in New York, the newly retired Holzman became a consultant who was never consulted, swept into a small office in a quiet corner of Madison Square Garden. Still, Red didn't mind. In fact, Holzman loved retirement. "Some guys retire, their friends tell 'em, 'You won't like it,'" Red said. "I loved it. I've always been a great relaxer."[101]

Without the calming presence of Holzman on the sideline, and with a rapidly aging team, the Knicks were in a rut. "This team has got to change the whole direction in which it's moving," Jackson said after the season's last game. Asked if the Knicks could be successful with their current roster, Jackson pulled out a timely analogy. "Hiring five movie stars for $5 million apiece doesn't mean a movie will be good."[102]

The 1976–77 Knicks had one of the league's highest payrolls, led by the quartet of McAdoo, Haywood, Frazier, and Monroe. Newly installed Coach Reed further muddied the waters when he told reporters the Knicks "would be so much better off if they had a guy like Dave Cowens, who exemplifies hustle and drive. Every guy would play harder because he does." Reed was right, of course, but every team in the league would have been better off with a Hall of Fame center like Cowens in the lineup. McAdoo, understandably sensitive to Reed's remark, fired back. "I don't think the Lakers and Knicks of those days that Reed . . . [is] talking about would be able to win as much today. The league," McAdoo argued, "is tougher as a whole."[103]

Much of the tension among the Knicks came from unfiltered statements made to the press and published in local newspapers. Likewise, on the streets of New York, verbal posturing became an important component of the Black youth culture emerging in the South Bronx. DJ Kool Herc's Merry-Go-Round not only provided an instrumental break encouraging dance battles but also allowed time for speaking rhythmically on the microphone. As Grandmaster Caz remembers, "MCing evolved from the DJ having a microphone to make announcements . . . then people started to embellish on how they said things."[104] Rapping to the beat, what Caz calls MCing, originated from many sources: prison toasts, the dozens, and maybe Jalal Nuriddin's 1973 *Hustlers Convention* album (released under the name "Lightnin' Rod").[105] Toasts were "violent, scatological, obscene, and misogynist," one historian writes; in prison they had been "used for decades to while away time in situations of enforced boredom."[106] Think of dirty "your mom" jokes. On the streets of the South Bronx, toasts became a competition to see who could come up with the most-obscene insults. In the Herculoids, the king of toasts was Coke La Rock who, at Herc's first party back on Sedgwick Avenue, grabbed the microphone to shout out greetings to his friends. Over time, he began to rhyme his shout-outs ("You rock and you don't stop!"), entirely improvisational. As with Herc, folks began borrowing La Rock's technique, and soon MCs throughout the South Bronx were rapping as part of their performances.

Despite the coaching change, the summer of 1977 was relatively quiet for the Knicks. On a corporate level, the team was still navigating its relationship with the Nets, who wanted to move from the Nassau Coliseum on Long Island to New Jersey's Meadowlands Sports Complex, where a multisport arena planned next to an extant horseracing venue and Giants Stadium. "New Jersey is a valuable part of our franchise territory," Burke argued.[107] Commissioner O'Brien agreed. "Operation of the N.B.A.," he reasoned, "is grounded upon the principle that teams must be accorded exclusive territorial rights."[108] Ultimately, the Nets did move to New Jersey in the summer of 1977, but for four seasons they played in the RAC—the Rutgers Athletic Center—forty miles down I-95 from the Meadowlands, much to the chagrin of Meadowlands manager David "Sonny" Werblin.

With the Nets situation temporarily resolved, the Knicks turned their full attention to the NBA draft. The Milwaukee Bucks made Indiana University center Kent Benson the top pick—teams still loved big-bodied, white centers from programs like IU—while the Nets plucked Brooklynite Bernard King out of the University of Tennessee with the seventh pick.

Selecting tenth overall, the Knicks chose University of Minnesota guard Ray Williams. "This is great," Williams gushed to reporters, "it's the only ball club I was with since I was a kid."[109] Williams, born and raised in the Bronx with his older brother Gus—then a Golden State Warrior—would sneak into Knicks games by picking up ticket stubs outside the Garden.[110] He vividly remembered watching the iconic Knicks teams from the era of Eden and desperately wanted to be a part of the next great New York basketball dynasty.

Williams was long, lean, and muscular. "I don't think Ray ever lifted weights," former trainer Mike Saunders told me, "but he had a body like Adonis. He could do anything on the court."[111] Before college Williams had led Westchester County's Mount Vernon High to two state basketball championships. As teammate Mike Glenn informed me, "Ray was just stronger than everyone on the team. They left Ray alone."[112] Little did Knicks fans know, but drafting Williams marked the first step in a real rebuilding of the team.

Summers as a New York Knick in the late seventies meant a break from the grueling schedule that began with training camp in early October and stretched to April or May. Including preseason, regular season, and the playoffs, they played at least one hundred games and traveled thousands of miles crisscrossing the country, spending countless hours in airports or scrunched into seats on commercial flights. No private jets for NBA players back then. It was easy to lose track of days or even forget what city you were in. By Memorial Day, Knicks players scattered across the country. Some left New York City for home elsewhere, and those who stayed did their own thing. Few players lived in Manhattan. Frazier had to because, well, he was Clyde. But most of his teammates rented apartments in nearby communities like Flushing, Queens (only a thirty-minute commute to the Garden), or across the river in New Jersey.

Thus, few Knicks were in New York City when, on July 13, 1977, lights across the five boroughs flickered and then went out entirely. The weather was hot outside, pushing 100°F even at 9:30 pm, so thousands of New Yorkers were hanging out on stoops or curbs when the streets went dark. At Shea Stadium, Chicago Cubs pitcher Ray Burris stopped mid-windup in his pitch to Mets third baseman Lenny Randall; Mayor Beame, seeking reelection that fall, paused mid-sentence during a speech about mortgages; Rahiem of the group Grandmaster Flash and the Furious Five was shooting hoops at his housing complex; and actors from the Broadway musical *The Wiz* broke character and chatted with patrons to pass the time in the semi-dark, hoping it was just a brief outage.[113]

It wasn't. And the looting started about fifteen minutes later.

Blackout looting was "an explosion a long time in the making," explains one historian. "Thousands of residents were angry and frustrated enough to generate an unprecedented rampage of destruction focusing on neighborhoods of concentrated poverty and public and private disinvestment."[114] Poor and disempowered New Yorkers were already on edge, and a loss of electrical power acted as a catalyst for action. Almost simultaneously, looters broke into Black- and white-owned businesses indiscriminately across the city, from Harlem through Brooklyn, and the Upper West Side through Midtown.

"You take your chance when you get your chance," said a Brooklynite clutching a half-empty wine bottle in one hand and a television, stolen from a nearby store, in the other. Looters hit all five boroughs with no rationale for the destruction. It was not a political protest or outgrowth of civil rights activism, and there were no demands for change or chants from the marauders. In the eyes of at least one police officer, "A bunch of greedy people took advantage. That was it, plain and simple," the cop told a reporter. "Don't go with all that sociological bullshit."[115]

In fact, the police force—or the lack thereof—was one of the biggest problems that day. Many cops ignored the callout, and those who reported did so in areas far from the looting, near where they lived in "white ethnic enclaves on the outskirts."[116] Nearly 40 percent of the off-duty police force refused to report, angry at how City Hall had treated them in the past. Still, cops on the job managed to arrest nearly four thousand looters while showing relative restraint. [117] "If we'd have shot just one person," a Brooklyn officer said, "we'd have a war on our hands."[118]

Within a day, the electric company had restored power to the city, calling the outage an "act of God" and blaming lightning strikes. Mayor Beame disagreed and charged the utility with "gross negligence."[119] The electric company later admitted that human error and systematic machine failure caused the surge.[120] Either way, the aftermath of the blackout was shocking.

Particularly hard hit was the South Bronx. Even there, despite the devastation, President Jimmy Carter refused to declare New York City a disaster area, calling the damage man-made. Carter visited in October as residents yelled "Give us money!" and "We want jobs!" at his passing motorcade. "It was a very sobering trip for me to see the devastation that has taken place in the South Bronx," he admitted. "But I'm impressed by the spirit of hope and determination by the people to save what they have."[121] As noted earlier, the creation of the Cross Bronx Expressway in the 1960s exacerbated existing poverty in the area, prompting white flight to the suburbs, which further eroded the local tax base. Banks stopped granting loans to businesses and potential homeowners in these redlined districts, and by the mid-seventies "it was more profitable to burn than to build."[122]

The blackout of July 1977 also jump-started the nascent hip-hop culture emerging from the devastation of the South Bronx. Some would-be deejays scored sound systems in the looting, taking advantage of the chaos to grab an otherwise unaffordable stereo. Yet others saw in the blackout an opportunity. "I look at the blackout as the official birth date of hip-hop," says James TOP. "It was really established in the summer

Figure 3. President Jimmy Carter greets residents of the South Bronx, circa October 5, 1977. Hum Historical/Alamy Stock Photo.

of 1977."[123] Rahiem agrees. "The blackout is what changed the scope of things," he argues. "It really gave the majority of kids who would have probably been victimized or involved in gang violence in some way, it gave them an option. Gang violence began to diminish because being involved in hip-hop culture, it gave latchkey kids something."[124] Sure, their new record players and mixers might have been stolen, but they justified their actions because the equipment was too expensive for them to purchase.

On October 12, 1977, the Knicks were wrapping up their preseason tour. After playing the Celtics in Dayton, Ohio, they were headed to Landover, Maryland, for a game against the Nets. But more New Yorkers were interested in baseball, as the Yankees were hosting the Los Angeles Dodgers in game two of the World Series. During the game, cameras cut to a live shot a few blocks from the stadium on the west side of the South Bronx where fires engulfed a nearby school. Announcers discussed the blaze several times throughout the broadcast, and journalists spun their discussion into the phrase attributed to, but never uttered by, Howard Cosell: "ladies and gentlemen, the Bronx is burning."[125] In one Bronx neighborhood, Hunts Point-Crotona Park East, the police station earned the nicknames "Fort Apache" and "The Little House on the Prairie" because it was "the only building left standing in a desert of rubble."[126]

The conflagrations continued for years after the Bronx burned on national television. But in the early 1980s, big insurance companies decided to stop pay out claims on tenement housing in the South Bronx. "In the year before they stopped paying insurance," one historian explains, "thirteen hundred buildings were destroyed by fire in the Bronx. The year they stopped, only twelve were."[127]

Thanks to the popularity of the World Series, and the attention paid to the area by President Carter after his predecessor metaphorically told the city to drop dead just two years earlier, the South Bronx became "an iconography of urban ruin in America."[128] Soon after Cosell's phantom call and Carter's visit, this area of New York City became synonymous with depredation and decay. Charlotte Street, which runs just three blocks between Crotona Park and Jennings Street, was mostly empty lots and burned-out shells of tenement buildings, taking on an air of apocalyptic neglect. As such, the residents of this neighborhood were cast as victims to be pitied and ignored, lepers best seen from a distance on a television program warning of the ills of urban living. Why did graffiti artists growing up in the South Bronx tag subway cars? Why did young deejays spin records at Crotona Park, scratching them or back-spinning to create a catchy beat? They wanted to be a part of something bigger than themselves; they wanted to attain a measure of individualism and personal autonomy in a nation that typecast them as pitiful victims.

And so, from this burning Bronx, which city administrators pledged millions to rehabilitate, a cultural phenomenon would emerge that not only engulfed the neighborhoods around Yankee Stadium but would also spread throughout the world.

1975–76 Knicks
Record: 38–44
Playoffs: Did not qualify
Coach: Red Holzman
Average Home Attendance: 16,408
Points Per Game (102.7–14th of 18)
Points Allowed Per Game (103.9–7th of 18)
Team Leaders:

> Points: Earl Monroe (20.7 per game)
> Rebounds: Spencer Haywood (11.3 per game)
> Assists: Walt Frazier (5.9 per game)
> Steals: Walt Frazier (1.8 per game)
> Blocked Shots: Spencer Haywood (1.0 per game)

All-Stars: Walt Frazier
Notable Transactions: Traded Gene Short and a 1979 first-round draft pick to the Seattle SuperSonics for Spencer Haywood

1976–77 Knicks
Record: 40–42
Playoffs: Did not qualify
Coach: Red Holzman
Average Home Attendance: 15,727
Points Per Game: (108.6–7th of 22)
Points Allowed Per Game: (108.6–18th of 22)

Team Leaders:

Points: Bob McAdoo (26.7 per game)
Rebounds: Bob McAdoo (12.7 per game)
Assists: Walt Frazier (5.3 per game)
Steals: Walt Frazier (1.7 per game)
Blocked Shots: Bob McAdoo (1.3 per game)

All-Stars: Earl Monroe and Bob McAdoo

Notable Transactions: Drafted Lonnie Shelton in the second round of the 1976 NBA draft; traded John Gianelli and cash to the Buffalo Braves for Bob McAdoo and Tom McMillen

3

"THE FLASHIEST LOSERS IN THE LEAGUE"

1977–1978

"Start spreadin' the news, I'm leaving today," the song starts. After "today," New York crowds loudly join in: "I want to be a part of it: New York, New York!" Originally performed by Liza Minnelli for the 1977 Martin Scorsese film *New York, New York*, the song became more famous after Frank Sinatra covered it a year later in a performance at Radio City Music Hall. Sinatra's 1980 recorded version peaked at number 32 on the Billboard Hot 100 Chart, and in subsequent decades the song has probably been played at more bar mitzvahs, weddings, and Yankees games than any other. But in the fall of 1977, it was brand-new, just in time to become the theme song for a new mayor.[1]

The 1977 mayoral election in New York City was one for the ages. Better put, the Democratic primary was one for the ages, as Republicans had little chance of winning the mayoralty in the seventies. The primary was a crowded field, and incumbent mayor Abe Beame faced five prominent challengers, including New York secretary of state Mario Cuomo and outspoken former congresswoman Bella Abzug. The biggest issues facing these candidates were the economy and crime, as New York hovered on the brink of bankruptcy while David Berkowitz, better known as the Son of Sam killer, remained on the loose. Between the summers of 1976 and 1977, Berkowitz killed at least six people (and wounded nine others), seemingly at random. He did not limit his attacks to just one borough, committing crimes in Brooklyn, Queens, and the Bronx and terrorizing New Yorkers until being arrested in August 1977, when Mayor Beame was finally able to tell reporters, "The people of New York can rest easy tonight."[2] Despite being the incumbent, Beame failed in his reelection bid, and, in the end, it was Abzug's former colleague in the US House of Representatives, Ed Koch, who would emerge victorious despite polling just 2 percent when the year began.

After winning the election, and even with the Son of Sam behind bars, Koch knew he faced a monumental task. As he later wrote, "When I came into office the city was on its rear end."[3] Tall and balding, with tufts of hair poking out like a monastic tonsure, Koch was notoriously confrontational. "His in-your-face humor and incessant flow of words . . . making impolitic jabs at opponents as 'wackos' in his fast New York twang," writes one biographer, "Koch fashioned himself as a personification of New York."[4] His campaign slogan was particularly hard-hitting, asking voters, "After eight years of charisma [referring to John Lindsay], and four years of the clubhouse [Beame], why not try competence?"[5] Even his inaugural address was stirring. "From its earliest days," he began, "this city has been a lifeboat for the homeless, a larder for the hungry, a living library for the intellectually starved, a refuge not only for the oppressed but also for the creative."[6]

Not all New Yorkers fixated on the mayoral election or the Son of Sam in the fall of 1977. Less than a week after the Bronx burned on live television, New York Yankees slugger Reggie Jackson smacked three home runs to lead his team to a World Series title and gain the nickname "Mr. October." He was the most popular athlete in New York City. But a few years earlier, at the height of the Knicks dynasty, Walt Frazier had been the most popular. On the court, Frazier had orchestrated Coach Holzman's beloved free-flowing offense by always finding the open man, and he had spearheaded the league's stingiest defense, earning seven straight All-Defense team honors. Off the court, Frazier transformed into Clyde, the coolest cat in the Big Apple, as famous for his stylish attire as for his athletic prowess. Frazier drove his Rolls-Royce (New York license plate "WCF" in homage to himself, Walt "Clyde" Frazier) to the hippest bars and wore full-length mink coats and his trademark hats. In 1970, he became one of the first NBA players to endorse a sneaker, as Puma released the low-cut suede "Clyde." All the kids in New York City wanted a pair, and they

Figure 4. Walt Frazier. © Larry Berman—BermanSports.com. Used by permission.

quickly became a part of Gotham's underground sneaker culture, worn by playground ballers and B-boys alike.

But by the time of Jackson's historic three-homer game, Clyde was clearly past his prime as a basketball player. "[Coach] Reed must find a way for the 32-year old Frazier to change his style of play," Sam Goldaper wrote in the *Times*. "Pro basketball ways have changed and Frazier has not." Frazier said all the right things, of course, when asked about his willingness to adapt. "Willis is the coach," Frazier insisted, "and if he wants me to change, then, I'll change." Asked about the possibility of being traded to another team, Frazier laughed. "There are not too many teams that want a 32-year old guard with three more years left on his contract and my salary [$450,000 per year]."[7]

In a preseason game against the Milwaukee Bucks, Frazier scored 19 points, grabbed 7 rebounds, and handed out 8 assists. "Clyde has a new enthusiasm," Monroe gushed to reporters. "Clyde is talking, he appears happier, he's putting out more."[8] Sure, maybe Frazier was happier. Or maybe the Knicks drafting a point guard, Ray Williams, in the first round of the draft lit a fire under him.

It didn't matter. A week later, Frazier was gone. Unbeknown to his teammates, president Mike Burke and general manager Eddie Donovan had been actively shopping Frazier for some time. Atlanta seemed a likely landing spot, but new team owner Ted Turner turned down the Knicks in the hopes that rookie head coach Hubie Brown could spark his young Hawks without an expensive superstar on the roster. Los Angeles general manager Jerry West, an old nemesis of Frazier, was interested, but Lakers owner Jack Kent Cooke backed out, skittish about adding another big contract. Finally, the Cleveland Cavaliers, a season removed from their "Miracle of Richfield" playoff run, entered the fray. The Cavs desperately wanted to become legitimate title contenders and hoped Clyde would be the missing piece to take them to the top.

Frazier was floored. "After playing in New York for 10 years, I wanted to finish my career there," he said.[9] He was especially hurt that Reed, his former teammate, had not called to let him know personally. "My agent met me at my apartment in the city to inform me," Frazier wrote in an autobiography.[10] Later he reflected on the move. "I guess the cool image started working against me," he said. "When we won, people said 'Frazier's cool, he never shows emotion.' When we lost, they said, 'Look at

Frazier, he doesn't care.' "[11] No matter what fans thought, Frazier's agent was livid, informing reporters, "He's not going to report to Cleveland—that's for sure."[12]

Technically, Frazier was not actually traded to Cleveland. Instead, he was sent to the Cavaliers as compensation. Part of the settlement of the Oscar Robertson lawsuit called for a team losing a player via free agency to receive a player or draft pick as compensation. In 1977, the Knicks signed the franchise's first free agent: Cavs guard Jim Cleamons, a seven-year vet who Burke and Donovan viewed as a younger, cheaper, and more willing role player than Frazier. Cleamons was part of the first true class of NBA free agents (Gail Goodrich, who relocated from the Lakers to the Jazz, was the only significant free agent in 1976), and only a few players changed teams. Other than Cleamons, the major signings were the Bullets adding Bob Dandridge from the Bucks, Truck Robinson joining Goodrich in New Orleans, and Jamaal Wilkes and Gus Williams leaving the Warriors for the Lakers and SuperSonics respectively.

So, Cleveland received Frazier as compensation, but to many fans it seemed like the Knicks had just traded Clyde for a journeyman.

With Frazier exiled to Ohio, expectations for the Knicks in their first season under Reed were split. On one hand, given their talent, the Knicks were bound to improve their 40–42 record. "Last year," new *Times* reporter Tony Kornheiser wrote, "they played as if they were strangers coming together for playground pickup games. . . . The Knicks were the flashiest losers in the league." Sage veteran forward Phil Jackson agreed. "There were too many guys reading stat sheets . . . Willis is gonna surprise people. He's not going to have the slightest trouble getting people to play hard for him."[13]

But Reed and the man he replaced on the bench, Red Holzman, were less convinced. "I don't know what happened with the team last year," Holzman admitted. "Maybe the guys will do more for Willis. Who the hell knows?"[14] For his part, Reed tried to downplay inflated expectations. "Let's be realistic," he told reporters. "We're not a team that's going to win the title. I'd be happy if we made the playoffs."[15] In training camp, Reed got a glimpse of his players' motivation. "One of Willis' innovations," Jackson explained, "was to make the players run two miles on an oval cinder track within a prescribed time period. McAdoo ran the course in twenty-seven minutes, Ticky Burden did it in twenty-eight minutes, and I kind of limped in just behind them."[16]

It was not what Reed hoped for from elite professional athletes. To put their times in perspective, American Garry Bjorklund finished thirteenth in the 1976 Olympic 10,000 meters, a little over six miles in roughly the same amount of time it took the Knicks trio to jog two miles.

With less-than-ideal effort given during the preseason, and modest expectations from a rookie head coach, New Yorkers were not sure what to expect when the Knicks opened the 1977–78 season at home against the Kansas City Kings. With no big-name addition to the team, attendance was low: around fourteen thousand showed up for opening night. Sharp-shooting Kings forward Scott Wedman led all scorers with 29 points, but Jackson and Monroe—the two remaining members of the 1973 championship team—combined for 43 to lead the Knicks to a 120–113 win. Putting up 120 points and playing an up-tempo style was a refreshing change, and afterward Monroe was ecstatic. "We feel if we can get the ball out and we're running we can be competitive," he told reporters. "It's a big change from last year and I love it—it's my game."[17]

Four days later, New York hosted their old nemeses from Washington and dropped 141 points on the Bullets, including 79 in the second half. In that game, New York tied a club record with 61 made field goals, as eight Knicks scored in double figures, led by Monroe's 22. Perhaps most importantly, several rookies contributed substantially. Ray Williams handed out 7 assists and scored 12 points in twenty-one minutes off the bench, and, after the game, Frazier told reporters, "[He'll] break all of my records. And that includes my record for assists."[18]

But Williams was not the only rookie sensation for the Knicks that night. In the 1977 draft, New York had used its second-round pick on Toby Knight, who poured in 17 off the bench in the team's win against Washington. Knight was born in the Bronx and raised on Long Island but had headed west to play college ball at Notre Dame. Knight was a wiry and strong six-foot-nine. A natural left-hander, Knight often drove to the basket before finishing with a short jump shot or layup around the rim. He never became a star in New York—a serious knee injury in 1980 would derail a promising career—but Knight provided the team with much-needed versatility thanks to his ability to play either forward spot.

Three days after their big win against the Bullets, the 2–0 Knicks hosted the Cavaliers. A sellout crowd, the first in nearly four years, packed Madison Square Garden to cheer the return of Clyde to the Big Apple. Before the game, Frazier admitted he was nervous. "New York fans," he told the Knicks' radio broadcaster Marv Albert, "are about as sentimental as traffic cops."[19] But out of respect for Clyde, Knicks fans stood and cheered for several minutes when he was introduced. "I thought the ovation would go on all night," Frazier said afterward. "Tonight was the greatest. They still love me."[20] The Knicks and Cavs finished regulation tied at 105, and with less than two minutes left in overtime Cleveland clung to a three-point lead. In an ending straight out of a Hollywood movie, Frazier hit a game-clenching free throw and then deflected an errant pass to preserve the 117–112 win for his new team. After the game, Clyde visited his old haunts—PJ Clarke's (at the corner of East Fifty-Fifth and Third Avenue), Maxwell Plum (on First Avenue, described as a "flamboyant restaurant and singles bar"), and, of course, Harry M's (located under Madison Square Garden).[21] Instead of another night in a hotel, Clyde slept in his apartment on East Fifty-Seventh, where a few years earlier he had hosted teammates to watch the Kings revive the Knicks' playoff hopes. Looking back, his game-clenching performance in the Garden was a rare highlight in what would be his career-ending three-year stay in Cleveland. "The Cavaliers never accepted me," he wrote later. "To them, I was New York. I was always an outsider on that team."[22]

After a strong start, the Knicks hit a rough patch in late November. Unlike in previous years, when the Knicks shook up their roster midseason, the front office decided to stand pat. "If we have a bad season, it's going to be with the players we have," Reed insisted. "We're going with the horses we've got."[23]

Skill level, even without Frazier, was not the issue; the Knicks featured several of the most talented players in the NBA. The problem was discipline.

The Knicks drilled and scrimmaged for several hours per day throughout the preseason and then eased up on their practice schedule after opening night. In the late seventies, the team practiced at Pace University, in downtown Manhattan's business district. Players arrived in the late morning, having Mike Saunders (who replaced Danny Whelan as the team's trainer in 1978) tape their ankles or help with therapy. By 11:00 a.m. (maybe noon, depending on the day), players were on the floor, running through drills and reviewing the game plan for the next opponent. When the basketball arena at Pace flooded in early 1979, the team moved to LaGuardia Community College in Queens, just a few blocks away from Peter Parker's stomping grounds as Spiderman (in Forest Hills). But the routine stayed about the same.[24]

Still, hoping to instill more discipline, Reed installed a series of fines. Showing up late to practice, missing a team bus, or forgetting equipment resulted in a $25 fine . . . plus a $5 per minute charge for tardiness. Emblematic of the Knicks' lack of discipline was their December 3 loss to the Bucks in which they committed an astounding 40 turnovers, including 10 by Ray Williams alone. Two weeks later, the Knicks traveled to Milwaukee and, despite a team-record 63 field goals, lost 152–150 in triple overtime. "Sometimes I think Willis wants us to play like robots," McAdoo complained after a close loss in mid-December.[25] But even more problematic than McAdoo's grumbling was the increasingly strained relationship between Reed and another star big man.

In Seattle, Spencer Haywood played for four coaches, including Bill Russell, who Haywood viewed as a father figure. When Russell pushed for the Sonics to trade Haywood to New York, the young forward felt betrayed. A deteriorating situation with Reed, also a Hall of Fame center, revived many of those same feelings for the now twenty-eight-year-old. Haywood had worked hard in the 1977 off-season, dropping twenty-five pounds of fat by spending hours on a Nautilus machine, and reported to training camp in the best shape of his career, despite battling a drug addiction of which few were aware.[26] But in a mid-December game against Phoenix, Reed penciled in a new group to start the game; Monroe and Cleamons would open at guard, while McAdoo, Jim McMillian, and Lonnie Shelton would begin in the frontcourt. Haywood watched the tip-off from the bench, an unfamiliar spot for the five-time All-Star. He played just thirteen minutes that night and lashed out after the game. "You don't have to humiliate me," he vented to reporters about Reed. "If you want to make a change, fine . . . but I don't think they're going to pay me that kind of money to sit on the bench." Haywood insisted he wasn't demanding a trade but admitted that "maybe I can go to New Orleans or someplace else where they need a forward who can score."[27] "I just wish

Willis would tell me what I should do," he said. "I'm treated like I have the plague."[28]

Haywood and Reed met in private to diffuse the situation. "I think we resolved everything," Haywood told reporters afterward. Yet Reed seemed confused by Haywood's outburst. "I don't know why Spencer does these things," he said. "If a guy has a problem, let's talk about it and we'll deal with it."[29] "When you are winning," Reed continued, "everyone understands. When you are losing, they will gripe. We can be a competitive team if we play it my way."[30]

On Christmas Day, the Knicks showed how good they could be when they worked together, pulling out a surprising 113–110 win over the favored Sixers behind 30 points from McAdoo and 27 from the suddenly rejuvenated Haywood. Subsequent wins against the Nets, Jazz, and Cavaliers pulled them to 20–15, the third-best record in the Eastern Conference.

But just hours after the ball dropped in Times Square to mark the beginning of 1978, the Knicks experienced a shocking change.

Six months earlier, the Knicks had officially become a subsidiary of Gulf & Western Industries. Gulf & Western, which already owned 81 percent of the stock holdings of the Madison Square Garden Corporation, added the Knicks, the NHL's New York Rangers, and a few other entities to their holdings, paying double the market value for the properties as part of their hostile takeover.[31] "I was called into Michael Burke's office," Mel Lowell told me, "and I was told something was going to happen . . . 'if you'd like to remain an employee,' [Burke said], keep your mouth shut." At the time, Lowell was a tax manager on the eighteenth floor of 2 Penn Plaza. A few months later, apparently having kept his mouth shut, he became vice president of sports operations, conducting all business and financial affairs for the Knicks and Rangers, including budgets and contracts.[32]

Then, on January 1, 1978, Gulf & Western named a new chairman of Madison Square Garden—effectively the new operating owner of the Knicks.

Sonny Werblin was a native New Yorker, the son of a paper bag manufacturer from Flatbush. Werblin had attended Rutgers and started working with the Music Corporation of America (MCA) as an office boy in 1933.[33] By age forty, Werblin was the president of MCA, with a well-deserved reputation for putting together big-time entertainment deals like the *Ed Sullivan Show* and for working with well-known performers like Elizabeth Taylor and Ronald Reagan.[34] "Not only did Mr. Werblin know Mr. Reagan as an actor," Lowell informed me. "Mrs. Werblin knew Nancy. They were very close. His secretary would buzz him and tell him 'President Reagan is on the phone.' "[35]

In the mid-sixties, sports fans took notice when Werblin led a syndicate to purchase the American Football League's New York Titans. He renamed them the New York Jets and signed star University of Alabama quarterback Joe Namath to a record-breaking deal. After selling his shares of the Jets, Werblin oversaw the construction of the Meadowlands Sports Complex out of 588 acres of New Jersey swampland. As he had done with the Titans/Jets and the Meadowlands, Werblin jumped in with both feet after agreeing to a deal with Gulf & Western. He signed Fred Shero, one of the NHL's top coaches, to lead the Rangers and picked up star forwards Ulf Nilsson and Anders Hedberg to anchor the team's top line. The Rangers improved from thirty wins to forty and reached the Stanley Cup Finals in Werblin's first year at the helm.

Could he work the same magic for the Knicks?

Werblin had a deserved reputation for being hands-on: "from million-dollar negotiations to the water pressure of the showers in locker rooms," one journalist wrote.[36] He installed a lounge in Madison Square Garden for the wives and girlfriends of Knicks and Rangers and spent time after every game talking to players in the locker room. "He was the perfect owner," Hubie Brown told me about Werblin, "Sonny was a physical force. He was the greatest master of making everyone feel comfortable in their jobs."[37] Werblin was even hands-on in contract negotiations. "Sonny was born on March 17, 1910." Lowell laughed, recalling the memory. "How do I know that?" he asked me rhetorically. "Every contract I did with a player had to end with $317.10"[38] A five-million-dollar contract, then, would actually pay out $5,000,317.10—it was just another of Sonny's quirks.

Sonny also talked to newly elected Mayor Koch about cleaning up the area around the Garden to make it more fan-friendly. "Although the Garden's location might seem the ideal spot," he told reporters, "it falls way short. The Garden presents tremendous difficulties for the fan. I don't think you want to buy a ticket," he continued, "and then have to buy your car back after the show is completed."[39] Maybe he had a point.

Two years earlier, a "band of youths" roamed midtown after a concert at the Garden, "terrorizing, attacking, and robbing passers-by." Nearly two hundred kids took part, ranging in age from 13 to 18. One police detective said, "They were like guerrillas in combat . . . they just hit and run."[40]

Still, even while badmouthing the Garden publicly, Werblin told his employees to refer to the Garden as "The World's Most Famous Arena."[41] If you can't make it, fake it.

The Knicks and Rangers were Werblin's most public projects, but the Garden was booked almost every night of the week. Executives packed Suite 200, a luxury box at the arena, to hobnob with business bigwigs. "Suite 200," Sonny's son, Tom, explains, "was celebs all the time."[42] As Lowell remembers, "Monday night was wrestling. Tuesday night was basketball. Wednesday night was basketball. Thursday night was a concert or boxing. Friday was a concert (salsa was big then); Saturday was a Knicks home game. Sunday was hockey."[43]

Werblin knew business and how to generate publicity. But what did he know about basketball? Journalist Harvey Araton had his doubts, writing that Werblin "didn't know a pick-and-roll from the first pick of the college draft."[44] Stanley Asofsky, who watched hundreds of Knicks games from his courtside seats, was even more candid. "I'd love to give Werblin a basketball IQ test," he said. "If his life depended on it, he'd be a cadaver every day of the week."[45]

Just two days after Werblin took over as the chairman of Madison Square Garden, the Knicks began their annual January road trip, giving the Garden time to hold its "Holiday on Ice" extravaganza. In 1978, though, the usual two-week trip was extended an additional week for an indoor tennis tournament. There was no way the old Knicks would have been bumped for the Colgate-Palmolive Masters, even if the tournament did feature nineteen-year-old John McEnroe upsetting tennis legend Arthur Ashe in the finals. All told, the long January excursion included eight games in eighteen days, sending the Knicks to Chicago, Kansas City, Portland, Oakland (Golden State), Seattle, Los Angeles, Phoenix, and Denver before returning to New York.

Team travel in the late seventies was far different than in the modern NBA, in which teams fly on chartered jets. "We traveled commercially," trainer Mike Saunders told me. "A lot of the flights didn't have first-class seats." For flights that did have better accommodations, the head coach and nine players (ranked in terms of seniority) were afforded first-class tickets, per the league's collective bargaining agreement. Sometimes, if the Knicks had back-to-back games in distant cities, they would charter. Usually, though, the players flew the same commercial flights as everyone else.[46]

Unsurprisingly, given the cramped travel conditions, the Knicks struggled on the 1978 road trip, losing five straight. For their game in Denver, Burke devised a unique strategy: oxygen tanks. After watching pro football players using oxygen when they played at high altitude against the Denver Broncos, Burke asked the Nuggets for a few. "It was an unusual request," Nuggets vice president Bob King admitted. But Denver provided the tanks, which may have helped the Knicks break their losing streak with a 143–141 overtime win.[47]

Before the trip sent the Knicks west, Reed reevaluated his early-season strategy of playing a dozen players every night and shortened his rotation. For Cleamons, the team's new point guard, it was a welcome change. "He was too nice," Cleamons told me of his first-year head coach. "Because he was so nice, we had three rookies, Ray Williams, Toby Knight, and Glen Gondrezick, and Willis wanted to give those rookies a chance to play. To me," Cleamons continued, "he should have told those rookies to sit their asses down."[48]

Reed also seemed to give up on the "passing game" preached by his predecessor, Red Holzman, in favor of a more isolation-heavy brand of basketball. McAdoo certainly approved of the switch. "If I'm scoring," McAdoo said, "it's going to be hard for us not to win."[49] Although McAdoo scoring thirty points didn't necessarily correlate with team success, making him the undisputed first option on offense did establish a hierarchy on a team of talented players. "I don't think Mac could accept a secondary role," Haywood told reporters. McAdoo, never shy about his immense talents, agreed. "You play people equally, and that's saying you have equal talent," he said. "We don't have equal talent."[50]

McAdoo was becoming a more comfortable on-court leader in his first full season with the team, but he was still uncomfortable with big-city living. Rather than residing in Manhattan, like Frazier, or near the Knicks' practice facility in Queens, like many of his teammates, McAdoo first rented a house on Long Island. But traffic congestion caused McAdoo to relocate to North Jersey and the small town of Ramsey (population twelve thousand), an hour and a half round-trip commute to and from the Garden.[51] "I get to have some trees," McAdoo explained. "I couldn't live on 33d and Park."[52]

The commute did not prevent McAdoo, however, from enjoying the downtown nightlife. The release of *Saturday Night Fever* in 1977 catapulted John Travolta into movie stardom and shone a spotlight on the music, culture, and dancing of the disco era. Even today, play the song "Stayin' Alive" and see how many people put one hand on a hip and the other in the air with pointer finger extended. But disco existed long before Tony Manero tore up the dance floor at 2001 Odyssey. In New York City, its birth (like that of hip-hop) began at a house party. This one was on Valentine's Day 1970 at a loft on Broadway in Manhattan where David Mancuso played an eclectic array of dance music. And just as was the case with hip-hop, such parties soon outgrew the space, and clubs sprang up to meet the demand. By 1978, more than one thousand discos existed in the NY metro area, including some like Le Jardin that encouraged straight and gay, white and Black to dance together.[53]

In the summer of 1978, a new club named Xenon opened on West Forty-Third in Manhattan. Although the paint on the walls was still wet, McAdoo and twenty-five hundred fellow New Yorkers showed up for opening night.[54] Xenon pumped disco music through their house speakers as dancers strutted atop Go Go boxes. Some club-goers bopped along to the beat; others took in the scene from a table or bar, just enjoying being in the moment. It stood in stark contrast to the grittiness of the South Bronx, but those two worlds were starting to move closer to one another, and, by the early 1980s, venues like Xenon employed deejays to spin hip-hop records for dancing, replacing disco music at the center of club life.

McAdoo stood out in every crowd, and reporters rushed to him for his reaction to the new club. "This place is smokin'," he told them. "I like it, it's nice."[55] McAdoo gave Xenon a thumbs-up but really dug Studio 54. "I was almost a regular there," he told me. "They would see me coming, and it would be like parting the Red Sea . . . there would be a hundred people out there, trying to get in. And they would see me coming up, and the guards would part, bring me right on in."[56] Xenon was about dancing and fashion; Studio 54 was Hollywood. People went there to celebrity-watch or, like McAdoo, to be seen.

Sometimes teammates joined McAdoo at the dance clubs. Butch Beard thought they were too loud, although he admitted to me that he would "pop in occasionally."[57] Bernard King hung out there at Studio 54 as a Knick and one night "blacked out from drinking" ("I don't remember it, but it happened").[58] Micheal Ray Richardson later became a regular at Studio 54 (and at a well-known swinger's club called Plato's Retreat), often waking up his roommates—Mike Glenn and Ray Williams—to join him in his partying.[59] Glenn knew, though, that he had to have a star with him if he wanted to cross the sacred velvet rope. "If you wanted to get into Studio 54," he said, "you had to go with McAdoo or Earl [Monroe] because they could get you in."[60] Monroe straddled both worlds. On one hand, he was a New York City celebrity—only a half-step below Frazier. On the other, he was already producing musical acts and was growing increasingly interested in the established disco and nascent hip-hop scenes.

In February, a few months before Xenon's grand opening, the Knicks stumbled into the All-Star break losers of three straight. At 26–25, the Knicks remained second in the Atlantic Division but, for the first time since 1969, had zero All-Star game starters; only McAdoo even made the team. But the break did give Reed and Haywood time to mend fences. "I wanted to talk to Willis about a couple of things," Haywood told the *New York Times*. "I had to straighten out a couple of things. I was sort of unhappy with myself and my playing time." For his part, Haywood was pleased, telling reporters that, "for the first time Willis understands." As usual, Reed was guarded about his feelings regarding his disgruntled star. "I just told him," he vaguely explained, "that for the rest of the season I wanted more offense from him." In the Knicks' first game after the All-Star break, Haywood gave Reed more offense and exploded for 37 points—his highest total since joining the Knicks.[61]

Two weeks after Haywood's scoring outburst, the Knicks hosted the Seattle SuperSonics, then in the midst of one of the greatest turnarounds in NBA history. After a 5–17 start, the team replaced head coach Bob Hopkins with Lenny Wilkens. Wilkens reshuffled the starting lineup, led the team to a 42–18 record the rest of the way, and reached the NBA Finals for the first time in franchise history. In their mid-February tilt, the Sonics and Knicks traded the lead back and forth; Seattle led 61–60 at the half and then went on a 38–19 third quarter tear as the Garden crowd began booing the Knicks. "I'd rather play on the road," Beard said after the game. "If that's the way they treat us, then we're better off playing without the people here."[62] Despite thousands of less-than-supportive fans, the Knicks outscored the SuperSonics 42–23 in the fourth quarter to eke out a 122–120 win. Most of the comeback was achieved using an unusual lineup, with McAdoo at center, flanked by Beard and three rookies: forwards Toby Knight and Glen Gondrezick and guard Ray Williams—sit their asses down indeed! McAdoo led all scorers with 37 points before fouling out, and Beard pumped in 20 to lead the come-from-behind victory.

Despite an electrifying win over the future NBA runners-up, which kick-started a five-game winning streak, the Knicks remained inconsistent. Reed embraced an up-tempo style, but that could lead to both easy baskets and too many turnovers. Asked to compare the current Knicks to the title-winning teams earlier in the decade, McAdoo told reporters, "We have more quickness. We're a fast-breaking team. We're different kind of players."[63] Even when they lost, the Knicks put up gaudy point totals. They would finish third in the league in points scored (113.4 points per game) and scored at least 100 in each of their last nineteen games. Unfortunately, they finished dead last in opponent points per game, giving up 114 on average. On defense, Phil Jackson later wrote, "this team didn't have a clue."[64]

With such a porous defense, the Knicks were unable to catch the 76ers to win the Atlantic Division and finished a dozen games back at 43–39. But that was good enough to secure a return to the playoffs and a first-round meeting with the Cavs.

Unfortunately for fans of both the Knicks and Cavaliers, Frazier would watch the series in street clothes after injuring his foot in mid-February. Dr. James Nichols, the Knicks' team physician, told the media Frazier had a stress fracture; Cleveland coach Bill Fitch dismissed it as a "sprained little toe."[65]

The Knicks throttled the Frazier-less Cavs in the opener of the best-of-three, 132–114, behind 41 points from McAdoo and double-digit scoring from five other Knicks, including 16 off the bench from Haywood.

In game two, the Knicks and Cavs found themselves deadlocked at 107 with two seconds left. Instead of forcing the ball to their All-Star center, the Knicks went to Haywood, who already had 25 points on the night. Haywood sank the mid-range jump shot, giving the Knicks the game and the series. The next day, a suddenly philosophical Haywood reflected on his time in New York. "I thought I should have played more this season," he told reporters. "But I wanted to fit in, and I didn't really know how. If I didn't score, I'd get benched because I wasn't producing offense. If I did score, my defense was blamed. My job now," he continued, "is to please Spencer. I was pleased with myself last night."[66]

Riding high after their opening round victory, the Knicks set their sights on upsetting the top-seeded 76ers. On paper, the Knicks could match up with almost any team in the league, but the Sixers were on a different level. Guards Doug Collins and Lloyd Free (who would change his name in 1981 to World B. Free) ignited Philadelphia's high-powered offense, and the forward tandem of Julius Erving and George McGinnis was the best in the league. Even young center Darryl Dawkins was developing into more than just a physical presence who liked to name his spectacular dunks (e.g., "In Your Face Disgrace"). And "Jellybean" Joe Bryant, whose wife was pregnant with a son they would name Kobe, contributed half a dozen points per game coming off the bench. Still, the Knicks remained confident. "We have a team feeling of love and devotion to each other now," Haywood told the *Times*. "We think we can beat anybody."[67]

As it turned out, Haywood was overoptimistic. In game one, the Sixers blasted the Knicks; their 130–90 win marked the worst playoff loss in over 170 games of Knicks postseason basketball.[68] "Clowns," Haywood called his team after the game. "We gave a display of selfish basketball. That's what we were—clowns." He shook his head in disgust. "In the playoffs and on national television, too."[69] Game two was closer, but the result was much the same: a nineteen-point loss that could have been far worse. "We should have stayed home," Haywood said. "It was like a rerun of the last game. . . . I don't like the idea that we're not fighting."[70] Unfortunately, few Knicks liked to fight and mix it up inside. Haywood and McAdoo preferred to play with finesse, either tossing in long-range jump shots or sweeping to the rim on picturesque drives to the hoop. Only Lonnie Shelton, a six-foot-eight, 240-pound bruiser who reminded everyone of a young Willis Reed or Dave DeBusschere, liked to play physically.

"He's the only aggressive player in a Knick uniform too often," Haywood admitted. "He is really just playing the way all of us should play."[71] Despite his willingness to battle, Shelton was quiet and unsure about the team's chances. "I don't know what we can do to beat them," he admitted. "Maybe we can't."[72]

As it turned out, Shelton was right: they couldn't. The Sixers easily won games three and four to sweep past the Knicks and into the Eastern Conference Finals where, despite being heavy favorites, they lost to the eventual NBA champion Washington Bullets.

While Wes Unseld and Elvin Hayes powered the Bullets to the franchise's first (and to date only) NBA title, the Knicks faced another off-season of disappointment. Reed, after just one season on the bench, was already feeling the heat. "I don't like when people say I'm a lousy coach," he admitted to reporters. "When they say I'm doing a bad job, and when they say I have a center when I don't."[73] Unsurprisingly, McAdoo took offense to the perception that the team lacked a real center. "This club needs people in certain positions," he said, "but I can't see how mine is one of them." In 1977–78 McAdoo put together a very McAdoo-esque season: 27 points per game on 52 percent shooting and 13 rebounds per game to earn an All-Star spot. But he was not the prototypical NBA center. McAdoo was six-nine and 210 pounds of lean muscle. He stood out while in a crowd outside Xenon or Studio 54 but was a few inches shorter (and often a few dozen pounds lighter) than most of his contemporaries. "People are gonna blame me for it, I know it," McAdoo predicted, "They'll say we needed a big center."[74]

Cleamons, signed before the season after coming from the Cavs, believed that the 1977–78 season was a lost opportunity for the Knicks. Not only should Reed have played the rookies less, but too few players were willing to sacrifice personal stats for the good of the team. "If we could have had a balanced attack on both ends of the floor. . .," he sighed. "We had the personnel," he told me. "But we just couldn't put it all together."[75] Cleamons sacrificed. He always did. After three straight seasons averaging double figures in Cleveland as a role player for a very good Cavs team, he scored just seven points per game in his first season starting in New York. The Knicks' offense revolved around very good one-on-one scorers. They could score, sure, but Monroe was thirty-three years-old, and McAdoo needed to play next to a strong defender and rebounder who could mix it up inside. Shelton fit that bill, but Haywood was too talented (and was owed too much money) to sit on the bench. Shuffling those frontcourt spots seemed to be a top priority heading into the off-season.

As the Knicks struggled to develop an on-court identity under Reed, New York City, under Mayor Koch, struggled to shed its reputation as a center of moral depravity. President Carter's visit to the South Bronx might have made that neighborhood a symbol of urban decay and poverty, but reports about Times Square made that locale America's under-the-mattress porno mag.

Today Times Square is a glitzy neon light show assaulting the senses and is probably best known as the location where the ball drops on New Year's Eve. But in the late seventies, it was a much different place, where assaults of more than just the senses regularly took place.

Entrepreneurs built the first peep show in Times Square in 1966. A dozen years later, shops playing "loops" (short pornographic films) in coin-operated peep show booths littered Times Square, numbering in the hundreds. What emerged in the 1970s was an "Erotic City," in the words of one historian: "Manhattan's biggest erogenous zone."[76] Stores with names like Sugar Shack and Honey Haven enticed passersby while thousands of sex workers showcased their wares up and down Eighth Avenue. Some movie houses showed pornographic films during which customers were allowed to engage in sexual acts. *Midnight Cowboy*, which won Best Picture at the 1970 Academy Awards, painted a gritty portrait of the area, as Joe Buck (played by Jon Voight) navigates Times Square with the help of sleezy "Ratso" Rizzo (played by Dustin Hoffman). Although fictional, *Midnight Cowboy* hit pretty close to the mark.

In the early eighties, Mayor Koch demanded a cleanup of Times Square, empowering the Office of Midtown Enforcement with closing down repeat offenders. As one regular says of the city's on-again, off-again interest in the area, "public sex was largely a matter of public decency—that is to say, it was a question of who was or who wasn't offended by what went on in public venues."[77] Ultimately, the threat of AIDS—particularly problematic among New York City's homosexual male population that frequented these downtown theaters—resulted in a 1985 health ordinance shutting down gay movie houses and beginning the whitewashing of Times Square.

But even as the mayor's office worked to clean up Times Square (and the seemingly ever-present graffiti from subway cars), a new musical phenomenon was emerging organically from north of the Harlem River that would soon become the soundtrack to life in the city.

1977–78 Knicks
Record: 43–39
Playoffs: Won Eastern Conference first round versus Cleveland Cavaliers; lost Eastern Conference semifinals versus Philadelphia 76ers
Coach: Willis Reed
Average Home Attendance: 15,288
Points per Game: (113.4—3rd of 22)
Points Allowed per Game: (114.0—22nd of 22)
Team Leaders:

  Points: Bob McAdoo (26.5 per game)
  Rebounds: Bob McAdoo (12.8 per game)
  Assists: Earl Monroe (4.8 per game)
  Steals: Butch Beard (1.5 per game)
  Blocked Shots: Bob McAdoo (1.6 per game)

All-Star: Bob McAdoo
Notable Transactions: Signed Jim Cleamons as a free agent; sent Walt Frazier to the Cleveland Cavaliers as compensation; drafted Ray Williams in the first round of the 1977 NBA draft

4

"Meminger's Law"

1978–1979

Music producer Sylvia Robinson was looking for a new sound. It was 1979, and Robinson hoped to capitalize on the underground popularity of the hip-hop music created by deejays like Afrika Bambaataa and Grandmaster Flash in the South Bronx. What her label, Sugar Hill Records, produced became the first commercially successful rap album, *Rapper's Delight.*[1] Robinson cared little about authenticity; instead of recruiting the pioneers of the movement like Bambaataa, Flash, or Kool Herc, she created her own hip-hop group and dubbed them the Sugarhill Gang.

Henry Lee Jackson, better known as Big Bank Hank, was working at a pizza shop when he got his big break, using lyrics borrowed from his buddy Grandmaster Caz to impress Robinson. When Caz heard "Rapper's Delight" on the radio, he was furious. *He*, not Hank, was "Casanova Fly"! Deejays throughout New York City mocked the Sugarhill Gang's hit single. DJ Disco Wiz called it "a total farce," and Caz dubbed it "some cornball shit." "Rapper's Delight" lacked originality. It was stolen from Caz or, at the very least, pieced together using common street slang. Still,

Michael "Wonder Mike" Wright defended his group's song, arguing that "there's no denying there's a lot of shoutouts and phrases that were just like the common vocabulary at the time."[2] And, in the end, it doesn't really matter: whether original or not, "Rapper's Delight" transformed— you might even say created—rap music.

"The game of hip-hop changed," Grandmaster Flash admitted. "'Rapper's Delight' just set the goal to whole 'nother level. It wasn't rule the Bronx or rule Manhattan, or rule whatever. It was now how soon can you make a record."[3] "I did not think it was conceivable that there would be such a thing as a hip-hop record," Chuck D, leader of the rap group Public Enemy, explained later. "I'm like, record? Fuck, how you gon' put hip-hop onto a record?"[4] Hip-hop was spontaneous and organic, and rapping was about quick thinking, not written lyrics. Still, regardless of its authenticity, "Rapper's Delight" spread hip-hop music to the mainstream. As Whipper Whip of the Fantastic Five admits, "it was actually great. After a while, it became the phenomenon that set up a whole new genre. It showed the whole world what hip-hop was."[5]

After the success of their debut, self-titled album, the Sugarhill Gang— Wonder Mike, Master Gee, and Big Bank Hank—had high hopes for their sophomore offering, *8th Wonder*, an album featuring an ancient Egyptian–motif cover. Its reception was lukewarm. The group performed the title track on the television show *Soul Train*, and it reached number 82 on the Billboard Hot 100—and would be sampled twenty years later by Kobe Bryant in his short-lived, forgettable rap career. Another song, "Apache," added lyrics to the tune made popular by the Incredible Bongo Band in the early seventies. It did a little better on the charts, reaching number 53 before falling off. The trio released two more albums for Sugar Hill, *Rappin' Down Town* and *Livin' in the Fast Lane*, before disbanding in 1985. Their place in hip-hop history is contentious, but, whether you believe them to be posers or authentic, they helped push rap to the mainstream, and even today "Rapper's Delight" gets airplay.

"Rapper's Delight" transformed hip-hop music, introducing to the mainstream something that had remained mostly hidden for half a dozen years in the parks and playgrounds of the South Bronx. Before Wonder Mike, Big Bank Hank, and Master Gee began rappin' to the beat, deejays like Herc, Flash, and Bambaataa created a musical sensation. From the beginning, this new cultural movement—later dubbed hip-hop—connected rap music, graffiti, and B-boy dancing to urban playground basketball. It was no coincidence that "Rapper's Delight" shouted out the New York Knicks and Rucker Park. By the time the Sugarhill Gang released their debut album, hoops and hip-hop were already becoming inseparable, Black-driven enterprises.

Like MCs and rappers, playground basketball players created their own vocabulary. In 1980, two sportswriters released *The In-Your-Face Basketball Book*: a hoops bible, almanac, atlas, and how-to guide rolled into one. "The pick-up game breeds colorful phrases and nicknames," the authors explained, "truncating words like 'competition' and 'reputation' into 'comp' and 'rep.'"[6] Clearly the book was aimed at folks outside the city (mostly white, suburban teenage boys). Within the decade, many consumers of hip-hop would also be white, as both playground ball and rap music became packaged for mainstream consumption.[7]

Some of the slang in *In-Your-Face* is easy to pick up: to "take the train" is to travel and a "chump" is a "weak player." But some of the terms are quintessentially New York City. "Meminger's Law," the book says, is "an edict promulgated by New York schoolyard product and former pro Dean Meminger. It decrees that, if you don't play ball, you can't hang out."[8] Decades later, the phrase "ball is life" became popular; in the early eighties, that was Meminger's Law. "The asphalt was a meeting ground for my extended family," Onaje X. O. Woodbine recalls. "During games we shed tears together, laughed, fought, and bonded; our whole lives were centered on the court." Basketball was more than a game. It was, Woodbine explains, an "urban lived religion."[9]

In addition to a vocabulary lesson, *In-Your-Face* included a primer highlighting the rules of the court. "The schoolyard is an unpoliced world," it noted. "So many of the standards of conventional basketball go unenforced that the lesser felonies become accepted."[10] On the blacktop, players called their own fouls, leading to inevitable arguments—and sometimes fights—over disputed calls. Part of gaining ghetto celebrity status, or at least street cred, was the willingness to absorb punishment without calling a foul. No blood, no foul. Calling a weak foul led players on both teams to question your masculinity. Rap music was tough. B-boying was tough. So playground basketball had to be tough too.[11]

Unlike hip-hop, basketball was not born in New York City. But eighty years after James Naismith drew up rules for a new game to teach his students at the International YMCA Training School in Springfield, Massachusetts, the center of the basketball world was squarely in the Big Apple.[12] The Garden of Eden Knicks won NBA titles in 1970 and 1973, and the New York Nets won ABA titles in 1974 and 1976. But decades before that, Nat Holman's City College of New York teams ruled college basketball, winning both the NCAA and NIT titles in 1950, while *USA Today* later recognized Lew Alcindor's Power Memorial team as the best high school basketball squad of the twentieth century.[13] Even beyond these legendary teams, New York City was the mecca of the blacktop basketball world. Period. In 1970, Pete Axthelm wrote *The City Game*, exploring New York's informal basketball scene. "There's a love of the game in this city that is very difficult to put into words," one playground baller told Axthelm. "You start off when you're very young and you never get it out of your system. You might be married to a woman, but basketball is still your first love."[14]

By the summer of 1978, basketball was still crucially important in New York City Black culture, and the Knicks once again had hard decisions to make to improve a team mired in mediocrity. They were on the periphery of the playoffs most years, unable to make a serious run at the NBA title or rebuild with high draft choices. Maybe the newest innovation in the NBA, free agency, could help them quickly turn their fortunes around. A year earlier, Gail Goodrich became the first big-name free agent to switch teams when the New Orleans Jazz signed him away from the Los Angeles Lakers. Hoping to keep deep-pocketed teams from buying a title, Commissioner O'Brien awarded the Lakers staggering compensation (three first-round picks, one of which became Magic Johnson) for the thirty-three year old Goodrich, who played just two and a half seasons for the Jazz before retiring from the NBA. Now several elite players might be available. Would the Knicks risk losing multiple draft choices to sign a superstar? They would certainly try.

The biggest prize was undoubtedly Denver Nuggets guard David "Skywalker" Thompson, a six-foot-four dynamo who, at age twenty-three, was already one of the league's most exciting players. Thompson averaged 27 points per game in 1977–78, and Garden chairman Sonny Werblin was understandably attracted to what adding Skywalker might do, on the court and at the box office, for the Knicks. "I've watched Thompson since he was at North Carolina State," Werblin told reporters, "I know he's a great player."[15] With Monroe on his last legs and scheduled for free agency himself, Thompson seemed the ideal replacement. But before New York could make an offer, the Nuggets dropped a bombshell in mid-April, announcing a five-year, $4 million deal with Thompson, making him the highest-paid player in NBA history. The Knicks didn't even have a chance to negotiate with the would-be free agent and now faced a familiar predicament: Plan B.

One rumor making the off-season rounds had Bob McAdoo and Lonnie Shelton headed to Los Angeles in exchange for Kareem Abdul-Jabbar, a native New Yorker. When asked about a potential return to the Big Apple, Abdul-Jabbar replied, "I would not be averse to it."[16] Abdul-Jabbar, of course, remained in L.A. and won five titles with the Showtime Lakers before retiring in the spring of 1989. So much for that as Plan B.

Without Thompson or Abdul-Jabbar, Burke and Donovan reviewed the list of potential college draftees and worked furiously to move up in the draft. Finding a willing partner across the river in New Jersey, the Knicks traded their own number 13 pick and reserve forward Phil Jackson, who wanted to retire and transition to coaching, for the Nets' number four pick and a 1979 first rounder. The seemingly one-sided deal made more sense when the teams revealed that the Knicks also agreed to waive the $3.2 million indemnity still owed them from the ABA merger two years earlier.[17] Giving up two first-round picks was a high price for the Nets to pay, but it finally ended the teams' long-standing dispute over territorial concessions.

Now holding the fourth overall pick, New York brass crossed their fingers that University of Kentucky center Rick Robey, the stereotypical "big center" Reed wanted to play alongside McAdoo, would fall to them. With the first pick, the Portland Trail Blazers took Mychal Thompson, the first foreign-born top choice in league history. Next, the Kansas City Kings selected guard Phil Ford before the Indiana Pacers grabbed Robey. "We preferred the big man," Reed admitted after the draft, "but couldn't get one."[18]

With Robey unavailable, the team chose guard Micheal Ray Richardson. Two choices later, the Boston Celtics selected a slow-footed underclassman forward from Indiana State. Yes, the Knicks and four other teams had a chance to take Larry Bird in the 1978 draft—and passed.

(Bird would opt to stay in college for his senior season and signed with the Celtics in 1979.)[19] New York fans were shocked. Few of them had ever heard of Richardson, who had started for four years at the University of Montana and became the first Grizzly drafted into the NBA. Robey's Kentucky team won the NCAA Championship in 1978, but Richardson's Grizzlies had failed to even gain an invitation to the NIT.

Knicks fans questioned the Richardson pick, but NBA super-scout Marty Blake loved Micheal Ray. "Super pick," Blake said. "Super kid. He's got great quickness."[20] Reed desperately wanted Robey but said the right things about the newest Knick. "Richardson plays similar to Walt Frazier," Reed said. "He can rebound, he can play big people, and he has a good knack for stealing the ball. He's very mobile."[21] Micheal Ray was excited to join the team, although his response revealed a lot about what Knicks fans would come to expect from the eccentric Richardson. "I wanted the Knicks all along," Richardson told reporters. "And when this guy, Elwood Donovan, called me, I just started screaming 'yeah, yeah.' "[22] Eddie (not Elwood) Donovan remained hopeful the team could still make some moves, telling reporters, "We're still in the market for Robey."[23]

No Kareem. No Robey. And so the Knicks were once again desperate for a traditional center. One possible fit—the Knicks rarely aimed low—was reigning league MVP Bill Walton. Walton wanted out of Portland and included the Knicks on his list of preferred destinations. "If that's true," Donovan told reporters, "then we have to be interested."[24] According to Walton's advisor Jack Scott, a well-known sympathizer of the Symbionese Liberation Army linked to the Patty Hearst kidnapping, Walton liked New York's progressive "medical policies."[25] What that entailed was never very clear, but what the Blazers did make immediately clear was that they wanted a center in any trade for Walton. Portland shot down offers from the Knicks centered around McAdoo or Haywood, so the deal fell through. In the end, it was probably for the best. Walton signed with the San Diego Clippers after sitting out the entire 1978–79 season with injuries and only played fourteen games over the next three years before a brief career resurgence with the mid-eighties, Bird-led Celtics.

With Walton, Kareem, and Robey off the table, New York turned to Sonics center Marvin "The Human Eraser" Webster. Webster started his career in Denver where he played two unremarkable seasons with the

Nuggets before being traded to Seattle. In the Pacific Northwest, he blossomed into one of the league's best young centers, averaging 14 points, nearly 13 rebounds, and 2 blocked shots per game. At seven foot one, the Human Eraser was the traditional center that Knicks execs so desperately wanted. Webster flew to New York for dinner with Burke and Donovan and then had a three-hour meeting with Werblin before becoming the Knicks' first-ever big free-agent signing after inking a five-year, $3 million contract.

On paper, Webster was a perfect fit for the Knicks. "It's the first time I've played on a team with somebody bigger than me," McAdoo admitted. "I won't have to be responsible for blocked shots or defense on the tall guys."[26] But some observers wondered how Webster would react to the bright lights of the big city. Webster grew up in Baltimore but attended tiny Morgan State University and seemed more comfortable out of the spotlight than in it. His wife had grown up down the block from McAdoo, and, like his new teammate, Webster preferred a slower-paced lifestyle. During his first training camp with the Knicks, Webster's wife gave birth in Greensboro while Marvin was at practice. He had to be driven from training camp in West Long Branch, New Jersey, to Newark Airport to fly to North Carolina. "Drive myself?" Webster responded to reporters' questions about his mode of transportation. "I don't even know where Madison Square Garden is [much less the Newark Airport]."[27]

Haywood, clearly jaded, watching the team bring in another big name, big-money frontcourt player, offered a dire warning for Webster. "I came here all alone, expected to replace Reed and DeBusschere by myself. I suffered," Haywood said, "but it made me a better man." The thing is," he continued, "in New York, all the attention and the fans and the press can be so detrimental. Marvin's got to learn they aren't the archenemy. If he's not ready for all of this, he could get crushed."[28]

As it turned out, Haywood could have been speaking about another new Knick when it came to dealing with big city life: their top draft choice, Micheal Ray Richardson. If anyone proved unready for the pressure of playing in the Big Apple, it was him. Richardson grew up in Denver and was lightly recruited as a six-foot-three high school forward. He ended up at the University of Montana, the only Division I school to offer him a scholarship, and quickly grew close to head coach Jud Heathcote. Having been raised, along with his five siblings, by a single mother, Richardson latched onto Heathcote as a surrogate father figure. While a freshman, Richardson and his girlfriend got pregnant, and the two quickly married. After the season, Heathcote bolted from Missoula for East Lansing, Michigan, where he led Michigan State to the 1979 NCAA championship. Losing Heathcote devastated Micheal Ray. "Don't go!" Richardson begged his coach. "You're like a father to me . . . You can't leave me. I don't have a father."[29] Richardson was despondent and considered dropping out of school altogether but stayed and blossomed into an All Big-Sky performer, growing to six-foot-five while in college.

Despite having a wife and child at home, Richardson embraced the trappings of his relative fame. First, he gave himself the nickname "Sugar," explaining to reporters it was because he had "so many girlfriends" or in homage to boxer Sugar Ray Robinson or even because he was "s-sweet on the court."[30] A stutter and lisp bothered Richardson, despite his outward bravado. "Sometimes it was impossible for anybody to understand what I was trying to say," Richardson later said.[31]

No speech impediment could keep Sugar from taking full advantage of his newfound celebrity, however. While some athletes from small schools, like Webster, avoided the spotlight, Richardson embraced his arrival in the Big Apple. As his sister later said, "It's like they put Jethro in New York."[32] He bought a brand-new Mercedes-Benz 450SL, adding a custom stick shift with "Sugar" embossed in large gold letters.[33] Micheal Ray did everything at breakneck speed. "He must've been ADHD or something before that stuff was recognized," teammate Mike Glenn recalls. "His whole life was that speed. He'd drive a car and even cabs would get out the way. His whole life was in that fast lane."[34] "He was always traveling 90 miles an hour in a 45-mile zone," trainer Mike Saunders remembers. "He drove this new Volkswagen Bug at one point, and I remember driving up [one-way] Eighth Avenue and he's coming the opposite direction, coming down Eighth Avenue in reverse."[35]

Soon after joining the Knicks, Richardson grew close to fellow guards Glenn and Ray Williams. Calling themselves "The Family," the trio of young Black guards soon became inseparable.[36] As Glenn remembers, "we had this little threesome; [if] you messed with one of us, you messed with all of us." Glenn, who grew up in Georgia and then attended Southern Illinois University (Walt Frazier's alma mater), and Richardson, a Denver native, were far from home in New York City. But Williams was from Mount Vernon, just north of the Bronx, and treated Richardson and Glenn like younger brothers. "We'd go out and party together," Glenn said. "We'd go up to Ray's house, and his mom would say 'What do you want me to cook you, fish or chicken? And Ray'd say 'Cook 'em all, Mama!' "[37] They found housing near each other in Flushing, Queens (a few miles north of where Run-DMC were then hooking up) and hung out constantly. Despite an age gap, the trio also bonded with McAdoo. "When the younger guys . . . came in," McAdoo says, "the culture changed a little bit. And I would hang with those guys. Those guys wanted to hang with me. We'd see each other socially and stuff."[38] Watch out, Studio 54!

While the Knicks played in Madison Square Garden in front of tens of thousands of fans, pickup games on asphalt courts around the city garnered few fans, and teams changed daily. Sure, kids on the playgrounds emulated their Knicks heroes and hoped to one day don the blue and orange. But they laced up their shoes for games played on hoops without nets and courts without painted lines.

Sometimes, though, the two worlds collided.

At Rucker Playground, at 155th Street and Eighth Avenue, across the Harlem River from the South Bronx, the best of New York streetball sometimes collided with the best of professional basketball. Today it is impossible to imagine elite pro players showing up at a playground in Harlem on a sweltering August afternoon to take on a crew of men who never even played college ball. But Rucker was different then. Annual tournaments began in 1946 and by the mid-seventies were fixtures on the playground scene. Blacktop heroes (ghetto celebrities) like Earl "The Goat" Manigault and Joe "The Destroyer" Hammond faced accomplished professionals like Wilt Chamberlain and Dr. J, who later described playing at Rucker as "a bone-chilling experience."[39]

On the streets of Harlem, unlike anywhere else in the world, Erving could play second fiddle to blacktop legends like Herman "The Helicopter" Knowings. "In a Rucker League game," one report insisted, "Helicopter went for a ball fake in the lane. As his man waited for him to come down, Herman treaded air, witnesses swear, until the referee whistled a three-second violation."[40] Bunyanesque descriptions of playground hoops are common: no cell phone footage can prove or disprove the play. As

Nelson George writes in *Elevating the Game*, "The tales told of Rucker are not of team ball but of individual forays, not of careful geometric designs but of gravity defied and good sense ignored."[41] Rucker was "a place God designed to expose greatness," legendary baller Pee Wee Kirkland explained. "It wasn't corporate, it was real, man. . . . It was in your heart and in your soul and that's the essence of street basketball, man."[42] Sounds a little like early hip-hop, doesn't it?

By 1972, the Rucker Tournament featured a ten-team, round-robin schedule in which each squad played nine forty-minute games. This was its peak. By the late seventies, most pro players had stopped showing up. The arrival of free agency helped them make too much money to risk an injury.[43]

Many streetball players dreamed of one day playing for the Knicks; few ever got a tryout, and only one ever made it all the way to Madison Square Garden.

Harthorne Wingo grew up in North Carolina but moved in 1968 to New York where he quickly established a reputation ("rep" for readers of *The In-Your-Face Basketball Book*) on the streets as an excellent baller. He lived in the Bronx, wheeling racks of clothing by day and dunking on fools by night (and on weekends). "Up here they take ball a little more serious at that time than they did in North Carolina," he laughed decades later.[44] Wingo played against playground legends like Hammond and Kirkland as well as NBA stars like Dr. J and Tiny Archibald. Wingo played well enough in these games to gain the attention of the Allentown (Pennsylvania) Jets, a team in basketball's minor leagues. A year later, Wingo traded his Allentown jersey for a spot on the bench of the title-winning 1973 Knicks. His NBA career lasted four seasons, but he personified the rare overlap between playground baller and professional athlete.

Like B-boys, who performed for ghetto celebrity status, elite playground ballplayers occupied rarified air. But the pressure on talented young Black New Yorkers was intense. "Dudes on the street will encourage a big-time ballplayer to be big-time in other ways," one player remembers. "They expect you to know all the big pushers, where to buy drugs, how to handle street life. . . . [If] you're not strong enough, well, you find yourself hooked."[45] In the mid-seventies, journalist Rick Telander moved to Brooklyn and integrated himself into the hoops culture of the streets, later writing *Heaven Is a Playground* about his experiences. Telander got to know the players and joined them for hours of pickup basketball. "It is a common saying in the ghetto of Brooklyn," Telander wrote, "that if a boy is bad he joins a gang; if he is good he plays basketball."[46] Later, after hip-hop became an ingrained part of urban life, one street baller remembers, "Every boy in my neighborhood understood that there were three common routes of escape from the ghetto. You could become a gangster, a rapper, or a ballplayer . . . since I couldn't fight or rhyme on the mic, basketball was my refuge."[47]

Among the young men Telander befriended was a talented teenager named Albert King. "Everybody's trying to tell me what to do," King told Telander at the time. "They try to compare me to Connie Hawkins, saying I'm the next Hawk and that I'll get myself messed up the way he did."[48] Hawkins was a Brooklyn playground legend whose pro career was cut short because of accusations of point-shaving, leading to an NBA ban that lasted until the Hawk was in his late twenties. After Telander's book was published, King accepted a scholarship to Maryland and played nine seasons in the NBA. His older brother, Bernard, was even better and, nearly a decade after Telander roamed the asphalt courts of Brooklyn, became a demigod as a Knick.

New York newspapers in the late seventies regularly covered the battles between Yankees owner George Steinbrenner and manager Billy Martin. Unfortunately, by the fall of 1978, the relationship between Sonny Werblin and Willis Reed was threatening to become just as dysfunctional. "Werblin," one journalist wrote, "is ticked off at Willis' constant dictates to the front office on how to spend the Garden's money on the Knicks." Werblin, never one to be bullied, told the same reporter, "I can be as tough as Steinbrenner."[49] Reed was hired before Werblin assumed control of the team and, despite a 43–39 record in 1977–78, his days coaching the Knicks bench seemed to be numbered. Sonny had made a coaching change for the other Madison Square Garden inhabitants, the Rangers, early in his tenure as Garden chairman, and it helped the team to ten more wins and a finals appearance.

Could a Knicks coaching change be far behind?

Only 12,075 fans showed up for opening night in the Garden in October 1978 to watch the Knicks host Houston. Rockets forward Rudy Tomjanovich, making his first appearance since nearly dying on the court ten

Figure 5. Head coach Willis Reed. © Larry Berman—BermanSports.com.
Used by permission.

months earlier as a result of an on-court fight with Kermit Washington later dubbed "The Punch," scored twenty points to lead his team to an emotional 111–107 win. Two weeks after the Houston game, the Knicks, now 4–4, left for a six-game West Coast swing, which sent them from Phoenix on Halloween night through San Diego, Los Angeles, Portland, Seattle, and Denver.

Away from New York City, the relationship between Reed and Knicks management grew increasingly strained. "It hurts a team every time it hears or reads that the coach is going to be fired," Reed admitted. "It hurts our gate and killed team spirit. Either I'm in or out. They should make that determination and tell you guys about it so you can stop asking me about it." Prompted by reporters to respond to Reed's comments, Burke told them, "everyone's job is always on the line every day whether you work for Con Ed or the Knickerbockers."[50] This was a nonanswer as far as Reed was concerned, so he asked for a vote of confidence, "a show of support from Sonny Werblin."[51] The back and forth in the papers continued. "He hasn't spoken a word to me or to Mike [Burke] since he left on the road trip," Werblin told the *Daily News*. "But we'll be meeting Friday, as soon as he gets back into town."[52] The road trip ended on November 9 with a disheartening loss to the Denver Nuggets in which George McGinnis and David Thompson (both long coveted by the Knicks and the former recently traded by the Sixers to the Nuggets) combined for 57 points.

Back from the West Coast swing, Reed finally had his long-awaited meeting with Werblin, Burke, and Donovan. After just thirty minutes, Reed emerged, head hung low. All he would tell reporters: "You'll have to get the details from Mr. Werblin and Mr. Burke." Reed had been fired, and Werblin was more than happy to explain, insisting, "No coach gives me an ultimatum."[53] In barely more than one full season as a head coach, Reed led the Knicks to a 49–47 record despite roster turnover and an influx of young players. "We, as players, couldn't understand why they got rid of Willis," McAdoo told me. "We thought Willis was doing a great job."[54] Glenn agreed. "It was a surprise," he told me decades later. "We thought it was Willis's team. He was molding us, and we were around .500. We thought we were going to have a good year. Then Willis was gone."[55] Hoping to set the record straight, Werblin sat down with reporters to explain his decision. "It wasn't the won-lost record," Werblin said.

"We didn't like the 'we and they' syndrome." And he reiterated, "No coach gives me an ultimatum."[56]

Fortunately for Werblin, the Knicks had a championship-winning coach already on the payroll. Following his retirement in 1977, Red Holzman was paid as a team consultant, although he did little work. Now Werblin wanted him back on the bench. "But Sonny," Red replied, "I'm enjoying retirement. I'm the women's tennis champion of my club," he joked. "I'm having fun."[57] But Werblin was persistent and finally convinced Red to return.

The team Holzman inherited was much different than the one he had left just fifteen months earlier. When Red first retired, Walt Frazier and Earl Monroe joined Phil Jackson and Bill Bradley as holdovers from the '73 title winners. Now Monroe was holding out for more money, Frazier was in Cleveland, Jackson played for the Nets, and Bradley was the junior US senator from New Jersey. "I took over a team I didn't make," Holzman wrote. "In a way they were a bunch of strangers." Not only were these Knicks new to Red, they were also part of a younger generation. "The guys I was now coaching were a new breed, self-centered, and sometimes just plain selfish," he said. In particular, Red noticed that there was a divide on the squad, and "the younger and older players were in constant contention with each other."[58] On one side, young players like Richardson, Williams, Glenn, and Toby Knight were athletic and excelled in the open court with a fast-breaking style of play. On the other, vets like Haywood, Butch Beard, and Jim McMillian were unsure about where they fit into the team's long-term plans. "The New York dream was fading for me," Haywood wrote later. "I was closing in on age thirty and the Knicks were convinced that my savior days were behind me."[59] Beard, expecting play regularly at guard, questioned the Knicks' front office decisions. "After going out and spending all that money on [Marvin] Webster, they turn around and ignore the veterans. Who knows what their [sic] doing?"[60]

When the Garden was Eden, Red allowed the players to police themselves; now he had to set a curfew. For a while, the Knicks rented hotel rooms across the street from the Garden so players could relax on game days after morning shootarounds. "Unfortunately," Red recalled, "some of them abused the privilege. Some of the players didn't use the rooms for the rest we intended."[61]

The most notable clique on Holzman's new Knicks, of course, was "The Family." For his part, Glenn embraced the coaching transition. "Red told us about how to carry ourselves," he told me. " 'The New York Knicks uniform needs to mean something to you because it means something to me. You wear that with pride and carry yourself in a certain way. You represent the New York Knicks.' And no one coach in my whole career ever put it quite like that."[62] But Williams and Richardson were slower to accept the change. Williams was six foot three and a muscular 190 pounds; Richardson was a sleeker six foot five. Both had long arms and incredible quickness and terrorized opponents on defense. But, as Holzman later wrote of his starting backcourt, "[they] were not thoughtful players but they had so much talent that they were able to excel at times to get by on raw ability."[63]

Just hours after Werblin replaced Reed with Holzman, the Knicks re-signed Monroe, clearly intended to ease Red's transition back to the bench. As Mike Lupica wrote in the *Daily News* of Monroe, "His basketball intelligence—the Knicks' collective on-court IQ is approximately 48—is badly needed among Reed's pre-schoolers."[64]

Fan expectations were high following the coaching change. More than 18,000 showed up for Red's return, easily the highest attendance of the season. They were treated to a 111–98 win over their old rivals from Boston. Cleamons, stuck on the bench under Reed, played forty minutes in the win. "Willis did not know how to use me," Cleamons told reporters later; he was not alone in this assessment.[65] "Willis wasn't a very good coach," Jim McMillian charged, while Haywood was more conciliatory, simply telling reporters that, "there was a lack of communication with Willis. . . . [Red] has explained it better. He says, if we lose, the team loses, not an individual."[66]

New York won its first five games under the new-old coach, and, with Holzman at the helm, Haywood finally looked like the man sent to save the Knicks three years earlier. "Red Holzman is the best thing that happened to Spencer Haywood right now," Haywood told reporters after scoring 35 points in a win over the Jazz. "He's gotten through to me that starting and scoring points is not everything."[67]

If movie scriptwriters wrote the story of the 1978–79 Knicks, Haywood would fulfill his promise to save the Knicks, Red would win his third title and retire again, and every other player would slide seamlessly into their roles. But this was not Hollywood; it was New York City in the era of *Taxi Driver*. So, while the Knicks did start to gel under Red, their short-lived fairy tale was over by the end of December. McAdoo missed almost a month with a toe injury, Haywood came back to earth after his hot start, and the team lost 10 of 14, capped by a 109–94 Christmas Day drubbing at the hands of Dr. J and the Philadelphia 76ers. "This isn't a lost cause yet," recently retired guard (and now assistant coach) Beard told reporters. "But if a lot of people begin to panic, it will be. This can become contagious."[68]

Lost in the transition from Reed to Red was the fragile psyche of Richardson, who found himself in the all-too familiar position of having to adjust to a new coach and father figure. Compounding the problem, Holzman seemed unsure about how to fit Richardson into the lineup. Sometimes he played backup guard, behind Cleamons, Glenn, Williams, and Monroe, and sometimes he replaced Knight at small forward. Theirs was a love-hate relationship as Holzman became another surrogate father for Richardson. Red called Richardson "Meshuggah," Yiddish for crazy. [69] "He liked that," Holzman said later, "he was from Denver and must have thought I was speaking French."[70] Still, Sugar was growing increasingly frustrated and called a press conference. Reporters made sure to pack an extra pencil; they knew Richardson would have something juicy for them to print.

He didn't disappoint. "My first announcement," Richardson later recalled telling them, "was that Holzman didn't know what the fuck he was doing. My second announcement was I wanted the Knicks to trade me."[71] Even the *Post* toned down the language in its coverage of the conference, quoting Richardson saying, "I wanna get out of here. I'm being mistreated here. I wanna go somewhere where I can play. When I get back to the hotel, I'm gonna call my agent in Houston and see what he can do."[72]

Richardson was tired of being yanked in and out of the lineup, especially after playing just a dozen minutes in the team's January 4 loss to the mediocre Cavaliers. He felt that the younger guys were being overlooked— outplaying the veterans but losing playing time to them. "We'd play lights out and get us right back in the game," Richardson said years later, "then Holzman would reinsert the vets, and we'd go back to getting the shit kicked out of us." Richardson by then regretted his trade request. "I was a young kid who never had a father to teach me how to be a man. I was impulsive, pig headed, and didn't know what was right and what was wrong. Not only did I feel unloved, but I felt unlovable."[73]

And so, on January 5, the Knicks announced a trade.

No, they didn't trade Micheal Ray. He was a young player with a team-friendly contract, unlike the man they traded, Spencer Haywood.

Haywood, whose clashes with Reed became a regular part of their player-coach relationship, had flourished in the twenty games he played under Holzman and was crushed to learn he had been traded. "I don't want to leave," he told reporters. "I only want to win with the Knicks."[74] Later, though, he admitted he needed a fresh start. "I didn't want to leave my wife [supermodel Iman], but I just had a bad experience in New York," he explained. "The press was very mean to me. There were a lot of lies spread out about me."[75]

Holzman tried to spin the trade, which sent Haywood to the New Orleans Jazz for center Joe C. Meriweather, as a positive for both parties. "Spencer's the kind of guy who should be playing," Holzman said. "He can score a lot of points and he'll probably get a good opportunity down there."[76] On paper, exchanging a former All-NBA talent like Haywood for a role player like Meriweather seemed to make little basketball sense; Haywood was averaging almost 18 points and 6 rebounds per game while Joe C. averaged 6 and 5. But while Haywood needed the ball to excel, Meriweather was content boxing out, setting hard picks, and blocking shots. In his first game with New York, in fact, Meriweather sealed the victory by grabbing a key rebound, gaining him a cult following of fans who longed for a return to the grittiness of DeBusschere, Reed, and the old Knicks.

The Haywood trade ended a tumultuous era in Knicks history. From his first press conference (when he told reporters at first that if the team needed saving, then he'd save) to the team's acquisition of McAdoo, and through near-constant battles with Reed, Haywood served as a cautionary tale for teams trying to buy a winner. For his part, Haywood was happy in New Orleans during his time there. A jazz aficionado, Haywood fell in love with the Big Easy and in thirty-four games with the team averaged 24 points per game. But in 1979, the Jazz moved to Utah and traded Haywood to the Lakers. In L.A., Haywood teamed with Kareem Abdul-Jabbar and rookie sensation Magic Johnson. "It's like a dream situation for me," he said at the time, "Here I am for the first time in my career with a bona fide, official team."[77] But the drug habit he developed in New York soon reared its ugly head. "The Devil got in there, man, and it was controlling me completely," he admitted later. "I wasn't myself."[78] Haywood added, "I wasn't the only Laker doing coke. I got high at least once with eight other players on the team. But the others who indulged were either smart enough or lucky enough to get away from it."[79]

Some NBA players used cocaine recreationally and infrequently. Haywood, though, became a heavy user while with the Knicks and started mixing cocaine and heroin with alcohol and Quaaludes to stabilize the high. "It was like having sex and winning the lottery and scoring fifty points all at once," he explained.[80] In the 1980 playoffs, Haywood would struggle with the pressure of prime time, and when he admitted his drug problem to interim Lakers head coach Paul Westhead, he was thrown off the team. Despondent, Haywood did eighteen hits of crack that night and paid a hit man to cut the brakes on Westhead's car. Fortunately, Haywood's mother found out and convinced Spencer to call off the attack.[81] Informally blackballed from the NBA, Haywood played in the Italian League before retiring after a brief comeback with the Washington Bullets. Three decades later, Haywood earned induction into the Naismith Basketball Hall of Fame, introduced by the eclectic trio of Lenny Wilkens, Bill Walton, and Charles Barkley.

After dealing Haywood to New Orleans, the team continued its up-and-down play under Holzman. Burke attributed their struggles to a lack of mental discipline; McAdoo thought they should play more up-tempo; Knight argued that the team should institute a full-court pressing defense.[82] The Knicks were pulling in all directions at once, and fans were growing impatient. A six-game slide capped off by a 107–104 loss to Golden State at home was the final straw, and fans began loudly booing the home team. "I never got booed before I came to New York," McAdoo complained afterward. "We're out there trying to play and you can't shut out the booing. We go on the road and you don't hear the fans booing home teams. It's just here."[83] The loss dropped the team to 22–30. And so, after a seven-game losing streak, the front office decided it was time for another major shakeup.

On February 12, a reporter for the *Post* asked McAdoo about being traded to the Celtics for a backup center and three first-round draft picks. "If it's true," McAdoo told him, "it'd be a shock for me. No, it doesn't make any sense at all."[84]

It was true. But McAdoo was right: it didn't make any sense at all . . . for the Celtics.

Without consulting their coach or general manager, Werblin and Burke negotiated the McAdoo deal with Celtics co-owners John Y. Brown and Harry Mangurian.[85] "John and his fiancée [former Miss America and CBS telecaster Phyllis George], my wife and I and Harry and his wife were sitting around bemoaning the fate of our teams," Werblin explained to reporters. "John Y. suddenly asked me, 'What have you got to sell or trade.' 'Anybody and everybody on the team,' I told him."[86]

In Boston the story was reported differently. In that version, George enjoyed watching McAdoo play and asked her fiancé to trade for him. "You want him, little lady?" Brown supposedly asked her. "You got him."[87]

No matter how the deal went down, McAdoo was livid. It was even worse because McAdoo found out secondhand. "Nobody called me or anything," he told me. "I never went through anything like this. I thought I had found a home."[88] Later McAdoo lashed out at the Knicks front office. "Me and Spencer have been scapegoats," he told reporters. "We had team play, but we just weren't winning."[89]

Boston fans were not happy that Brown shortsightedly traded three top draft choices for a sullen McAdoo. They flooded radio call-in shows and newspapers to complain.[90] As it turned out, the fans were right to question Brown's decision; the Celtics had an even worse record than the Knicks at the time and already had an All-Star center, player-coach Dave Cowens, blocking McAdoo's path to playing time. Still, in his short stint in Boston, McAdoo managed to average more than twenty points per game, although Celtics fans were less than pleased with his effort, serenading him with chants of "McAdoo; McAdon't; McAwill; McAwon't."[91] As Red Auerbach, Boston's team president, later admitted, "Dave [Cowens] tried to teach him our system, the Celtic ways, but he was not interested in learning. He was only interested in his average and playing minutes."[92] McAdoo's time as a Celtic was mercifully brief, and a few months after arriving in Boston he was the key piece in the deal that ultimately landed the Celtics the rights to Kevin McHale and Robert Parish.[93] Unlike Haywood, McAdoo enjoyed a career resurgence after eventually landing in L.A., transforming into a dangerous scorer off the bench. In fact, McAdoo became a key cog in the Lakers' 1982 and 1985 NBA title teams, averaging double-figures as Abdul-Jabbar's primary backup. Like Haywood, McAdoo eventually earned induction into the Naismith Basketball Hall of Fame.

The spring of 1979 was déjà vu all over for Knicks fans; five years earlier New York lost multiple Hall of Fame frontcourt players almost overnight. But this time it was intentional and seemed to be part of a larger plan. "We have come to the conclusion that stars are less important," Burke told reporters. "We have decided to build a winner with a group of players. We will try to have a balanced squad that will play as a team rather than as individuals."[94] Following the Haywood and McAdoo trades, unheralded second-year forward Toby Knight became the team's leading scorer, averaging better than 20 points per game, including a 30-point outburst against the Bulls in mid-March. The backup center the Knicks received from the Celtics, Tom Barker, lasted less than two dozen games in New York. When he arrived, the team didn't have a jersey with his number on it, so trainer Mike Saunders wrote a big number six on the back of a blank jersey with a piece of chalk.[95]

Flipping McAdoo and Haywood for a pair of backup centers and some draft picks was a long-term play. In the short-term, the Knicks were a young and inexperienced squad. Fortunately, Monroe took his role as elder statesman very seriously. "We lost one game at the Garden," Glenn told me, "and Earl just blasted us out. He started yelling 'You guys think it's funny! This ain't funny. They come up in the Garden and kick our butts in here. We should be ashamed. Have some pride."[96] Now in his eleventh NBA season, Monroe put together a solid campaign, averaging about a dozen points per game in twenty minutes of playing time. It was a far cry from his halcyon days as a playground legend and NBA superstar in Baltimore, but, as Werblin admitted, "Earl had a good season. . . . He's a great player."[97] Monroe was frustrated, though, in the direction the team was headed. "I had always been a winner," he said later, "then everything else just culminated here. Losing, losing, losing. It got to be unbearable."[98]

Harvey Araton, writing for the *Post*, best summed up the Knicks' 1978–79 season in a column he penned in early April, after an eight-game losing streak ended the team's slim hopes for a playoff berth. "Thirty-one wins, fifty-one losses, eight straight closing defeats," he began. "The worst club record since 1966, the lowest attendance in 10 years, a declining TV audience, a deposed coach, two stars traded, the GM on the hot seat, and the ignominious experience of finishing behind the Nets."[99] Interest in the Knicks was ebbing in the Big Apple, and everyone was pointing fingers. "The excitement's gone," Monroe told sportswriters. "People used to come here, and maybe the games weren't so flashy, but they appreciate what the old Knicks did, and pretty soon they'd appreciate the game. Of course, that's when teams would draft and trade to fill their needs. Now they draft and trade for names to fill their arenas."[100]

During the playoffs, as Knicks players sat at home watching the Super-Sonics win the NBA title in a rematch against the Bullets, scouts prepared reports for the upcoming NBA draft. There was no question who the top pick would be. Michigan State guard Magic Johnson was a six-foot-nine whirling dervish fresh off leading the Spartans (under Richardson's former coach Jud Heathcote) to the NCAA title. And, in a case of the rich becoming richer, Magic was headed to L.A., thanks to the Jazz having signed Goodrich a few years earlier.

It was not clear who would be drafted next, by the Bulls (second pick overall) and the Knicks (third pick). *New York Times* reporter Sam Goldaper asked fans to write in with their opinions, and they suggested Johnson's Michigan State teammate Greg Kelser or perhaps DePaul guard Gary Garland, son of gospel singer Cissy Houston and half-brother of Whitney Houston.[101] As it turned out, they drafted neither.

The NBA draft was nowhere near the media circus it would later become; in 1979, it was scheduled for noon on a Monday at the Plaza Hotel, and, for the first time in league history, it was open to the public. League execs scoffed at the idea of televising the proceedings, inviting fans to attend "in person because they wouldn't have done well if it was on TV." To their surprise, hundreds showed up more than half an hour before the first pick to witness the proceedings firsthand.[102]

Holding the third overall selection, their highest choice since drafting Cazzie Russell in 1966, the Knicks chose University of San Francisco center Bill Cartwright after the Lakers took Johnson and the Bulls plucked forward Dave Greenwood out of UCLA. With their remaining first-round choices (thanks to the McAdoo deal), the Knicks selected Larry Demic (ninth overall) and Sly Williams (twenty-first).

"If Willis Reed had a love affair with New York," Cartwright's agent Bob Woolf told reporters, "then in a couple of years, Bill Cartwright will have a marriage."[103] Knicks scout Hal Fischer loved Cartwright's potential. "He is a great outside shooter . . . he has good moves to the basket. He's very intelligent and unselfish . . . three years from now, he'll be untouchable."[104]

Cartwright grew up near Sacramento, California, in the town of Elk Grove where, along with his parents and six sisters, he worked hard to make ends meet. His mother cleaned people's houses, and his father was a farm laborer; at nine, Bill joined his dad in the fields. "If I never see another irrigation ditch," he joked after being drafted, "it will be too soon."[105] During Cartwright's sophomore year in high school, he sprouted to six foot nine and started dating Sheri Johnson, the daughter of the school's vice principal. Sheri was white, and Bill was Black, creating an interesting situation in Elk Grove, where less than 10 percent of the population was African American. "People didn't say much to our faces," Sheri recalled of their biracial courtship. "I guess if we hadn't been 'somebody' things might have been a little different."[106] Bill and Sheri married at the end of Bill's college career, and she joined him in New York City after the draft. "First thing I thought was *Wow, what a big frickin' city!*" Cartwright told me of his inaugural visit to New York. "But I felt I was ready for it. Wasn't intimidated. Wasn't worried. Wasn't scared. Just ready to play."[107]

Drafting Cartwright made sense in a vacuum; he was a talented center in a league that valued quality big men. But there were some red flags. One was Cartwright's agent. A few months before the draft, Woolf negotiated Larry Bird's record-breaking rookie contract with the Celtics, calling for a hefty $650,000 annual salary and a no-trade clause, a rare commodity in the late seventies. "Let me say this," Donovan told reporters the day after the draft, "no no-trade contracts." Holzman agreed. "We won't get into a no-trade situation with Cartwright. Marvin [Webster] has one and we'd like to keep our options open."[108] Drafting Cartwright also guaranteed friction between the new draftee and the two incumbent centers: Meriweather (traded to the team in mid-season for Haywood), and Webster (signed to a huge contract nine months earlier). "I didn't come here to play forward," Cartwright said. "I don't know about Webster's condition. I just know he's a good player from what I've seen on television."[109] At the time, Webster was in Greece, vacationing and rehabbing his knee, when Holzman called to tell him about Cartwright. "I'm still the center," Webster told reporters who tracked him down for comment. "I don't plan on going anywhere, either."[110]

All in all, 1979 was a pivotal year in New York City. The Sugarhill Gang's "Rapper's Delight" earned unprecedented mainstream play, placing Gotham squarely at the center of a new urban cultural phenomenon. And for the Knicks, the summer of 1979 led to more questions than answers. Who would start at center? Could Webster and Cartwright (and Meriweather) play together? Would Monroe come back for a twelfth season? If nothing else, one thing was sure: the Knicks were not going to buy their way out of this slump. They would rebuild as they had a decade earlier, through the draft and player development rather than buying stars. Well, unless one came up for sale.

1978–79 Knicks
Record: 31–51
Playoffs: Did not qualify
Coach: Willis Reed (6–8); Red Holzman (25–43)
Average Home Attendance: 13,310
Points per Game: (107.7—18th of 22)
Points Allowed per Game: (111.1—13th of 22)
Team Leaders:

> Points: Bob McAdoo (26.9 per game)
> Rebounds: Marvin Webster (10.9 per game)
> Assists: Ray Williams (6.2 per game)
> Steals: Ray Williams and Bob McAdoo (1.6 per game)
> Blocked Shots: Marvin Webster (1.9 per game)

All-Stars: None
Notable Transactions: Drafted Micheal Ray Richardson in the first round of the 1978 draft; signed Marvin Webster as a free agent and sent Lonnie Shelton to the Seattle SuperSonics as compensation; traded Spencer Haywood to the New Orleans Jazz for Joe C. Meriweather; traded Bob McAdoo to the Boston Celtics for Tom Barker and three first-round draft choices

5

"Black, White, Green, or Red"

1979–1980

On October 10, 1979, the New York Knicks released backup forwards Glen Gondrezick and John Rudd, cutting their roster down to the league-mandated eleven. Releasing Gondrezick and Rudd, both white, left the Knicks with eleven players. Eleven Black players. And so, when they took the court two days later in Atlanta against the Hawks, the 1979–80 Knicks became the first all-Black team in NBA history.

Cutting Gondrezick and Rudd bucked a long-standing tradition in professional basketball. As David Halberstam explains in *Breaks of the Game*, "on many teams the lower bench positions were often filled by marginal white players, kept aboard principally as a bone to the fans. The blacks resented this," Halberstam wrote, "and they had a word for it, when a white was kept instead of a black. He's stealin', they would say, just stealin' it."[1] Walt Frazier agreed. "The unstated 'rule' in the NBA at the time," he said, "was basically that if you were black, you were play-ing."[2] When Frazier joined the league in the late sixties, "the ratio was supposed to be about 60 percent white and 40 percent black." A decade later, nearly three out of four NBA players were Black, and even end-of-the-bench spots were now open to more talented African Americans.

Publicly, Knicks executives—all of whom were white—downplayed the historical significance of an all-Black roster. General Manager Eddie Donovan told reporters that "if we had kept Gondo [Gondrezick] and Rudd just because they were white, we would have lost the respect of our other players."[3] Madison Square Garden chairman Sonny Werblin agreed. "When you're bad, you worry about getting good players," he said. "You don't care whether they're black, white, green or red. There was no black-white decision to make, none whatsoever."[4] Werblin's best friend and right-hand man, Jack Krumpe, argued that it was the media who created a controversy. "It was a merit system," he told me, "we didn't have good players, but it wasn't because of their color."[5] And team trainer Michael Saunders recalls "no issues whatsoever. I was very happy with management that we didn't keep a token white player or anything like that."[6] In fact, Krumpe insisted in telling me that they never even "used words like 'token.'"[7]

Even Philadelphia 76ers star Julius Erving, probably the most high-profile Black player in the NBA at the time, said much the same when asked about the all-Black Knicks by *Jet* magazine reporters. "The game transcends color," he told them, "when the ball drops into the net from 20 feet out, nobody thinks of the color of the man who tossed it. The ball is brown," Erving continued, "but what fan is conscious of it?"[8]

A week after cutting Rudd and Gondo, on October 18, 1979, the Knicks traveled to Detroit to play the Pistons in the first NBA game featuring only Black players (the Pistons had one white player, but he never left the bench). Asked about the historical significance of the contest afterwards, Coach Holzman shrugged his shoulders and said, "so?"[9] "What if we had 10 blacks and one white?" Red asked a reporter. "Or nine and two? Is that going to change people's opinions? What if the 11 best players turned out to be all white? Would the same people then want me to keep a token black or two?"[10] Still, before making final cuts, Red drew up a list of his top eleven players and instructed his assistant coach, Butch Beard—who was Black—to do the same. Both chose the same eleven.[11] Beard asked Holzman if he realized every player was Black. "Red looked at me," Beard remembered, "and said, 'We are choosing the best team in talent, not in color. I don't care if they are all green.'"[12] Red also told the *New York Amsterdam News*, a local Black newspaper, that playing time was entirely up for grabs. "Every job is open," Holzman said, "even women are welcome if they can cut the mustard."[13]

Still, not everyone was standoffish or interested in sexist joking when it came to discussing race. And soon a high-profile personality connected to the team publicly addressed the racial situation of the 1979–80 Knicks. Ex–head coach Willis Reed, fired almost exactly a year earlier, told *Jet* magazine that he didn't feel New York was ready for an all-Black team. Although he did not elaborate on his reasoning, he admitted he "would have kept one White player."[14]

Privately, though, the debate was more delicate. "It was a very contentious situation," Mel Lowell recalls. "I'm not going to discuss the hate mail and other things that would come in." In fact, Werblin called Lowell, one of the Knicks' vice presidents, into his office, and told him the team needed a "home run hitter who was white." Lowell and Werblin flew to Los Angeles to meet Sam Schulman, the owner of the Seattle SuperSonics, to discuss a potential deal for Jack Sikma, a young center nicknamed Goldilocks for his long blonde hair. "Mr. Werblin wanted Sikma to be on the Knicks," Lowell told me, "we must have done about ten permutations of trades and draft picks" before Schulman called off the deal. So Werblin and Lowell flew back home, right into a media firestorm.[15]

Issues of race became inseparable from discussions of the NBA in the late seventies. During the decade, the racial makeup of the league changed from about half the players in the league being Black, to more than three in four. "There is a 'checkerboard' in the NBA," Milwaukee Bucks' owner Marvin Fishman wrote in his 1978 book *Bucking the Odds*, "and everyone is aware of it—the players, the owners, everybody. For best results at the gate, you want a mixture." In 1968, the Bucks almost selected Bill Hosket from Ohio State (the Knicks chose him tenth and he ended up as a member of the 1970 title team); instead, Fishman recalled, "we decided that we really didn't want to draft the best white player. We wanted to draft the best player." The Bucks chose Charlie Paulk, an African American forward. But two years later, they chose Hosket's white teammate Gary Freeman, passing on future Hall of Famers Tiny Archibald and Calvin Murphy in the process.[16] "White people have to have white heroes," Cavaliers owner Ted Stepien told reporters. "I myself can't relate to black heroes, I'll be truthful—I respect them, but I need white people." Like

Fishman, Stepien insisted that "you need a blend of black and white. I think that draws and I think that's a better team."[17] Interviewed for a *Basketball Digest* article a few months after the debut of the all-Black Knicks, commissioner Larry O'Brien fielded several questions about the racial makeup of the NBA. "I don't think that the owners think in terms of color," O'Brien said. "I just don't find anyone focusing on how many blacks and whites are on the floor . . . [and] I feel the fan and viewer basically is color-blind." Asked specifically about the Knicks, O'Brien insisted, "When the Knicks wound up with an entirely black team . . . lots of stories were written that it would adversely affect the team." "When they move into playoff contention," he said, "it will be reflected in attendance."[18] O'Brien hoped to cultivate Black attendance at NBA games but also to grow the league's market share of Black viewers on television.[19]

TV viewers in the late seventies and early eighties were bombarded with issues of racial tension. The 1977 miniseries *Roots* revolutionized television broadcasts with its portrayal of Kunta Kinte and his offspring through generations of slavery, while sitcoms with predominantly Black casts like *Sanford and Son* and *The Jeffersons* addressed institutional racism in a humorous, if often crass, manner.[20] And in a 1981 episode of *Diff'rent Strokes*, Willis Jackson charged his white coach with racism after being cut in favor of a white player and sued the school because of its affirmative action policy.

And then there was Archie Bunker. In a 1980 episode of *Archie's Place*, a spin-off of *All in the Family*, airing just two days before Americans elected Ronald Reagan to the presidency, Bunker was convinced that "Zimbabwe" was "a forward for the Knicks. Big tall colored guy." Not every New Yorker was as culturally insensitive as Archie or George Jefferson or Fred Sanford, of course. But in an era when Bunker symbolized blue-collar white Americans, an all-Black basketball team on the nation's biggest stage created many uncomfortable conversations about race and pro sports.

By the time *Archie's Place* had its short TV run, the hip-hop scene, centered just a few miles from Bunker's fictional Queens residence, had already changed dramatically. When DJ Kool Herc started mixing James Brown music on his turntables in the early 1970s, B-boys and B-girls downrocked on the dance floor while the Herculord sound system shook walls of nearby buildings. Now rappers took center stage. "B-boying was the main thing about a Kool Herc party," Kurtis Blow recalls, while "a Flash party was more about Flash and you standing out in front of a stage watching Flash on those turntables cut it up." So popular were people like Flash, Melle Mel, and DJ Hollywood that, Blow says, "all the breakdancers became MCs."[21]

But for several years after DJ Kool Herc hosted his first party on Sedgwick Avenue, this movement lacked a unifying name. The first person to use the term "hip-hop" was probably Keith "Cowboy" Wiggins around 1978, while Lovebug Starski began using it in his performances around the same time, and Afrika Bambaataa adopted it as a cultural signifier.[22] And Michael Holman, writing in the *East Village Eye*, was the first to use the term in print when, in 1982, he called it an "all inclusive tag for the rapping, breaking, graffiti-writing, crew fashion wearing street subculture."[23] Yet Holman's inclusive tag fell just a little short. Because by the time he used the term "hip-hop," there was another central element to that culture: basketball.

Rucker Park in Harlem best exemplified this connection. In their 1979 hit, the Sugarhill Gang name-dropped the Knicks and Rucker, which had tournament games featuring an MC hyping the participants. The MC boasted, rapped, and rhymed on the microphone, and often tried out nicknames on star players—Julius Erving was "The Claw," "Black Moses," "Magic," and "Little Hawk" before instructing the MC to "just call me the Doctor."[24] Likewise, several Knicks players had playground nicknames. Earl Monroe, as already noted, was "Black Jesus," "Black Magic," and "Earl the Pearl," while Harthorne Wingo was "Wingy," and Dean Meminger was "Dean the Dream."

The connection between hip-hop and playground basketball was made stronger in 1982, when Harlem rapper Greg Marius created the Entertainer's Basketball Classic (EBC). The next generation of streetball players gained their reps in the EBC, as Rafer "Skip-2-My-Lou" Alston and Ed "Booger" Smith became legends for their ball handling wizardry. By the 1990s, the And1 crew was making waves with their streetball mixtapes, and hip-hop sensation Puff Daddy and Def Jam Recordings sponsored teams in the EBC.[25]

Big-time tournaments like the Rucker and EBC featured MCs with microphones. But even pickup games on hot asphalt courts required the perfect soundtrack. "Basketball and music were founded on rhythmic schemes," the 1980 edition of the *In-Your-Face Basketball Book* informed readers. "Pop music is the food of face," its authors argued, "and live music always beats the [boom]box."[26] Deejays like Disco Wiz practiced their craft on basketball courts while b-boy and b-girl crews worked up new dance moves. It was part of the same culture, accessible to anyone who could lace up a pair of sneakers (required footwear for anyone interested in the hoops or hip-hop scenes).

Rucker Park is the most important and well-known asphalt court in the United States. In the era of the rise of hip-hop, it was available only to the best of the best. "Unless you're All-World, or at least All-City, plan to watch, not play," *In-Your-Face* advised. Everyone else had to find a different spot to ball. Some ended up at the Cage on West Fourth Street and Sixth Avenue in Greenwich Village; others at the Valley in the Bronx, where 107.5 FM (WBLS, the city's top R&B station) played on boomboxes. Still others dropped in at the Hole in Brooklyn, on Monroe and Sumner (WXLO 98.7 FM, playing disco and R&B, was the preferred radio station there), or joined former Knicks guards Dean Meminger and Dick Barnett at the Stuyvesant Town Courts on Eighteenth Street and First

Figure 6. The Cage. Gustavo Rossi/Alamy Stock Photo.

Avenue in Manhattan.[27] Players of all ability levels could find someplace to play in the city.

Like hip-hop music, playground basketball in New York City was dominated by Black men, but white players from both inside and outside the city made pilgrimages to sites listed in *In-Your-Face*. A few years after writing *In-Your-Face*, the authors published a sequel: *The Back-In-Your-Face Guide to Pick-Up Basketball*, including descriptions of even more courts and additional info about the games played there. The sequel described the level of play, number of courts, roughness of the games—and the racial makeup of the regulars. Using seasonings as a stand in for race ("salt stands for white; pepper for blacks"), the authors emphasized that its racial descriptions were "in no way endorsing the epidermal status quo" and encouraged readers: "if more white dudes sought out pepper places, and more bros took their games to salty locales, the world would be . . . you know what we're saying."[28]

Whether playing on a salty or peppery court, ballers of all races were concerned with their shoes. And they weren't alone; B-boys and B-girls had to make sure their kicks were scuff-free and stylish before they danced. [29] In the early seventies, Adidas ruled both hip-hop and basketball fashion. Most college and pro players wore white leather Adidas Superstars, following the lead of Adidas pitchman Kareem Abdul-Jabbar. In New York, Superstars were so highly sought that potential buyers had to prove they played high school basketball to purchase a pair (at Carlsen Imports on Lower Broadway, the only store in the city that sold them).[30] But then Walt Frazier, the most famous of the celebrated Knicks, signed with Puma to launch the Clyde, a colored suede shoe with thick rubber outsoles. The Clyde, for which Frazier earned $0.25 per pair sold, instantly competed with the Superstar as the most sought-after kicks in the city, for both basketball players and B-boy dance crews.[31] "If you got into hip-hop, you would get into sneakers," *SLAM* magazine editor-in-chief Russ Bengtson explains, "and through sneakers you would maybe get into basketball."[32] Wearing the wrong shoes was like wearing the wrong gang colors. If you wanted to be authentic, a pair of sweet suede Clydes or leather Superstars better be on your feet. Keep those raggedy-ass canvas Chuck Taylors in the closet.

October 1979 (just a few weeks after the release of the Sugarhill Gang's "Rapper's Delight) was a busy month on the sports calendar: the "We

Are Family" Pittsburgh Pirates beat the Baltimore Orioles in a thrilling seven-game World Series, legendary distance runner Bill Rodgers won his fourth-straight New York City Marathon, rookie quarterback Phil Simms debuted for the hometown Giants, and Larry Bird and Magic Johnson kicked off Hall of Fame NBA careers. With so many distractions, the all-Black Knicks might have been forgotten to history but for a pair of columns published that month in a local newspaper.

Two weeks after opening day, journalists Harvey Araton and Peter Vecsey penned side-by-side articles in the *Post* addressing fan reaction to the all-Black Knicks squad. Araton was generally optimistic about New Yorkers' responses. "Not one 'give us a White Hope' banner has appeared" in Madison Square Garden, he wrote. "The other night, there were 17,000 people to watch the Knicks play the 76ers, and to those who had insisted that New York will not support an all-black team, I say you have lost Round 1." Years later, Araton regretted downplaying the significance of the moment. "I should have been whistled for flagrant naivete," he wrote, "race was the elephant in the arena, the microcosm of the society at large, whether people were willing to see it or not."[33]

The fall of 1979 marked the arrival of Reagan's America, even though his election as president was a year away. Many Americans were already tired of the economic stagflation, expanding governmental bureaucracy, and racial unrest that dominated national politics in the late seventies. Reagan provided a symbol of change, popularizing the term "welfare queen" and demonstrating a willingness to engage in targeted anti-Black efforts by framing racial discontent in terms of states' rights. The implication was that hardworking whites were funding government programs benefiting lazy people of color. When Reagan visited the South Bronx in 1980, he told reporters that he "hadn't seen anything like this since London after the Blitz."[34] For Reagan, like Carter before him, the South Bronx—the birthplace of one of the most important American cultural exports in the nation's history—was less a real place than a cautionary tale. You can imagine, then, how an all-Black team in the largest city in the nation might rankle its (mostly white) fan base.[35]

Still, Araton's column reflected his hope that color-blind New Yorkers would embrace an all-Black NBA team. Vecsey, though, was far more negative about hometown support of the new-look Knicks.

"Judging from my mail," Vecsey wrote, "a number of fans have no desire to watch only blacks perform. Especially when it costs big bucks. Several bigots have gone so far as to suggest they be renamed the 'N-----bockers.'"[36]

Yes, Peter Vecsey dropped the N-word in a newspaper column. In 1979.

To be fair, Vecsey couched his own statements in anonymity, identifying these "bigots" only as "a random sampling of season-ticket holders" to distance himself from use of the offensive term.[37] "I had heard people on the street use it," Vecsey insisted, although Araton said "nobody ever called them that."[38]

Knicks players were privately livid after reading Vecsey's column. "Nobody wanted to be called that," Hollis Copeland said. "I thought it was in poor taste. But we just kind of let it go. We didn't want to make a big stink."[39] "It wasn't like it was celebrated," former Knick Rory Sparrow told me decades later. "It was more negative press than congratulatory."[40] Bill Cartwright, the team's first-round draft pick, agreed. "You would think New York, which is a mecca for folks to enter from different countries around the world, wouldn't have any problem."[41] Two members of the Family blamed the media. Ray Williams said, "The press made a big deal out of it, and the guys on the team thought that was unfair." Mike Glenn agreed: "It's only the press who makes something out of it." Turning the question back at Vecsey, Glenn asked, "Do you write stories about how there's all white guys on the Boston Bruins?"[42] As Spike Lee, then finishing up his degree from Morehouse College, remembered, "I don't know how that thing started, but it wasn't started by black people."[43]

Howie Evans, a reporter for the *New York Amsterdam News* provided an alternative view of the importance of the Knicks from the perspective of a Black journalist. "This is a team that absolutely must prove itself," he wrote. "All eyes will be on the New York Knicks. They have taken a bold step. In the greatest city in the world, racism is rampant and growing more blatant each passing day . . . minorities in this city are in a death-struggle for survival."[44] Maintaining a roster composed entirely of Black players meant more than just wins or losses. The eyes of the nation would be on these Knicks, tracking every win as not only a victory against another NBA team, but as a triumph for the Black race. Just as Billie Jean King's "Battle of the Sexes" win over Bobby Riggs was a boon for women's rights; the success or failure of the 1979–80 Knicks could advance or hamper the cause of Black people in New York City and indeed across the country.

While it is impossible to know whether Vecsey actually heard people on the street use the slur as he reported, its racist underpinnings certainly fit the attitudes among some New York City whites at the time. A few months after the debut of the all-Black Knicks, Dr. Frank T. Bannister Jr. penned an article for *Ebony* magazine titled "Search for 'White Hopes' Threatens Black Athletes." "White fans are beginning to show their uneasiness," Bannister wrote. "They are searching for reassuring White symbols of power in the sports world." Not only were most NBA superstars Black. Bannister said, "Resentment surfaced early this season in pro basketball when the New York Knickerbockers became an all-Black team."[45] League-wide, Bannister continued, "91 per cent of the fans during the regular season are White, and these fans are demanding more White players—good, bad, or indifferent." During the 1980s, he predicted, there would be a greater number of white players, as white owners and general managers would acquiesce to fans demanding greater racial representation. He was wrong; in fact, the proportion of Black players in the league grew to over 80 percent by the mid-1990s before an influx of European white players brought the figure back down to around 75 percent.[46]

It is significant that this blackening of the Knicks took place as the Black population of New York City was shifting throughout the five boroughs. In his study of Canarsie, a neighborhood in southeastern Brooklyn, Jonathan Rieder explains that local residents experienced a "time of danger and dispossession" as their Jewish and Italian ethnic whiteness was reinforced by "the fear of external dangers." Graffiti, an important aspect of hip-hop culture, as well as rap music, demonstrated to local residents a "sign of blacks' reluctance to observe the most basic proprieties" and "added to the visual estrangement." These were white, ethnic Americans claiming to be victims of reverse racism; it was their neighborhood under attack from an invading, dark-skinned menace—"hoodlum blacks [who] act like animals" one resident complained—just like white players clinging to spots on NBA rosters. "When the blacks say 'Black Power,' 'Black this,' 'Black that,'" one Canarsie resident said at the time, "it has a religious connotation. . . . We are white, and we have to fight for what they are taking from us. White is also a religious term. Let's take back what is ours."[47] It isn't hard to imagine white residents of Canarsie—or

Flatbush or Bed-Stuy or Tribeca—dropping the N-word when describing their local, all-Black basketball team.

Players' skin tone was the most controversial issue facing the Knicks that fall, but it was not the only contentious issue for the franchise. In 1946, New York joined the Basketball Association of America (BAA) using a logo featuring a cartoonish Knickerbocker decked out in royal blue and orange—the official colors of the city since its birth as part of the Dutch colony of New Amsterdam. The name "Knickerbocker" can be traced to Washington Irving, best known for his short stories "Rip Van Winkle" and "The Legend of Sleepy Hollow," who also wrote under the nom de plume Diedrich Knickerbocker.

For thirty-two seasons, the Knickerbockers embraced this manufactured heritage and used some variation of Dutch national colors—wearing white jerseys at home and blue on the road, trimmed in orange. But in 1979, the team introduced new kits, swapping out the royal blue and orange for dark blue and maroon. "I was tremendously offended by it," trainer Michael Saunders told me, still incensed forty years later. "I think it was Mike Burke . . . what college has those colors? The University of Pennsylvania. That's where he went to school."[48] Also for the first time, the word "Knicks" replaced "New York" across the stomach, below the players' number. It was a radical change and lasted until 1983, when the team quietly switched back to a more traditional look.

Knicks' execs hoped the new uniforms would help their young team establish their own identity separate from the Golden Age Knicks. But who would lead this new generation of Knicks? Ray Williams, entering his third year, told reporters "I believe I can be that leader," but he remained inconsistent as the lead guard.[49] Maybe Micheal Ray Richardson, a nightly triple-double threat and purveyor of countless "Sugarisms" in interviews. Or maybe it could be Cartwright, drafted third overall that summer. Moving east certainly marked a major life change for Cartwright, relocating from Sacramento into an apartment in Weehawken, New Jersey. During training camp, he also learned that adjusting to life in the NBA was about more than just learning a new offense. "Really kind of finding your way around" was a challenge for Cartwright, who latched onto a quartet of fellow rookies: Larry Demic, Sly Williams, Geoff Huston (from Brooklyn), and Hollis Copeland. [50]

Figure 7. Knicks forward Larry Demic goes to the hoop against Laker center Kareem Abdul-Jabbar, watched by Knicks guards Ray Williams, and Micheal Ray Richardson, in the fourth quarter of a game at Madison Square Garden, February 6, 1980. AP Photo/Ray Stubblebine. © 1980 AP. All rights reserved.

The young, all-Black Knicks started the 1979–80 season with three wins and three losses in their first six games but looked more like a cohesive team than they had in years. Yet only 7,911 fans turned up to watch the Knicks defeat the Indiana Pacers on October 23, the lowest total since the new Garden opened in 1968. Those in attendance saw lanky forward Toby Knight score 34 points, Cartwright add 24 points and 11 rebounds, and Richardson finish one assist shy of a triple-double, contributing 17 points, 11 rebounds and 9 assists in the team's 136–112 drubbing of the Pacers. "When the public realizes that we're for real," Werblin predicted, "they will be back."[51]

The young Knicks showed glimpses of being real, hovering around .500 all season despite an inexperienced roster, but the public stayed away. Given that attendance was down league-wide, it is probably wrong to ascribe the downturn in New York City solely to the racial makeup of the Knicks. Sure, the NBA was becoming increasingly populated by dark-skinned players, but does that entirely explain fan apathy? And why did fans stay away even as the team was young, exciting, and reasonably successful? The neighborhood around Madison Square Garden was no more dangerous than it had been for most the 1970s. Ticket prices were not significantly higher than when the team was a perennial title contender. Yet fewer and fewer fans turned out for the games.

Whatever the cause, Garden was pitifully empty for most of the winter. In front of fewer than 9,000 fans—in an arena seating more than twice that—the Knicks pulled out one of their most memorable wins of the season on November 20. With one minute left to go in the third quarter, New York trailed the visiting Houston Rockets 98–75. The game seemed virtually over, thanks to Rockets' All-Stars Calvin Murphy and Moses Malone, and New Yorkers began filing out, deciding that a drink at Charley O's was preferable to watching the Knicks that night. A few hundred fans stuck around, and with eight minutes left the Knicks still trailed by 18. Six minutes later, New York had sliced the lead to 7. A final rebound and layup tied the game at 117–117, and in overtime the Knicks pulled out an unlikely 130–125 win. It was Red Holzman's six hundredth career win as a head coach.[52]

Hoping to give the Knicks' young guards more playing time, Burke traded guard Jim Cleamons to Washington in early December. Two years earlier, Cleamons's arrival had marked the end of the Walt Frazier era.

Now he was dealt a few days before the Knicks celebrated Walt Frazier Night, honoring the recently retired Clyde. "When I saw that [announcement of Walt Frazier Night]," Cleamons told me decades later, "I said I wouldn't be around to see that happen."[53] He was right. A day after trading Cleamons, the Knicks traveled to Washington, and Richardson scored the game-winning three-point play after driving around Cleamons, his teammate a day earlier. This time, Richardson did get a triple-double, finishing with 16 points, 10 rebounds, and 10 assists.[54] Williams might have been the locker room leader of the young Knicks, but Micheal Ray was emerging as the team's best player.

While Richardson and Williams began to gel in the absence of Cleamons, another veteran, this one with a long and storied history as a Knick, was on his last legs. After the Cleamons trade, Earl Monroe was almost eight years older than his next-oldest teammate, Marvin Webster, but still occasionally showed glimpses of his electrifying one-on-one ability. "You see a lot of guys trying to emulate him," former Bullets teammate Wes Unseld told reporters. "They try to shoot like him, spin off the ball. He has kids everywhere trying to be like him. He was the first 'Magic.' Anyone after him is second-rate." Glenn agreed. "You call Earvin Johnson 'Magic' and he's not even 'Magic Jr.' "[55] Glenn and Unseld clearly undervalued Johnson, but their points stand. It was time to honor the great Earl Monroe, to remember him not as a hobbling backup guard for a middling team dominated by younger players, but as "The Pearl," "Magic," "The Lord's Prayer," and "Black Jesus," the playground legend and basketball superstar.

Monroe played his last game as a Knick on March 27, 1980. But a day earlier, fans got one last taste of the Monroe of old. Against the resurgent Boston Celtics—powered by rookie forward Larry Bird—Pearl came off the bench and, in fifteen minutes of action, poured in 25 points, including a 10-for-12 performance from the field. Boston won by eight, but it was vintage Pearl.

By the end, Monroe was clearly of a different generation than most of his teammates: the last remaining link to the old Knicks. "Earl kind of went to the beat of his own drum," Saunders told me. "Earl would go to the airport on his own, wouldn't necessarily take the team bus to the airport."[56] He had arrived in New York in 1971 following four outstanding seasons in Baltimore where he averaged over twenty points per game. But after the trade to the Big Apple, Monroe set aside individual success for the good of his new team. He averaged 15.5 points per game in helped the Knicks win an NBA title in 1973.

Monroe rarely talks about his last years as a Knick, preferring to discuss the days when the Garden was Eden or his time as a young superstar with the Bullets. Woody Allen, a lifelong Knicks fan who watched Monroe play hundreds of times from his seat behind the scorer's table, later reflected about Pearl's time in the Big Apple. "I, amongst all my friends, couldn't help wondering if Earl Monroe's great sacrifice, the voluntary reigning in of his flamboyant theatrical court genius to become a cog in an organized unit, wasn't too high a price to pay for a ring."[57] Monroe won a ring but never became the once-in-a-generation superstar he had seemed destined to become in Baltimore.

As a Knick, Monroe developed numerous outside interests. In 1972, he started in the entertainment business managing the Aleems, a Harlem-based duo who had performed with Jimi Hendrix a few years earlier. Under Monroe, they released an album as the Prana People, which realized modest success in dance clubs around the city. More importantly, Monroe was hooked on being a part of the music business. He founded Pretty Pearl Records, which evolved into Reverse Spin Entertainment, eventually moving to an office in Studio 902, nine floors above West Thirty-Eighth Street.[58]

Many of Monroe's forays into music were in promoting R&B, soul, and funk. Some of the bigger acts he worked with were Joe Simon, whose 1972 hit "Power of Love" sold more than a million copies and reached the top of the R&B charts, and Millie Jackson, known for her 1974 soul album *Caught Up.*

But Monroe was also involved in early hip-hop recordings. He helped promote the Fatback Band who in 1979 released their hit single "King Tim III (Personality Jock)," one of the first commercially successful hip-hop songs: rap in its earliest form.[59] A slight reference to basketball appears in the song's first lines, when Tim Washington (King Tim) raps, "Slam dunk, do the jerk / Let me see your body work."

By the time the Fatback Band released their album *XII*, rap was making occasional appearances on pop charts. "King Tim III" peaked at number 26 on the R&B chart, while "Rapper's Delight" made it all the way to number 36 on the pop chart (the Billboard Hot 100) that summer. Despite some success, the folks at *Billboard* predicted that rap was "a passing novelty that will soon go the way of all fads."[60] Yet in the Bronx, the hip-hop scene was exploding. Performers expanded their reach beyond the borders of the South Bronx and began engaging in verbal battles for street cred across the city. The Cold Crush Brothers and Fantastic Five engaged in a legendary rivalry, peaking when the two sides battled in July 1981 for a $1,000 prize. Tapes of the battle circulated through the city, and soon their notoriety reached filmmaker Charlie Ahearn, working on a documentary about hip-hop.

Connecting music to sport was not unique to the playgrounds of urban New York City. Before rap and hip-hop, basketball was most often linked to jazz: improvisational and with room for both group performance and solo work.[61] Basketball and jazz were also—as historian Todd Boyd points out—"two arenas where Black people have had the best opportunity to express themselves." With the pioneering work of DJ Kool Herc on the soundboards and Earl the Pearl on the courts, hip-hop and basketball both thrived in urban environments. Especially in the seventies hip-hop symbolized Black culture, providing a "soundtrack to a lifestyle."[62] "Rap," journalist Pete Croatto writes, "connected with basketball and the NBA on a deeper level . . . rap's popularity came from kids, the same group that the NBA would ultimately target." Ron Thomas, *USA Today's* basketball editor, "The NBA decided that it was going to make being a black league, it was going to accept it as its culture—what we could call now its brand."[63]

Instead of pushing back from identifying as a predominantly African American league, in the mid-eighties the NBA began embracing the connection between its players, fans, and hip-hop culture. "They wanted to appeal to the youth," Christopher "Play" Martin (from the group "Kid 'n Play") remembers. "That was the sound of the youth. That's what they loved. That's what appealed to them. That was the language, the style, the culture."[64]

Basketball also, inadvertently, created perhaps the best-known New York–based hip-hop group of the generation: Run-DMC. As the story goes, Joseph Simmons (DJ Run) hung out with Darryl McDaniels (DMC) at the Two-Fifth Park in Hollis, Queens, the center of the neighborhood's social life. In the summer of 1978, the duo played ball all day

long at Two-Fifth or Jamaica Park and then went home for quick showers before returning to listen to MCs rap and deejays spin records on
turntables brought from home. The two remained close in high school,
even as they moved apart from each other. Joseph fought with his older
brother, promoter Russell Simmons, to get a shot at producing a record
while Darryl (enrolled in a private school in Harlem) was exposed to
jam tapes of Afrika Bambaataa and Grand Wizzard Theodore. A few
years later, they added Jason Mizell (Jam Master Jay), the leader of the
Hollis Crew, and began performing around the city.[65] The rest, as they
say, is history.[66]

While Run-DMC were just emerging onto the scene, the NBA geared up
for its annual All-Star game in 1980. More than 19,000 fans showed up in
Washington, D.C., to cheer on three superstar rookies: Larry Bird, Magic
Johnson, and Bill Cartwright. Not since 1954, when Ray Felix, Don Sun-
derlage, and Jack Molinas took the court, had three first-year players
suited up for an NBA All-Star Game. This time Magic scored 12 points
for the West squad, while Bird and Cartwright scored 7 and 8 respectively
in helping the East to a 144–138 win.

Cartwright was slowly gaining recognition as an elite offensive center. In mid-March, he scored a last-second basket to give the Knicks a
111–110 win over the visiting Atlanta Hawks, capping an outstanding
21-point, 16-rebound effort. *Sport* magazine argued that he was a contender for Rookie of the Year, favorably placing Cartwright with "Bird
and Johnson at the head of the freshman class." Statistically, Cartwright
certainly merited that recognition; after all, he finished the season as the
rookie leader in points scored, field goal percentage, and minutes played—
the first player to pull that off since Abdul-Jabbar (then known as Lew
Alcindor) a decade earlier.[67]

Shortly after his heroic performance against the Hawks, Bill Cartwright and his wife, Sheri, celebrated their most important moment of the
season—the arrival of their first child, a son named Justin. Before and after
Justin was born, the Cartwrights spent a lot of time listening to their home
stereo, which played records from their favorite bands: James Brown, the
Platters, and the Shirelles. Road trips meant time away from Sheri and
Justin, so Bill brought a portable cassette player, which he hummed along
to while listening through his headphones.[68]

Bill and Sheri were also adjusting to living on the East Coast and in a much bigger city than where they had grown up (Elk Grove, California, population 11,000). "Country folks have their problems for sure," Bill admitted. "Like their tendency toward complacency when they have big problems. City people, on the other hand are too competitive," he told reporters. "They're uptight and sometimes blinded by their competitiveness. Yeah, I'll take that country life."[69] Maybe not the most comforting words for Knicks fans, but Bill had already demonstrated a willingness to mix it up on the court, including a preseason dust-up with Golden State Warriors center Robert Parish. "He hit me, and so I hit him back, and we squared off, and that was it," Cartwright told me. "Got to let people know that you're coming and that you're not scared. If you want to throw some punches, we'll do that. If you want to play, we'll do that."[70]

Cartwright was a rock for the Knicks, but race remained an all-encompassing aspect of the season for the all-Black squad. "If you get the lead and didn't keep the lead, it was implied that our players weren't smart enough to keep the lead," assistant coach Beard recalls. "That's how things were said."[71] The team lost plenty of leads that season and hovered around .500 for most of the year; in fact, Cartwright's last-second basket against the Hawks pulled the Knicks to 38–38 with six games left on the schedule. The Knicks only needed to win two or three games to guarantee themselves a playoff spot. Instead, they dropped three in a row.

"We have to be synergetic," Hollis Copeland said following their latest loss. "I don't know how you spell it, but it means we have to be together."[72]

After a win over the Cavs, New York traveled to Boston for an incredibly important game against the despised Celtics. Both teams played with solid "synergetic-ism," to steal a phrase from Copeland, in an old-school, physical Boston–New York classic. Two old-timers suited up for the game: Monroe for the Knicks and Dave Cowens for the Celtics. But neither of the two got involved in the game's physicality. Early in the first quarter, Toby Knight fouled Bird, knocking the rookie into the basket support. As Bird limped off the court, Celtics coach Bill Fitch called on little-used reserve Jeff Judkins. As soon as play restarted, Judkins grabbed Ray Williams in a bearhug and tried to wrestle him to the ground. Officials called a foul and Judkins checked back out, spending the rest of the game on the bench. Later, Richardson and Nate Archibald got into a shoving match, as did Knicks reserve forward Larry Demic and former apple of the Knicks' eye Rick Robey. New York somehow led by four points late in the game, but another long-toothed Knicks-killer, Pistol Pete Maravich, in his only season as a Celtic, poured in twelve fourth quarter points to lead Boston to a 129–121 victory.

Playing the Celtics tight was great, but the Knicks needed more than a moral victory and now their final game—against the division-leading Philadelphia 76ers—was a must-win if they wanted to make the playoffs.

In front of 19,591 screaming fans (they could still pack the Garden for important games), the Knicks clung to a 101–99 lead with just eleven seconds left on the clock. Philly scored to tie the game at 101, and Holzman called a timeout. Richardson threw away the inbounds pass and Dr. J collected it and drove hard to the basket, colliding with Knight as he flipped in the game-winning layup. "It was an obvious offensive foul," Holzman complained afterward. "He stuck his knee in Toby's chest . . . it was an offensive foul."[73] Despite Holzman and 19,591 referees screaming for a foul, the official officials kept their whistles silent, and Philly escaped with a two-point win. "If this is the end for us, then it's some damned way to finish," Demic told reporters.[74] "Our last game of the year," Holzman recalled later, "kind of symbolized the season for us."[75] Once more, the Knicks' slim playoff hopes rested with another team. If the Nets beat the Bullets, the Knicks were playoff-bound; but if Washington won, New York was out of luck.

Of the Knicks' players and coaches, only Richardson, joined by an older brother and their girlfriends, traveled to Piscataway, New Jersey, and the Rutgers Athletic Center to watch the Bullets-Nets game in person. The rest of Richardson's teammates sat around the radio listening to WVNJ's John Sterling's play-by-play. Midway through the fourth quarter, the Nets cut the Bullets lead to one, giving New York hope. But a late Washington run, powered by ageless center Wes Unseld's 14 points, 20 rebounds, and 5 assists, gave the visiting team a 93–87 win. "It's all over now," Richardson grumbled in an interview.[76] "There ain't nothing to think about. There ain't nothing to say. It's been rough."[77]

The next day, Holzman called a team meeting. It was short and sweet but not well-attended. Webster and Monroe were no-shows, both unhappy with their roles on the team. Holzman ignored his absentee veterans and heaped praise on their young teammates. "These kids deserve credit," Red told reporters. "I've got a good feeling about these kids."[78] In particular, Holzman pointed out Richardson's efforts in earning his first All-Star nod. Micheal Ray "did everything but take tickets this year," Holzman said.[79] He wasn't far off. For the first time in league history, a player led the NBA in three categories as Richardson paced the circuit in assists and steals but also (uh-oh!) turnovers.

The 1979–80 Knicks, best known for being the first all-Black team in NBA history, finished the season 39–43. It was an eight-game improvement over the previous year, and only a series of unfortunate breaks—a no-call on a Dr. J charge, a fourth-quarter explosion from gimpy-kneed "Pistol Pete," and a last-minute Bullets win—kept them from postseason play.

It was also a young team. Richardson and Cartwright rightfully earned most of the accolades for the Knicks' modest success. Cartwright averaged almost 22 points per game as a rookie while shooting nearly 55 percent from the field. But Toby Knight and Ray Williams were almost as important. Knight averaged 19 points on 53 percent shooting from the field as a slashing small forward, while Williams finished second on the team (and seventeenth in the league) with 21 points per game while handing out 6 assists and grabbing 5 rebounds per game. Ray also began to feel more comfortable in this, his third NBA season, and he seemed poised to assume the leadership of the team as Monroe was phased out. "It's a whole new atmosphere here this year," Williams said after the season. "This year we socialize more and we're closer. I think maybe because it's such a young team and so many of the guys are single that we've had the time. I feel," he continued, "like I've finally found my place here."[80]

1979–80 Knicks
Record: 39–43
Playoffs: Did not qualify
Coach: Red Holzman
Average Home Attendance: 12,405
Points per Game: (114.0—4th of 22)
Points Allowed per Game: (115.1—20th of 22)
Team Leaders:

   Points: Bill Cartwright (21.7 per game)
   Rebounds: Bill Cartwright (8.9 per game)

Assists: Micheal Ray Richardson (10.1 per game)
Steals: Micheal Ray Richardson (3.2 per game)
Blocked Shots: Joe C. Meriweather (1.8 per game)

All-Stars: Bill Cartwright and Micheal Ray Richardson
Notable Transactions: Drafted Bill Cartwright in the first round of the 1979 NBA draft

6

"Colorful yet Colorless"

1980–1981

We've had a crazy man called the Son of Sam
And Earl Monroe, the hoopster pro
—"Big Apple Rappin'," Spyder D, 1980

Even after the release of "Rapper's Delight" in 1979, hip-hop remained mostly an underground sensation, barely spreading beyond the boundaries of the five boroughs. Spyder D was from Hollis, Queens, where the center of the hip-hop world was slowly shifting. The members of Run-DMC were still in high school, but Russell Simmons (Joseph "Run" Simmons's older brother) was a popular promoter in the city and included both Kurtis Blow ("Basketball is my fav-o-rite sport") and Spyder D among his clients. They rapped about a lot of things but often came back to two topics they knew best: living in New York City and basketball.

Just like the Knicks, hip-hop was essentially a nonwhite production. Latino and Black young men performed as MCs and deejays, while few white people witnessed live shows. Still, Afrika Bambaataa, one of hip-hop's earliest pioneers, had a vision. "I've got to grab that Black and white audience and bridge the gap," he said. In 1981, Bambaataa performed in the Mudd Club—his first exposure to a predominantly white crowd. His popularity grew across racial lines, aided by Blondie's hit song "Rapture" (a pop song with some rap elements . . . and a shout-out to Fab 5 Freddy), and Bambaataa started playing at the Roxy Club, a popular roller-skating rink and disco located in Manhattan near Tenth Avenue and West Eighteenth. The area around the Roxy was not as gentrified as it

Figure 8. Veteran Knicks guard Earl Monroe drives past Jim Barnett of the Utah Jazz, 1974. © Larry Berman—BermanSports.com. Used by permission.

would become but even then was known as a progressive art district—not the usual venue for hip-hop artists to perform. Still, Bambaataa and others persisted, and soon, as B-boy Frosty Freeze later recalled, "the downtown scene connected with the uptown scene."[1] Bambaataa also fused musical styles, creating "electro-funk" in the process—his song "Renegades of Funk" (not to be confused with Rage Against the Machine's version a decade later) is the best example of this genre.

By late 1982, rappers were mixing with white fans in downtown clubs, and Bambaataa's hit "Planet Rock" sold over six hundred thousand twelve-inch singles, many to white suburban kids enamored with this new underground sound.[2] "If hip-hop had depended only on the Sugarhill Gang's breakout song, and it had not come downtown and experienced the cultural and media embrace and explosion" journalist Michael Holman argues, "it would not have happened the way it did." "What put rap music on the map," he continues, "was when the culture was encapsulated as a multifaceted diamond of dance, writing, song, music, lyrics, visuals, graffiti, and then presented to the world."[3]

One person with a foot in both Uptown and Downtown New York City was Earl Monroe. Monroe might have been a hoopster pro in the eyes of Spyder D, but he was about to be a former pro. In the 1980 expansion draft, in which the NBA added the Dallas Mavericks, the Knicks left five players unprotected, including Monroe. The Mavs passed on the thirty-five-year-old, who never again played in the NBA. It was a sad end to an amazing career. Since retiring in 1980, Monroe has had nearly fifty surgeries, including vertebral fusion. "They done made him the bionic man!" Willis Reed joked later. "I used to ask him, 'All that twirling you used to do, would you have done it if you knew your knees would be as bad as they are? . . . He thought about it awhile and said, 'Welllllll, yeah, but maybe not quite as much.' "[4]

With the expansion draft completed, and the last link to the old Knicks unceremoniously dumped, the team turned its attention to the NBA's annual collegiate draft. New York held the twelfth pick, and everyone in the city, from fans to the team's front office, had a single name atop their wish list: UCLA sharpshooter Kiki Vandeweghe. Kiki's father, Dr. Ernie Vandeweghe, played for the Knicks in the 1950s before joining the air force. While Ernie was stationed in Germany, he and his wife had a son whom they named Kiki. Moving stateside to California, Kiki grew to be

Figure 9. Almighty Kay Gee and JDL of the Cold Crush Brothers perform at South Bronx High School, 1980. Photo by Joe Conzo Jr. (Division of Rare and Manuscript Collections, Cornell University Library. © Cornell University.)

an outstanding high school basketball player who was smitten with the idea of playing for his dad's old team. "I like the people in New York and I identify real well 'cause of my father," he told sportswriters before the draft.[5] The feeling was mutual.

Was the Knicks' infatuation with Kiki because he had connections to the team and was an excellent outside shooter? Or was it because he represented a potential Great White Hope for an all-Black squad? It was probably a little of both.

So enamored of one another were Kiki and the Knicks that other NBA teams began to question whether to draft Vandeweghe knowing that, like Bill Bradley a generation earlier, Kiki had other options. He openly talked about attending law school, applying for a Rhodes scholarship, or taking postgraduate classes to delay his entry into the league. With the first overall pick, the Golden State Warriors passed on Vandeweghe to select Purdue center Joe Barry Carroll. Next, the Utah Jazz chose high-flier "Dr. Dunkenstein" Darrell Griffith before Boston made Kevin McHale the newest Celtic with the third pick. Adding McHale (and Robert Parish, as part of a trade that sent the first overall pick—acquired in the

McAdoo-to-Detroit deal—to Golden State) created Boston's legendary front line and the foundation for one of the greatest dynasties in NBA history.

New Yorkers grew more excited with each pick that moved Kiki and the Knicks closer to their dream scenario. Then with the eleventh selection— just one before the Knicks—the expansion Mavericks ruined everything and chose Vandeweghe. The New York crowd chanted obscenities and booed the Mavs. Kiki was distraught. "I'm a Knick fan," he admitted. "Maybe some day I'll play here . . . there's a hope."[6] With Vandeweghe off the board, the Knicks scrambled, ultimately deciding on guard Mike Woodson from Indiana University. "We might have drafted Kiki if he was available," Holzman admitted. "But Woodson has added value because he can also play the big [shooting] guard. We will concentrate on having him fit in."[7]

Woodson, at least, was excited to join the Knicks. That summer, Mike Burke and his partner joined the newest Knick and his girlfriend on a double date to a Yankees game, where Woodson met Reggie Jackson, who joined the foursome for a late dinner at McMullen's, "one of the swingingest and most popular pub-restaurants on the East Side."[8] Woodson was floored. "This is the most wonderful thing that has ever happened to me," the rookie (and future Knicks coach) gushed.[9]

Other than adding Woodson, the 1980 off-season was an unremarkable one for most of the Knicks. Some players relaxed all summer, barely picking up a basketball or running farther than to the refrigerator and back. But others used the downtime to develop off the court. Mike Glenn, heading into his third season in New York, worked on Wall Street that summer while pursuing an MBA. He also started a summer camp for hearing-impaired children. Glenn's father coached basketball at the Georgia School for the Deaf, so he had grown up around deaf kids, Glenn explained to me decades later. "They taught me sign language and the sport of basketball. They were my best friends."[10] When Knicks' PR director Kevin Kennedy approached Glenn about a tournament for deaf schools, Glenn decided to go one step further and create a summer camp at the Mill Neck Manor School for the Deaf, located on Long Island. For the next four decades, Glenn would welcome hundreds of children and NBA players to the camp and early on earned the J. Walter Kennedy Citizenship Award in 1981 for his efforts.[11]

Glenn was excited to join his teammates for training camp that fall, and expectations were high for the young Knicks team. Talented guards Ray Williams and Micheal Ray Richardson seemed destined to team up in All-Star games for the rest of the decade, while Bill Cartwright was already one of the best centers in the league and showed up in tremendous shape after dropping twenty pounds with an off-season regimen of running and lifting weights.[12] And Toby Knight, who had come out of nowhere in 1979–80 to average almost 20 points per game, signed a three-year contract extension in the offseason, which should have secured the Knicks' core for several more seasons. All four were under twenty-six years old. The future was bright in the Big Apple.

"Training camp was long," Cartwright remembers. "It was a month of two-a-days. So we went down to practice in Monmouth College in South Jersey. Nothing special. Stayed in a regular hotel and went to practice twice a day and ran in practice really hard. By the end of camp, you were in great shape. Training camps were different back then," he explains. "[You] got into shape if you weren't in shape."[13]

But then, in a meaningless exhibition game after weeks of grueling two-a-days, Knight tore cartilage in his knee while chasing down a rebound.[14] Suddenly the Knicks had lost a twenty-point scorer just days before the season began. Hoping to replace Knight internally, the Knicks turned to Sly Williams. But even if Williams, who had averaged less than ten minutes of playing time per game as a rookie, became a competent starter, the Knicks desperately needed depth behind him. So Burke and Donovan once again started working the phones.

At the top of their wish list was Campy Russell, engaged in a bitter contract dispute with the Cleveland Cavaliers. The Knicks offered Cleveland two first-round picks for Russell, but the Cavs turned them down. Instead, Cleveland traded Russell to Kansas City, who then flipped him to New York. In return, the Knicks sent one first-round pick and blue-collar big man Joe C. Meriweather to the Kings. "I was happy with it," Russell told me of hearing about the trade, "I wanted to be with a contending team." [15] It had been a few years since the words "contending team" could unironically refer to the Knicks, but bumper stickers found around the city in the summer of 1980 echoed those sentiments. "The New New York Knicks" one sticker read, while another predicted "A Year Better."[16]

Twelve months after becoming the first team in NBA history composed entirely of African American players, the 1980–81 Knicks again featured an all-Black roster. And once again Peter Vecsey was writing about it for the *Post*. "At least one white, long-time season ticket holder tells me," Vecsey wrote, that "as long as the team remains exclusively black and conspicuously lacking in charisma (colorful yet colorless) . . . pale faces will abstain."[17] It was no secret that NBA executives searched high and low for the next Great White Hope. In the early seventies, Pete Maravich was that guy; then it was Bill Walton, maybe Jack Sikma, and then Larry Bird and maybe even Vandeweghe. Every team wanted a white superstar because, as they reasoned, most of their fans were white and would relate more easily to a white player than a Black player. Unsurprisingly, then, the *Sports Illustrated* cover athlete for the 1980–81 pro basketball preview issue was the newest Seattle SuperSonic, Paul Westphal, a white guard.

The Knicks got off to a strong start to the 1980–81 regular season, winning five of their first six. Ray Williams was so excited about his team's hot start that, after leading the Knicks to a 114–109 win over the Milwaukee Bucks, he told reporters, "I wanted this victory more than I wanted Ali to beat Larry Holmes."[18] Muhammad Ali had lost to Holmes a week earlier in Las Vegas in what was billed as "The Last Hurrah."

Williams and New York continued their winning ways, and when they landed in Denver for a November 7 game against the Nuggets, they stood at 7–3. "I feel like I've been reborn," Russell, freed from the doldrums of Cleveland, told reporters.[19] The game in Denver was physical, and in the second half it quickly escalated when Marvin Webster squared off with Denver center Dave Robisch. Webster threw a left hook that connected with Robisch's chin and then shoved an official who tried to intervene, drawing an immediate ejection.[20] After the game, which the Knicks won by nine, Webster's teammates razzed him for his pugilistic performance, chanting "Ali . . . Ali" when he boarded the team bus. "Inside the airline terminal in Salt Lake City," the *Post* reported, "Ray Williams passed the hat to raise money for Webster's automatic $250 fine."[21] As it turned out, the league's ruling was much harsher. The December 1978 punch by Lakers forward Kermit Washington that nearly ended the career of Rockets forward Rudy Tomjanovich had resulted in greatly increased punishment for fighting. So Webster, instead of $250, owed the league $2,000 for decking Robisch.

Unlike the Garden of Eden Knicks, who tended to go their separate ways after games, this new generation of players seemed to enjoy socializing with one another. A few weeks after Webster's right hook, Ray Williams made the society pages in *Jet* magazine for his early December birthday bash. As befit one of the new faces of this fresh and young Knicks team, Ray and some teammates met at Justine's in Manhattan, a Black-owned disco five blocks from Madison Square Garden on Thirty-Eighth Street. There Williams "celebrated his birthday in grand style," which included "a soul food buffet and a giant X-rated birthday cake."[22]

The young Knicks were winning on the court and growing together as a team off it. Even the forward positions, which looked like problem areas in October after Knight's knee injury, were becoming a strength as the combination of Russell and Sly Williams proved to be greater than the sum of its parts. "Sly and I played well together because we complemented each other," Russell told me. "We both could handle the ball. We both could pass the ball. We both could rebound the ball."[23] Williams and Russell were long, lanky, and athletic, able to switch to cover guards or even centers, helping the Knicks force a lot of turnovers. On the other end of the court, they rarely turned the ball over themselves, allowing the Knicks to control the tempo of games.[24]

Sly, Campy, Ray, and Cartwright all contributed to the team's hot start, but Micheal Ray Richardson was quickly becoming the face of the franchise. "I think I'm the leader of this team," he told reporters. "The guys look for me to get them the ball, and I want to. I get off on passing, and they get off on scoring and you kill two birds with one stone."[25] Hoping to keep their young core intact and trying to get a discount before Richardson got even bigger, the Knicks convinced the third-year guard to sign a contract extension in late 1980. He would receive a few bonuses before the three-year deal, worth a total of approximately $1 million, would kick in before the 1982–83 season. "What I completely fail to fathom," Vecsey wrote of the contract at the time, "is why Richardson agreed to such skimpy terms."[26]

If Sugar was as talented as everyone believed him to be, why not hold out for a mega-deal like the one the Los Angeles Lakers were negotiating with Magic Johnson (a startling twenty-five-year, $25 million contract signed the next summer) or even something like the Nuggets had given David Thompson a few years earlier ($800,000 per year)? It was simple. Richardson wanted to be a Knick. He wanted to be wanted. And so he signed a contract that probably cost him millions of dollars. Perhaps as a thank-you for his diligence in re-signing Sugar, in December Eddie Donovan was offered and inked a three-year contract extension that also earned him a promotion from general manager to vice president. Donovan was also promised that Holzman would succeed him as GM when Red chose to re-retire.

The Knicks' early season success brought back fond memories for the team's Hall of Fame head coach. Sportswriters often asked Holzman to compare his team with the title winners of a decade earlier. At first, Red brushed off the questions, telling reporters that "what's past is past." But after being asked repeatedly, Red finally decided to answer truthfully. "This team I've got now has more raw talent than my other team," he admitted. "But thinking-wise, and defensively, the old team was better." This was great copy, but it didn't play well in the locker room. "I'm not saying the fans should forget Frazier and the Old Knicks," Webster told reporters. "I'm just saying 'Look at us, we're pretty good too.'" Glenn agreed. "Ever since I've been here," the fourth-year guard told reporters, "I've been hearing about the old Knicks. We just got tired of hearing about it. It's like having a new wife and having to hear all the time about what the old wife did."[27]

By 1981, Holzman was the team's only remaining link to the old Knicks. Henry Bibby, a rookie on the title-winning team in 1973, still played in the league. But he was a bench player for the San Diego Clippers who probably spent more time chasing his three-year-old son (and future NBA guard) Mike than he did playing. Phil Jackson was still in the league, as an assistant coach with the Nets, but the other '73 Knicks had moved on with life after basketball.

Assistant coach Butch Beard, who played for Seattle when the Knicks won their last title, might have linked the old Knicks and the New Knicks most clearly, having played in both eras and coached under Holzman for several seasons. Like many former players, Beard lamented the lack of fundamentals in the modern game and compared it to the generational gap facing America in the early '80s, when the post-boomers came of age. Young men and women in their early twenties were in elementary school during most of the sixties and only knew about Martin Luther King Jr. and Malcolm X because they had read about them in their textbooks. They did not remember the assassinations of those leaders, nor those of John and Bobby Kennedy. Their memories were of Jimmy Carter, stagflation, and the terror at the 1972 Olympic Games. It was a different generation. "The real problem," George Vecsey (Peter's brother) asserted, "is that kids today don't have discipline. They can't learn." Beard told Vecsey, "In the old days, you tried to make basketball players into athletes. Today you try to make athletes into basketball players."[28]

Perhaps it was that generation gap, or maybe just the changing nature of professional basketball, rather than the race of the players on the court that kept fans away from Madison Square Garden. Even with the team's success early in the 1980–81 season, tickets were not a hot item. A December 16 game against the Jazz (in their second season playing in Utah) drew barely ten thousand fans to see rookie Darrell Griffith and All-Star forward Adrian Dantley come to town. Russell and Cartwright led the Knicks that night with 22 points apiece as the team pulled out a strong 112–97 win, but the attendance figures were troubling. In the early seventies, home games regularly sold out: more than nineteen thousand fans packed the arena forty-one times a year (not including the playoffs). As the seventies progressed, attendance slowly dropped, and this was only loosely tied to the team's won-loss record. In 1975, the 40–42 Knicks averaged over eighteen thousand fans per game, but the 1978 team won 43 games in front of around fifteen thousand per game. In 1981, the Knicks won 50 games but barely drew ten thousand per game. Sonny Werblin claimed that spring that Madison Square Garden had lost $3.7 million in 1980, roughly the amount they paid the city of New York annually. "How long can you expect a company to keep losing money?" he asked reporters, ultimately hoping to drop the Garden's annual tax bill closer to what new Los Angeles Lakers owner Jerry Buss was paying for Inglewood's Forum: approximately $1 million per year.[29]

Unfortunately, the situation facing the Knicks reflected a league-wide trend that many outsiders blamed on the racial makeup of NBA rosters. Attendance across the league was down 10 percent for the 1980–81 season. And with fourteen of twenty-three teams sporting losing records by mid-December, the NBA was increasingly becoming a league of haves and have-nots. For the season, the SuperSonics led the league in attendance with over sixteen thousand per game, while Cleveland and Detroit eked out barely five thousand. In Cleveland's Richfield Coliseum, which could seat twenty thousand, and the Pontiac Silverdome, with a basketball capacity of twenty-two thousand, the stands appeared almost entirely empty on television and sounded like a crypt over the radio.

Identifying the problems was easy. Solving them would be much more difficult. One factor the NBA had to consider was the length of the season. In 1980, teams opened on October 12, right in the middle of the Major League Baseball playoffs. During the first week of the NBA schedule in 1980, the Philadelphia Phillies beat the Kansas City Royals in an exciting six-game World Series and captured the highest television viewership in MLB history with a 32.8 Nielsen rating.[30] Going head-to-head against the MLB playoffs seriously handicapped NBA ratings in the early season and cost the league a prime opportunity to capture new viewers. Unsurprisingly, the Sixers—with the Philadelphia baseball team headed to their first World Series title—felt the crunch in October. "The whole city was engrossed in baseball the way they should have been," Sixers general manager Pat Williams admitted. But not even the end of the baseball season helped his team: "Now the interest is in pro football and the Philadelphia Eagles, rather than us."[31]

Williams blamed the loss of interest in basketball on both season start date and the perception that the NBA had lost the parity it celebrated in the seventies. "I can't remember such a dramatic difference between the top and bottom teams," Williams told the *Times*. "We have seven or eight elite teams while the others are floundering . . . when teams like Detroit and Dallas come into your building, it's tough getting people to come and see them." Speaking of Dallas, Knicks president Mike Burke blamed league expansion for his team's decline in attendance. "We were against expansion," Burke declared. "Nobody is thrilled about seeing San Diego."[32] The San Diego Clippers were not an expansion team—they had relocated from Buffalo in 1978—but after a 2–7 start to the season, the Clippers were tied with the Mavericks for the NBA's worst record.

Whether a later start to the season, greater parity, or an end to expansion might help the NBA, many owners and league executives realized that one potential solution to decreasing viewership was a still-emerging technology: cable television. In New York, the Madison Square Garden (MSG) Network began showing Knicks games on pay television in 1970.

But the rest of the nation was slow to catch up. Then, in September 1979, the Entertainment and Sports Programming Network (ESPN) debuted on cable with its flagship program *Sportscenter*. Eventually, when cable use became more widespread and profitable, ESPN would provide twenty-four-hour coverage, giving sports junkies an around-the-clock fix while showcasing the best in pro basketball and other sports. For now, the NBA had to deal with flagging ratings on free TV. The 1979–80 NBA Finals, featuring the Los Angeles Lakers and Philadelphia 76ers, was famously preempted by CBS in favor of reruns of *The Dukes of Hazzard* and *Dallas*. Although not as well known, maybe because they lacked the flair and drama of Magic Johnson's unforgettable 1980 game six performance, four of the six games in the 1981 finals were also tape-delayed, causing the Boston Celtics and Houston Rockets series to play in the lowest-rated NBA Finals in the twentieth century.

After the heart-wrenching assassination of John Lennon, gunned down outside his apartment near Central Park in December 1980, the Knicks managed to string together eight straight wins later that winter.[33] It was their longest winning streak since 1973 and, just like with the old Knicks, every player contributed to winning basketball: Richardson averaged 15 points per game during the stretch, Russell and Ray Williams chipped in 18 apiece, Sly Williams added 16, and Cartwright led the way with almost 22 per game. The Knicks were playing smart, unselfish team basketball, rarely turning the ball over on offense while forcing turnovers on defense without fouling. Nearly all their shots were taken either near the basket or from the mid-range, although they attempted the fifth-most three-pointers in the NBA that season (around three per game). As Holzman explained, "you don't count on winning games with 3-pointers. You never look for a 3-pointer when you're ahead."[34] Unsurprisingly, the Clippers and Cavaliers were at the top of the league in three-pointers attempted and at the bottom of the standings. Only Boston, thanks to Larry Bird, made the playoffs by shooting more three-pointers than did the Knicks.

As the end of the season approached, the young Knicks remained optimistic about making the playoffs. Only three of their players had postseason experience, and just one, Ray Williams, remained from the last Knicks team to make the playoffs, in 1978. But it was Richardson who was on the cusp of superstardom as the season entered its final days. On

March 21, the Knicks hosted the Cavaliers, led by All-Star small forward Mike Mitchell. Mitchell scored 26 points but was outclassed by the Broadway-worthy show Richardson put on for the New York faithful. Barely eleven thousand fans showed up, but those in attendance saw peak Micheal Ray, who finished with 27 points, 19 assists, 15 rebounds, and 2 steals. After the game, Mike Glenn gushed to reporters about his friend's play. "Nothing Sugar does amazes me anymore," Glenn told them. "He's incredible. He reminds me of the small town storekeeper who also serves as the sheriff, the fire chief and the justice of the peace. Sugar is an incredible player, the best point guard in the league."[35] Hyperbole, perhaps, given where Lakers' point guard Magic Johnson was headed. But in 1981, Magic missed three months with a knee injury, feuded with coach Paul Westhead, and demanded a trade, missing the All-Star game for the only time in the twelve seasons before his 1991 retirement. Although Sugar missed out on first- and second-team All-NBA honors (Dennis Johnson and George Gervin made first team, Tiny Archibald and Otis Birdsong the second), Richardson had a brighter future than any of the four and might have had a better season: he earned first-team All-Defense honors and was one of only two players to average at least 15 points, 5 rebounds, and 7 assists per game. The other was Larry Bird.

After fifty wins in the regular season—the highest win total for the Knicks between 1973 and 1989—New York's opponent in the first round of the 1981 playoffs was the Chicago Bulls. The Bulls, winners of their last eight games, were not only the hottest team in the NBA but also the tallest. Guards Ricky Sobers (6'3") and Reggie Theus (6'7") joined forwards Larry Kenon and Dave Greenwood (both 6'9") and monstrous center Artis Gilmore (7'2") to overpower smaller teams. The Knicks were better equipped than most to deal with this size, but none of the Knicks (even Cartwright, who was of a similar height) was as physically imposing as Gilmore, a muscular 240-pounder whose Afro made him seem closer to eight feet tall than to seven. Gilmore was confident that he could dominate the Knicks on the inside. "I think they have to establish another game," he bragged. "I'm gonna be there to block their shots if they bring it to me."[36] In the regular season, Gilmore averaged 18 points, 10 rebounds, and more than 2 blocked shots per game, leading the league in field goal percentage by connecting on almost 70 percent of his attempts. He rarely shot outside of five feet, but he didn't need to. He usually bullied his way to the rim for offensive rebounds and dunks.

Game one in the best-of-three series started well for the hometown Knicks. Despite a disappointingly low attendance (14,822—nearly 5,000 less than a full house), famous fans dotted the arena. Woody Allen, taking a break from working on *A Midsummer Night's Sex Comedy*, which opened the following July, joined Mia Farrow at courtside while Ken Howard, who played fictional high school basketball coach Ken Reeves in CBS's *The White Shadow*, and players from the New York Rangers, New York Giants, and New Jersey Nets held seats in the lower bleachers. When the Knicks jumped out to a 22–8 lead, the fans were loud, chanting "De-fense! (clap, clap), De-fense!" every time the Bulls got the ball. "When the Garden is rocking and the team is good," Rory Sparrow told me, "I'm not sure there's a better place to play basketball."[37] "It was like the glory days," mused one sportswriter. "Then it stopped. The Knicks went cold. The Bulls dominated them, outrebounded them, outshot them, outthought them."[38]

Most glaringly, New York had no answer for Gilmore. The mighty one finished with just 13 points on nine field goal attempts, but he dominated the interior, pulling down a game-high 16 rebounds and blocking 7 shots. "He intimidated us," Glenn admitted after the game. Reserve forward Larry Demic saw it a little differently. "He's a bitch," Demic said of Gilmore, promising that the next game would be different.[39] Most of the blame for New York's game one collapse, though, fell squarely on the shoulders of Cartwright. Like Gilmore, Cartwright took just nine shots, but he managed just 8 rebounds and 1 blocked shot. And, in one third-quarter stretch, Cartwright missed a layup, shot an airball, committed a turnover, and watched Gilmore swat away two other shots.[40] "Oh nooo, Mr. Bill," Gary Myers wrote in the *Daily News*, referencing a recent *Saturday Night Live* sketch of clay figurine Mr. Bill. "Sluggo stomped all over Cartwright." Cartwright, as usual, was unruffled. "I'm not going to lose any sleep over it," he told reporters. "I'm just going to do what I'm supposed to do next time."[41]

More than twenty-two thousand packed Chicago Stadium for game two as the Bulls hosted their first playoff game in four years. Again New York jumped out to an early lead, this time thanks to an intense full-court pressing defense used to harass the Bulls guards. At halftime, the Knicks' lead was 14, but Richardson and Ray Williams each had several fouls, forcing them to dial back their aggressiveness in the second half. Relieved of the pressure, the Bulls found their mojo and slowly chipped away at the Knicks' lead before Theus took over, following up a subpar game one with a sizzling 37-point game two performance, including making 17 of 18 free throw attempts. During the regular season, the Knicks excelled at limiting their fouls. Now the Bulls were living at the line. At the end of the third quarter, the Knicks clung to a seven-point lead, but free throw problems from Richardson and Williams (who combined to shoot 12 for 21 from the charity stripe) allowed the Bulls to inch closer, and Sobers's eight-footer as time expired sent the game into overtime. With ten seconds left in the extra period and the Bulls up by one, Theus drove the lane, and his shot was blocked by Webster (replacing the ineffectual Cartwright). But the ball kicked away, and all ten players scrambled for possession; before either team could secure the ball, the final buzzer sounded. The game—and the Knicks season—was over.

Sly Williams sat in the locker room after the game, tears streaming down his face. He had a breakout season, replacing Knight far better than anyone could have expected. But the emotion of how it ended was overwhelming. Across the room, Ray Williams looked shocked, amazed that he and his team had blown a double-digit lead and lost in overtime. Only Richardson seemed to take the loss in stride. "It's over, we can't do anything now," he said. "We have nothing to be ashamed of."[42] Holzman agreed. He looked at Donovan, who was consoling players in the locker room, and told him, "Let's get down to working on next year."[43]

Would the Knicks who walked off the court in Chicago be the same ones who suited up for New York in the fall? They were a young team who had finished 50–32 but many questions remained. Could Sly, a wiry six-foot-seven 210-pounder, hold up against the league's top power forwards over a full season? Could the Knicks afford two highly paid centers, one who specialized on offense (Cartwright) and the other on defense (Webster)? And would the Knicks open the checkbook wide enough to keep free agent Ray Williams in the Big Apple? His brother Gus had sat out the entire season in a contract dispute with Seattle; Ray was younger and more athletic, probably in line for a bigger payday. But with Richardson signed to a team-friendly, multiyear contract, did the Knicks really need another playmaking guard?

Peter Vecsey perhaps best summed up the problems facing the Knicks in the offseason. "I've never seen a team win as much as the Knicks did this season, yet receive so much well deserved grief from the media, and turn off so many fans," he wrote. "Fundamentally impure players assembled by one of the most feeble, unimaginative management teams since the Pittsburgh Condors [who folded after two ABA seasons]," Vecsey continued, were "neither enjoyable nor fun to be around." Ray Williams fired back at Vecsey. "I'm tired of all the negative press this team constantly gets," he complained. "If you guys don't like how we play, don't pick on us. We didn't put this team together. We aren't the GM and we aren't the coach. We just follow orders and do the best we can under the circumstances."[44]

Looking back, 1980–81 was a false spring for Knicks fans. "All the players on that 1980–81 team knew their roles," Holzman reflected years later. "We had a good system."[45] "They didn't understand," Russell told me wistfully in 2017. "Our chemistry was so dynamic it allowed us to win games even though we were not able to outrebound most teams . . . it was a better thing to . . . create turnovers and get easy baskets."[46]

Once again, with an earlier-than-hoped-for end to their season, the Knicks had their eyes on landing a big fish in the summer of 1981. One was Otis Birdsong, a young All-Star guard for the Kings who had just earned a spot on the All-NBA second team. He averaged almost 25 points per game, sinking over 54 percent of his shots, and, as a better outside shooter than Ray Williams, seemed like a perfect fit next to Richardson in the Knicks' backcourt. To beef up the team's front line to better compete with bullies like Boston and Chicago, the Knicks were looking at Mitch Kupchak. In 1981, decades before becoming a punchline as a Lakers and Hornets executive, Kupchak was a rugged six-foot-nine power forward. He was also white and had grown up on Long Island. That summer, both Birdsong and Kupchak were free agents, looking to sign big contracts.

While negotiating with Birdsong and Kupchak, New York traded its first-round draft pick (seventeenth overall) to the Cavaliers for veteran guard Randy Smith. Smith had been an All-Star for the Buffalo Braves in 1976 and 1978 thanks to his exceptional athleticism; one coach made him wear a weighted belt in practice so his teammates could keep up.[47] In New York, management hoped he could mentor the young Knicks guards as well as provide insurance in case the Knicks failed to sign their big free agent targets. Smith was also a native New Yorker, having grown up on the South Shore of Long Island before going to college at Buffalo State. "New York is definitely my home," Smith told reporters, "I feel I can play 25 or 26 minutes a game and give a nice contribution."[48] On paper, the deal made sense for both teams. New York didn't need another rookie, and Holzman told reporters, "We felt we would never get a player of Randy Smith's quality on the 17th pick."[49] And the Cavaliers regained a first-round pick after trading a host of draft choices under owner Ted Stepien, which had forced the NBA to institute the so-called Stepien Rule limiting pick trading.

In retrospect, the Knicks probably wished they'd had a pick after all, as the 1981 draft was one of the best ever. Top choice Mark Aguirre would average 20 points per game over a thirteen-year NBA career, while third choice Buck Williams would be an All-Star power forward for the Nets before transitioning into an excellent role player for Portland. But the pick between Aguirre and Williams was the best of the bunch: Isiah Thomas. Thomas would become the heart and soul of the Bad Boy Detroit Pistons teams of the late eighties and in 1997 be named one of the fifty greatest NBA players of all-time. Outside the top three, Tom Chambers, Larry Nance, Rolando Blackman, and Danny Ainge (hated by Knicks fans in later years) all would have solid NBA careers. Unfortunately, the Knicks picks were forgettable. Only Frank Brickowski, a third-round choice, would play more than forty NBA games, and he never even suited up for New York after being cut in the preseason.

With only Randy Smith to show for a lackluster 1981 draft day, the Ray Williams situation took a bizarre turn. Werblin informed reporters he had inside intelligence that Williams was going to sign with the Cavaliers for $700,000 a year plus a bonus of $0.50 per ticket the team sold above five thousand per game. Based on the Cavs' attendance in 1981, that totaled an extra $20,000 dollars per season, give or take.[50] Cleveland owner Stepien had already inked center James Edwards and forward Scott Wedman to above-market deals, so signing a guard like Williams made sense, especially since they now had Randy Smith's contract off the books. But other owners were incensed at Stepien's liberality. One told reporters, "He set the early free-agent pattern by offering crazy salaries, and we're going to have to live with it. It seems that the average going price for a free agent

is $750,000; some of them had been getting less than $200,000 per year."
Stepien defended his spending, arguing, "I had to induce them to come to
an unglamorous market." "I didn't create free agency," he insisted, "but
as long as it's there, I want to take advantage of it."[51] Werblin was adamant that the Knicks were not going to follow suit, telling Harvey Araton
of the *New York Post*, "There is no way in the world that I'm going to pay
Ray Williams $700,000 a year."[52]

As noted earlier, free agency arrived in the NBA in 1976, as Gail
Goodrich left the Lakers for the Jazz. A few big names changed teams in
the late seventies, but rules changed when the collective bargaining agreement in 1980 called for the free agent's team to retain the right of first
refusal, allowing them to match any free agent offer sheet signed by the
player. Now only exorbitant contracts like those offered by the Cavs to
Edwards, Wedman, and maybe Williams made it likely that players could
change teams. Not until Tom Chambers in 1988 would unrestricted free
agency allow unfettered player movement. And while Stepien was willing to open his checkbook to improve his team, the Knicks continued
to largely rely on an outdated model of trading young players and draft
choices for established NBA veterans to build their squad.

Still, Williams's contract dispute highlighted a constant problem during
Larry O'Brien's tenure as NBA commissioner: team ownership. Stability
was a real concern; between 1971 and 1982, the league had forty-five different ownership groups. As Larry Fleisher, general counsel for the NBA
Players' Association (NBPA), explained, "[New owners] buy in and take a
very active role for two years or so, until the novelty wears off. Then they
begin to disappear and are gone completely after four years, maximum
five."[53] By early 1982, some team payrolls were as much as ten times greater
than they had been a decade earlier, with TV ratings on the decline.[54]

O'Brien met with owners constantly to discuss potential solutions.
Some of the ideas were drastic, such as a franchise merger of the Utah
Jazz and Denver Nuggets, and maybe of the Indiana Pacers and Kansas
City Kings.[55] More realistically, the owners, aware of the approaching
expiration of the collective bargaining agreement on June 1, 1982, wanted
a salary cap. But the NBPA would not agree to that without a fight. Owners grumbled about salary escalation, but they were the ones offering the
contracts and signing the checks. "We have no intention of saving them
from themselves," Fleisher told reporters. "They say they're a sick and

dying industry. That's ridiculous."[56] To make matters worse for owners, during these contentious negotiations in which they claimed poverty, the 76ers signed free agent Moses Malone to the richest contract in NBA history, proving—to players at least—that some owners were far better off financially than they were leading people to believe. Malone's signing galvanized players. As future commissioner David Stern explained in late 1982, "We are not at an impasse but we're getting there."[57]

Unsurprisingly, Ray Williams was determined to take advantage of the market created by free-spending owners. So he found himself a new agent to represent him during these negotiations. "Ray wanted a black agent," Fred Slaughter told *Black Enterprise* magazine, "and Gus [Ray's older brother] referred him to me." Slaughter was a thirty-eight-year-old former dean of admissions at the UCLA School of Law and a member of the 1964 Bruins national championship basketball team. He was also a new breed of sports agent: a Black man representing other Black men. "Clearly the white agents don't want me to do well," Slaughter said, "and they undercut me whenever possible. Some general managers and owners have been tougher in dealing with me than they would have been with whites."[58] Whether or not Werblin and the Knicks played hardball with Slaughter because of his race, Fred was blunt in replying to allegations that Williams to the Cavs was a done deal, telling reporters, "Cleveland ain't offered us bleep."[59] Also, per free agency guidelines of the day, the Knicks retained the right to match any contract Williams might sign with another team. "They call this free agency," Slaughter said, "but it isn't really very free."[60] With the two sides at a standstill, Knicks fans began to fear that Ray would join his brother on the sidelines and sit out the entire season.

And so, heading into the 1981–82 season, the Knicks were again in flux. With Williams unsigned, the chemistry the team built in putting together their best season since winning the 1973 title was in jeopardy. Would Williams be a Knick come October? Or would the team continue to try to buy a contender—maybe whitewashing the team in the process?

1980–81 Knicks
Record: 50–32
Playoffs: Lost Eastern Conference first round versus Chicago Bulls
Coach: Red Holzman

Average Home Attendance: 13,328
Points per Game: (107.9—12th of 23)
Points Allowed per Game: (106.3—9th of 23)
Team Leaders:

>   Points: Bill Cartwright (20.1 per game)
>   Rebounds: Bill Cartwright (7.5 per game)
>   Assists: Micheal Ray Richardson (7.9 per game)
>   Steals: Micheal Ray Richardson (2.9 per game)
>   Blocked Shots: Marvin Webster (1.2 per game)

All-Stars: Micheal Ray Richardson

Notable Transactions: Drafted Mike Woodson in the first round of the 1980 NBA Draft; traded Joe C. Meriweather and a first-round draft pick to the Kansas City Kings; received Campy Russell from the Cleveland Cavaliers as part of a three-team trade

7

"The Ship Be Sinking"

1981–1982

On August 1, 1981, less than a mile west of Madison Square Garden, television history was made when MTV launched from its studio on West Thirty-Third and Tenth Avenue. The Buggles' "Video Killed the Radio Star" was the first music video aired—although only a limited number of households in New Jersey could watch on opening day.[1] Warner Communications (which once owned the Cosmos and brought Pelé to the United States in 1975) initially balked at the notion of a cable TV channel devoted exclusively to music videos, but MTV quickly became a cultural sensation. Among other accomplishments, MTV introduced mainstream white audiences to Black stars like Prince and Michael Jackson.

But even more influential locally was a different music television program: *Video Music Box*. Although it never gained the mainstream popularity of MTV, *Video Music Box* first aired in 1983 on WNYC (channel 31) and remains decades later, thanks to Brooklynite Ralph McDaniels.[2] "MTV . . . were obviously on some rock stuff," McDaniels recalls, "it was dope, but I knew what my community wanted to hear."[3] Soon viewers could see not only mainstream groups like Madonna and Hall & Oates, but also hip-hop acts like Grandmaster Flash, Kurtis Blow, and Biz Markie.

That October, after months of tense negotiations, the Knicks parted ways with Ray Williams, refusing to match an offer sheet he signed with the New Jersey Nets. Ray showed up in poor shape when he arrived in the Meadowlands, and his new teammates immediately nicknamed him Boom Boom, Big Butt, and Mr. Butterworth because "he was so thick and rich." Ray didn't care, he was just happy to be out of New York, livid that "they [said] they can't pay players."[4] Ray wanted $750,000 a year, but New York offered less than half that; in the end, he settled for half a million dollars a season with the Nets.

Williams was not the only member of the Family to leave in the fall of 1981, as Mike Glenn signed with Atlanta that October (it was a big mistake for the Knicks not to bring him back, Holzman later admitted).[5] "We very much wanted to stay together," Glenn told me of the trio, "and we thought we could make our mark. Then they decided to make some other moves and tried to leapfrog back up to the top again without continuing the step-by-step."[6] Losing his two closest friends was crushing to the team's best, and most emotionally fragile, player, Micheal Ray Richardson. "They were connected," Cazzie Russell explained to me. "Losing that took a lot out of Micheal Ray . . . and he did not want to play with those other guys."[7]

Feeling abandoned and alone, Richardson turned inward and, for the first time in his life, experimented with cocaine. "When I was in college, I didn't drink; when I was in high school I didn't drink," Richardson recalls. But in New York, as Richardson became a star, things changed. "You figure you're in control of everything, that you can do whatever you want to do, that you're invincible."[8] So he snorted a line of cocaine at a party. Just one. "That first hit felt like the best thing that ever happened to me," Richardson said. "I was invisible and invincible. . . . I spent the next seven years trying to duplicate that very first high. And from the get-go, basketball didn't seem as important as getting off." "Man!" he recalled thinking at the time, "that shit was gooooood!"[9]

Losing Williams and Glenn was not the only major roster change that offseason. In fact, even before Williams signed with the Nets, the Knicks and Nets came together on a trade that sent second-year guard, and future Knicks head coach, Mike Woodson across the Hudson for Mike Newlin, coming off back-to-back seasons of over 20 points per game for New Jersey. Besides dealing a young player for an established veteran, adding Newlin meant the Knicks were no longer an all-Black team. That fact drew few headlines at the time, but looking back it was the end of a brief but incredibly important, pioneering era in NBA history. Replacing Woodson with Newlin made sense on paper (this would be a common theme in the years ahead for the Knicks), but ultimately even Holzman admitted that trading for the white shooting guard was a mistake. "Newlin never fit in," Holzman wrote in his autobiography. "He lacked intensity except when it came to spending time taking what he told people were Bible lessons over the telephone."[10]

A backcourt of Richardson, Newlin, and Randy Smith made sense to Knicks execs. Richardson was dynamic but erratic, and he might be steadied by Smith's veteran poise, while Newlin's silky outside shooting touch could only help. Without Williams, though, the Knicks were a much different team, especially on defense. "We went from being able to dominate most teams' backcourts to not being able to do that anymore, with the speed, quickness, strength, offensive ability and defensive ability of those two guys," Campy Russell told me.[11] As compensation for losing Williams in free agency, the Nets sent Maurice Lucas, a bull-strong three-time former All-Star in his late twenties, across the Hudson, giving the Knicks a bona fide power forward for the first time since Spencer Haywood left in early 1979. It helped that Lucas had a reputation as an enforcer, famously squaring off against Darryl Dawkins in the 1977 NBA Finals as a member of the Portland Trail Blazers. New York had lacked toughness in their series against Artis Gilmore and the Bulls; Lucas would provide that. He was also, as David Halberstam observed in *Breaks of the Game*, "acutely conscious of race and the double standards in both American life and his chosen profession."[12] Another perfect fit on the almost-all-Black Knicks.

Losing Williams and adding Lucas would be a bust, but basketball insiders at the time praised the deal for New York. "It was a good trade for the Knicks," Celtics coach Bill Fitch said in 1981, "It's the missing link for them."[13] In the *Post*, Harvey Araton concurred, writing that "the Knicks needed a couple of vets like Archie [Bunker] needed Edith" and "needed a rebounder the way Ozzie needed Harriet."[14] For his part, Lucas was confident in his ability to help the team win. "I don't see myself as any kind of savior," he said, "but I think I can provide a missing element,

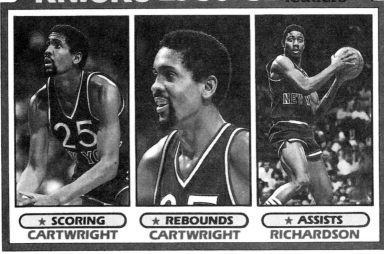

Figures 10a–d. 1980–81 New York Knicks Topps basketball cards: a) team leaders Bill Cartwright and Micheal Ray Richardson; b) Cartwright; c) Marvin Webster; d) Richardson. Topps® trading cards used courtesy of The Topps Company, Inc.

one that's been missing here for a while."[15] Sportswriter Roy S. Johnson wrote, referencing Reggie Jackson joining the Yankees in 1977, "So now, it is Maurice Lucas . . . who stirs this drink."[16]

While sportswriters bandied pop culture references about the newest Knick, newspaper headlines focused on the upcoming mayoral election. Unlike four years earlier, when he came out of nowhere to take down incumbent Abe Beame to win the mayoralty, Ed Koch was a clear favorite to win reelection in 1981. When Koch was first elected, New York City was in crisis mode, and in the short term his austerity politics helped balance the budget. But in the long run Koch's time as mayor shifted the city's political outlook from the liberalism of John Lindsay and Beame to a neoliberal constituency, cutting budgets and city services while promoting business development. Key to Koch's plans was future president, and Knicks' season ticket holder, Donald Trump, whose extensive Manhattan developments helped "revive New York as a center of glitz and glamour."[17] Unfortunately, fiscal retrenchment created greater economic disparity than ever before in the Big Apple, and the percentage of the population under the poverty level jumped from 15 percent in 1975 to over 23 percent by 1985.[18]

In addition to economic austerity, Koch hoped to appeal to residents fearful of crime by embracing a law-and-order platform. Koch saw graffiti-writing and hip-hop culture as troubling signs of juvenile delinquency—a stepping-stone to criminal behavior and disorder—so he instituted anti-graffiti efforts to protect city subway lines. Abandoned buildings likewise reminded New Yorkers of turmoil and unrest. So city officials put huge decals in windows to make them look lived-in to commuters traversing the Cross-Bronx.[19] And parks inhabited by nascent hip-hop artists became another target of the Koch administration. "Everything about hip-hop was illegal," Paradise Gray of the Latin Quarter argues. "Do you know how many laws were broken just to do an average street jam? We broke into the light poles. . . . We cut the wires and we stole electricity. . . . We didn't have no permits to do our jams. . . . And we dared the police to try to fuck with us."[20]

"Nine out of 10 times," Gordon J. Davis, a Koch-appointed parks commissioner, said at the time, "what people mean when they say the park is lousy is not only that it's not clean, but that there are kids smoking dope and there are graffiti and there are Blacks and Hispanics where there were once Italians and Jews."[21] Although rarely explicitly racist, Koch and his administration usually listened to those nine out of ten, promoting New York City as place that was safe for white people to work, live, and visit.

Another way Koch hoped to push through his agenda was through privatizing public space and encouraging gentrification.[22] Brownstones and lofts in SoHo would become artist havens with the development of a bohemian gallery district and the Garment District, just northeast of Madison Square Garden, as the center of the fashion world. To residents of these gentrifying neighborhoods, though, it felt like an assault. "These invaders have already turned low-income, blue-collar neighborhoods on Manhattan's West Side into havens of quiche-eating, boutique-shopping professionals," an article in *Ebony* proclaimed.[23]

In 1981, Koch earned nearly three-fourths of the vote citywide, even winning the Republican nomination. Flying high after achieving his sought-after mayoral landslide, Koch ran for the governorship of New York in 1982. But he failed to appeal to upstaters, and he withdrew, licked his wounds, and returned to his duties in New York City, beaten if not humbled. Writing about Koch's 1984 memoir, *Mayor: An Autobiography*, his friend Dan Wolf calls it "the best love story since *Tristan and Isolde*, only Ed Koch plays both parts."[24]

Lost in the shuffle of an extensive on-court turnover and a headline-grabbing mayoral race was a key organizational change in the Knicks' front office as president Mike Burke announced his retirement after six years at the helm. "The restless nature commands me to move along to a fresh challenge," Burke told the *Times*.[25] True to his word, Burke left New York City for his cattle and sheep farm in County Galway, Ireland. Jack Krumpe, Sonny Werblin's best friend and long-time business partner, replaced Burke in the Knicks front office, although no one could truly replace the silver-maned playboy in the New York City social scene.

Madison Square Garden's non-sporting events continued no matter who was in charge. In 1979, Pope John Paul II had traveled to the United States, preaching to huge crowds across the country. Twenty-thousand people packed into Madison Square Garden that October 3 to see the pope; ten days later, half that number turned out for the Knicks' home opener against the Bullets. The following summer, the Democratic

National Convention met in New York City, calling for the reelection of President Jimmy Carter, who would be routed by Republican candidate Ronald Reagan. And in May 1982, long after Holzman and the Knicks were eliminated from playoff contention, Reverend Sun Myung Moon would marry more than two thousand couples in a "blessing ceremony" in the Garden; most of couples were matched by the reverend himself and had known each other a very short time.[26] Dubbed "Moonies," a potentially derogatory term, adherents of the Unification Church of the United States drew a great deal of attention in the mid-eighties before trailing off in popularity by the 1990s.

> *Now way back in the days when hip-hop began*
> *With Coke La Rock, Kool Herc, and then Bam*
> *Beat boys ran to the latest jam . . .*
> —"South Bronx," Boogie Down Productions, 1987

Boogie Down Productions released "South Bronx" in response to MC Shan's song "The Bridge," which seemed to promote Queensbridge as the true birthplace of hip-hop, causing a feud known as the Bridge Wars. It was just a decade after Coke La Rock, Kool Herc, and Afrika Bambaataa debuted, but already the history of hip-hop was important to the movement.

When it was released in 1979, "Rapper's Delight" was widely panned by many in the hip-hop community as being inauthentic. But even before the Sugarhill Gang bang-banged the boogie to the boogie, hip-hop appeared to be a passing fad, headed the way of disco or punk rock.[27] Audiences who had packed apartment or playground parties in the mid-seventies to listen to La Rock, Herc, and Bam (Bambaataa) moved later in the decade to dance clubs where deejays spun records, bartenders slung booze, and peddlers dealt a little Panama Red. B-boying, graffiti art, and street deejaying had largely disappeared, replaced by club deejays who adopted Bronx-style techniques and raps, picking songs with a snappy beat and accessibility, like "Rapper's Delight," rather than scouring record stores for obscure albums.[28] Crowds at the clubs wanted to drink, smoke, and have fun, not watch or take part in a B-boy dance-off.

Created in the South Bronx by young, impoverished Black and Latinx women and men, hip-hop shifted to appeal to a broader demographic.

During the early eighties, middle-class Black New Yorkers, working closely with white-dominated record labels, began creating music appealing to young white suburbanites (the NBA's target audience too), providing, as one historian explains, "an age-old image of blackness: a foreign, sexually charged, and criminal underworld against which the norms of white society are defined."[29] White kids in the burbs tried to "perfect a model of correct white hipness, coolness and style by adopting the latest black style and image."[30] They watched *Beat Street* and *Body Rock*, memorized the lyrics of "Rapper's Delight," pulled on Adidas Superstar sneakers, and enjoyed the sanitized version of hip-hop, shined up to be as non-offensive as possible.[31]

And it wasn't just white kids who embraced Black culture. In 1980, Louie Robinson, a prominent Black journalist, wrote a piece for *Ebony* magazine titled "The Blackening of White America," exploring the phenomenon of white athletes embracing elements of Black culture. "Black athletes have not only brought to the playing fields fresh and awesome talents to thrill American sports fans," Robinson wrote, "but they have also insinuated into the language of the locker room a pungency and coloration that could launch a new riot at Attica or San Quentin as White players have suddenly taken to speaking in the 'mutha tongue.'"[32]

In the eighties, rap music would become the voice of the youth, both white (Generation X) and Black (the hip-hop generation). Young women and especially men growing up in this era witnessed tremendous social dislocation and uncertainty. What resulted was a period of "rising alienation" in which "young whites were drawn to hip-hop" as "an appealing antiestablishment culture."[33] In other words, hip-hop became Generation X's answer to rock 'n' roll. "Hip-hop was counterculture," one Gen Xer recalls. "It gave youth a voice to tell the truth and exposed the ills of society, especially racism and our hypocritical government."[34] One producer would say late in the decade, "Rap in the '80s is equivalent to the Motown Sound of the '60s."[35]

Rap during much of the eighties was subject to the same push-and-pull factors as the NBA and the Knicks. Record labels wanted to sell albums to both Black and white kids. And hip-hop pioneers like Afrika Bambaataa and Kurtis Blow always sought inclusiveness in their music and culture, just as pro basketball co-promoted the duo of Larry Bird and Magic Johnson—celebrating Black and white athletes. As Bakari Kitwana writes in *Why White Kids Love Hip-Hop,* "The NBA, second only to hip-hop, has been a primary source of cross-racial interaction."[36] But this inclusiveness missed the point of rap-as-counterculture; it isn't cool to listen to the same music as your parents or dress like your uncle. And watering down rap for mainstream consumption brought it to the cusp of urbaneness. As Charles Whitaker wrote in 1990, "Hollywood has co-opted it and so has Madison Avenue. Sanitized for mass appeal, rap is used to promote a wide range of products—from hamburgers to automobiles."[37] Hardly the antiauthoritarian authenticity hip-hop promoted from its gritty origins in the mid-seventies.

By the mid-1980s, other elements of hip-hop would also diverge. Graffiti slowly disappeared from New York City subway cars, while B-boying found itself replaced by catchy, faddish group dances like the Wop and the Cabbage Patch. Only rap music continued as a stand-in for hip-hop culture. Sure, a few groups of legit B-boys like the New Rock Steady Crew remained. But they were, as author Jeff Chang says, "the last b-boys standing." One member of this crew, Crazy Legs, tried to re-create the theme of many kung fu movies, traveling around the city to challenge the remaining B-boys to dance-offs.[38] But soon there was no one left to battle.

As rap continued to grow in popularity among white kids around the city, some white fans wanted to hear white rappers. In 1981, three middle-class Jewish New Yorkers, Michael Diamond (Mike D), Adam Yauch (MCA), and Adam Horovitz (Ad-Rock), formed a new group from members leaving a hardcore punk band called the Young Aborigines. They rechristened themselves the Beastie Boys and transitioned to hip-hop, releasing "Cooky Puss" in 1983. It became a huge hit in the city's downtown club scene, and soon the trio worked with Rick Rubin, who formed Def Jam Recordings with Russell Simmons, on producing an album. The result, *License to Ill,* became the first rap album to reach the top spot on the Billboard 200, catapulting the Beastie Boys into the American mainstream and giving white rappers their first national stage. "Russell [Simmons] opened the door for Run-DMC to take over white America," says Dante Ross, a music executive, "and now [with the Beastie Boys] white America had their own white boys. And he knew that that shit was going to go big."[39]

Like the Sugarhill Gang, the Beastie Boys encountered questions about their authenticity. "One of the first hip-hop shows we played was at this club called Encore in Queens," Mike D remembers. "So we get there and we, this bunch of white kids from Manhattan dressed in Puma suits, step out of the limo. The first comment we heard was, "Who the f*ck are you guys, Menudo?"[40]

The Beastie Boys eventually managed to transcend race, and Knicks execs hoped their new-look, no-longer-all-Black Knicks could do the same when they opened the 1981–82 season. Cartwright sat out opening night against the Nets with a knee ligament sprain, forcing Lucas, a member of the opposing team just a week earlier, into a prominent role. Lucas responded with 25 points and 12 rebounds to help his new team to a hard-fought 103–99 road victory. "No jump-shooting team has ever won an NBA championship," Richardson told reporters after the game. "If you've got the guys to go inside, you go to them."[41] Early returns on Lucas were favorable. In his first month as a Knick, he scored in double digits in eleven straight games, highlighted by a dominant 28 points and 19 rebounds in a win over the Pistons to kick off December.

There were other instances of individual brilliance in the early going. On November 10, Richardson secured a triple-double with 20 points, 15 rebounds, and 12 assists, and a week later Cartwright tied a league record by sinking all nineteen of his foul shots. But overall the team was wildly inconsistent, and Holzman struggled to cope. He shuffled the lineup for the team's November 19 game against Atlanta, starting Sly Williams and Randy Smith in place of Cazzie Russell and Mike Newlin, but the team lost 89–84. "The fans are down on us," Smith said after the game, in which spectators at the half-full Garden roundly booed the Knicks. "I hope they would give us a little longer to prove ourselves."[42] By Thanksgiving, the team was 4–8 and playing like they had already written off the season. "After every defeat, the scene in the Knicks dressing room is the same," Sam Goldaper wrote in the *Times*. "Campy Russell talks of the need for developing a half-court game, playing together and patience. Marvin Webster, the captain, tells of the necessity for more concentration and better response to pressure . . . [and] Coach Red Holzman trie[s] to say as little as possible."[43]

On Thursday, December 3, the team reached a new low. Little more than eight thousand fans filed into Madison Square Garden, less than half its capacity, to watch New York host the lowly Bullets and recently signed forward Spencer Haywood, back in the NBA for the first time since allegedly putting a hit out on his coach. Haywood only scored six points in a reserve role, but Greg Ballard dominated the Knicks forwards, scoring 33 points in a 114–88 drubbing. After the game, Werblin was livid. He stormed into the Knicks locker room and, according to several players, "told the team he was embarrassed by its showing." "He said he was disappointed by the Knicks' play, that the club was a 'disgrace' to New York and that the crowds at the Garden were growing smaller and smaller." Then Sonny refused to speak to the media. "I agree with Mr. Werblin that we played very bad," Webster told the *Times*. "I don't know if we deserved him being that mad at us."[44] Two nights later, whether inspired or embarrassed by Werblin's outburst, the Knicks blew out Boston, the defending champs, in front of almost nineteen thousand fans.

With the team hovering around .500, stringing together a five-game winning streak and then losing four in a row, Richardson dropped a bombshell. After being ejected from a mid-December game against the Pistons for complaining too much to the referees, Sugar announced that he wanted a new contract, and, if the team refused to renegotiate, he wanted out. "I wish they would trade me," he told the *Times*. "Maybe a change of scenery would help." Told of Richardson's request, Holzman said, "Sugar is a very intense player. He's an emotional player."[45] Donovan agreed. "When Sugar doesn't have control of himself, it's impossible for him to have control of the team. But when Sugar is under control . . . he is looking to make the play and for his shot secondly."[46] Donovan also reminded reporters that Richardson had signed a new deal just one year earlier and that he still had several seasons under contract before he could leave via free agency.

A week later, after a Christmas Day loss to the Nets, Richardson was still frustrated about the direction of the team and his long-term contract. In the process, he gave perhaps the most quotable interview in league history.

"What do you think is happening to this team?" one reporter asked.
"The ship be sinking," Richardson replied, deadpan.
"How far can it sink?" Nat Gottlieb of the *Newark Star-Ledger* chimed in.
Micheal Ray sighed. "The sky's the limit."[47]

Even when Richardson and the Knicks did win, there seemed to be a steep price to pay. In January 1982, a gambler who usually wagered a few hundred bucks on Knicks games started laying down $10,000 bets on New York. And, unlike the Knicks, he was winning—beating the spread on six out of seven games. The FBI investigated, trying to determine whether any NBA players were on the take. "Hell no," Richardson said later, "I never did anything like that."[48] The FBI report tied their findings to the drug culture becoming prevalent in the league, citing a source who alleged that "none of the players receive any money for the tip, but simply do it as a courtesy to their dealer."[49] Without any solid leads or corroborating physical evidence, the FBI closed its case. The bookie, whose identity was redacted along with the names of the suspected players in the released FBI documents, escaped unscathed.

Beyond allegations of gambling and FBI investigations to deal with, January was a rough month for the Knicks. Almost nightly the team set a record low for attendance in Madison Square Garden, bottoming out on January 10 when only 7,558 fans bothered to show up to watch the Bullets trounce the home team.[50] Newlin, who led the Nets in scoring the year before, was relegated to bench duty on a bad Knicks team and began venting to reporters. "My role is top cheerleader. There is nothing I can do about playing time, except be ready when I'm called. . . . It's a comedy here."[51] This rubbed some of his teammates the wrong way. "There is no discipline on this team," an unnamed player was quoted in the *Times* as saying. "Nobody is willing to make a sacrifice but everybody is looking to score."[52]

Another Knick upset with playing time was Sly Williams, who played outstanding basketball in 1980–81 as the nominal power forward in an up-tempo attack taking advantage of his athleticism. Now with Lucas on board, Williams was forced to the bench. And, like Newlin, he was unhappy in his new role. "I don't think they're giving me what is my correct amount of playing time," Williams told the *Sporting News*, "I deserve to start."[53] Making matters worse, Sly sprained his toe and struggled to recover while his agent, Joe Moniz, was negotiating a contract extension for him. With Sly on the mend, those talks stalled, and Moniz advised his client to avoid rejoining the team until his toe was completely healed. Injured and distracted by contract negotiations, Williams missed several practices, appointments with Knicks team doctor Norman Scott and trainer Mike Saunders, and the team plane bound for Boston on January 26. After fining him $100 for each event, Holzman finally suspended Sly indefinitely without pay.[54] "I was shocked," Sly told the *Post*. "I wasn't running out on them or anything," he explained. "It was just bad timing on a situation that had to do with my contract."[55]

After just one game, Red reinstated his troubled forward. For some fans, this confirmed that Holzman was out of touch, and one Knick told reporters anonymously, "Red has lost all control of this team."[56] When asked if he planned on replacing Holzman, recognized just six months earlier by *Basketball Digest* as the coach with the most job security in the league, Werblin shrugged his shoulders. "We'll have to see."[57]

The Knicks' struggles were minor when compared to those facing New York City in the early 1980s. Losing a few basketball games was nothing when weighed against the seeming disorder presented by trash and graffiti littering subway trains that were dangerous on their own. The murder rate had been steadily climbing (it would peaked in 1990, with 2,245 murders that year) but, perhaps more importantly, the public perception was that the city was unsafe.[58] "Anyone who uses the New York subway after 11:00 pm," one reporter noted, "is either intrepid, without travel alternatives, looking for trouble, or plain dumb."[59] Rather than being recognized as an organic, wild art form, graffiti was becoming more than an eyesore in some places. The Bronx County Courthouse, for example, is a limestone building in the Art Deco style built in the 1930s. But vandals marked the front to such an extent that one journalist, exasperated at the constant tagging, wrote, "How can we let a courthouse be overrun by barbarians? If it means repainting the facade of that building every day or having a twenty-four-hour guard detail, that courthouse must be reclaimed from the clutches of the barbarians who do not respect the law or public property."[60]

Despite negative perceptions by some New Yorkers, graffiti art was finding a new outlet: album jackets. In 1982, in preparation for the first international hip-hop tour—dubbed "The Roxy Tour"—Disc AZ and Celluloid Records released seven LPs, recorded by hip-hop groups like Fab 5 Freddy and PHASE 2. PHASE 2 was best known as a graffiti artist who popularized the use of bubble lettering, but he also rapped, performing at the Roxy in Chelsea, Manhattan, after which his song "The Roxy" was named. It was another graffiti artist, though, whose work graced the album jackets produced for the tour. Futura 2000 toured with the Clash in 1982, painting backdrops as the band performed. And when the seven albums produced for the Roxy Tour were lined up side-by-side, they formed a single piece of extensive and impressive graffiti art.[61]

Album covers represented the beginning of graffiti being recognized as legitimate and commercial art. In the 1970s, artists painted under the cover of darkness, with an ever-present threat of being arrested. Over the following decades, the idea of graffiti became chic, especially in gentrifying areas of the city where alley and building pieces were commissioned by property owners. During the 2020 COVID-19 pandemic, artists took to the streets again, painting without permission. "The streets were sanitized with pieces that were cool and nice and done with permission," one graffiti artist recalls. "Now we're back to the roots."[62]

With Sly sidelined, Newlin still sitting on the bench, and Red's job in jeopardy, the Knicks began to slip down the standings. During the slide, Nets coach Larry Brown was reprimanded by the league for tampering after he sent a note to Marvin Webster that read, "Keep your head up; we'd still like to have you."[63] On the heels of that message, rumors of Webster going to New Jersey made the rounds, as did talk of a blockbuster that would have seen Webster rejoin the Nuggets in exchange for guard David Thompson.

Thompson had been a superstar in the late 1970s but was now seen as damaged goods. Thompson first tried cocaine during the 1976 ABA finals as a twenty-two-year-old dealing with sky-high expectations and pressure. For several seasons in Denver, he managed to keep his drug use from drastically affecting his play and was rewarded with a then-record $800,000 per year contract. But by 1981, when he should have been in his prime, he was a shell of his former self, averaging career lows in every category. "Thompson became the most wasted talent—in a marketing, creative, aesthetic sense—the NBA has ever had," Spike Lee would later assert.[64]

Just behind Thompson on that list might have been Micheal Ray. Unbeknown to Knicks fans, Richardson managed to keep it together on the court while spiraling out of control off it, using marijuana and cocaine regularly to cope with his sense of isolation, boredom, and anxiety. Richardson reached a breaking point on February 21, 1982, with a game against Houston scheduled for the afternoon. "I'd gotten so high that I completely forgot about the game," Richardson said. "I'd just smoked a bowl at 8:35 a.m. when I suddenly remembered that in less than five hours I'd be playing in a nationally televised game! Fuck me!" He showered, drank a quart of OJ, ate a quick lunch, and hustled to the Garden. "While I was loosening up," he remembered, "I kept telling myself that I'd never do this again. 'Please God. Get me out of this one and I'll go cold turkey. I'll check into a rehab clinic. I'll do anything.' "[65] For the tens of thousands of fans watching the broadcast on CBS, Richardson put on a show and nearly earned a triple-double, scoring 20 points, pulling down 8 rebounds, and handing out 11 assists in leading the Knicks to an upset win over the visiting Rockets.

Did Richardson keep his pregame promise? Of course not. Instead, he celebrated his success, recalling later, "I got stoned for the next twenty-four hours."[66] Richardson had no problem finding illicit drugs in the city. Conservative author Herbert London wrote, "Walking the streets of New York is like observing an open-air drug bazaar."[67] Other players and coaches knew about the rampant drug use on the team and in the league, but even now players are hesitant to name names. "I had a friend in the city who would call me up and say, 'Hey, man: so-and-so is up here buying drugs," assistant coach Butch Beard recalls. "There were things I didn't even bother telling [Holzman], because he wasn't ready to hear that." Holzman was hard-pressed to deal with this new generation of athletes— the forerunners of the coming hip-hop generation. As Beard remembers, "those early-eighties teams were wild as hell, and the city gobbled them up."[68]

Richardson was not the only Knick from this era to struggle with a drug addiction. Before Haywood moved to New York in 1975, he had used marijuana recreationally and had an occasional drink.[69] But with his wife, Iman, frequently out of town on photo shoots, Haywood began to experiment with harder drugs and soon was using regularly.[70]

Haywood, Richardson, and Thompson were just a few of the high-profile Americans struggling with drug addiction at the time. In the summer of '76, around the time Haywood began dating Iman, New York suffered through a "Great Dope Famine"—marijuana was hard to find, so dealers started to sling "Mexican brown heroin," a minimally refined narcotic.[71] Michael Weinreb writes, "In 1977, a *Newsweek* story compared cocaine to Dom Perigon and beluga caviar, and quoted Jimmy Carter's drug czar, who claimed that 'there's not a great deal of evidence of major health consequences from the use of cocaine.' (He was operating largely under the assumption that the drug was so prohibitively expensive most Americans couldn't afford to get addicted.)" But movie stars, popular musicians, and big-time athletes had the cash to fund a drug habit.[72] Richard Pryor famously set himself on fire freebasing while filming a movie in 1980, and two years later John Belushi died from an overdose after mixing cocaine and heroin. In sports, Montreal Expos outfielder Tim Raines slid headfirst into base so as not to break glass vials of cocaine he stored in his back pocket; Dock Ellis threw a no-hitter while tripping on LSD; and Utah Jazz forward Terry Furlow died in a car crash in May 1980 with traces of cocaine found in his system.[73]

Three days before Furlow's death, presidential candidate Ronald Regan clinched the Republican Party nomination. When he swept into office that fall, it was on the strength of white voters; just 10 percent of nonwhites cast their ballot for the former Hollywood actor. Reagan also declared a "war on drugs" at a time when Black men were explicitly linked to drug culture. Nationally, marijuana, heroin, and first-time cocaine use were actually on the decline by the time of Reagan's inauguration. But his administration decided there was a drug crisis.[74]

In the early eighties, many Americans connected hard drugs to Black men. So, as the NBA employed more and more Black athletes, the perception was that more and more players used coke and heroin. Historian Todd Boyd writes, "Indulgent actions of these players [drug users] had come to dominate perceptions of the league itself, one now being not so subtly touted as a collection of overpaid, underachieving, selfish, arrogant n-----s," and "the NBA came to be thought of as simply another example of black criminality."[75] League officials encouraged athletes struggling with addiction to voluntarily seek treatment. To counter drug users unwilling to come forward, they hired outside experts to authorize drug testing of suspected players, subjecting those players to as many as four tests over a six-week period. Any player testing positive three times, or convicted of a crime involving the use or distribution of cocaine or heroin, would be permanently banned any player with three positive tests.[76] Outside the NBA, punishments were even harsher. As Carol Anderson explains in *White Rage*, Reagan's administration worked to "demonize and criminalize blacks and provide the federal resources to make incarceration, rather than education, normative."[77] This became especially true in the mid- to late 1980s, when crack arrived in urban America, turning "Gotham into Gomorrah" and, in the words of artist and hip-hop scholar James "Koe" Rodriguez, "put New York City ghettos in a headlock."[78] Richardson was one of those young men put in a headlock, and in 1987 he filed suit against an NBA-appointed psychiatrist who, Micheal Ray alleged, ordered him to buy crack to somehow help shake his drug habit.[79]

Even with Richardson's drug problem, frustrated bench players, and trade rumors swirling, the Knicks still had a shot to make the playoffs in the spring of 1982. So Donovan and Werblin began working the phones, targeting Supersonics guard Paul Westphal, still unsigned after suffering a stress fracture and unhappy with the Sonics' contract offers as he rehabilitated. Werblin and Sam Schulman, the Sonics' owner, had an acrimonious relationship dating to the Spencer Haywood deal, and this grew worse when, in mid-February, New York signed Westphal to an offer sheet that stipulated that the Knick would pay the former All-Star roughly $150,000 for the last third of the season. To prevent Seattle from matching, Werblin inserted several unique clauses, including a bonus if Westphal's team won 40 games. The Knicks had almost no chance of winning 40 while Seattle, sitting at 36–18, was all but guaranteed to do so.[80] Per the collective bargaining agreement, Seattle had fifteen days to match the Knicks offer. Schulman was irate. "I'll tell you this, " he told KIRO radio in Seattle, "there is no way the Knicks are going to get Paul Westphal. Not only that," he continued, "they're going to suffer for what they've done."[81] Schulman demanded arbitration, certain he would beat Werblin this time.[82] But on March 7 the arbitrator ruled in favor of New York, and Westphal became a Knick.

Four days after the arbitrator's decision, the NCAA kicked off its high-profile postseason tournament, which ended in a Final Four featuring the Louisville Cardinals, the Houston Cougars (powered by the Phi Slama Jama duo of Clyde Drexler and Akeem Olajuwon), the North Carolina Tar Heels, and the Georgetown Hoyas. In the finals, the Tar Heels, led by James Worthy and Sam Perkins, pulled out a thrilling 63–62 win best remembered for the memorable buzzer-beater by a freshman guard named Michael Jordan. But the real blue-chip prospect who became a national sensation during the tournament was Georgetown freshman Patrick Ewing. Ewing finished the championship game with 23 points and 10 rebounds in a losing effort, but his performance put him on the radar of every NBA team.

In New York, Ewing was at the top of the list of collegiate players scouted by Dick McGuire, the team's longtime head scout. But while McGuire would work for the Knicks until his death in 2010, changes were afoot in the Knicks front office. Holzman joined the Knicks in 1959 as a scout and became the team's head coach in 1967 when Ned Irish flipped his role with that of McGuire. When Red started, most players made less than the coaches, and many held down off-season jobs to pay the bills. Over the years, Holzman had a few close friends on staff but was most comfortable around Frankie Blauschild, the team's traveling secretary. "[Blauschild] was attached to Red like Velcro," John Hewig, the Knicks' director of communications at the time, recalls. "He always traveled with one of those Pan-Am plastic blue bags on his shoulder. And in it . . . they'd get those little bottles. Two-ounce bottles of scotch and vodka. And in that bag, that was all he had. It was filled right to the top. And they'd check in and Frankie would be in the other end of Red's suite . . . and Frankie would come limping down through the hallway into Red's suite and he'd sit down and pull out two or three bottles of that stuff. And Red and Frankie would drink scotch. Three or four bottles every night and sit around and talk. And they wouldn't answer their door and Red wouldn't take phone calls and stuff. That was their time." Red agreed. "On the road I was prepared for any emergency," he joked in his autobiography. "I always made sure I had a bottle of scotch in my bag for medicinal purposes."[83]

By the spring of 1982, Blauschild (and his son Keith, the ball boy) were still around, but Red knew his time as the Knicks coach was coming to a close. So he called Hewig and asked to meet him at a club located in the Garden.

"Red had a scotch," Hewig told me. "It was about five o'clock in early March, and he said, 'You know, I'm not coming back—I'm done.'" Before meeting with Hewig, Holzman had gone to Werblin, who asked his coach, "What's it like in the morning after you lose, when you get up?" Red had responded, "I look at my wife Selma and thank God she's still with me, and I know that my daughter Gail is well taken care of . . . so life's pretty good for me."[84]

> "This is the morning after a loss?" Werblin wanted to know.
> "Yeah, or a win. Whatever. But I'm pretty happy," Red replied.
> And Sonny said, "Well, maybe you shouldn't coach anymore."
> And Red said, "That'd be fine with me."[85]

After their cocktail and dinner, Red walked with Hewig around the Garden, before fans filed in for the game. "This is a very funny place," Red told him. "You know, when this place is full it's the most beautiful building in the world. It's so loud and intimate, and everybody is putting their arms around you. But when there's five thousand people in here like there will be tonight, it's the ugliest place I've ever been."[86]

By the end of the season, five thousand wasn't far off. Win or lose, the team continued to break low-attendance records at the Garden, including a record low (6,917) to watch the Knicks lose to the Bulls. As bad as the official numbers were, sportswriter Sam Goldaper believed the actual attendance was even worse.[87] "Really about half," he wrote in the *Times*, "including Sonny Werblin, Eddie Donovan, and several seats with coats in them." He estimated the actual total at closer to 2,000.[88] "I had bigger crowds in grade school," Lucas joked, reasoning that maybe a lot of people were in church on Wednesdays. For his part, Richardson was not in a joking mood about the lack of spectators, but he understood. "Who wants to come out and see losers?" he asked the *Post*.[89]

Knicks management hoped Westphal might turn around the team's fortunes on the court and at the box office, giving them a white star they had lacked since Bill Bradley's retirement half a dozen years earlier. At thirty-one, Westphal might not have been the same player he was when he made four straight All-NBA teams for the Suns in the late seventies, but he still knew how to put the ball in the basket and how to run an offense, both of which the Knicks desperately needed.

Before signing with the Knicks, Westphal had an impressive pedigree dating back to his high school days in California. Instead of joining UCLA, which was in the middle of winning nine NCAA titles in a ten-year stretch, he shocked everyone by signing to play college ball at USC.[90] Westphal helped turn the Trojans around, and in 1972 he became a Boston Celtic.

Three years later a trade sent him to Phoenix. In Arizona, the ambidextrous guard became a superstar, drawing many comparisons to retired Lakers legend Jerry West. Westphal did not fit the stereotypical profile of a white guard in the seventies, though. "He loved to dunk," wrote Boston sportswriter Bob Ryan, who called him "one of the true white leapers in the game."[91] In 1979, Westphal peaked athletically: he not only earned first-team All-NBA honors but also won the league's "HORSE" competition, reached the finals of the Dewars' Celebrity Tennis Classic in Las Vegas, and won a made-for-TV three-on-three half-court tournament with teammates Sam Jones (a retired Boston Celtic) and David Steinberg (a well-known comic). Westphal was so competitive that Jimmy Walker (better known as J. J. on *Good Times*) threatened to sue the then-Phoenix guard after suffering a cheek bruise from a rough Westphal drive.[92] A year later, unhappy with the Suns organization, Westphal asked for a trade. He ended up in Seattle, who sent guard Dennis Johnson to Phoenix, in what was supposed to be a win-win, that rare NBA deal where both sides benefited. Instead, Johnson led the Suns to a 57–25 record while injuries derailed Westphal, who played in less than half the games for the 34–38 Sonics. So, when the Knicks called to express interest in Westphal, he jumped at the chance for a fresh start.

Westphal debuted for the Knicks on March 13, 1982, but Sly Williams—recently returned from his one-game suspension—was once again nowhere to be found. The Knicks tried to reach him, but his phone was out of order; later his brother called the team, explaining that Sly had eaten some bad Italian food. And so the Knicks suspended him again. Sly rejoined the team for five games in late March before being suspended for the third time of the season.[93]

With Sly missing, New York dropped eight of its last nine games to finish a dismal 33–49, last place in the Atlantic Division and far out of playoff contention. "When you don't have anything to play for," Webster told the *Times*, "it's difficult to go out onto the court. You can only play for your own pride." Campy Russell was also frustrated. "I had high expectations," he said. "But we never really materialized. . . . This is the biggest disappointment of my eight years in the league."[94] Westphal played serviceably for the Knicks, averaging a shade under twelve points per game, but the team was just 4–14 after his signing. Years later Westphal lashed out at the lethargy of the Knicks teams he played for, charging that Coach Holzman canceled practices because of poor attendance. "To not have practices because you know guys won't even bother to come to them?" Westphal remembered. "It was certainly a low point in Knicks history."[95]

Interviewed leaving the season's last game, a fan summed everything up with one simple phrase: "Thank God it's over."[96]

To be fair, there were a few bright spots in the dreary season besides Richardson's "ship be sinking" quote. Sugar made his third-straight All-Star team and finished seventh in the league in assists, while once again leading in steals. And Russell led the NBA in three-point percentage, shooting an impressive 44 percent from behind the arc. "That was the last thing in the world I expected," Russell laughed as he told me decades later. "When they called me and told me that, I said 'What?' I didn't take three pointers. The three-point shots I took were primarily because we were down and were trying to get back in."[97] For the season, Campy connected on 25 of his 57 three-point attempts, the lowest total made shots for a three-point percentage leader in NBA history. (As of 2023, a minimum of 82 three-pointers made is required in order to qualify for league leadership.)[98]

Once again, uncertainty surrounded the team in the 1982 off-season. Everyone knew Holzman was done coaching, but would he move back into a consulting role? Or would he retire with Selma to their Long Island home? And who would replace him on the bench? Rumors mentioned Dave DeBusschere, but what about Jerry Colangelo, recently named Executive of the Year as the general manager of the Suns? Or maybe Dave Gavitt, a former coach of Providence College and then commissioner of the Big East Conference?

1981–82 Knicks
Record: 33–49
Playoffs: Did not qualify
Coach: Red Holzman
Average Home Attendance: 10,834
Points per Game: (106.2—16th of 23)
Points Allowed per Game: (108.9—12th of 23)
Team Leaders:

Points: Micheal Ray Richardson (17.9 per game)
Rebounds: Maurice Lucas (11.3 per game)

Assists: Micheal Ray Richardson (7.0 per game)
Steals: Micheal Ray Richardson (2.6 per game)
Blocked Shots: Marvin Webster (1.1 per game)
All-Stars: Micheal Ray Richardson

Notable Transactions: Received Maurice Lucas as compensation for the New Jersey Nets signing Ray Williams; signed Paul Westphal

8

"A POLICY OF PATIENCE"

1982–1983

Racial tension was high in the early eighties throughout the United States. But in New York City, it peaked in the summer of 1982 with the killing Willie Turks, a New York City transit worker. Turks and two Black friends stopped at a bodega on Avenue X in Brooklyn to buy bagels and beer late on June 22. After leaving the store and returning to their car, they were confronted by a group of white men. Turks and his friends tried to drive away, but their car broke down, and Turks, dragged out of the car, was beaten to death by a crowd of fifteen to twenty whites. Six white men were charged and four convicted (by a jury consisting of eleven white men and women and one Latino) of manslaughter but found not guilty of murder. While handing out their sentences, Judge Sybil Hart Kooper admonished the convicted: "There was a lynch mob on Avenue X that night," she said. "The only thing missing was a rope and a tree."[1] The local Black community was incensed at the apparent lack of justice. "They let him off with nothing!" one bystander yelled after the verdict was read.[2] But Willie Turks's death, argues historian Jason Sokol, "caused only a minor stir in New York." "His name did not become a battle cry. . . He was just a black man who had been stomped to death, and who faded from the city's collective memory."[3]

Race remained an issue for the Knicks that fall as well. Red Holzman's retirement created a great deal of buzz in NBA coaching circles. When he had last left, in 1978, his replacement was already in place. But Willis Reed's tenure running the Knicks lasted less than a hundred games before Red was called back to coach. In 1982, one of Reed's teammates, Phil Jackson, was just starting his coaching career after landing the head job with the Albany Patroons of the Continental Basketball Association. Jackson would go on to win eleven NBA titles coaching the Bulls and Lakers, but he wasn't even a candidate to replace Holzman in '82.

Instead, on May 10, the *New York Post* leaked a story claiming that Sonny Werblin planned to bring in DeBusschere and former Hawks coach Hubie Brown to run the Knicks. Werblin denied the rumors but a week later introduced the duo as the team's new general manager and head coach respectively. "Werblin hired Hubie at the 21 Club [a trendy Manhattan restaurant] at lunch one day in late May," former director of communications John Hewig explained to me years later. "And at dinner at 21, he hired Dave DeBusschere to be the general manager. And he didn't tell either one that he'd hired the other one."[4] Publicly, DeBusschere backed Brown's hiring, telling reporters "I picked the coach," and that "I was hired first and in my discussions with Sonny, Hubie was the one guy who we felt would be a great coach to bring in here."[5]

Privately, it was a different story.

Brown grew up in Elizabeth, New Jersey, less than an hour's drive from Manhattan, in a working-class Irish Catholic neighborhood. Hubie worked hard and received a scholarship to attended Niagara University, where he earned multiple degrees in education before becoming a high school coach in tiny Little Falls, New York. Brown was ambitious and soon gained a reputation for running the best basketball clinics on the East Coast. In 1972, he joined the Milwaukee Bucks as an assistant on a staff led by his former Niagara teammate Larry Costello, and two years later he replaced "Magnolia Mouth" Babe McCarthy as the head coach of the ABA's Kentucky Colonels. Hubie led the Colonels to the 1975 ABA title and joined the Atlanta Hawks after the two leagues merged, earning NBA Coach of the Year honors in 1978 with a scrappy Hawks squad.

"My guys barely make the minimum," he bragged to *Sport* magazine at the time. "They're hungry. Coachable. . . . I'm not burdened with long-term six-figure contracts."[6]

Hubie loved players who overcame physical limitations through hard work and effort, and he had little patience for talented loafers. "We play like blue-collar workers," he explained. "We bring our lunch pails with us and we wear you out."[7] Not everyone was sold. "Hubie's tough on players," Bucks general manager Wayne Embry explained. "He has a tendency to demand a lot and when he doesn't get it, he puts the players down. Players just don't respond to that."[8] Cotton Fitzsimmons, a fellow NBA coach, was even more blunt. "He can't believe that anybody else is doing as good a job as he does. Sometimes when you talk to Hubie," he said, "you get the impression that he invented the game."[9] "I don't care who likes me," Brown shot back, "I don't like everybody myself."[10]

DeBusschere, of course, also had a blue-collar upbringing, raised in Detroit before embarking on a long and successful NBA career. After retiring from the Knicks in 1974, DeBusschere joined the ABA's New York Nets in a front office role and a year later was named league commissioner and then was instrumental in coordinating the 1976 merger. He left basketball for a while, dabbling in business with a boxing magazine, a TV ad sales firm called "Total Video Inc.," and restaurants in both Boston and Manhattan's Upper East Side.[11] "I get to the office early and I stay late," DeBusschere told the *Times*. "I read the business sections of the newspapers every day. I even go to that before the sports page."[12]

Whether or not it would pay immediate dividends, bringing in Brown and DeBusschere represented a significant shift for the Knicks. Jack Krumpe, the team president, explained, "The word to use is stability. We brought in Dave and Hubie in hopes of building a foundation. . . . I'm committed to a policy of patience." Patience was often preached and rarely practiced in the Knicks front office, but the team finally seemed to be at peace with the past. The *Times* noted, "The frustrations the Knicks have experienced in recent years may have resulted from living too much off memories." "John Gianelli," the article continued, "could never be Willis Reed; Spencer Haywood could not become Dave DeBusschere. Ray Williams and Micheal Ray Richardson could not be Walt Frazier and Earl Monroe. But they were asked to." Even though DeBusschere had played on the title-winning teams, the dawning of the DeBusschere and Brown era provided a break with the past and an opportunity for a fresh start. "The fans do tend to live in the past and there is an attachment to the old Knicks," DeBusschere admitted. "But these are new players and they have to establish their own mystique."[13]

Brown and DeBusschere were both driven, and from the start there was tension between the two men. "They didn't like each other," Hewig explained to me.[14] Maybe it was their history dating to the ABA, when DeBusschere was the commissioner and Brown a prominent coach. Or maybe it was simply a clash of personalities; both were outspoken, and each had their own idea of how to return the Knicks to prominence. "I have complete control over all basketball operations," DeBusschere told reporters. "Period."[15] Pressed by journalists about who might be on the trading block, DeBusschere admitted that Cartwright was "probably our No. 1 asset, if we wanted to trade him."[16] A few weeks earlier, he had told reporters "They're all safe. Until we [Knicks executives] meet."[17] For his part, Hubie told the *Daily News* that he considered just three assets untouchable: their first-round pick in the draft, Micheal Ray Richardson, and Cartwright.[18]

Brown and DeBusschere had to get up to speed quickly that spring, as trade rumors heated up with the approaching NBA draft. Cartwright and Webster were the two most-mentioned Knicks in trade talks, as management had all but given up hope they could play together. "I still want to stay here," Webster said, "but I don't want to be no backup center."[19] Neither did Cartwright. Unfortunately, Bill had yet to replicate his outstanding debut; as a rookie he averaged 22 points and 9 rebounds, meriting mention in the same breath as fellow rookies Larry Bird and Magic Johnson. That dropped to 20 and 8 in season two, and 14 and 6 in his third season ('81–82). Cartwright was not really regressing, he was just being used less on offense as backcourt players like Ray Williams, Richardson, and Paul Westphal took more shots. Defensively, he was solid if unspectacular. So his talent was wasted if his teammates rarely worked the ball to him on the offensive end. To complicate matters, in addition to Webster and Cartwright, the Knicks still had Maurice Lucas, a power forward probably better suited to playing center. Something had to give.

With the first pick of the 1982 NBA draft, the Lakers—to no one's surprise—selected All-American forward James Worthy, kicking the team's "Showtime" era into high gear. Next, the San Diego Clippers picked DePaul big man Terry Cummings before the Utah Jazz snatched Georgia forward Dominique Wilkins (later traded to Atlanta). Dallas and Kansas City chose Bill Garnett and LaSalle Thompson respectively, putting the Knicks on the clock with the sixth pick. Knicks fans desperately wanted Clark Kellogg, a bruising six-foot-seven forward from Ohio State, and chants of "We want Kellogg!" echoed through the Felt Forum (now the Hulu Theater), located beneath Madison Square Garden. When Commissioner O'Brien came to the microphone and announced the Knicks's choice, University of Minnesota guard Trent Tucker, the crowd of about two thousand loudly booed. "I would have liked a warmer welcome," Tucker joked when asked about fans' response.[20] Despite fan resentment, Tucker seemed like a perfect fit for Hubie's system; he was a rangy six-foot-five athlete who led Minnesota to a rare Big Ten conference championship. He modeled his game after Frazier, and his ability to play both guard spots would allow Hubie to shift Micheal Ray to small forward in some three-guard lineups, a group that he hoped could press teams defensively with a collection of long, lanky athletes.[21]

Adding Tucker was not the only significant move the Knicks made that off-season. In early July, they cleared their logjam at center—somewhat—by shipping Lucas to Phoenix in exchange for forward Leonard "Truck" Robinson. "I'm glad to be going to a team with a big dude," Truck told the *Post*. "There are few cities in this league where every player wants to play," he said. "And New York is one."[22] The team also replaced Campy Russell, who tore ligaments in his knee, with rail-thin Pacers forward Louis Orr, and assistant coaches Butch Beard and Hal Fischer with Mike Fratello and Richie Adubato. Beard and Fischer remained with the organization—Beard became the voice of the Knicks on MSG television and WOR radio, while Fischer returned to his former assignment as a scout.

More telling was the direction Brown was going with his choice of assistants. Fratello and Adubato spent their summers with Brown coaching at the famed Five Star Basketball camps held annually in upstate New York. Five Star founder Howard Garfinkel called Brown, "Picasso, Pavarotti, Sinatra with a basketball."[23] Soon the trio of Knicks coaches joined up-and-coming Boston University coach Rick Pitino, Louisville's Denny Crum, future Pistons coach Chuck Daly, and legendary Indiana University coach Bob Knight as celebrated members of the "Five Star Group."

With Brown's Five-Star staff in place, DeBusschere worked to get his new coach a few "Hubie Brown-type players."[24] In the early eighties, a "Hubie Brown-type" meant someone who was "accountable" and a "team player," with "discipline" and a "high IQ." Hubie told me that he expected his guys to give "their heart on a daily basis," and that all twelve men on the team would always be ready to play.[25]

Mike Newlin and Randy Smith, brought in to stabilize the backcourt a year earlier, were gone. Neither fit into the defensive scheme Hubie planned to employ. Instead, DeBusschere hoped Tucker, Orr, and swingman Ernie Grunfeld, who Hubie said had a lot of "mental toughness," could fill their roles off the bench. [26] Grunfeld, now best known as the longtime (and long-suffering) general manager of the Washington Wizards, was born to Holocaust survivors from Romania. He immigrated to the United States in 1964 as an eight-year-old who spoke no English. Occasionally Ernie's father took him to Knicks games, and the youngster picked up the language playing basketball in Queens.[27] At the University of Tennessee, Grunfeld became the school's all-time leading scorer and earned a second-team All-American nod, even as he was overshadowed by teammate Bernard King in the "Bernie and Ernie Show" (a marketing ploy dreamed up by the Vols' PR department).

As DeBusschere and Brown shaped the Knicks' roster in the Garden, hip-hop continued to expand beyond its South Bronx roots.

"Rapper's Delight" is widely regarded as the first commercially successful rap song. But the first authentic hit from some real B-boys? That was probably produced by Grandmaster Flash and the Furious Five. As with most groups at the time, they focused on live performances instead of albums or cassette tapes. But in 2007, they became the first hip-hop act inducted into the Rock and Roll Hall of Fame, mostly because of their 1982 hit "The Message" (on the album of the same name). The lyrics have been sampled so often folks can be forgiven for not realizing their origin. "Don't push me / 'Cause I'm close to the edge / I'm trying not to lose my head."

"The Message" was groundbreaking, transforming rap from party music into social commentary. Later called conscious hip-hop or political hip-hop, the song spoke to living in urban poverty. There was no "hip hop and you don't stop to the bang, bang boogie" nonsense here. Instead

Figure 11. Knicks head coach Hubie Brown during a May 3, 1984, game against the Celtics at Boston Garden. Trent Tucker is on the bench. AP Photo/Paul Benoit.

the lyrics are sobering. "I can't take the smell, can't take the noise / Got no money to move out, I guess I got no choice." This was real, speaking to the frustrations of young Black men and women living in poverty—in the South Bronx or elsewhere—matching, as historian Jeff Chang argues, "a rising disgust with Reaganomics."[28]

Unfortunately, the group soon divided over disputes about royalties and created two separate crews; one led by Grandmaster Flash, the other by Melle Mel. They reunited half a dozen years later, but their second (and only other) album, *On the Strength*, was neither as well-conceived nor as well-received as *The Message*. *Rolling Stone* ranked "The Message" number 51 on their list of 500 greatest songs of all-time in 2004; it was the highest-ranking hip-hop song and highest position for any song released in the 1980s. It also became the first hip-hop recording chosen by the Library of Congress as part of its National Recording Registry.

It was a transformative summer for the Knicks and for rap music, for sure. But the biggest on-court change in New York City took place in the weeks leading up to the first game. Richardson, still privately battling a drug addiction, was very excited about the opportunity to play for Hubie. "I never saw a guy so organized," he told Werblin. "I'm learning. I'm learning."[29] But Richardson never got his chance to prove he was a Hubie Brown guy. The new coach was looking to clean house and told the *Times* that he "had to get rid of a couple of drug users before he would feel comfortable with his new team."[30] Although Brown did not name names, when Sugar tried to renegotiate his contract (again), he was as good as gone. Hubie said later, "He was constantly worrying about his contract and he was letting it affect his attention and concentration and that became a source of disruption for the team."[31]

On the other side of the country, Brooklyn native Bernard King, like Richardson, was frustrated with his team's front office. Twenty-six years old, King was a free agent coming off his first All-Star appearance and averaging 23 points and 6 rebounds per game for Golden State. But negotiations with Warriors owner Franklin Mieuli were going nowhere. Sensing an opportunity to make a deal that would pay dividends both on the court and at the box office, the Knicks offered King a contract for nearly $4 million spread over five years. Mieuli was outraged.[32] He took as long as possible to decide whether to match the Knicks' offer, calling a press conference at New York City's Sheraton Centre Hotel to make the announcement that King would remain with Golden State. Mieuli blasted the Knicks to the press, calling them "a carpet-bagging conglomerate . . . [that] used to be run in dignity by Ned Irish."[33] "Bernard is part of our inventory," he complained. "We found him, developed him and what stature he has attained is due to us."[34] King and his agent, Bill Pollak, disagreed. "Franklin never intended to keep Bernard," Pollak said later. "When he matched the offer sheet, one reporter here said he welcomed Bernard back with closed arms."[35]

Publicly, King issued a statement regarding Mieuli's determination to match. "I accept Golden State's decision with mixed emotions," King wrote. "Having grown up in New York City, I always dreamed of playing in a Knick uniform before my mother and father at Madison Square Garden. . . . It almost became a reality."[36]

Privately, King was fuming about being treated like a piece of property. He refused to report to Golden State, claiming Mieuli had withheld a signing bonus owed him. Neither Mieuli nor King was happy with the outcome.

Fortunately, the Knicks had something the Warriors wanted.

On October 22, just a week before the start of the regular season, the Knicks stunned the basketball world by announcing a trade sending Richardson to the Warriors for King. Sugar was heartbroken. "I'm gonna wear Hubie's butt out when we play them," he promised. "It's gonna be an ego game."[37] While Richardson was feeling hurt and unwanted, King was ecstatic. "My God, I was excited," he remembered later.[38] "I wanted to play in New York. I wanted to play for the Knicks." King did have some reservations about playing for Brown, however. As King told reporters, "I don't know Hubie personally, but the man is a winner and a teacher, and I want to learn and improve. And I will under Hubie Brown."[39] King was well aware of Brown's deserved reputation for belittling and demeaning his players. "The thought of having to put up with Hubie Brown's abuse made me seriously consider turning it down," King later wrote in his autobiography.[40]

On opening night, October 29, 1982, the Knicks hosted the Philadelphia 76ers, who were headed toward the NBA title. The crowd booed the visiting Sixers but erupted when King made his Knicks' debut. "The cheers," he wrote later, "made it feel like a homecoming."[41] New York fell behind early but clawed back to keep the game close until the very end, when Philadelphia pulled away for the win. Still, the Knicks had reason for optimism. It was the first opening game sellout in years, and the first sellout for any game since Dave DeBusschere Night in March 1981.[42] On the court, Hubie judged the team's effort "terrific" and claimed he "didn't hear one boo out there," an unofficial first for an Garden crowd in years.[43]

Following their exciting opening night loss, the Knicks left New York for a four-game road trip. After losing to Milwaukee, the Knicks held a nine-point lead in Golden State to open the fourth quarter before falling by two. Richardson watched from the bench, already suspended by his new team for trying to renegotiate his contract again. New York sportswriter Harvey Araton took to calling Richardson "Micheal Raise" and dubbed the Warrior backcourt, Richardson and World B. Free, "Sugar-Free."[44] Two more losses, to Seattle and Portland, dropped the Knicks to 0–5, pushing the volatile Brown over the edge. As King wrote in his autobiography, Hubie decided to take out his frustrations on the team's new superstar. "You worthless piece of shit!" Hubie allegedly yelled at King in the locker room after the game. "You're no fuckin' All-Star! You're no All-Pro! You ain't shit! You're a dog!"[45] Two days later, King wrote, he confronted Hubie about the incident. "Don't you ever, under any circumstances, dare to speak to me in the manner you did again. Do you understand?" King remembered that Hubie paused and then told him, "It will never happen again." "And it didn't," King wrote. "Not with me. But he continued talking to my teammates like that. He saw nothing wrong with it. To him, it was perfectly acceptable."[46]

Despite the losing streak, which peaked at seven straight to open the season, and the flare-up between he and Hubie, Bernard supported his new coach. "Hubie Brown was a great coach," King wrote. "Not a good coach, a *great* coach."[47] Brown understood that changing the team's fortunes would take time, but he also knew how important that turnaround was to New York City. In the preseason, Hubie wrote three things on the chalkboard for his players to focus on: "1) The only thing that matters in New York is to win. 2) Play an exciting style of basketball. . . 3) Victory equals fun for everyone."[48] Brown drilled his players incessantly, running long, grueling sessions when many coaches were beginning to lighten their practice regimens. The hard work paid off when the Knicks finally broke their long losing streak by beating the Washington Bullets to improve to

1–7. "It was a victory we needed," a sweat-soaked Brown told reporters after the game. "It takes pressure off everyone—management, the coaches and the kids."[49]

While Brown might have used the term "kids" to refer generically to his team (he was, after all, pushing fifty—nearly twenty years older than his oldest player, thirty-two-year-old guard Paul Westphal), he was more accurately describing his inexperienced backcourt. With Richardson in Golden State, the point guard position fell to a trio of rookies: Ed Sherod, Vince Taylor, and Tucker. DeBusschere insisted the team did not need a pure point guard, asking reporters sarcastically in the preseason, "Why can't both guards handle the ball?"[50] But it became apparent that the young backcourt was woefully inconsistent. King liked to receive passes while on the move, bulling his way to the basket for high-flying slam dunks or close-range jump shots. But the Knicks guards were reluctant to push the pace with fast breaks. In fact, the Knicks finished the season last in the league in pace of play (the number of possessions per game). In an early December game at cavernous Richfield Coliseum in Ohio, only two thousand fans turned out to see the Cavaliers (the next-slowest team in the league) host the Knicks. After a high-scoring first quarter, the teams reverted to form and chants of "Boring! Boring!" echoed through the near-empty stadium by the second half.[51]

Struggling rookie guards were frustrating but also expected. Two-time All-Star power forwards, on the other hand, were not supposed to play so poorly. In stints with the Bullets, Hawks, Jazz, and Suns, Truck Robinson had earned a well-deserved reputation as a relentless rebounder and powerful inside scorer. In 1977–78, he led the league with 15.7 rebounds per game while scoring almost 23 a night. Even by 1981–82, his last season in Phoenix, Truck averaged 19 points and almost 10 rebounds per game. Now he was shooting under 50 percent from the field and less than 60 percent from the line, both near career lows. Making matters worse, Knicks fans began yelling "No!" when he caught the ball, urging him to pass rather than shoot, killing his confidence.[52] As Robinson struggled, the boobirds became louder and more difficult to ignore. "People can boo," Robinson said. "I don't like it, but that's their prerogative."[53] Soon Brown also lost confidence in Robinson and replaced him in the starting lineup with Sly Williams, back in the team's good graces after being suspended several times by Holzman the preceding season.

By midseason, Knicks execs realized that they had failed in their roster construction. Hubie conceded, "We need a point guard," while DeBusschere admitted, "The trade for Truck has not turned out the way we would have liked." Werblin, never one to mince words, told the *Times*, "the whole season has been most upsetting. I never expected something like this would happen."[54]

Like Robinson, Cartwright was also falling out of Brown's good graces. As a rookie, Cartwright drew favorable comparisons to fellow first-year All-Stars Larry Bird and Magic Johnson. By the fall of 1982, Larry and Magic were superstars while Cartwright was becoming an afterthought. He was still a strong offensive player, averaging almost 16 points per game, but he was a non-factor on the defensive end, averaging 1.5 blocks and pulling down just 7 rebounds a night. "Cartwright is too passive," the *Sporting News* wrote, "and that's difficult to change."[55] He had his moments, to be sure, including a 21 point, 18 rebound performance against Hubie's old Hawks, but Cartwright was increasingly relegated to being the second or even third most important offensive player on a mediocre Knicks team. Harvey Araton, writing for the *Daily News*, opined that the Knicks should trade Cartwright "for a draft pick or a warm body or a cold turkey on rye with lettuce and tomato."[56]

Cartwright fans held out hope and seemed to be rewarded when, after an ankle sprain sidelined King for several weeks in late January, the team posted a 9–5 record and their center showed flashes of his early career brilliance, topping 20 points nine times. Asked about his turnaround, Cartwright told reporters, "It's simple. I'm just getting the ball."[57] "With Bernard out," he continued, "Paul [Westphal], Truck, and myself have been shooting it up more. If you shoot more," he added sagely in his gravelly voice, "you score more."[58]

While Cartwright and the veterans shouldered the scoring load in the absence of King, the team shored up its problems at point guard by trading for Rory Sparrow. As a kid, Sparrow had patterned his game after Pete Maravich, but now Hubie called him "one of the best defenders in the league" and "one of the people [the Knicks needed] to build a future on."[59]

Hubie was excited to work with Sparrow but got a little too enthusiastic during a February 25 game in Indiana when, in the second quarter, he split his trousers down the back. Brown emerged from the locker room for the second half wearing a sports jacket . . . and red, white, and blue Knicks warmup pants.[60] To his credit, Hubie had good reason to be excited; Cartwright shot 9 for 10 in the first half against the Pacers and finished the game with 32 points in the Knicks' win.

Three days after Hubie's wardrobe malfunction, more than one hundred million Americans tuned in to CBS to watch the final episode of the hit television show *M*A*S*H*. In the special two-hour finale, series regulars like Hawkeye Pierce and Margaret "Hot Lips" Houlihan witness the final ceasefire of the Korean War and say "goodbye, farewell and amen" (the episode's title) to the 4077th surgical unit.

Alan Alda—the actor who portrayed Hawkeye Pierce—was a big Knicks fan and soon had more reason to attend games than he had in several years. "It was almost like the old-time chic at Madison Square Garden last night," Michael Katz wrote in the *Times* following the near-sellout crowd assembled to watch the Knicks and Sixers game in early March. "The stars, like Woody Allen, Mia Farrow, and Peter Falk, returned from wherever stars go when their team is not winning."[61] With King back off the injured list, the team finally seemed to gel. "Before," Westphal explained, "Bernard was the only one scoring and Hubie was going to him out of necessity. Now we're playing the way Hubie wanted us to all along."[62]

Despite an improved offense, defense remained the calling card of the team, as the Knicks blitzed opponents to force turnovers. "If we score on the trap," Hubie explained, "we stay with it until you prove to us you can beat it or until fatigue sets in. Some nights," he admitted, "the trap works. Some nights, it doesn't. It still comes down to people."[63] By mid-March, the trap was working, and the team was four games over .500. Asked to compare the mid-March Knicks to the same team two months earlier, which started 14–26, Cartwright shrugged his shoulders and told the *Times* "We're no longer that team."[64]

One reason for the turnaround was Hubie's use of what he referred to as his "second unit." Brown's starting lineup was very traditional: Sparrow ran the offense, Westphal and King created shots from the wings, Robinson battled for rebounds, and Cartwright provided solid low-post offense. The "second unit" was entirely different. For one thing, there was no traditional point guard or power forward; Tucker, Grunfeld, Williams, and Orr were all between six foot five and six foot eight, best suited to playing on the wing. At center, Webster anchored the defense, reminding folks why he earned the nickname "The Human Eraser," allowing his teammates to gamble for steals or double-teams knowing he had their backs. Sure, Hubie wasn't entirely sold on Marvin, and he sometimes enlisted the help of Knicks' VP Mel Lowell. "Can you stand here," Mel told me Hubie asked him during one practice, "and every time someone who Marvin is guarding gets the ball, say 'Marvin, put your hands up!' He's 7-foot-2 and he doesn't put his fucking hands up!"[65] Statistically, Marvin remained underwhelming, averaging just five points and five rebounds a night. But now, for the first time as a Knick, he seemed confident in his role—and even Hubie admitted as much. "I can't say enough about what this second unit has meant to us," Hubie said. "Not only are they quicker than our first unit, but they play a different style . . . they are able to change the tempo of the game, and it confuses opposing defenses."[66]

The Knicks' surge in the spring of 1983 coincided with the first public inklings that the newest Knick had a darker side. King was naturally intense and quiet, generally keeping to himself and rarely socializing with teammates. Then, in late March, the *Times* published a long article detailing King's history of alcoholism and sexual violence. "I wasn't the bad boy in the headlines," King claimed, blaming police harassment for his poor reputation, which included five arrests in eighteen months as an undergraduate in Knoxville. He did understand, though, that he was becoming dependent on alcohol. [67] "My problem wasn't that I drank because my body needed it," King now says, "I drank because it was the only way I could enjoy myself." Although always sober for games, King admits that his alcoholism took control of his life as a Net. "I believe if the Nets had not traded me, I wouldn't be alive today, due to the fact that I did a lot of driving under the influence of alcohol." Not even sending King to Salt Lake City had sobered him up; three months after joining the Jazz, police arrested King on charges of forced sexual abuse, sodomy, and possession of cocaine. He received a fine and a one-year suspended sentence and then checked into St. John's Hospital and Health Center in Santa Monica, California, causing him to miss the end of the 1979–80 season. His time in Utah was brief. "I had a serious problem," King says, "and they didn't care."[68] In September 1980, the Jazz dealt Bernard to Golden State for a backup center before King revived his career, and reputation, with the Warriors.

Just as news of Bernard's checkered past broke in the local papers, an emerging phenomenon in New York City's largest borough was about to explode in popularity. Yes, many young people heard "Rapper's Delight." And some bought copies of "Planet Rock" or "The Message." But few people outside the Bronx knew of Grandmaster Flash or the Cold Crush Brothers in early 1983. That year, a film produced by Charlie Ahearn gave outsiders a taste of real hip-hop. *Wild Style* had a limited release in 1983—*Return of the Jedi* and *Terms of Endearment* dominated at the box office that summer and fall—but the film and its soundtrack quickly became cult favorites.

Wild Style was part documentary and part fictional film featuring dozens of hip-hop pioneers. Melle Mel called it "the one movie that captured the true essence of hip-hop."[69] Basketball played a particularly important role in the film. "I was later at West Fourth Street one time, and that's probably one of the best streetball game spots in all of New York," Ahearn recalls. "And there was a DJ on the other side of the court practicing records, and that combined with this whole thing of Grandmaster Caz writing his rhymes while he's playing basketball, it was maybe one of my favorite inspirations of making the film."[70]

In one particularly memorable scene, the Cold Crush Brothers and the Fantastic Five square off on a basketball court. They start with a rap battle (appropriately dubbed the "Basketball Throwdown"), invoking several well-known NBA players in their rhymes, including Master Rob rapping that "I'm the M like all the pretty girls, I serve your monkey ass like Earl 'The Pearl.' " Once the pickup game between Cold Crush and the Fantastic Five starts, the rappers try to one-up each other on the court as well, bragging after every made shot or highlight-reel move. Even though one rapper boasts about his team's "Eighteen-to-oh" lead, the score clearly takes a backseat to style.[71] *Wild Style* brought hip-hop to film audiences and remained influential decades later. In fact, a 1997 Sprite commercial re-created the basketball court rap battle, featuring Tim Duncan and Kobe Bryant, with Missy Elliot rapping alongside Grandmaster Caz of Cold Crush and Prince Whipper of the Fantastic Five.

By late 1983, hip-hop was spreading out of the South Bronx to the far reaches of the world. "There was a lot of parties, and a lot of underground music was making the scene," Rory Sparrow told me. "It was original, it was loud, it was in your face, and it was real. You knew it was going to

Figure 12. The Cold Crush Brothers rehearsing for the basketball scene in the Bronx in Charlie Ahearn's film *Wild Style*. From left: unknown, JDL, Charlie Chase, Charlie Ahearn (behind Caz), Grandmaster Caz, and Fab 5 Freddy. Photo by Joe Conzo Jr. (Division of Rare and Manuscript Collections, Cornell University Library. © Cornell University.)

catch on, you just didn't know how big it was going to get," he said. Later in life, Sparrow traveled to Africa as an NBA ambassador, and he told me about his experience. "In the middle of Africa is hip-hop. Basketball on red clay . . . [There's] one television in the village, but they knew basketball and they knew hip-hop."[72]

New York City had just one professional hoops team—the Knicks. But dozens of high school and college squads played within the five boroughs. In March 1983, the Big East first held their postseason tournament in New York City, at Madison Square Garden. St. John's, led by a pair of New Yorkers (head coach Lou Carnesecca and leading scorer Chris Mullin) defeated Boston College in the final. Even in defeat, BC's head coach Gary Williams, born in New Jersey, admitted that he loved playing in the Garden. "It was a great experience coming to New York to play in this tournament," he told reporters. "This is the best place in the world to have a basketball tournament."[73]

From 1938 until 2021, Madison Square Garden also hosted the National Invitational Tournament (NIT). The NIT was the premier post-season college basketball tournament for decades before the NCAA's March Madness eclipsed it during the early seventies. Now, with the Big East tournament, MSG had its own signature collegiate event, and New York became, as George Vecsey described it, "the spiritual as well as the geographic center" of the Big East.[74]

New York City was also the epicenter of high school basketball. As Rick Telander describes in *Heaven Is a Playground*, playground basketball produced amazing teenage talent like the King brothers (Bernard and Albert). Dozens of other stars from the seventies and eighties played their high school ball in and around New York as well, including Lew Alcindor of Power Memorial, Tiny Archibald from DeWitt Clinton, Julius Erving from Roosevelt, World B. Free from Canarsie, the Williams brothers (Gus and Ray) from Mount Vernon, and Pearl Washington from Boys & Girls in Brooklyn.

New York State banned high school basketball state championships from 1933 until 1978 due to concerns about eligibility and gambling, so many of these star players never had the opportunity to compete for a state title. So winning a local title, like the PSAL (Public Schools Athletic League) or CHSAA (Catholic High School Athletic Association) meant even more then than it does now. At Power Memorial, Alcindor helped his team to a 95–6 record and three City Catholic High School titles. By 1983, the recently reinstituted state tournament had four classes—A for the largest down to D for the smallest—and was held in the Glens Falls Civic Center, about two hundred miles north of New York City. Kids from downstate were well-represented in the tournament finals. That year in Class A, North Babylon (of Long Island) defeated Springfield Gardens (of Queens); Bishop Loughlin (Brooklyn) won the Class B title; Wayandanch (Long Island) finished second in Class C; and Our Saviour Lutheran (Bronx) won the Class D championship.

In later years, Madison Square Garden hosted a handful of high school games—including the PSAL championship—but in March 1983, the team brought back the doubleheader, a format that had been successful under Ned Irish in the 1940s and 1950s. This time, it was the Knicks battling the Portland Trail Blazers a few hours after Mullin and Carnesecca led

St. John's to the Big East title. Rory Sparrow's last-second three-pointer (one of only two made three pointers for Sparrow that season—the team made just 33) gave the Knicks a 97–95 victory and a 32–30 record on the season. It was their eighteenth win in twenty-two games. In early April, the Knicks clinched a playoff berth.

It should have been a time to celebrate, but instead rumors swirled around the team about the future of their hot-headed head coach. Two weeks before the end of the regular season, Nets coach Larry Brown resigned to take over at the University of Kansas, where he would eventually lead Danny Manning and the Jayhawks to an improbable 1988 NCAA title. Now there was some speculation that the Nets would replace one Brown (Larry) with another (Hubie). "The way I hear it, the deal has been done," the *Daily News* reporter wrote. The Knicks, though, denied that Hubie was going anywhere; they were supposedly working out a multiyear contract extension.[75] For his part, Hubie was livid that Larry's abrupt departure led to questions about his own future in New York. "I have not asked permission to talk to the Nets, and the Nets have not talked to me," he insisted. "It all started with the little guy who left a great team to look for happiness on the plains. I hope to hell he gets it," he continued, "because he has made my life miserable for me, my family, and my team."[76]

Despite losing their coach in midseason, the Nets finished 49–33 and earned homecourt advantage in their best-of-three first round playoff series against the 44–38 Knicks. Darryl Dawkins, the Nets' eccentric center who liked to give his rim-rattling dunks names like the "Yo Mama" and the "Spine-Chiller Supreme," dubbed the series between the two New York–area teams the "Function at the Junction." "This is the first time since I've been in New York that people are getting excited about a playoff series," Webster told reporters. "And it's about time."[77]

Nearly sixteen fans packed into Brendan Byrne Arena in East Rutherford, New Jersey, for the Nets-Knicks game on April 20, 1983. On paper, the series appeared to be an even matchup. The Nets' stars were forwards Buck Williams, who averaged 17 points and 12 rebounds in just his second NBA season, and Albert King, Bernard's younger brother and a key figure in Rick Telander's book *Heaven Is a Playground*, who chipped in 17 points per night. Another familiar face was the Nets' new starting point guard, Micheal Ray Richardson, acquired after just half a season in Golden State. Unfortunately, Richardson's running mate in New York, Ray Williams, had already left New Jersey, shipped to Kansas City, and Sugar was struggling mightily with drug use. He even went AWOL for several days before the playoffs began. As teammate Len Elmore explained to me decades later, "He wasn't particularly ready to play; it was somewhat of a distraction, there's no question about it."[78]

Despite the focus on the Nets' star forwards and the whereabouts of Richardson, backcourt play decided the first game in the best-of-three series. Richardson reappeared, and he and Darwin Cook, the Nets' other starting guard, shot poorly and turned the ball over half a dozen times while Sparrow put up 22 points on just 12 shots and handed out 7 assists for the Knicks.

Oh, and Bernard dropped 40 on his little brother Albert. "I wanted this badly," Bernard said after the game. "The team wanted it badly."[79]

The Nets were reeling, still adjusting to life after Larry Brown. During the regular season, New Jersey had the best defense in the league, but they surrendered 40 to King in game one and now, with their season on the line, had to travel across the Hudson River for a win-or-go-home game two. New York jumped out to a nine-point lead in the first quarter and stretched it to 23 at half (62–39). The rowdy capacity crowd at the Garden cheered loudly, starting a "We want Philly" chant even before halftime began. The Nets refused to give up and slowly chipped away at the lead, but then Grunfeld iced the game by hitting all ten of his free throws to gain a 105–99 win for the Knicks. Hubie, soaked in sweat, was in a jovial mood after the game, swigging a beer while answering questions from reporters. Asked about their upcoming series against Philadelphia, Hubie said, "What the hell? Bring 'em on. Those guys in that locker room believe in themselves now."[80]

Before the 1983 postseason, reporters asked Sixers center Moses Malone for his playoff prediction. Malone, rarely quotable, responded "Fo' Fo' Fo'," meaning that each series would last just four games, resulting in a twelve-game playoff sweep for Philadelphia. Malone, named the league's MVP for the second straight season after averaging 25 points and 15 rebounds per game, had missed the last four games with knee soreness and claimed to be about 75 percent healthy at the time. Fortunately for Malone, he had one hell of a supporting cast to back up his bravado. Julius Erving may not have been the otherworldly high flier he had been when he played in the ABA half a dozen years earlier, but Dr. J could still be counted on for twenty points and at least one highlight reel dunk almost every game. In the backcourt, Maurice Cheeks, the Philadelphia point guard, played hard-nosed defense and directed the offense, while shooting guard Andrew Toney earned the nickname "The Boston Strangler" for his post-season play. "He was a deadeye shooter with the demeanor of a hired gun," one columnist wrote of Toney, "a grim gamer, in awe of no one."[81] If the Knicks could force Erving and Cheeks to shoot from the outside, and if they could keep Toney away from the basket, and if Moses's bum knee kept him from dominating, then they might have a chance.

Unfortunately for Knicks' fans, a hobbled Malone played game one like a man on a mission, finishing with 38 points, 17 rebounds, and 3 blocked shots. "If that's 75 percent," teammate Clint Richardson joked afterward, "I'd hate to see him healthy."[82] Losing the game was bad, but the Knicks suffered a more painful blow in the second quarter when King slipped and re-sprained his right ankle, the same injury that had forced him to miss a month earlier in the season. Norman Scott, the Knicks' team physician, began working on a special shoe designed to support King's ankle, but New York, already an underdog, would have to try to even the series with their best player hobbled.

Like Moses had in the first game, King gamely battled through pain in the second. Before tipoff, King had electrotherapy on his injured ankle and put on supportive orthotics to cushion the impact. Even injured, King willed New York to a twenty-point first-half lead. "It's like he's playing for his life," Erving told reporters after the game, "a man possessed."[83] But then Malone took over. After halftime, Moses scored 19 and pulled down 10 boards, dominating his matchup against Cartwright, who finished with 0 points and just 4 rebounds (against 30 and 17 for Malone). "The contest between the redoubtable Moses and Cartwright jumped off the court and slapped you right across the face," wrote Harvey Araton.[84] Behind Malone, Cheeks, and Erving (who combined for 76 points), Philadelphia overcame a twenty-point first-half deficit to pull out a deflating 98–91 win.

Down 2–0 in the best-of-seven series, it would have been easy for the Knicks to fold. Instead, "Hubie Brown's scrappy little army," kept game three close, trailing by just one at the end of the third quarter.[85] With just five seconds left in the fourth, the Knicks tied the game, giving Philadelphia a chance to win in regulation or for New York to force overtime. The Sixers tried to work the ball to Erving, but the Knicks double-teamed Dr. J, forcing a pass to little-used reserve Franklin Edwards. Edwards tossed up a ten-foot shot off the backboard as time expired. It dropped through the net, and the Knicks lost again. "We couldn't have played any harder," Hubie told reporters after the game. "It is physically impossible for us to play any harder."[86]

Now trailing 3–0, every game was a must-win. Unfortunately for Knicks fans, the Sixers jumped out to an eight-point lead at halftime of game four and never looked back. This time, with five seconds left, the Knicks were down by six. There would be no last-minute heroics. Then something surprising happened. Instead of booing the home team for losing, Knicks fans packing Madison Square Garden gave their team a standing ovation, even while being swept. "If we played like this in any other series against any other team, we win," King said later. "The ovation we got from the fans was the nicest thing that ever happened to me."[87] Hubie agreed. "No man likes to go out 0–4," the coach told reporters, "But I'll tell you something, it was no knockout."[88] In four games, the Sixers outscored the Knicks by just twenty-two total points. And in the next series, the Milwaukee Bucks ruined Malone's prediction, losing in five games instead of four, but then Philadelphia swept the Los Angeles Lakers in the finals, giving the Sixers their first NBA title since 1967.

In the 1983 offseason, the Knicks hoped to build on their playoff success, looking forward rather than backward. But that summer, the past came rushing back as the Naismith Basketball Hall of Fame inducted Dave DeBusschere and Bill Bradley, joining Willis Reed (1982) and Jerry Lucas (1980) from the Knicks' title teams. Eventually seven players from the '73 team (DeBusschere, Bradley, Reed, Lucas, Monroe, Frazier, and Phil Jackson) as well as Coach Holzman earned plaques in Springfield.

While New Yorkers celebrated the nostalgia of two old Knicks joining the Hall of Fame, team execs were working overtime to make changes to the new Knicks. There would be several new faces, as Campy Russell and Toby Knight (who combined for $600,000 in salary and zero games played in '82–83) were gone. Likewise, the team's starting backcourt of Westphal and Sparrow as well as sixth-man Sly Williams and backup center Webster were all free agents. And although he still had several years left on his contract, the team was unsure about what to do with Cartwright. When they drafted him in 1979, the Knicks thought Cartwright was their center of the future and someone they could pencil in for 20 points and 10 rebounds a night for the next decade. But while Cartwright was a very good offensive center, his defensive and rebounding flaws were exposed by Malone in the playoffs as they had been by Gilmore a few years earlier. Kareem Abdul-Jabbar, now thirty-five years old, was a free agent, and DeBusschere tried to convince him to finish his career in New York. But there was no way Kareem was leaving the Showtime Lakers. He re-signed with L.A. and won three more titles before retiring in 1989 as the NBA's all-time leading scorer. With Abdul-Jabbar off the table, rumors of a possible Cartwright-for-Sikma swap with Seattle made the rounds, but it never materialized. Instead, the Knicks had a shot at another big man who could both help New York and hurt one of their archrivals.

In mid-June, Werblin and DeBusschere met with free agent Kevin McHale of the Boston Celtics about potentially signing in New York. McHale came off the bench for Boston, backing up center Robert Parish and forwards Larry Bird and Cornbread Maxwell, but was widely regarded as one of the NBA's premier defensive players. He also possessed a dizzying array of post moves that twisted defenders in knots. Boston loved McHale and wanted to keep him, but New York hoped a big money deal and a guaranteed starting position could convince him to trade Celtics green for Knicks blue and orange. Upon hearing that DeBusschere and Werblin had met with McHale, the Celtics quickly signed three of the Knicks' free agents (Webster, Williams, and Sparrow) to offer sheets, forcing New York to decide within fifteen days whether to match or to risk losing three quality players for nothing.

Red Auerbach, the Celtics' president, thought the Knicks had no chance of signing McHale. "They're just wasting their time," Auerbach told reporters, "McHale won't play for the Knicks, you can bet on that."[89] And although McHale's agent insisted that his client was listening to other offers, Red was right. McHale re-signed with Boston on a huge multiyear deal and stayed with the Celtics until his retirement in 1993. Hoping to salvage something from the McHale fiasco, the Knicks matched the Celtics' offer sheets on all three of their free agents.

Missing out on a superstar in free agency again, New York turned to the NBA draft to shore up their team. For the first time since 1979, when the Lakers took Magic Johnson, the first pick in the draft was a no-brainer, as the Houston Rockets chose Ralph Sampson, a three-time consensus first-team All-American from the University of Virginia. The Indiana Pacers then selected Steve Stipanovich from Purdue, a plodding center who would play just five NBA seasons, as the Knicks waited patiently for their pick, twelfth overall, to come up. Whether they were willing to admit it or not, the Knicks targeted one of two guards: Jeff Malone, a sharpshooter from Mississippi State, or Derek Harper, a hard-nosed player from Illinois. Unfortunately, Malone and Harper were the tenth and eleventh picks. Then, while some fans chanted "We want Drexler! We want Drexler!," referring to University of Houston high-flyer Clyde Drexler, the Knicks selected University of Arkansas guard Darrell Walker, a player from Chicago who earned the nickname "Junkyard Dog" for his toughness. In hindsight, passing on Drexler—a future Hall of Famer—was a mistake, but Walker was another great fit in Brown's defense-oriented scheme (although he and Hubie would clash repeatedly).[90] Keeping his remarks to the press brief, Walker told them simply that, "I'm going to play hard every night."[91]

While the Knicks struggled to build their team, either through free agency or the draft, the league had more pressing problems.

After being hired in 1976, Commissioner O'Brien had been forced to quickly learn on the job, shepherding the league through merging with the ABA and making sticky decisions like the McGinnis ruling. Two years later, O'Brien continued to cement his legacy by hiring an attorney with extensive knowledge of the league's operation as its general counsel. It didn't take long for that attorney, David Stern—a rabid Knicks fan whose father ran "Stern's Deli" on 8th Avenue between 22nd and 23rd streets—to emerge as the de facto leader of the league.[92]

Stern was promoted to vice president in 1980 with an eye on expanding the NBA's footprint through extensive marketing and television deals. In 1982, his efforts bore some fruit as the NBA and CBS signed an $88 million contract extension; but this deal paled in comparison to the $2.4 billion earned by the NFL across multiple networks and called for fewer nationally televised games than did the previous contract.[93] Stern also helped create NBA Entertainment, which emphasized promoting its players. "We were really the first league to sort of marry the pop culture, music, entertainment, with NBA players and its lifestyle," Don Sperling, the senior VP of NBA Entertainment remembers.[94] One of the company's early developments was a tagline Stern helped create: "America's Game: It's Fantastic."[95] Commercials for the league used the phrase over and over, finally getting celebrities to utter the line on camera. Peter Falk was the first, captured after a Knicks game at Madison Square Garden.[96]

Despite Stern's efforts to build the league's brand, the biggest concern in the NBA around the time the Knicks drafted Walker was the collective bargaining agreement set to expire on June 1, 1982.

Fearing a strike like the one Major League Baseball had experienced a year earlier, O'Brien asked owners to explore the possibility of employing replacement players, an option the NFL had used during the 1987 work stoppage. Instead, hoping to avoid losing the whole season—and especially the playoffs, which were a financial windfall—owners agreed to provide the players with copies of their team financial statements. Reviewing the documents, players' counsel Larry Fleisher could see that some teams actually did have legitimate financial struggles. But, he noted, most losses were not due to player salaries. In Cleveland, for example, Ted Stepien spent more on advertising than his team took in as revenue.[97]

Krumpe, representing the Knicks in these negotiations, remained quietly in the background; his team was in good shape financially. But Werblin was on the record about his feelings on players' rights. "In three or four years, every player will become a free agent, and if they change teams, it will hurt the game," Werblin told the *Times*. "Players will be moving from one team to another and there will be no loyalty and no players the fans can relate to the way there used to be."[98]

By the spring of 1983, after playing for almost a year without a collective bargaining agreement, player reps established an April 2 deadline to get a deal in place. As he had done before, Fleisher decided to use the annual All-Star Game to meet with players. Abdul-Jabbar explained the player's position to the press: "We're not making any demands. We're just trying to maintain what we have." Sonics owner Sam Schulman wanted none of it. "I dare them to strike," he told reporters. "The players are overpaid. A strike would enable us to return to normalcy and start all over again."[99]

As the deadline for the strike approached, the Knicks decided to vote after practice one day whether to support the movement. Their vote was unanimous, 12–0, in favor of the strike. "The vote took five minutes," player rep Marvin Webster explained. "We don't have any other choice. There was very little discussion. The guys felt they knew the issue and if they had to strike they would."[100]

On April 1, 1983, at the Waldorf Astoria in Manhattan, after twenty-six negotiating sessions spread over ten months, O'Brien announced a new collective bargaining agreement, just hours before the players' deadline. Players gained a share of league revenues—initially set to 53 percent—while the owners gained what they had long sought: a salary cap. "Both sides basically got what they wanted," O'Brien told reporters. "League parity is now possible because teams in large cities won't be able to spend more on players than those in smaller areas. Yet players who already have big salaries will not only keep them, but still have the right to move—the right of free agency."[101]

Beginning in 1984, the salary cap went into effect. For that season, the cap was $3.6 million per team, but each year the figure would be readjusted based on gate receipts, television revenue, and other forms of income, projecting a rise to $4 million within two seasons. The five teams with the largest payrolls (the Lakers, Nets, Knicks, SuperSonics, and Suns) could re-sign their own free agents but could not bid on players who would increase their team's salary. Additionally, the league continued its outmoded practice of restricted free agency; not until Tom Chambers signed with the Suns in 1988 could NBA players relocate without compensation owed their original team.

As the new bargaining agreement took effect, there were no earth-shattering changes for the Knicks. Abdul-Jabbar remained in L.A., Sikma stayed in Seattle, McHale was still a Celtic, Webster and Sparrow were back in the fold, and Darrell Walker was penciled in to replace Westphal, who finished out his career in Phoenix. With few off-season moves, the Knicks had no reason to suspect that 1984 would bring the team the highest of highs and lowest of lows.

1982–83 Knicks

Record: 44–38

Playoffs: Won Eastern Conference first round versus New Jersey Nets; lost Eastern Conference semifinals versus Philadelphia 76ers

Coach: Hubie Brown

Average Home Attendance: 10,703

Points per Game: (100.0—20th of 23)

Points Allowed per Game: (97.5–1st of 23)

Team Leaders:

> Points: Bernard King (21.9 per game)
> Rebounds: Truck Robinson (8.1 per game)
> Assists: Paul Westphal (5.5 per game)
> Steals: Ed Sherod (1.5 per game)
> Blocked Shots: Marvin Webster (1.6 per game)

All-Stars: None

Notable Transactions: Drafted Trent Tucker in the first round of the 1982 NBA Draft; traded Maurice Lucas to the Phoenix Suns for Truck Robinson; traded Micheal Ray Richardson to the Golden State Warriors for Bernard King

9

"To the Hoop, Y'All"

1983–1984

On October 15, 1983, Knicks head coach Hubie Brown, who had celebrated his fiftieth birthday a few weeks earlier, checked into Lenox Hill Hospital on Manhattan's Upper East Side, complaining of chest pain and left arm stiffness. Although doctors diagnosed him with angina, Hubie told reporters he came "from a family with a high rate of heart attacks" and admitted a "need to slow down." Brown was always animated on the sidelines while coaching, stomping up and down the court, yelling at players and referees in usually equal measure. Part of the problem, at least as his wife Claire saw it, was his lack of hobbies. "I always tell her," Hubie said, "my hobbies are: I read, I do clinics and give talks like crazy. I'd much rather do those things than play golf or tennis."[1]

Some of Hubie's coworkers, though, were concerned that other stresses might have contributed to the health scare. A few days before he checked into Lenox Hill, an issue of *Sports Illustrated* hit newsstands with a profile on Hubie in which several NBA coaches took shots at him. Cotton Fitzsimmons said, "Sometimes when you talk to Hubie you get the impression that he invented the game," while Doug Moe called him "an average coach who happens to be great at promoting himself." Most problematic for Hubie, though, was the piece's quotation of comments he had made about Stan Albeck, one of his former assistants and now Larry Brown's replacement as head coach of the Nets. "Albeck is a washerwoman," Hubie was quoted as saying, "who calls six people every day to find out the latest gossip."[2] Hubie claimed the interview had been done off the record and that his comments were taken out of context, but director of communications John Hewig told me years later, "That whole year, wherever we went, the first question in the postgame press conference would be, 'Hubie, how could you say those things?'"[3]

Maybe it was a lack of hobbies or a magazine article that had induced Hubie's chest pains. Or maybe it was the usual on-the-job stress of being the Knicks head coach. But it was becoming increasingly obvious to Knicks insiders that Hubie and Dave DeBusschere were like oil and water. One NBA official joked, "[They] have about as much in common as a brown sock and a black sock." Publicly, both men continued to toe the party line, insisting that everything was fine. "You don't have to be friends," DeBusschere told reporters. "You don't have to have a relationship where it's one of bosom buddies. What we have is a professional relationship." Brown agreed. "An awful lot of people do not want us to succeed," he said (a classic Brown line—he loved being the underdog). "I think an awful lot of people were kind of shocked with our results last year."[4]

More troubling in the long run was word that Gulf & Western wanted to raze Madison Square Garden and build an office tower above Penn Station. A spokesman for Gulf & Western denied the rumors and reminded reporters of the deal the company had signed in 1982 agreeing to keep their teams (the Knicks and Rangers) in the city for at least a decade, accepting losses up to $3 million annually in exchange for a large tax abatement and union concessions. Recent reports that the Garden lost around $2 million annually then, while troubling, fit the criteria G&W had established earlier. Governor Mario Cuomo, in his first term in office, was not satisfied. "Over the years we've lost the Dodgers from Brooklyn, the Giants and the Jets to the Meadowlands," he told reporters. "That's wrong. We've done something wrong."[5]

For better or worse, Brown and DeBusschere's 1983–84 Knicks started the season with a similar roster to the group that took the 76ers to four hard-fought games in the '83 playoffs. The only significant losses were Paul Westphal, who had signed with Phoenix and retired as a Sun, and Sly Williams, who was shipped to the Atlanta for Rudy Macklin. The Knicks had added first-round draft pick Darrell "Junkyard Dog" Walker, whom NBA coaches, somewhat ironically, compared to Micheal Ray Richardson for his defensive ability and length.[6] Then, in mid-September, the Knicks welcomed back Ray Williams. In the fall of 1981, Williams had left New York for a huge multiyear deal with the Nets. But showing up to his first training camp in New Jersey in such poor condition that teammates dubbed him "Mr. Butterworth" was not a good sign. Journalists would saddle him with the nickname "The Big Apple Turnover." Less than a year later, the Nets traded him to Kansas City, and now he was back for a second tour as a Knick.

In 1981, New York had replaced Williams with veterans like Westphal, Randy Smith, and Mike Newlin. Now Williams was expected to be a locker room leader. "I've changed since I first came into the league," Williams told reporters. "In my first years I know people criticized me for being out of control." Williams reigned himself in on the court and off it as well. "When I was younger and with the Knicks, [Richardson] and I used to stay in the street until the street told us to go home. We'd be out all night and then we might go straight to practice, me and Mike. And we still had plenty of energy to practice."[7] When asked about Williams's comments, Richardson agreed. "We were young and living in New York," Sugar said, adding wistfully, "if only we could have stayed together a little longer, until maybe we were both a little wiser."[8]

While one-third of the Family was back with the Knicks, the others had veered off in different directions. Mike Glenn was a role player for the Hawks before transitioning into the business world as a consultant for Merrill Lynch. Glenn had also started the Mike Glenn All-Star Basketball Camp for the Hearing-Impaired, described in chapter 6. Richardson, however, was not doing so well. He would play sporadically for the Nets from 1982–84 before bouncing back and playing regularly again in 1985, when—despite a continued drug problem—he would earn a spot on the All-Star team as well as the NBA's Comeback Player of the Year Award after averaging more than 20 points per game. "Once again,

I was hobnobbing with the A-list," Richardson recalls. "But once or twice every week, I was dashing up the stairs and swivel-hipping my way past needled-out junkies on my way to score."[9]

Drug-related problems ultimately caught up with Richardson, and by the end of his comeback year, his marriage was crumbling, he was working with his seventh different agent, and was driving his seventeenth different car. The next year, his wife Leah issued a restraining order. Richardson was arrested trying to break into her house, and the NBA demanded a drug test. When Richardson failed, Commissioner David Stern banished the once-promising Richardson from ever again playing in the NBA. "This is a tragic day for Micheal Ray Richardson," Stern said at the time. "Nothing less than the destruction by cocaine of a once-flourishing career."[10]

Richardson was devastated and blamed the NBA for making an example of him to scare its white players into getting clean. "Getting kicked out of the NBA was the lowest point of my life," he recalls. "I was a punk-ass kid from nowhere, so the NBA thought I was expendable . . . Believe me, when I got kicked out, all of them white druggies threw away their pipes and got clean in a hurry. The NBA got exactly what they wanted." After being blacklisted, Richardson played overseas for a more than a decade, finishing his pro career at the age of 47 for a French team.[11] "I don't know if moving to Europe saved my life, but I know it helped me," Richardson admitted. "It got me out of the environment I was in."[12] He divorced his wife, remarried, and sobered up, finally turning his life around. Fifteen years after he was banned from the NBA, Stern quietly helped Richardson find a position with the Nuggets in their community relations department, although Sugar still feels unwanted by the league that once welcomed him with open arms.[13]

When Micheal Ray played for the Knicks, Stern was the league's legal counsel. That changed in November 1983 when Madison Square Garden's media room hosted a historic press conference. Despite some behind-the-scenes grumbling about promoting from within, rather than making a splashy headline–grabbing hire, the NBA announced that Stern would be replacing Larry O'Brien as the commissioner of the NBA in February 1984. O'Brien was succinct in his statement to reporters, telling them simply that "I think my job here is done."[14] Fittingly, Stern, who grew up in the city, took the subway to the announcement.[15]

After taking office in 1978, Mayor Koch embraced austerity politics to shrink New York City's financial deficit. He also proved confrontational in battling unions and striking workers while striving to balance the budget.

Koch's administration faced other challenges during his second term in office that were less tangible than bankruptcy. The *New York Times* first reported an outbreak of what doctors deemed a "rare and often rapidly fatal form of cancer," primarily afflicting young homosexual men, in 1981.[16] Soon this epidemic, now known as AIDS, gained national attention, although Larry Speakes, the press secretary for President Reagan, blew off questions about the disease and dubbed it the "gay plague."[17] Likewise, Koch, who later acknowledged that "its effect on the public psyche with respect to contagion could be compared to that of leprosy of yesteryear, an uncontrolled irrational fear," remained publicly silent as the epidemic spread throughout the city.[18] By early 1984, tens of thousands of New Yorkers were infected, and the city's hospitals soon filled with patients afflicted with AIDS. Although privately concerned about the spread of the disease, Koch's administration responded only sporadically and then seemed more intent on shutting down gay movie theaters in Times Square than in combating the epidemic.[19] The NBA too did little publicly about AIDS until, in 1991, Magic Johnson suddenly retired from basketball, announcing that he had tested positive for HIV, a virus that can lead to AIDS. Before this, AIDS and pro basketball occupied two different worlds, but Johnson's announcement threw them into sharp relief as players grew immediately concerned about issues of blood contamination and unprotected sex.

Besides AIDS, the other hot-button issue Koch dealt with particularly poorly during his tenure was race. No one would ever accuse Koch of being politically correct. During his 1977 campaign, he used the term "poverty pimps" and argued that the governor should have called out the National Guard during the blackouts to violently curb the looting.[20] As mayor, Koch claimed color-blindness. He simply assumed people of color could, like his Jewish family had done in the 1950s and 1960s, overcome societal difficulties. What he overlooked, though, was the government assistance his family had received to succeed. So, when racial conflict escalated in the seventies and eighties, Koch's Archie Bunker–like approach seemed out of touch.

In the fall of 1983, the Knicks' PR department compiled their annual yearbook, which included a couple of gems about current players. Truck Robinson told a story about how he got his nickname from a teammate as a rookie with the Washington Bullets in 1974, Ernie Grunfeld shared his love of antique quilts, and Darrell Walker revealed his dream to play in the NHL. "Growing up in Chicago," he said, "the Black Hawks were really super tough. Everybody wanted to be a Black Hawk, including me."[21]

The yearbook also gave Knicks fans a chance to learn about newcomer Rudy Macklin, acquired from the Hawks in exchange for Sly Williams. Macklin was an avid video game player, and, when he joined the Knicks, Centipede was his game of choice. Released first as an arcade game in 1980, Centipede moved over to home video game consoles like the Atari 2600 and Apple II computer a few years later. In 1984, *Electronic Games* magazine released their fifth annual Arkie Awards, recognizing Centipede as the year's best computer action game, edging out Jumpman for the honor. Like Macklin, Truck Robinson was a gamer. "When I was younger, I found those games helped my shooting, because it was an instinctive thing," he told reporters. "After nine years of pro basketball and traveling, the games still help develop patience and help the eye and hand coordination. I find it relaxes me. But most important, it gets me away from the basketball world."[22]

What most people knew about Macklin was that he had made headlines in college at Louisiana State University because of his response to a huge national event. During the 1981 NCAA Final Four, President Reagan miraculously survived being shot by would-be assassin John Hinckley Jr. At the time, Macklin and his Tigers teammates wondered if the third-place game, scheduled for that evening, would even take place. It did, and LSU lost in the consolation round to Virginia, led by superstar center Ralph Sampson. After the game, a reporter asked Macklin if the attempt on Reagan's life affected his play. Macklin was upset about losing and tried to sidestep the question. But the reporters kept asking, and finally Macklin snapped. "He's no kin to me, OK?" he said. His quote made national headlines, and his family was inundated with hate mail from angry Americans across the country. "They're calling me a lot of vulgar things," he told reporters at the time. "They say I'm not American, that I shouldn't be allowed to play ball anymore."[23] "I was really down, and I was hurt, mentally and physically," Macklin explained to me decades later.[24] Macklin graduated as the all-time leading rebounder in LSU history and its second-leading scorer (behind only Pete Maravich), but all anyone could talk about during his post-collegiate career was his lack of patriotism.

Behind Walker, Grunfeld, Robinson, Macklin, and the rest of the Knicks, the team started the season with back-to-back wins over the Cavaliers and Bullets, despite inconsistent play. On opening night, the Knicks led by 22 in the third quarter but only won by seven. "When we were good, we were very, very good," Brown told reporters after the game. "And when we were bad, we were very, very bad."[25] The next night, the Knicks were again very, very bad as they missed seventeen straight shots during a 12-point second quarter but still hung on to win by three.

Four straight losses on an early West Coast swing dropped their record to 2–4, but Brown was unconcerned. "What we're demanding to do," he told the *Post*, "is press at 75 feet, man to man. Deny. Do all that, plus fast-break offense after every score."[26] He understood that took a lot out of his players physically but counted on his ten-man rotation to eventually wear down and outlast their opponents. Over the course of the season, Hubie's method began working, and the Knicks were able to clamp down defensively, leading the league in defensive rating and allowing the third-fewest points per game in the NBA. "I always want 10 guys to play," Hubie explained. "I want 10 guys to be happy and to develop their talent while young. Also in case of injury, we do not have to make any major adjustments."[27] Fortunately, the Knicks remained reasonably healthy through the fall and winter of 1983 and at the end of December had a 17–14 record, good for third in the Atlantic Division. "As the season went on," Cartwright remembers, "we played better and better."[28]

At the end of January 1984, New York started a three-game swing through Texas that would become part of Knicks legend. On January 31, they traveled to San Antonio to face "the Iceman" George Gervin and their old nemesis Artis Gilmore (now a Spur). The first half was an Old-West-style shootout, and the Knicks led by one: 67–66. Amazingly, King had scored nearly half the Knicks points by himself. "Bernard is Bernard," Hubie said later. "You don't even realize he's getting all those points. When (trainer) Mike Saunders turned to me near the end of the first half and said 'Bernard's got 29,' I nearly fell of the chair."[29] King kept rolling in the second half, and led the Knicks to a 117–113 win. Gervin scored 41 points in the loss, but King topped him, finishing with 50. He hit 20 of his 30 shots from the field, including a dunk at the buzzer, and 10 of his 13 free throws.

Hubie's system was supposed to emphasize depth, platooning two-deep at every position without bending to the will of individual stars. But King was different. "He does not freelance or razzle-dazzle or break plays or call for the ball or yell at his teammates," Hubie explained. "He just takes good shots when they are there."[30] Before the game against the Spurs, King ate a turkey sandwich and drank a vanilla milkshake, and, while basketball players might not be as superstitious as their baseball counterparts, no one blamed King when he ordered the same before his next game, against the Dallas Mavericks.

The Mavericks were well aware of King's 50 points the night before and were determined to hold the forward in check. When asked how to stop King, Mavs assistant coach Bob Weiss joked, "Tell him the tipoff starts at 9:05 [for the 7:30 game]." He promised reporters, "We'll do better against him. We'll hold him to 49."[31] King, though, was in no mood to joke. He rarely was. He knew the last Knick to get 50 points in a game had been Willis Reed in 1967 and that no Knick had ever scored 50 in back-to-back games. In fact, only three players in NBA history had accomplished that feat: Elgin Baylor, Wilt Chamberlain, and Rick Barry. Could King pull it off?

The Knicks trailed the Mavericks by eight at halftime, but King was again on fire, scoring 31 of his team's 50 points. And again Hubie had no idea that King was scoring so prodigiously. "He does it so quietly. I wouldn't have known it," Hubie said, "except that [assistant coach Rick] Pitino was yelling it in my ear."[32] With nine seconds left in the game, Sparrow held the ball out front, the Knicks now safely ahead by five. King had 48 points (on just 27 shots), but the Knicks on the bench weren't going to let Sparrow run out the clock. "Rory was dribbling and the bench was like 'Get B the ball!'" King said later. "Finally he dribbles over, he passes me the ball. I drive against Jay Vincent—never forget it—and I spun and he cut me off and I said 'I'm not gonna miss this shot.'"[33] Sparrow laughed. "If I didn't give it to him, my teammates would have killed me."[34] King's off-balance 22-footer gave him 50—again.

"King: 50 More!" the *Daily News* proclaimed in huge type the next day. "I've never seen anything like it," Hubie gushed. "Never. In high school, college, or the pros. There are just no words to describe him."[35] Trent Tucker told Darrell Walker after the second game, "This is something we can tell our kids, our grandchildren. We can tell them we were there when Bernard did it." Walker was stoked. "Bernard's a nightmare," he said. "You're worse-est nightmare. Woo-eee, it's a good thing he's on our side."[36] Even the Mavericks were impressed. "He's right up there with Larry Bird and Julius Erving," Mavs forward Mark Aguirre admitted.[37] "He was unbelievable. Unstoppable. To score 50 back-to-back on the road, that's a roll. He is on a roll. Rolling. Rolling Rolling."[38]

After a well-deserved day off, the Knicks took the court for their third game in their run through Texas, this time facing Houston and their rookie center Ralph Sampson. "We haven't had anything come through Texas like this since Santa Anna," Rockets forward Elvin Hayes joked. "King got 'em at the Alamo, then he went to Dallas and tore 'em up there. We can't just let him come through and rip up the whole state like a tornado."[39] Hayes and the Rockets did limit Bernard to less than 50 (25 less, to be precise), but the Knicks still won, 103–95. During King's three-game Texas swing, he scored 125 points on just 78 shots from the field. "Right now," Werblin told reporters, needing none of his usual hyperbole, "Bernard is as good a player as there is in the league."[40]

The 1984 All-Star Game, played for the first time in Denver, was a watershed moment in NBA history. For one, it marked the end of O'Brien's ten-year tenure as league commissioner. Stern stepped into the role the following week and would hold it for the next thirty years. But it also proved to be a step toward transitioning into the All-Star weekend extravaganza it would later become. A year earlier, Marvin Gaye's rendition of "The Star-Spangled Banner" shocked the crowd (and the players) assembled at the Forum in Inglewood. He sang it with soul. As Kareem Abdul-Jabbar explained, "It was so different that it reminded me of Jimi Hendrix's anthem at Woodstock. Marvin changed the whole template, and that broadened people's minds. It illuminated the concept 'We're black and we're Americans. We can have a different interpretation, and that's okay.' "[41] In '84, the Temptations sang the anthem (to far less fanfare), and the East defeated the West 154–145 in overtime, thanks in part to 18 points from Bernard King, the only Knick on the squad.

The '84 All-Star Weekend also reintroduced the Slam Dunk Contest, dormant since Darnell Hillman won seven years earlier. This time, Suns forward Larry Nance beat crowd-favorite Dr. J in the finals with a dunk nicknamed "Rock-the-Cradle." None of the Knicks participated in the contest.

The NBA also honored its history that weekend, as twenty-one retired greats took the floor for the Old Timers' Game. Fifty-eight-year-old Bill Sharman was the oldest player, while his teammate Pete Maravich was only thirty-five. Former Knick legend Earl Monroe led the West to a 64–63 victory, but the real winners were the legends who avoided injuries. Later renamed the All-Star Legends Game, the annual contest between retired players lasted another decade before they were canceled due to too many sprained ankles, pulled hamstrings, and bruised egos.

Under Stern, All-Star Weekend would transform into a cultural phenomenon over the coming decades, eventually serving as an event where hip-hop artists and NBA stars rubbed elbows. It became, as sportswriter and educator J. A. Adonde dubbed it, "the Black Super Bowl."[42] Eventually it would also link hip-hop and the NBA in a strong partnership.

In the early eighties, the most explicit mainstream link between basketball and hip-hop was Kurtis Blow's hit single "Basketball." Beyond its catchy lyrics ("Basketball is my fav-o-rite sport. I love the way they dribble up and down the court"), the song's music video became iconic after it aired on MTV, showcasing Blow in a blue track suit, a basketball game that turned into a karate showdown (Bruce Lee films were still all the rage), and a group of rapping cheerleaders. The song referenced Knicks greats Reed, Monroe, and King, while the music video featured photographs of Micheal Ray Richardson.[43] Blow was a pioneering voice in rap music, not only by spinning lines about the connections between basketball and hip-hop ("to the hoop, y'all!") but also as an alternative to other popular Black music in the 1980s, like that of Michael Jackson, Whitney Houston, and Tina Turner. Even Blow's light-hearted rap reflected, as one historian reminds us, "the hard times and hardships African Americans faced during Reagan's presidency."[44]

The two most forward-facing outlets of Black culture were basketball and hip-hop. Collectively, they were potential avenues of advancement and recognition for young men of color. On the court, Black players came to dominate play—the 1984 All-Star game featured nine Black starters as

Larry Bird was the only white player on the court at tip-off—and hip-hop was growing in popularity, emerging as "a way of being seen and, more importantly, of being heard when all other forces attempted to suffocate the Black voice."[45]

By mid-March 1984, the Knicks (who had only two white players; Grunfeld and little-used reserve Eric Fernsten) were rolling. At 41–25, they were just a half-game behind the 76ers for the third-best record in the Eastern Conference. King was clearly the Knicks' star, but his teammates were becoming increasingly comfortable in their roles, especially the team's five-man bench group. "When we come into the game," Grunfeld explained, "it changes the tempo. The first unit plays a power game with the offense geared to Billy Cartwright and Bernard King. When we come in, we're supposed to harass and force opposing teams into taking the quick shot. We're supposed to try and score off the breaks."[46] Starters King, Cartwright, Williams, Sparrow, and Robinson played more traditionally; reserves Grunfeld, Louis Orr, Tucker, Walker, and Marvin Webster offered a change of pace and, as Hubie anticipated earlier in the season, fit in flawlessly when minor injuries—like a Robinson ankle sprain in late February—forced the team to adjust on the fly. The only troubling medical report was that King dislocated both middle fingers in the span of a few games in late March and early April. But he came back strong, exploding with 44 points against the Detroit Pistons in his return.

The Knicks easily made the playoffs (eight of eleven Eastern Conference teams qualified), finishing the season with a 47–35 record, which earned them a first-round matchup against the 49-win Pistons. Five years later, Detroit's "Bad Boys" would win their first of two straight NBA titles powered by Isiah Thomas, Bill Laimbeer, Mark Aguirre, Rick Mahorn, Joe Dumars, and Dennis Rodman. Now they were led by Thomas and high-scoring forward Kelly Tripucka, but Laimbeer was already well on his way to becoming a Bad Boy. "Early in the first game," King said later, "I went up for a layup, and [Laimbeer] smashed my hand against the backboard. I know he did it on purpose . . . he was a dirty player."[47] Thanks to Laimbeer's physical play and 26 points from Tripucka, Detroit led by as many as 14 in the second half. Hubie was so irate at the officiating that he was ejected in the middle of the fourth quarter—his fourth ejection of the season—turning the team over to assistant coaches Richie Adubato and Rick Pitino.

Brown's ejections provided Pitino with the first NBA head coaching experience of his career. Prior to joining Brown's staff in 1983, Pitino led Boston University to the NCAA tournament. After two years on the sideline with Hubie, Pitino would return to the college game as the head coach of Providence College. After earning acclaim for taking the Friars to the Final Four in 1987, Pitino would return to New York as the new head coach of the Knicks for another two-year stint in the Big Apple before resigning to join the staff at the University of Kentucky where he would gain godlike status in the Bluegrass State.

But in 1984, whether spurred by Hubie's tirade, Pitino's tactical brilliance, or general chutzpah, the Knicks roared back in game one against the Pistons, and Walker stole the ball twice in the last two minutes (giving him seven for the game) to lead the Knicks on a late 9–1 run to pull out a 94–93 win. "Can we come back?" Thomas sullenly asked reporters after the game, "I don't know."[48]

Two nights later, the teams met again in Detroit. King, who scored 36 in the first game of the series, exploded in game two. He scored 46 (on 35 shots) and pulled down 6 rebounds. But late in the game, King lost his cool when one heckler yelled "isn't it time you had a drink?" and another came out of the stands to stand right behind the Knicks bench, touching King on the shoulder. King was enraged and took off after the fan; fortunately, Norman Scott, the team physician, got Bernard to stop.[49] King's demons obviously remained a touchy subject for the Knicks' forward, who had run afoul of law enforcement several times in the late seventies and early eighties. Dave DeBusschere told reporters, "I talked to a lot of people, and they all told me he had straightened himself out."[50]

Perhaps channeling his anger at Detroit fans into his on-court play, King averaged more than 40 points per game over the series. The Pistons had no answer. "We tried fronting him, backing him, everything," Detroit coach Chuck Daly recalled. "He was utterly magnificent. He shoots the ball on the way up and gets the shot off so fast he leaves you flat-footed."[51] But for all King's individual brilliance, the Knicks split the two games in Detroit and then the two at home to set up a decisive fifth game, scheduled for April 27 in the Motor City.

While the Pistons played in New York, the Pontiac Silverdome was being filled with dirt for a motocross event. So, instead of playing at their usual arena, the Pistons had to change venues for game five, moving thirty miles southeast to downtown Detroit's Joe Louis Arena. The Pistons had never played in Joe Louis, which was primarily used to host the NHL's Red Wings, and Detroit's team trainer had to give his players directions to find the facility.[52] More than twenty thousand Detroit fans, however, knew precisely where Joe Louis was and packed the historic arena to watch the Knicks and Pistons play in the winner-take-all fifth game.

King showed up battling flu and riding a streak of three straight 40-point games. The air was stifling in the arena—King compared it to playing in a sauna, and Sparrow called it "very intense." Fittingly, the teams went after one another like they were re-creating Joe Louis's immortal match against Max Schmeling. "It was like a 15-round championship fight, and the guy on his feet at the end wins," Daly recalled decades later.[53] Brown too would still vividly remember that game. "It was a hundred degrees outside and inside it was worse," he joked. "After five minutes I had my jacket off, had water in my shoes—I have a little short-sleeved shirt on. Chuck Daly, dressed impeccably at the other end, has a Brioni suit on that costs $5,000 and he's not taking it off." Brown chuckled at the memory. "I asked if he ever wore it again and he said 'I'd soaked it through the back so it looked like a navy blue suit.' So, they couldn't resurrect that suit."[54]

With two minutes left, it looked like the Knicks were going to win the fight on points, with a 106–98 lead after King scored points 33 and 34. But then Thomas, the Pistons' third-year point guard, took over. First he hit a pair of jump shots from the lane, then drew back-to-back fouls from Sparrow. With less than a minute left, Thomas took the ball and drove the length of the court, dribbling around and through all five Knicks defenders to score a layup and draw a foul; his free throw pulled the Pistons to within three, 112–109.

King and Thomas traded baskets before Isiah hit a three-pointer to tie the game at 114 with 23 seconds left. The crowd's roar became deafening. Walker turned the ball over on the inbounds pass, and suddenly the Pistons had the ball with a chance to win the game in regulation. Everybody at Joe Louis Arena—hell, everyone watching the game on television or listening on the radio too—knew the ball was going to Thomas. So did the Knicks. Walker was just a rookie but was also a dogged defender with long arms who stood three inches taller than the Pistons' lead guard. Thomas took the pass as his teammates fanned out around the perimeter. The crowd stood in anticipation, cheering and screaming as Isiah pounded the ball rhythmically against the hardwood. He then started his drive to the basket, hoping to make a shot or draw a foul. But Walker suddenly snaked his hand out and tipped the ball away as the clock ticked to zero, ending regulation.

More than twenty thousand fans sat down. This heavyweight fight was headed into overtime. "That game was the most intense I ever played," King later admitted, "it was the greatest."[55] Even though the Pistons missed eleven straight shots in the extra period, and Laimbeer fouled out, Thomas refused to give up, willing the Pistons back into the game with five quick points on a three-pointer and layup, pulling his team to within two. With less than a minute left, the Knicks worked the ball to Cartwright. Thomas tried to steal the ball from the Knicks center but was called for his sixth foul, sending him to the bench. Cartwright hit both free throws, icing the game and closing out the series. "I'll never forget this game," Tripucka said afterward. He was obviously exhausted, playing 47 of the games 53 minutes, and scoring 23 points in a losing effort. Asked by reporters what he was going to do after the game, Tripucka joked, "I guess I'll drink beer, eat Wendy's and get fat again."[56] Six years later, the Pistons would eliminate the Knicks from the playoffs en route to their second straight title. But in '84, it was New York moving forward.

In the summer of 1984, Los Angeles hosted the Olympic Games. Perhaps most known for the Soviet boycott, the Games nonetheless provided many memorable moments. Rafer Johnson became the first Black man to light the cauldron opening the Games, Carl Lewis won four gold medals in track and field, Mary Lou Retton won the gymnastics all-around competition, and the men's basketball team—coached by Bob Knight—won the tournament, powered by Michael Jordan and future Knick Patrick Ewing. And during the closing ceremonies, hip-hop was broadcast worldwide. As Lionel Richie performed "All Night Long," hundreds of young men (including future actor Cuba Gooding Jr.) conducted an extended, and extensively choreographed, breakdancing routine, complete with head-spins, toprock, ass-spins, and even some downrock.

B-boy dancing (called breakdancing by mainstream media, much to the chagrin of real B-boys and B-girls) witnessed a brief resurgence in popularity from 1983 to 1984. Part of its appeal was the hit 1983 film *Flashdance*, featuring Jennifer Beals as a ballet dancer who embraces street dancing to succeed in her audition. In that film, the Rock Steady Crew performs on the sidewalk as Beals's character is joined by a growing group to watch, spellbound. The next year, *Breakin'* and its sequel *Breakin' 2: Electric Boogaloo*, both set in California, recognized modest box office success but became cult hits. (The soundtrack for the sequel included the first album credit for a very young Ice-T.)

For Beals, and for kids who took up the B-boy mantle, hip-hop dance became a form of expression, a way "to use your body to inscribe your identity on the streets . . . a physical version of two favorite modes of street rhetoric: the taunt and the boast."[57] Dancing paralleled rap, using sharp moves instead of sharp words as a means of self-expression. Soon it was a national phenomenon, even featured on the cover of *Newsweek*, but it would be a short-lived fad. The problem, as one journalist wrote,

Figure 13. The Eastwood Rockers and spectators, July 26, 1984. The crew members went by the names of Muller, MC, Freakie Friday, Trix, and Hower. Trinity Mirror/Mirrorpix/Alamy Stock Photo.

was that "rap had product. It had something you could sell."[58] Break-dancing didn't. And so, despite its popularity that summer, B-boying once again faded from the national conscious by the end of the year.

Heading into their second-round playoff series with Boston, a few months before those Olympic Games, the Knicks knew they were in for a battle. The Celtics, who would probably peak two years later with their legendary 1986 title-winning team, boasted a 62–20 record. League MVP Larry Bird (who averaged 24 points, 10 rebounds, and nearly 6 assists per game—and had been passed up by the Knicks in the 1978 draft) led a potent frontcourt, joined by Sixth Man of the Year Kevin McHale, Cedric "Cornbread" Maxwell, and All-Star center Robert Parish. Their backcourt, bolstered by the recent addition of Dennis Johnson from the Suns, played strong defense and fit perfectly around Bird and company. During the regular season, the Knicks and Celtics split their six-game series, with each team winning twice on the road, and a thrilling double-overtime Knicks win in late November was still fresh in both team's minds.

Before game one of the Eastern Conference semifinals, several Celtics provided the Knicks with quality bulletin board material. Reserve forward M. L. Carr told reporters, "Bernard has scored his last 40 points," while Maxwell promised, "We're going to stop the bitch."[59] Yet King remained serene. "The game's played on the court, not in the newspapers. Good players don't talk that way," he said.[60] McHale was usually a prankster and instigator but this time tried to smooth everything over. "Max didn't mean anything by the remark," he told the *Times*, "everyone on this team talks funny."[61] But Bird also got in a few jabs, telling reporters, "I don't feel I get the calls Bernard gets and he always complains. If I get half the calls he gets and got to the line 10 times a game, I could average 30, too."[62] The bad blood went beyond verbal sparring, of course, and tensions flared early in the first game. It was clear—as Grunfeld said later—the Celtics and Knicks "really hated each other."[63]

Boston won game one, 110–92, as Maxwell held King to 26 points. As usual, it was Bird carrying the load for Boston, flirting with a triple-double, scoring 23 points, hauling down 9 rebounds, and handing out 12 assists, many of them to McHale, who led Celtics scorers with 25.

Game two followed a similar script, with the Celtics pulling out another win in Boston behind 37 points from Bird and 24 from McHale.

King managed only 13 and, while it was great that Cartwright suddenly came alive and dropped in 25 points against arguably the best frontcourt in NBA history, the 116–102 loss put the Knicks halfway toward elimination. "I don't have a calculator," Maxwell told reporters after game two, "but for [King] to average 40 or more, he's got to score 60." Up two games to none, McHale—who had downplayed Maxwell's pre-series comments—came up with his own analogy. "Right now they're lying down in the grave," he boasted. "We've got the shovel in our hands. They've got the heartbeat. We have to keep throwing dirt on them."[64]

For game three, hoping to stave off the gravedigger, Hubie made a few adjustments, playing the starters a little more and the bench unit a little less. He also decided to bring Ray Williams off the bench, using Tucker in the starting lineup instead. But maybe most importantly, the battle shifted from the parquet in Boston Garden to the hardwood of Madison Square. Vendors teemed outside the arena, hawking T-shirts and hats that read "St. Bernard" on the front and "Our Savior—1984 Season" on the back.[65] Everyone in the Garden for game three expected King to put the Knicks on his shoulders and carry them to victory. Instead, three Knicks scored more than 20 apiece; Ray Williams chipped in 22 off the bench, King scored 24, and Cartwright poured in 25, including 11 of 12 from the free throw line. But the real stars might have been the fans. "Our crowd was so raucous," King later explained, "you'd have thought an earthquake tremor was rumbling through the arena."[66] Maybe the Garden could be Eden again?

Boston remained confident going into the fourth game of the series, but the Knicks came out hot, racing to a double-digit lead in the first quarter, and never looked back, winning 118–113 thanks to 43 from King. Bird complained that New York was playing a zone defense. Pitino fired back. "If you watch what we're doing, we're going after the ball. We're rotating our defense. That's not a zone," he told the *Daily News*.[67] Bird was clutching at straws, trying to distract the Knicks, who clearly had the momentum after their second straight win. Later, when asked about a rivalry between him and King, Bird admitted that he didn't guard Bernard. "I had no chance guarding Bernard," he laughed. "Maxwell didn't either, by the way."[68] Maxwell was curiously quiet after King's scoring outburst in game four. "They can dig all the graves and throw all the dirt they want," Williams told reporters.[69] McHale allowed, "Now we're fighting over the shovel," but he added, "If it takes me to get them motivated, then they're in the wrong league."[70]

Game five of the 1984 Eastern Conference semifinals might have been the most memorable blowout loss in Knicks history. Boston jumped out to an early lead and led by a dozen after the first quarter. By halftime, they had extended it to 21 points: 66–45. But the Knicks chipped away early in the third and pulled to within 13. Driving down the court on a fast break, Williams found Walker near the basket with a picture-perfect pass. Celtics' guard Danny Ainge, who gained quite a reputation for his sneakily dirty play, flew into Walker, forearms extended into his face—one reporter called it a "double-forearm shiver."[71] "I fouled him unintentionally," Ainge insisted, "I wasn't trying to hurt him. I was trying to prevent a three-point play. I wouldn't call it a flagrant foul."[72] The Knicks saw it differently. "He hit me in the chin and neck," Walker said, "and I just retaliated."[73] Walker threw wild punches at Ainge, and both benches cleared. Carr got in a few cheap shots, which nearly set off Bernard. "That's dirty basketball. He's a dirty player. That's unacceptable, especially from someone as insignificant as him," King told the *Post* afterward.[74] Referees ejected Walker and Ainge, and even Hubie got in on the action, although he ended up on the floor in the melee. "It makes you feel young to go out there," Hubie explained later, "but as soon as you bounce off one of those guys, you know why you should've stayed on the bench."[75] The NBA fined the two instigators ($500 for Walker, $750 for Ainge) and seventeen other players for leaving the bench ($150 apiece).[76] New York lost 121–99, but clearly the bad blood was running hot with two must-win games for the Knicks looming.

On May 11, almost twenty thousand fans packed Madison Square Garden to watch game six of the best-of-seven series. It was the rowdiest crowd the Knicks had seen in a decade. "The fans will be ready for a boxing match," King said. "They will be pumped up, and so will we. It's do or die. We don't want to die." Maxwell and his Celtics teammates knew they needed to jump out to an early lead to deflate the home crowd. "They're the most vocal in the league with their chants. It's really getting more intense," he admitted.[77] Maxwell's fears came to fruition, though, as New York, not Boston, jumped ahead early. "As we grew our lead," King remembered, "the fans' war cry got louder. We could hear it reverberating through the Garden: 'Boston sucks! Boston SUCKS! BOSTON

Figure 14. Fight at the Knicks-Celtics playoff game at the Boston Garden, May 9, 1984. AP Photo/Paul Benoit. © 1984 Associated Press.

SUCKS!" Despite the loud crowd, Bird scored 35 points, pulled down 11 rebounds, and handed out 7 assists. McHale added 16 points and 10 rebounds, and Gerald Henderson, often overshadowed by the Celtics' dominant frontcourt, scored 20. But it was not enough. King led all scorers with 44 points, and Cartwright again played like a man possessed (14 points and 14 rebounds) as the crowd "threatened to roar the roof off the Garden, and send it spinning into space." Even Maxwell had to admit that King was operating on another level. "He wasn't running down the baseline, he was flying," Cornbread told the *Daily News*.[78] King was at the peak of his powers. His quick first step forced defenders to back away from him on the perimeter, but, even when they knew it was coming, he would blow by them or bully them toward the basket for an easy turnaround jump shot. The fans were rabid after the game, charged up about the Knicks forcing a winner-take-all seventh game. "We needed a police escort to get away from Madison Square Garden," Bird remembered. "The bus driver had to drive the wrong way on a one-way street to get us out of there."[79]

Facing game seven, this time in Boston, both teams were on edge. "You always want to avoid a one-game series, especially with Bernard as hot as he is," McHale told reporters. "Getting into a situation like that, he can single-handedly get 100 points."[80] Looking back, the idea of King dropping 100 on the Celtics in 1984 seems laughable. But in the moment, anything seemed possible. King was scoring 40-plus by taking 25 or 30 shots. What if he shot the ball twice as much? King usually scored quietly, letting the points pile up in small groups of two or three baskets at a time. What if he simply told his teammates to clear out and let him take Maxwell or Bird or McHale off the dribble every time?

Stories about playoff games in Boston Garden during Red Auerbach's time as president of the Celtics are legendary. No hot water in the visitors' showers. Locker rooms so hot they felt like saunas. You name it, Auerbach probably tried it. So, with game seven looming, the Celtics made sure to tweak the Knicks at least a little. John Hewig vividly remembers that afternoon:

> We get there, and our dressing room is locked, and Hubie says to me, 'John, go get the maintenance guy to open the fucking door,' and his veins are popping. Its two hours before the game. So I'm walking around the bowels of the old Boston Garden. In maintenance, there's a young guy sitting with his feet up on the desk, and he's not the head guy, and I kind of knew the head guy a little bit. . . . I looked at the guy, and he said, "Can I help you?"
> I said, "I'm John Hewig from the Knicks, and I'm looking for Joe."
> He said, "Oh yeah, Joe. He's a good Catholic. He's at church, you know."
> I said, "We've got to get our dressing room door unlocked. Can you help me?"
> And he said, "No, the only one with the key is Joe."
> I said, "You don't have a key?"
> And he said, "No, but he'll be back at eleven." And this is like at ten fifteen.
> I said, "well, what am I supposed to tell my coach?"
> He said, "I don't know. You're from New York, aren't you?" And he knew all this. He'd been coached by Red Auerbach. He knew all this. So he says, "You know, I might have a solution. I've got keys to these two other dressing rooms that are on the other side of the building. They're small, but you guys could fit into them. Like six and six, if you wanted to do that."
> I said, "You're kidding, right?"
> He said no, he wasn't kidding
> And I said, "Okay, come with me, you're going to tell my coach this."
> Hubie is ranting and raving in the hallway: "What the fuck is going on?"

And he's stomping around as I'm walking up there with this guy. I said, "Hubie, the guy who has the key is at church. He's not going to be back until eleven. But this guy here has a solution." And he tells Hubie what it is. And Hubie says 'Okay, all right, boys, let's go. Follow me."

And we follow the guy, and we go halfway around the building, and he gets to the dressing room doors, and they're next to each other. And he opens them up with this key, and he says, "You guys gonna be fine in here," and the stink in there in both of them was horrendous.

And I've always said Red Auerbach had every employee in the Boston Garden go in there and take a shit Friday night, and then they turned the water off and closed the doors. And we went in, and the players and Hubie and everybody was like "oh God, what is this stink?"[81]

Across the arena, in their own locker room, the Celtics had no idea of what New York's players were dealing with. They just knew they had to win one more game against a hot Knicks team. Bird, normally confident to the point of cockiness, sat by his locker wringing his hands. "Very often I have strong positive feelings before big games," he remembered later. "But I wasn't sure about that seventh game. I knew that if Bernard stayed hot, it would go down to the wire. The only thing making me feel good at all was that we were playing in the Boston Garden."[82]

Thanks to Bird, Boston jumped out to an early 22–4 lead and by halftime still led 67–52. The Celtics breezed in the second half, winning by 17. "New York's M.V.P. won it for the Knicks Friday night [game six] in New York and the N.B.A.'s M.V.P. won it for us today," McHale smugly told reporters.[83] Maxwell, though, was drained. "I'm sick of Bernard King. I don't want to see him anymore . . . after seven straight games of Bernard King, I'm having nightmares about the guy."[84] Less than a month later, the Celtics defeated the Lakers to win the NBA title.

May 1984 seemed to be the start of something great for Knicks fans. Their team took the eventual champs to seven hard-fought games in the playoffs, King was one of the best players in the NBA, and most of his teammates were just entering their primes. Instead, the season marked the highpoint in the era after Eden.

1983–84 Knicks

Record: 47–35

Playoffs: Won Eastern Conference first round versus Detroit Pistons; lost Eastern Conference semifinals versus Boston Celtics

Coach: Hubie Brown
Average Home Attendance: 12,096
Points per Game: (106.9–17th of 23)
Points Allowed per Game: (103.0–3rd of 23)
Team Leaders:

Points: Bernard King (26.3 per game)
Rebounds: Truck Robinson and Bill Cartwright (8.4 per game)
Assists: Rory Sparrow (6.8 per game)
Steals: Ray Williams (2.1 per game)
Blocked Shots: Bill Cartwright and Marvin Webster (1.3 per game)

All-Stars: Bernard King
Notable Transactions: Drafted Darrell Walker in the first round of the
1983 NBA Draft

10

THE FROZEN ENVELOPE

1984–1985

You're the kind of guy that girl ignored
I'm drivin' a Caddy, you fixin' a Ford"
—"ROCK BOX," RUN-DMC, 1984

In March 1984, DJ Run, DMC, and Jam Master Jay (Run-DMC) released their debut studio album with Profile Records. The single "It's Like That / Sucker MCs" was a hit, and so was their self-titled album, fusing hard rock and hip-hop, a combination highlighted by their 1985 album *King of Rock* (the first platinum hip-hop album) and 1986 collaboration with Aerosmith, "Walk This Way."[1] Run-DMC also marked a change in generation. As Grandmaster Caz recalls, "That was the end of our era, when Run-DMC and them came into the game."[2] Run-DMC "offered a new sense of blackness," historian Todd Boyd writes. It was "a way of being seen and, most importantly, of being heard where all other forces attempted to suffocate the Black voice."[3]

On the court for the Knicks, more changes were afoot. Ray Williams, acquired a year earlier for a first-round draft pick, was let go. Worse, he signed with the hated Celtics, leaving the Knicks with little to show for the short-sighted trade. After retiring, Ray became a cautionary tale for young players in the league. By his fortieth birthday, Ray was divorced and bankrupt, having lost his New Jersey home. Soon he was living in Florida, working odd jobs, and by the mid-2000s living in his car, fishing to feed himself. Fortunately, a *Boston Globe* story in 2010 brought attention to Williams's situation. "They say God won't give you more than you can handle," Williams said at the time, "but this is wearing me out." Former teammate Mike Glenn understood better than most the problems players of his generation faced. "Ray is like many players who invested so much of their lives in basketball," he said. "When the dividends stopped coming, the problems started escalating. It's a cold reality."[4] Former teammates helped Ray, moving him back to Mount Vernon where he worked with kids in his city's parks department, before he passed away in 2013.

But in the summer of 1984, the earlier trade for Williams cost the Knicks a first-round choice in arguably the greatest draft in league history. University of Houston center Akeem (later Hakeem) Olajuwon went first to the Houston Rockets, Sam Bowie ended up in Portland with the second pick (some rumors had the Knicks acquiring Bowie for Cartwright), and the Chicago Bulls used the third pick on Michael Jordan. Sam Perkins, Charles Barkley, and John Stockton followed in the next dozen picks.

"We all just cried through the first couple of rounds," Pitino recalled.[5] The pickings were slim by the time the Knicks were on the clock—at the end of the third round, and they didn't add anyone who made an impact at the pro level.

"We are extremely happy with our progress this season," head coach Hubie Brown told reporters. "It gives us something to build on."[6] But the Knicks management was also right up against the new NBA salary cap—which sat at $4.6 million for the following season—and could only recoup part of the salary savings if they cut veteran role players. Plus, any significant cuts would decrease their depth, which had allowed them to run their two-unit system. "That's the depressing part," one unnamed Knicks official admitted. "We're not good enough yet, but we don't have the maneuverability to improve."[7] Despite promising fans that changes would be made, DeBusschere was hamstrung. "I don't think anybody fully understands the salary cap," he said, "including the league, ourselves, and the players' association. No one knows fully what can and cannot be done."[8]

Hoping to bolster the Knicks roster with players who could help immediately, DeBusschere signed Dallas forward Pat Cummings and Detroit swingman Vinnie "The Microwave" Johnson, to free agent offer sheets.

The Pistons matched New York's three-year, $1.4 million offer, but the Mavericks let Cummings go to New York on a four-year, $2 million deal. After missing on Johnson, the Knicks went after San Antonio Spurs guard John Paxson with a creative offer. Paxson was offered a six-year contract for an initial salary of just $75,000 in his first year, ballooning to $500,000 each of the last five years. Additionally, he would receive a $2.5 million signing bonus and $3.5 million loan.[9] Skirting the salary cap with a low base salary, but with exorbitant perks that might drive the value of the contract to eight figures, the Knicks hoped to manipulate the salary cap in their favor and keep the Spurs from matching. This proposal went to arbitration, and Paxson ended up re-signing with San Antonio, but the Knicks deserve credit for their creativity.

Innovative contract structures were a hallmark of the Knicks in the early salary cap era. Mel Lowell handled those negotiations and developed a flair for creativity. There were no Excel spreadsheets, and the math was still new to every franchise. "I used to try and come up with ways to beat the salary cap," Lowell told me, laughing.[10] DeBusschere and Lowell would regularly go out for drinks at a restaurant on Fifty-Ninth Street and First Avenue known as TJ Tucker's to discuss cap workarounds. Like the Knicks, another New York city institution got a makeover in the summer of 1984. Nearly one hundred years earlier, President Grover Cleveland had dedicated the Statue of Liberty, a gift from France, following a parade that started at Madison Square Garden. Now Lady Liberty needed a little body work done; her right arm was corroded and her head slightly off center. So the statue was closed to the public for more than two years while undergoing a multimillion-dollar facelift.[11]

As the 1984–85 season approached, the Knicks were in good position to move up the standings although, if anything, their Atlantic Division rivals improved as well. Boston remained the team to beat in the East, while the Sixers added Auburn's "Round Mound of Rebound," Charles Barkley, to their already potent lineup, featuring Moses Malone and Dr. J. The Bullets added high-scoring forward Cliff Robinson, while the Nets' backcourt of Richardson and Otis Birdsong, flanked by twenty-four-year-old All-Star forward Buck Williams, was young and exciting.

Then disaster struck, giving Knicks fans a taste of what the upcoming season would deliver. During the summer, Cartwright was out jogging, trying to stay in playing shape, when he stepped on a rock. "It kind of hurt my foot a little bit," he explains. "But being stubborn or stupid, I kept running on it." Eventually, Cartwright saw team physician Norman Scott, who diagnosed it as a stress fracture and fit the Knicks' center with a removable cast so he could swim to stay in shape. "I don't know how well he swims," Scott joked at the time, "but I guarantee he'll swim a lot better after these few weeks."[12]

With Cartwright out and Len Elmore (who spent one season with the Knicks) announcing his retirement to attend Harvard Law School, it looked like Webster might have to step back in as the team's starting center.[13] Then more disaster struck. Less than a month before opening night, Webster checked into the hospital, suffering from extreme fatigue. "He came to camp in poor physical shape," Hubie told the *Times*, "and we were hoping he would play himself into shape."[14] As it turned out, it was not a case of Webster being lazy; he was later diagnosed with hepatitis and acute anemia. Like Cartwright, Webster was expected to miss the first two months. A few days later, the prognosis changed again, and the Knicks announced that Webster would miss the entire season. The Human Eraser would play just fifteen more games in his NBA career.

Despite the injuries, opening night, October 27, 1984, was an exciting one for the hometown Knicks, hosting one of their playoff nemeses, the Detroit Pistons. Behind the play of Thomas, Tripucka, and Laimbeer, the Pistons jumped out to an early lead and managed to foul out the Knicks' big free agent acquisition, Pat Cummings, in just seven minutes of play. But New York came storming back and cruised to an easy 137–118 win, punctuated by 34 points from King.

The real story, though, was the team's backup center. With Webster and Cartwright (and Truck Robinson) sidelined, unheralded Eddie Lee Wilkins, their sixth-round pick, got a shot. He responded beyond anyone's wildest dreams, scoring 24 points and pulling down 10 rebounds thanks to his energy and hustle. And his excitement was contagious. "The kid played with such enthusiasm that he was getting himself involved," Pitino told reporters.[15] After every basket, Wilkins busted out a dance and pumped his fists in the air, ramping up the crowd. Maybe this kid could be the second-unit center Hubie loved.

New York's second game was less thrilling for Knicks fans. Wilkins was sidelined with a sprained foot (which eventually had to be put in a cast), leaving recently acquired James Bailey to back up Cummings, playing out of position at center. Bailey filled in admirably, but injuries were already taking their toll. The Knicks lost that second game, 117–111, to Utah, whose rookie guard John Stockton handed out the fourteenth assist and gained the fifth steal of his professional career. Twenty years later, Stockton would retire with 15,806 assists and 3,265 steals, both NBA records.

On November 8, the Knicks, with a gruesome 1–6 record, hosted another rookie sensation: Michael Jordan. Nearly twenty thousand fans packed the Garden to see the young Bull, who stole the show. As the clock wound down on the third quarter, Jordan stole the ball from Grunfeld and drove the length of the court for a one-handed dunk, tongue wagging the whole way, to extend Chicago's lead to 23. Knicks fans knew greatness when they saw it, and gave Jordan a standing ovation, even as their team dropped to 1–6 on the season.

Things went from bad to worse a few days after the embarrassing defeat to Chicago. While rehabbing with a light workout, Cartwright reinjured his left foot, fracturing the same bone he had hurt in the off-season. The cast went back on, and Dr. Scott estimated his return as January at the earliest. Because the Knicks were above the salary cap, they could only replace Cartwright with a player earning the league minimum, and they had a hard time finding any takers. It didn't help that one potential replacement already on the roster, Truck Robinson, was unhappy with his role. "Right now, all I want out of basketball is to get rich," he told reporters. "If the Jazz will pay me another year, I'd be happy to play for them." Robinson never played another game for the Knicks, or any other NBA team for that matter, finishing his eleven-year career with a forgettable twenty minutes in New York's 105–93 loss to Houston's Twin Towers of Ralph Sampson and Akeem Olajuwon. Hubie was happy to get rid of Truck, once the apple of the coach's eye. "The guy's a child," he told the *Sporting News.* "He's got to face the fact that he's not the player he once was."[16] Hubie wasn't done piling on his centers, either. Of an injured Cartwright, Hubie told reporters, "He's got limitations, and that's why he's making $500,000 instead of $1 million a year."[17]

Throughout the turmoil, one constant was King. Two days after Thanksgiving, now improved to 6–9, the Knicks hosted the Indiana Pacers. King hit 14 of his first 18 shots from the field, finishing 19 for 31, and knocked down 14 free throws to finish with 52 points, shattering the

Figure 15. Bernard King, shooting over Adrian Dantley of the Utah Jazz at Madison Square Garden, 1984. Adam Stoltman/Alamy Stock Photo.

record for points scored in the new Madison Square Garden, opened in 1968. "We tried everything on him tonight," said Pacers' coach George Irvine, "we doubled and tripled him, but when he gets going, he can't be stopped."[18]

With King at the top of his game, the Knicks won six straight to pull their record to a respectable 8–9. Then King pulled a groin muscle and missed two weeks; the Knicks lost six of the next seven and suddenly found themselves back at the bottom of the division. With King out, the low point came in a 112–83 loss at home against the Mavericks. It was the Knicks' worst loss in three years and set a Mavericks franchise record for fewest points allowed. Cummings had signed with New York, at least in part, because they were a team competing for a title. Now Rolando Blackman, Mark Aguirre, and Sam Perkins formed a strong, young core for Cummings's former team. The next night, the Knicks roared back from an early double-digit deficit to the Bulls, only to watch helplessly as Jordan hit a buzzer-beating twenty-footer, the first of many game-winners in his NBA career.

On December 11, King returned to the Knicks lineup in a game against the 76ers. Despite 23 points from Moses Malone, 16 from Erving, and 7 (along with 7 rebounds) from Barkley, King's 34 points were enough to give the hometown team the win. King went on a roll after returning from his injury. Including the game against the Sixers, King scored 34, 30, 21, 29, 28, and 43 in his first six games back, setting up a huge Christmas Day game against the cross-river rivals from New Jersey.

One of the most beloved, mainstream hip-hop songs from the late-eighties is Run-DMC's "Christmas in Hollis," with its music video featuring Santa Claus on a sled pulled by a dog. In the 1988 film *Die Hard*, the limo driver Argyle jams to the song while waiting on John McClane to take out the bad guys in Nakatomi Plaza. Less well-known today, though it was huge at the time, was another hip-hop holiday single: Kurtis Blow's debut "Christmas Rappin.'" Released by Mercury Records in 1979, Blow's rendition includes Santa joining a house party, dancing, handing out TVs and stereos as gifts. Then Blow raps, "The dude in red's back at the Pole / Up north where everything is cold / But if he were right here tonight / He'd say Merry Christmas and to all a good night."

On Christmas Day 1984, the *New York Post* published an article relaying the holiday wishes of the Knicks' players. Backup center Ron Cavenall said, "I have my Christmas present . . . playing for the Knicks." King cracked, "I wish someone would teach Trent Tucker how to play blackjack." James Bailey also joked, "[I hope that] Louis Orr and I could exchange some pounds—a few of mine for him, which would mean less for me." Orr, apparently not in on the joke, wished for "peace and love throughout the world," while exuberant rookie center Eddie Lee Wilkins said, "I just want Santa Claus to bring us a win."[19]

Early in their game against the Nets, it looked like Wilkins would get his wish. New York jumped out to a double-digit lead, stretching it to as much as 16 points late in the second quarter before finishing the half with a ten-point advantage. But the real story was King, who had 40 of his team's 64 at halftime. "We wanted to hold King to 40 points," Nets center George Johnson joked, "but not in the first half."[20] Nets' coach Stan Albeck—that old washerwoman—switched the 36-year old center onto King in the second half, reasoning that "there was no one else left on the bench to go but George."[21] King started to slow down, but still got to 50 in the third quarter and seemed well on his way to setting the Knicks single-game record. In 1959, Richie Guerin tallied 57 points against the Syracuse Nationals. And now, on Christmas Day 1984, King hit 19 for 30 from the floor, and 22 of 26 free throws, giving him an even 60 points. But Johnson's height bothered King. Bernard hit just 1 of 9 shots facing the bigger man, and the Nets won the game, 120–114. Micheal Ray Richardson scored a career-high 36 for the Nets, including 24 in the second half, to ruin King's herculean effort.

Bernard King scoring 60 points on Christmas Day 1984 is a happy memory for long-time Knicks fans, most of whom probably forget that the Knicks lost that day. For King, the individual record was far less important than the team's record. "I'd rather score 15–20 points and win the game," he groused afterward. "The record just doesn't mean as much. This game should have been a blowout."[22] Still, King generally remained upbeat, even as the team around him failed to match his level of play. "We have a deficiency," he admitted, "but I think in the second half of the year we'll be able to turn it around. And you'll see an improved basketball team."[23]

King was also very forward-thinking in considering how his game might evolve into the 1990s. "When I get into my 30s," he explained, "I want to keep playing. It is important for a player to do more than one thing if he expects to prolong his career." One thing King certainly recognized was how taller players with greater skill ranges might affect the league in the future. "There is a trend in this league toward bigger players, and I want to stay ahead of the trend. If you look at the way this league is going, you've got 7–4 centers shooting 25-foot bank shots."[24] He was probably referring to Ralph Sampson, the second-year sensation for the Rockets. But even someone as prescient as King would have been hard-pressed to imagine players like Dirk Nowitzki or Karl-Anthony Towns, seven-footers who stretched defenses far beyond what Sampson accomplished in the early eighties.

Even with King playing at an All-NBA level, the losses continued to pile up. With a 12–22 record as 1985 began, the Knicks clung to playoff hopes; the Pacers (9–22) and Cavaliers (6–22) remained behind them in the Eastern Conference. But King was playing hurt—and then had to take time off because of a series of nagging groin and ankle injuries. And after managing only six minutes of action in a sixteen-point loss to the Bulls on January 11, King shut it down for several weeks. After a loss to the lowly Pacers, Hubie was livid, estimating that his team managed only one basket in "20 or 21 possessions" during one stretch in the second quarter. Before he talked to the press, Hubie slammed the locker room door closed and yelled at the team for a solid fifteen minutes. It didn't help. Their January 12 loss (100–95 against the lowly Pacers) set a club record with their twelfth straight road defeat and dropped them to an abysmal 13–27 on the season. A week later, an exasperated coach Brown admitted to reporters, "It's evident we can't win with this team."[25]

After missing almost a month of action, King came back strong in early February, putting up 23 points in each of his first two games and scoring 40+ on back-to-back nights. Then, on February 16, Bernard torched the Nets for the second time in three months, scoring 55 points in another losing effort against New Jersey. As usual, King's stat-line was impressively efficient. He took just 33 shots from the field (connecting on 19) and hit 17-of-23 free throws. He also pulled down 11 rebounds for good measure. By mid-March, the Knicks were far out of playoff contention, but King was still putting in his work. He topped 40 points thirteen times during the season—half after recovering from ankle, groin, and shin injuries.

During this hot streak, the Knicks approached King about a contract extension, and Bernard—making a little less than $900,000 per year—was open to discussions. Larry Bird earned more than double King's salary, and Bernard's agent, Bill Pollak, hoped to extract a similar sum from New York. Later King recalled that he had an offer from the Knicks for a five-year contract at about $1.6 million per season, a little less than Bird made but a hefty raise nonetheless. But Pollak and King decided to wait it out, expecting that league-wide interest for a player of Bernard's caliber would only go up when the summer free agent battles began in earnest.[26]

On March 22, again playing the Pacers, King put on a clinic, scoring 45 points and hauling down 12 rebounds to lead his Knicks to a 118–113 victory, giving them 24 wins (against 46 losses) on the season. That day, Pitino announced he was leaving New York to take the head coaching position at Providence College. Two years later, he would rejoin the Knicks as their head coach before—ultimately—having his greatest success as a college coach at the Universities of Kentucky and Louisville.

A day after Pitino made his announcement, the Knicks suffered an even greater loss. It started like a normal late-season game between two struggling teams. The 24–46 Knicks stopped booking chartered flights when the team was eliminated from playoff contention and had to fly to Kansas City on an early-morning commercial flight to make their March 23 game against the 27–43 Kings. The game was close for the first three quarters, and the Knicks clung to a one-point lead entering the fourth. Kansas City surged ahead and, with less than two minutes left, threatened to pull away. But then Orr intercepted an inbounds pass and threw the ball ahead to a streaking King, who tried to slip a pass to Wilkins near the basket. It was tipped, and in the scrum, the ball made its way to Reggie Theus, waiting at half-court. Theus scooped it up and drove for a layup. King put his head down and sprinted back on defense, meeting Theus at the rim as both men rose toward the hoop. "He didn't have to chase down Theus," Tucker said later. "But Bernard made the extra effort. He always did."[27]

As King planted, his knee popped. From the bench, Hubie said it sounded like gunfire, "like somebody shot him with a rifle," he explained to me.[28] On the video, it sounds like King yells "oh shit" and then "oh God," while Marv Albert, doing commentary for WWOR (Channel 9), simply said, "Look out . . . King hurt himself as he gave the foul." Teammates and medical personnel on the Knicks bench, just a few feet from where King landed, rushed onto the court as Bernard slammed his fist on the ground in pain. Neither Dr. Scott nor Mike Saunders, the team trainer, immediately knew the extent of the injury. It was initially diagnosed as a severely sprained knee, and Hubie was optimistic in the postgame, telling reporters, "[I hope] it is not something that will be devastating for him in the future."[29]

With an abundance of caution, the Knicks had Bernard travel by ambulance to Lenox Hill Hospital for evaluation. There King learned he had a broken bone, a torn lateral meniscus, and a ruptured ACL. He and his agent interviewed several top orthopedists from across the country before deciding that Dr. Scott should conduct the needed surgeries to repair the damage. Forty-one metal staples held his knee together after surgery, and Bernard hallucinated about Bengal tigers thanks to a generous dose of morphine.[30]

Publicly, Bernard was optimistic about his recovery, and his teammate (and longtime friend) Ernie Grunfeld noted that his spirits were improving.[31] Privately, though, King was distraught. He and an old high school teammate sat together in the hospital room that first night without talking. "I just sat there in the wheelchair and cried," King admitted. "I couldn't handle the prospect of my career being over."[32]

In the nearly four decades since King blew out his knee, modern medicine has made great strides in treating many sports-related injuries. Today, the estimated recovery time for an ACL tear is generally between nine and twelve months.[33] But in 1985, it was a career-killer.

The Knicks lost the game against the Kings and then spiraled out of control, dropping their last eleven games to end the season 24–58. After their final game, an 88–84 loss in Milwaukee, Hubie lashed out to the assembled press. "Who can you depend on from day to day?" he asked. "Who do you go to on offense? Hell, you have no idea what he's going to do or where he is. We only have one guy (rookie Ken Bannister) who can post up, and the guards are shooting terrible from the outside."[34] For the season, Knicks players missed 324 combined games, setting a new league record (one they would top the next year). Clearly the team had to make some changes. Eight Knicks were entering free agency, while two of their star players (Cartwright and King) had suffered serious injuries. Cummings and Orr were probably their best returning players, and—while both had carved out nice careers—neither had been a good enough collegiate player to be drafted in the first round.

Suddenly there was a serious talent shortage in the Big Apple.

In the early days of the NBA, teams were allowed "territorial" selections in the draft to stock their rosters with regionally familiar talent. Beginning in 1966, the worst team in the Eastern Conference and the worst team in the Western Conference participated in a coin flip, with the winner receiving the first pick in the draft and the loser the second. In 1969, that process sent Lew Alcindor to Milwaukee while the Suns settled for Neal Walk. Five years later, Portland got Bill Walton while Philadelphia chose Marvin "Bad News" Barnes, who ended up signing with the ABA Spirits of St. Louis. And in 1979, the Lakers kicked off the Showtime Era with their choice of Magic Johnson while the Bulls ended up with Dave Greenwood.

After the 1984 NBA Draft, in which the Rockets made headlines for having lost on purpose to earn a better shot at University of Houston center Akeem Olajuwon, and two years after Clippers owner Donald Sterling admitted that his team could "win by losing" to earn a better draft pick, the NBA's Board of Governors determined that the bottom seven teams would have an equal shot at the top slot in the 1985 draft through a lottery system.

Recognizing an opportunity for publicity, new NBA commissioner David Stern decided to promote the event as live theater, televising the draw on CBS (Channel 2 in New York City) at halftime of the first game of the Eastern Conference finals. Instead of just two teams with a shot at the top pick, there were now seven. And one of them was the Knicks.

Even as the wheels came off for the team after Bernard's injury, the Knicks front office remained hard at work preparing for the upcoming draft. In early April, reporters got an insider's view of the team's "war room," a conference room with a wallboard listing the top one hundred college seniors and a handful of eligible underclassmen. The Knicks' big board was color-coded; players with a first-round grade were printed on an orange card, while powder blue cards designated later round options. One orange card included the name Chris Mullin, a local kid from Brooklyn who led St. John's to the Final Four. DeBusschere admitted he was a Mullin fan but told reporters, "If there is a good big man, you always have to take him."[35]

In the 1985 draft, there was only one "good big man"—at least one who was a surefire NBA superstar. And it was a player whose team who had bounced Mullin and St. John's out of the NCAA tournament that spring, Patrick Ewing. Born in Jamaica, Ewing developed soccer and cricket skills before immigrating to Massachusetts at the age of twelve. As an immigrant, Ewing often felt like an outsider and faced intense racism as a teenager. Later in life, it left him guarded and distrustful of the media.[36] Yet he developed into an elite athlete and signed to play collegiate basketball with Georgetown, where larger-than-life head coach John Thompson was turning the program into a national powerhouse by recruiting and developing talented centers like Ewing, Alonzo Mourning, and Dikembe Mutombo. Ewing made national headlines by dominating the 1982 NCAA tournament as a freshman (despite losing to freshman Michael Jordan and North Carolina in the finals) and then helping the Hoyas win it all two years later. Now, coming off a disappointing tournament final-game loss to Villanova, Ewing was clearly ready for prime time.

As the draft lottery approached, it was clear who would be chosen with the first pick. But the identity of the team he would land on was, of course, still up in the air. Each of the seven eligible teams was allowed to send one representative to the proceedings. The Knicks chose DeBusschere. Dave, always superstitious, brought a lucky horseshoe with him from a horse named On the Road Again and attended morning Mass at St. Joseph's Church near his home on Long Island.[37] "I said some prayers, like I always do," DeBusschere told reporters, "and then I thought, I'll be a little selfish and ask for Patrick Ewing in the lottery."[38] The seven men sat awkwardly next to one another at a long table, knowing the future of their franchise rested with which envelope Stern pulled from the hopper. All eyes were on the commissioner.

"We took every precaution with this lottery," Stern told reporters later. "An internationally-known accounting firm, Ernst and Whitney, that handles the Miss America pageant handled it for us. Jack Wagner sealed the seven envelopes with the team logos in a room all alone. We placed them in the drum and turned the drum while I turned my head. I didn't look at the drum until I pulled out the first envelope."[39]

Why envelopes? Later the league would turn to a clandestine system of ping-pong balls. But in 1985, as Brian McIntyre, then head of the league's media relations department, remembers, "We were afraid of having the thing pop open and all the balls fly out."[40] In fact, during a dress rehearsal, one of the envelopes did fall out of the drum. Stern was horrified at the thought of that happening on national television. So, with cameras rolling,

Stern pulled out the winning team's envelope, took a deep breath, and set it aside. Then he began selecting the remaining six envelopes one by one from the clear plastic drum, counting down the picks from seventh to second.

The first envelope Stern opened revealed the logo of the Golden State Warriors. Coach Al Attles dropped his head and smiled in disbelief. Instead of receiving one of the top two picks, as they would have been guaranteed under the old system, they now had to choose seventh. (Don't feel too bad for Golden State. They would pick Mullin, who would later successfully team with Mitch Richmond and Tim Hardaway as "Run TMC.") Next, Stern pulled the envelope of the Sacramento Kings—recently relocated from Kansas City—followed by that of the Atlanta Hawks. Kings owner Bob Cook and Hawks general manager Stan Kasten each sighed in resignation.

Only four teams remained: the Indiana Pacers, Los Angeles Clippers, Seattle SuperSonics, and the Knicks. On the West Coast, Seattle had recently hosted a St. Patrick Ewing Day, but their envelope was the next pulled, disappointing their representative, Coach Lenny Wilkens. In Los Angeles, the Clippers required switchboard operators to work on Sunday to field calls for season ticket requests in case they landed the first pick. As general manager Carl Scheer looked on, theirs was the next envelope Stern revealed. Now there were just two.

A CBS camera briefly showed three men side by side—Herb Simon (the Pacers owner who two years earlier had lost a coin flip that would have sent Ralph Sampson to Indy), Carl Scheer (general manager of the Clippers), and DeBusschere—before it zoomed in on Scheer, smiling in resignation, and then moved to DeBusschere, whose closed his eyes briefly, with his hands folded in front of his face. Then Simon and DeBusschere were shown at once, with a divided screen. Simon's eyes were wide, staring intently at Stern. Then the commissioner drew the final envelope. "The second pick in the 1985 draft," Stern began, furiously trying to tear open the envelope, "goes to . . ."

You could hear a pin drop in the Starlight Roof on the eighteenth floor of the Waldorf Astoria in midtown.

"The Indiana Pacers," Stern finished. Simon stood up and then sat down again as if unsure how to move properly. DeBusschere slammed his huge fist on the table and visibly exhaled as Pat O'Brien, covering the event for CBS, said, "The horseshoe worked. Basketball is back in New York City, my friend!"[41] Stern shook hands with DeBusschere and handed him the card bearing the Knicks logo. Then CBS cut to commercial. After Stern announced the Knicks pick, Ewing, O'Brien interviewed DeBusschere, who admitted to being "very nervous" but also said he was excited about winning the lottery and showing off a Knicks jersey with Ewing's name and number, 33, stitched on the back.

Almost immediately, conspiracy theorists cried foul. Stan Kasten, the Hawks' general manager, claimed a "high-ranking-team executive" had told him weeks before the lottery, "[Ewing is] going to the Knicks. It's all arranged." Ernst and Whitney, who ran the lottery, also audited accounts for Gulf & Western. Stern claimed he did not know about the connection, but could Jack Wagner, the law partner responsible for sealing the envelopes backstage, have thrown one in the freezer so Stern could tell by feel which one was the Knicks' envelope? Likewise, the video from that day has been broken down frame-by-frame like the Zapruder film of JFK's assassination and even analyzed by professional magicians for signs of trickery. Wagner did bang one envelope against the inside of the plastic drum—was it accidental?—and Stern clearly took a deep breath before reaching in to grab the first envelope. Was he feeling guilty? "If people want to say that [the lottery was fixed], fine," Stern said at the time. "As long as they spell our name right. That means they're interested in us. That's terrific." Later, Stern would walk that back, calling accusations of a lottery fix "crazy" and "ridiculous."[42]

Unsurprisingly, the Ewing draft lottery conspiracy was a hot topic around the water cooler. "Hopefully this is all a coincidence," the *Dallas Morning News* said, "but the NBA has put itself in a position where suspicion clouds the lottery situation. Ewing to the Knicks—there's just something too convenient about that arrangement."[43] "How could you blame everyone for thinking the lottery was an out-and-out hoax?" Peter Vecsey admitted.[44] Even Kevin McHale got in on the ribbing. "It was rigged," he deadpanned before starting to laugh, "just kidding, guys."[45] Hubie saw the outcome as divine providence. "It's kind of an atonement for the incredible suffering of last season," he said.[46] "We need medical miracles. But . . . it's been a great day for the Knicks."[47]

Even other teams understood, if reluctantly, the potential value of having a marquee player like Ewing in New York City. "There is no question in my mind that it was done fairly," the Clippers Scheer. "But I would be less than honest and candid if I didn't say it's good for the league."[48] Jack Krumpe joked with reporters, "I told them how to fix it 60 days ago. You call up Ernst & Whitney and you say 'If we don't get Ewing you're fired!'" Then, maybe understanding that this would only fuel the conspiracy theorists, he quickly qualified his statement. "If it was fixed," he told reporters, "I would've just gone to the beach."[49]

Rigged or not (that argument is not going away anytime soon), Knicks fans were ecstatic about the outcome of the lottery. "The Knicks will win the championship next season," one fan told reporters. The Madison Square Garden box office was flooded with season ticket requests. "For two or three hours after the lottery ended," one Knicks employee told the *Times*, "we received more than 1,000 calls." Krumpe also told reporters that the team might need to "redesign some of our season-ticket stratagems," hinting that their existing prices ($688 per seat for lower-level season tickets down to $344 for the mezzanine) might need to be increased with Ewing coming to town.[50] Even with a potential price increase, the number of season tickets almost doubled for 1985–86, skyrocketing from around 5,700 to nearly 11,000 after the lottery.[51]

In the Bronx, Spike Lee took a break from shooting *She's Gotta Have It*, in which he played a young B-boy bike messenger named Mars Blackmon, to buy his first set of season tickets. [52] It so happened that on the night of the lottery his girlfriend told Spike she was breaking up with him. "I considered the error of my ways," Spike remembered, "bit my lip. Picked up the phone. Punched the digits. Swallowed my pride. Time for commitment."[53] But the number he dialed wasn't his now-ex-girlfriend's; it was the number of the Knicks box office. Tickets would go on sale the next morning at eight, he was told, and the next morning he arrived three hours early. Spike's first seats were green seats in section 304 on the second promenade. Eventually he would have courtside seats. In the 1994 Eastern Conference finals, after Indiana Pacers' guard Reggie Miller hit five three-pointers in the fourth quarter of game five, NBA fans would gain the lasting image of Miller's throat-choking motions toward Lee at courtside.[54]

Knicks fans like Lee predicted a return to greatness for their beloved team. "In New York," Walter Leavy wrote in *Ebony*, "embarrassment has almost become a way of life. It's not a situation that New Yorkers cherish.

However, Ewing's arrival signals the beginning of a new era."[55] Surely after a decade of the team wandering the desert, Ewing would finally lead the Knicks to the promised land.

1984–85 Knicks
Record: 24–58
Playoffs: Did not qualify
Coach: Hubie Brown
Average Home Attendance: 11,154
Points per Game: (105.2—22nd of 23)
Points Allowed per Game: (109.8—12th of 23)
Team Leaders:

Points: Bernard King (32.9 per game)
Rebounds: Pat Cummings (8.2 per game)
Assists: Rory Sparrow (7.1 per game)
Steals: Darrell Walker (2.0 per game)
Blocked Shots: Ron Cavenall (0.8 per game)

All-Stars: Bernard King
Notable Transactions: Signed Pat Cummings as a free agent

Epilogue

The Ewing Era

More than a month passed between the draft lottery and the actual NBA draft. Powered by Magic Johnson and Kareem Abdul-Jabbar—who won Finals MVP honors for the second time (fourteen years after his first Finals MVP with the Bucks)—the Lakers beat the Celtics in a classic six-game series. Now the Knicks were center stage as the draft neared. But not everything was rosy in the Big Apple. David Falk, who grew up in Long Island and whose mother Pearl was a huge Knicks fan, represented Patrick Ewing as his agent, bringing his experience negotiating rookie contracts for James Worthy and Michael Jordan to bear in dealing with the Knicks. "It's not going to be as easy signing Patrick as everyone has publicly suggested," Falk cagily told reporters. "In 11 years of negotiations, I have never had one negotiation that I would say has been easy. And a center like Patrick Ewing comes along about once every 20 years."[1] There was no upper limit on what the Knicks could pay Ewing, except that they had to fit his contract under the existing salary cap, which was in flux because most of the Knicks' roster was eligible for free agency. "If they sign their free agents first," Falk warned, "they may not have enough left for signing Patrick."[2]

On June 18, at 1:08 p.m., Commissioner Stern announced the Knicks selection. To the surprise of no one, with the first overall pick of the 1985 draft, the New York Knickerbockers selected Patrick Ewing out of Georgetown University. Although the Knicks refused to comment on Ewing's salary after the sides agreed to a contract nearly three months later, Falk was only too happy to leak it to the press. Ewing was set to earn $17 million over six years, with the potential to earn $30 million if he stayed in New York for a decade.[3] It made Ewing the highest-paid rookie in NBA history. By 1987, he would be the highest-paid player in the league, and that did not include his multimillion-dollar shoe deal with Adidas, which released the Rivalry Hi in 1986.

Outside of adding Ewing, the Knicks had a quiet off-season in 1985. With all eyes turned toward their rookie center, King was happy to rehab his knee in peace. In August, five months after the injury, reporters caught up to Bernard at the "Bernie and Ernie All-Pro Basketball Camp" at St. Paul's School in Garden City, Long Island. Asked about his injury, King replied, "I don't want to talk about it. When I have something to say I will." He converted part of his home into a therapy center, so he could rehab away from the team and, more importantly, the media. "It is difficult for Bernard to go out places without people asking him questions," Norman Scott told reporters checking in on his famous patient. Scott also informed them that the rehab was "well ahead of schedule," but he cautioned, "The issue of when Bernard will be able to play is very unscientific."[4] Put bluntly, no pro basketball player had ever fully recovered from the knee injuries King suffered. Still, Scott remained optimistic. "I have never seen a person so dedicated. I never understood the game face he wears, but now I see it is real. He approaches his rehabilitation with the same game face."[5] Thirty years later, King would title his autobiography *Game Face*; it was a fitting description for his on-court and off-court stoicism.

With Ewing aboard, and seeing how well the pairing of Ralph Sampson and Akeem Olajuwon had performed for the Houston Rockets (a 48–34 record and, in 1986, an NBA Finals appearance), Hubie Brown decided to experiment with his own Twin Towers, inserting both Ewing and incumbent center Bill Cartwright into the starting lineup. Cartwright,

Figure 16. Number one pick Patrick Ewing (center), with NBA commissioner David Stern (left) and Knicks general manager Dave DeBusschere (right) at the NBA draft, Felt Forum/Madison Square Garden, June 18, 1985. AP Photo/Kevin Reece. © Associated Press.

who had missed the entire 1984–85 season with foot injuries, was a free agent but re-signed with the Knicks. "Free agency is something you should go through once," Cartwright said, "but it should also be avoided."[6] The pairing of Cartwright and Ewing got off to a rough start as the veteran busted the rookie's lip open in the team's first practice, on a hard collision near the rim. But the next day Cartwright smoothed everything over, telling him "Patrick, look, we're two aggressive centers and I want us to work together. We're going to have some collisions, but it's not personal." And the two became great friends. Cartwright reinjured his foot in a preseason game against Washington, but fortunately X-rays came back negative, and he was able to stay mostly healthy. Unfortunately, his teammates continued to fall to injuries. Walker sprained his wrist, and Tucker injured several ribs and his pelvis diving for a loose ball. Hubie admitted Tucker "could be hurt very badly."[7]

As his teammates battled through injuries, Ewing had struggles of his own. He was an intimidating presence on defense—Hubie joked that "I've seen guys drive the lane and start double-clutching and jerking around when Patrick's over sitting on the bench. Now that, my friend, is intimidation"—but he also had to adjust to the physicality of the pro game. In his first three preseason games, Ewing committed 17 fouls and was ejected for cursing out veteran ref Bennett Salvatore. Micheal Ray Richardson, suddenly Sugar the Sage, said, "He's got to learn that this ain't the Patrick Ewing League. These aren't kids. They're men."[8] Patrick also was part of a bench-clearing brawl when Pacers center Steve Stipanovich threw Ewing to the floor after the rookie caught him with an elbow to the throat. Both benches cleared, and both centers were ejected. Sparrow tried to intervene and earned a $500 fine for his efforts. "I went in to break up the fight," he joked, "not to be Hulk Hogan or the Iron Sheik."[9] Still, Ewing's teammates and coaches remained supportive. "I'm not going to tell the man to turn the other cheek," Hubie told reporters, and forward James Bailey said, "I'd hate to see Patrick draw his guns every night, but it's almost gotten to that point. We, as teammates, have to help him out a little more."[10]

With expectations that he would be an NBA superstar, Ewing had a giant bullseye on his back every game. But he had a better rookie season than the Knicks could have hoped for. He drew rave reviews everywhere he went and was constantly compared to Bill Russell. Throughout this, Ewing remained humble. "I don't consider myself a savior," he told reporters. "I want New Yorkers to think of me as somebody who works hard for a living, just like they do."[11] Ewing played 50 games in his rookie season, cut short by an injury in March, but earned an All-Star berth and Rookie of the Year honors, averaging 20 points, 9 rebounds, and 2 blocks a game for the season.

Despite his strong play, by the time Ewing went down in March the team's season was already in shambles. Cartwright, fresh off the pre-season foot scare, refractured his foot in late October and some fans (and even players) started calling him Medical Bill.[12] Cartwright played only two games the entire season as the team once again set a league record for missed games due to injury, and Brown never got the opportunity to see how his team might fare starting both big men together.

The low point might have come on December 10 when, despite winning 82–64 over the Pacers, the Knicks committed 32 turnovers. Only complete ineptitude from the Pacers, who shot just 25 percent from the field, gave the Knicks the win. The crowd booed unmercifully, and afterward DeBusschere told reporters, "I was both embarrassed and disappointed by our play."[13]

A few days later, King held a press conference—his first willing conversation with the media in nearly nine months. Flanked by his physical therapist, Dana Sweitzer, and team physician, Dr. Scott, King was confident. "I am a fighter," King told them. "Don't ever count Bernard King out." Scott agreed. "I asked Bernard about wearing a brace, but he doesn't need it," he told them. Sweitzer chimed in, "He has never had a plateau. He has made constant progress."[14]

With King on the mend, Cartwright rehabbing (again), and Ewing demonstrating that he could be a generational talent, there was reason for optimism in the Big Apple. But the Knicks of 1985–86 would end at 23–59, a virtual repeat of the preceding season, which meant that someone had to pay. The first to be shown the door was DeBusschere, fired and replaced by Scotty Stirling, a former executive with the Golden State Warriors, best known for engineering the trade netting Joe Barry Carroll for Robert Parish and Kevin McHale. A few months later, general manager Eddie Donovan followed DeBusschere out the door.

In the fall of 1986, the Knicks opened training camp at Upsala College in East Orange, New Jersey—a place Butch Carter called "complete shit" ("I hadn't played on a floor that bad since seventh or eighth grade").[15]

Before camp, the Knicks held a preseason meet-and-greet to introduce the new players and coaches. Kenny "Sky" Walker, a forward from Kentucky, was this season's high-profile rookie, and assistant coach Brendan Malone joined Bob Hill on Brown's coaching staff. As Malone explained to me three decades later, "[Hubie] introduced me and the staff and started introducing the players. Introduced Cartwright as a center. Introduced Ewing as a power forward. And Ewing said, 'I'm not a power forward, I'm a center.' And I said, 'Uh-oh, this is going to be very interesting.' "[16] Later Hubie shrugged it off, telling reporters that it didn't matter which position one played, but the meeting was off to a bad start.[17]

As Hubie continued around the room making introductions, he finished up with King, still rehabbing from his knee injury suffered a year and a half earlier. Hubie asked Bernard when he'd be back, and, as Malone told me, King said, "I'll be back in January."[18] Hubie was shell-shocked. He hoped to have his All-Star forward in the lineup on opening night and knew that a bad start to the season might mean he would become the Knicks' newest former head coach. As it turned out, Bernard was out even longer than January, and, after a 4–12 start to the season, Hubie was gone, replaced by Hill, who likewise received a pink slip at the end of the year. Former Knicks assistant Rick Pitino would be hired as head coach in July 1987.

Also gone was Darrell Walker, traded to the Denver Nuggets, just before the 1986–87 training camp opened, for a 1987 first-round draft pick, which the Knicks promptly shipped to the Bulls for Jawann Oldham (a journeyman center). Chicago would use that pick to trade for a skinny small forward from the University of Central Arkansas named Scottie Pippen. Walker, though, was happy to leave the Big Apple. "Hubie and I wasn't going to work," he explained to me years later. "I wasn't going to be talked to like I was a dog and wasn't going to accept that treatment. It was time to move on before it became a physical altercation."[19] The low point of their relationship came in January 1986, when Walker and Hubie started yelling at each other during practice, prompting the guard to commit an impromptu sit-in—right in the middle of the lane.[20] In hindsight, it is amazing the two never came to blows.

In 1986–87, with King playing just six games, the Knicks would duplicate their two preceding seasons, finishing 24–58. But things were about to improve. General Manager Al Bianchi, replacing Donovan, started to turn the team around, selecting Brooklyn point guard Mark Jackson from St. John's University in the first round of the 1987 draft.[21] Jackson brought fans back to the Garden with his moxie and grit, and under Pitino the Knicks would improve to 38–44 in 1987–88 and win the Atlantic Division of the Eastern Conference in 1988–89 with a record of 52–30. But Pitino would leave after two seasons to become the head coach at the University of Kentucky, and Jackson's play would decline after signing a contract extension in 1990 (he would be dealt to the Clippers in 1992).

Another big change took place in the office of New York City's mayor. Ed Koch served in that role until 1989, when he lost the Democratic primary election to David Dinkins, New York City's first Black mayor. During the last years of his tenure, Koch suffered a stroke that he blamed on scandals in his administration. Hundreds of officials serving under Koch were convicted of crimes related to payoff rings, using bribes to extend their political influence.[22] Yet Koch would remain an iconic figure in the city for decades. At the former mayor's eightieth birthday celebration at Gracie Mansion in 2004, then-mayor Michael Bloomberg would roast his predecessor. "When I was just a lowly millionaire in the 1970s," Bloomberg joked, "I wanted to be like Koch if I went into politics. I'd be tall, I'd be loud, and I'd be both a Democrat and a Republican."[23]

Koch truly embodied New York City during the seventies and early eighties, just as he symbolized the struggles in the Knicks organization, swinging wildly between hope and abject disillusionment. Koch's legacy, one biographer explains, is—at least in part—his "cockiness and racial divisiveness." But he also "bravely faced one of the worst crises in New York's history, restructured the city with minimal help from the federal government, and kept it solvent and growing for a generation."[24] In short, Koch prepared New York City for the Ewing era.

In early 1987, Ewing went down with a season-ending knee injury. [25] A dozen games later, King made his long-awaited return to the Knicks, more than two years after his own devastating knee injury. King checked the New York sports calendar to maximize exposure for his return. As he would later write in his autobiography, "With no one to share the stage on April 10, the spotlight would be turned squarely on Madison Square Garden for my comeback."[26] When Bernard checked into the game, Knicks fans gave him a three-minute-long standing ovation, shouting "We want Bernard!" at the top of their lungs. Unfortunately for Knicks fans, the

Bucks ruined King's return, limiting Bernard to just 7 points in twenty-three minutes off the bench. As it would turn out, Ewing's injury meant that no one ever had the opportunity to see if Patrick and Bernard could be the long-awaited co-saviors of the Knicks. "I wanted to be a Knick until I retired," King wrote later. "I was sure that if I stayed with the team and had a chance to play with Patrick Ewing, we would win a championship together."[27]

Instead, the Knicks declined to offer King a new contract that off-season. His agent, Bob Woolf, said, "It seemed that they were afraid to, that we might accept it."[28] Stirling, Bianchi, and the new Knicks brass didn't trust King's knee and wanted a clean break with the team's past. Despite Knicks fans chanting "We want Bernard!" through the entire pre-season, in the fall of 1987 King signed a free agent contract with the Washington Bullets and would then enjoy a career renaissance. While he never regained the explosiveness that made him one of the NBA's best in 1984, he became an even smarter and more determined player, peaking in 1990–91 when he was named third-team All-NBA after averaging over 28 points per game as a thirty-four-year-old. Watching closely was a young Brooklynite named Carmelo Anthony, who would come to pattern his game after King. More than two decades later, Anthony would break King's record for most points scored by a Knick in Madison Square Garden by dropping 62 in a 2014 game against the Charlotte Bobcats.

Despite their mandate to build around Patrick, the Knicks struggled to surround Ewing with talent, and he nearly left as a free agent in 1991 to become a member of the Golden State Warriors, where he would have teamed up with the high-scoring trio of Tim Hardaway, Mitch Richmond, and Chris Mullin.[29] Instead, he re-signed in New York and became the highest-paid player in the NBA.

Golden State played a fast-paced style under coach Don Nelson, and Hardaway, Richmond, and Mullin gained the joint nickname Run TMC. The name was a nod, of course, to the hottest hip-hop group in the country at the time, Run-DMC, the Queens-based trio founded in the early eighties. After their self-titled debut record in 1984 went gold, Run-DMC kept releasing hit after hit. Their 1986 album *Raising Hell*, might have been the peak of their success, featuring a collaboration with Aerosmith on "Walk This Way," a song first recorded by Aerosmith and released on the band's 1975 album *Toys in the Attic*. This new rock and hip-hop fusion of "Walk This Way" would reach number 4 on the Billboard Hot 100 chart. The trio from Hollis, Queens, became the first rap group to reach the top five on that chart. Although Run-DMC had struggles, including differences over their creative direction, battles with substance abuse, and—most tragically—the death of Jason Mizell (Jam Master J) in 2002, they revolutionized the hip-hop world, becoming the first act to have their music videos shown on MTV and the first to earn a Grammy Award nomination.

Despite their growing fame, Run-DMC recognized the importance of authenticity. "New York in the '80s was one of the most influential and innovative periods in history," Darryl McDaniels (DMC) said in 2019. "The punk rock, hip-hop and art scene were consistently producing some of the edgiest and most culturally relevant work from Uptown to Downtown." He name-checked Lou Reed, the Ramones, and Blondie in noting his influences. "When we were starting out, we were inspired by the artists and culture of our time."[30]

One of the songs on the *Raising Hell* album is "My Adidas." When Run-DMC cued it up, fans would pull off their Superstar sneakers and wave them in the air. For one Madison Square Garden show, Run-DMC convinced an Adidas exec to attend, and he was astounded at the response to the song. A few weeks later, Adidas—hoping to capitalize on the popularity of this group from Queens—signed the trio to a million-dollar endorsement deal, the first of its kind. After signing, Adidas called on their biggest superstar to help promote Run-DMC, and Patrick Ewing appeared in several cross-promoted events to hype the song (and, more importantly, the shoes).[31]

The connection between basketball and hip-hop continued to develop during the 1980s. In 1989, on their second album, *Paul's Boutique*, the Beastie Boys released the song "Lay It on Me," rapping, "More updated on the hip-hop lingo / My favorite New York Knick was Harthorne Wingo."[32] The EBC streetball tournament continued to grow at Rucker Park; NBA stars like Allen Iverson and Shaquille O'Neal released rap songs; and events like All-Star Weekend became a blend of hip-hop and hoops. Yet at the same time, in part due to the success of the Queens-based Run DMC, the center of rap music continued to shift away from the Bronx, as the East Coast versus West Coast battles of the 1990s pitted Californians Dr. Dre, Snoop Dogg, and Tupac Shakur against Brooklyn-born Notorious

B.I.G. and Mount Vernon–raised Sean "Puff Daddy" Combs. East Coast versus West Coast lasted for most of the decade, finally ending with the tragic murders of Tupac and B.I.G. Hip-hop outgrew the South Bronx, moving away from its birthplace as it became increasingly mainstream.

Ewing never released a rap album, nor did he develop into the dominant defensive player envisioned by DeBusschere and Brown when the Knicks drafted him in 1985. Instead, he became a consistently strong offensive player, with a reliable turnaround jump shot, and a very good defender who earned three All-Defensive second-team nods. Flanked by Charles Oakley and John Starks, and coached by Pat Riley, Ewing finally reached the NBA finals in 1994 and again made the finals under Jeff Van Gundy in 1999, but he never raised a banner in Madison Square Garden. Oakley, a bruising six-foot-seven forward, was the closest to a kindred spirit of the late seventies Knicks as the team could identify by the '90s. Oakley hung out with Tupac Shakur (2Pac) and regularly partied with Chuck D (of Public Enemy), Kid 'n Play, and Grand Puba. Oakley also counted LL Cool J among his good friends, and teammate Anthony Mason—a chiseled 250-pounder—served as a bodyguard for Cool J when he performed in Queens.[33]

Between winning the 1973 title and the arrival of Patrick Ewing a dozen years later, the Knicks struggled to achieve and sustain on-court success. Still, they served as pioneers in this transitional era in the NBA. They fielded the first all-Black team in 1979, had several of the most prominent drug users on their roster when the NBA instituted an ambitious anti-drug policy, led the charge in pursuing free agents, and butted up against the salary cap when it was put in place.

Their efforts mirrored the circumstances facing New York City between the mid-seventies and mid-eighties. Crippling economic conditions forced Mayors Abe Beame and Ed Koch to reevaluate and reprioritize municipal funding, while work done to reclaim Times Square and the Statue of Liberty emphasized a renaissance in the Big Apple (set to Old Blue Eyes singing "New York, New York"). At the same time, from the ashes of the burning Bronx, a new musical genre and Black culture emerged whole cloth, linked to basketball and taking the nation—and the world—by storm.

Although it took place after the glory days of the Knicks—when Madison Square was the Garden of Eden—this period marked a watershed moment in cultural history as basketball, Black culture, and the New York Knicks became inseparably linked.

Just a few years later, a white suburban teenager plugged *Tecmo NBA Basketball* into his Nintendo (blowing on the cartridge first, of course), selected Ewing and the Knicks as his team, and turned on some Dr. Dre (quietly so the parents wouldn't hear). That young man, who was me, made a connection between the New York Knicks, Black culture, and professional basketball without knowing one existed before—in New York City more than a decade earlier.

NOTES

Introduction

1. Thomas Rogers, "Celtics Top Knicks at Garden, 94–84," *New York Times*, November 9, 1973.

2. Peter L'Official, *Urban Legends: The South Bronx in Representation and Ruin* (Cambridge, MA: Harvard University Press, 2020), 2.

3. Kevin Baker, "'Welcome to Fear City': The Inside Story of New York's Civil War, 40 Years On," *Guardian*, May 18, 2015.

4. Michael Burke, *Outrageous Good Fortune* (Boston: Little, Brown, 1984).

5. "The Crisis of the Black Spirit," *Ebony*, October 1977, 142.

6. Jamel Shabazz, *A Time before Crack* (Brooklyn: powerHouse Books, 2005), 145.

1. "Then I'll Save"

1. Bill Verrigan, "It's a New Deal for Knicks," (NY) *Daily News*, October 25, 1975; Sam Goldaper, "Haywood Wants DeBusschere's No. 22," *New York Times*, October 25, 1975.

2. Mike Lupica, "Spencer Haywood Lights Up the Garden," *New York Post*, October 25, 1975; Goldaper, "Haywood Wants"; Bill Libby, *Stand Up for Something: The Spencer Haywood Story* (New York: Grosset & Dunlap, 1972), 282.

3. Verrigan, "It's a New Deal."(NY) *Daily News*.

4. Spencer Haywood with Scott Ostler, *Spencer Haywood: The Rise, the Fall, the Recovery* (New York: Amistad, 1992), 169.

5. Freddie Lewis discussion with the author, October 2016.

6. Phil Jackson and Hugh Delehanty, *Eleven Rings: The Soul of Success* (New York: Penguin Press, 2013), 55.

7. George Kalinsky and Pete Hamill, *Garden of Dreams: Madison Square Garden, 125 Years* (New York: Stewart, Tabori & Chang, 2004), 67.

8. Spike Lee with Ralph Wiley, *Best Seat in the House: A Basketball Memoir* (New York: Crown Publishers, 1997), 15.

9. Chris Herring, *Blood in the Garden: The Flagrant History of the 1990s New York Knicks* (New York: Atria Books, 2022), 122.

10. Leonard Koppett, "Knicks Reap Harvest of Awards," *New York Times*, May 15, 1973.

11. "Knicks Take Their Final Bows at City Hall," *New York Times*, May 16, 1973.

12. Mike Glenn discussion with the author, October 2016.

13. Harvey Araton, *When the Garden Was Eden: Clyde, the Captain, Dollar Bill, and the Glory Days of the New York Knicks* (New York: Harper, 2011), 296.

14. Phil Elderkin, "NBA Basketball," *Sporting News*, June 23, 1973, 53.

15. Pete Axthelm, *The City Game: Basketball in New York from the World Champion Knicks to the World of the Playgrounds* (New York: Harper's Magazine Press, 1970), 73.

16. Earl Monroe with Quincy Troupe, *Earl the Pearl: My Story* (New York: Rodale, 2013), 333.

17. Araton, *When the Garden Was Eden*, 69.

18. Sam Goldaper, "Knicks' Quiet Leader," *New York Times*, May 12, 1973.

19. Mort Zachter, *Red Holzman: The Life and Legacy of a Hall of Fame Basketball Coach* (New York: Sports Publishing, 2019), 150.

20. Willis Reed with Phil Pepe, *A View From the Rim: Willis Reed on Basketball* (Philadelphia: J. B. Lippincott, 1971), 166.

21. Walt Frazier and Ira Berkow, *Rockin' Steady: A Guide to Basketball and Cool* (New York: Warner Paperback Library, 1974), 14.

22. Walt Frazier with Dan Markowitz, *The Game within the Game* (New York: Hyperion, 2006), 14.

23. "Knicks' Frazier Says He Prefers Blacks to Whites," *Jet*, February 27, 1975.

24. Lee, *Best Seat in the House*, 42.

25. Thomas Rogers, "Knicks Bow 85–69," *New York Times*, October 21, 1973.

26. "Listless Knicks Battered by Bullets Here, 101–84," *New York Times*, October 24, 1973.

27. Joe Whittington, "NBA East," *Sporting News*, November 10, 1973.

28. Thomas Rogers, "Knicks Conquer Pistons," *New York Times*, December 27, 1973.

29. Sam Goldaper, "Pistons Beat Knicks, 96–91," *New York Times*, February 2, 1974.

30. Sam Goldaper, "DeBusschere's Special Stamp Goes on Big Victory for Knicks," *New York Times*, March 27, 1974.

31. At 68–14, the 1972–73 Celtics were one game better than the legendary 1985–86 Celtics, who posted a 67–15 record on their way to winning the 1986 NBA title.

32. Martin Lader and Joe Carnicelli, eds., *Pro Basketball Guide 1973* (New York: Cord Sportfacts, 1972), 83. ABC aired the "Jerry Lucas' Super Kids Day Magic Jamboree" in November 1972.

33. Araton, *When the Garden Was Eden*, 294.

34. Jackson and Delehanty, *Eleven Rings*, 58.

35. "Bronx Residents Lose Road Fight: Expressway Route Affirmed as Estimate Board Votes to Buy Mid-Section Land," *New York Times*, December 3, 1954; Matt Sedensky,

"Bronx up Close: Decades Later, Doing the Cross Bronx Expressway Right," *New York Times*, October 7, 2001.

36. Steve Hager, *Hip Hop: The Illustrated History of Break Dancing, Rap Music, and Graffiti* (New York: St. Martin's Press, 1984), 1.

37. Jim Fricke and Charlie Ahearn, *Yes Yes Y'all: The Experience Music Project Oral History of Hip-Hop's First Decade* (Boston: Da Capo Press, 2002); Jeff Chang, *Can't Stop Won't Stop: A History of the Hip-Hop Generation* (New York: St. Martin's Press, 2005).

38. Chang, *Can't Stop Won't Stop*, 18.

39. Ivan Sanchez and Luis "DJ Disco Wiz" Cedeño, *It's Just Begun: The Epic Journey of DJ Disco Wiz, Hip Hop's First Latino DJ* (Brooklyn: powerHouse books, 2009), 13.

40. Tricia Rose, *Black Noise: Rap Music and Black Culture in Contemporary America* (Hanover, N.H.: Wesleyan University Press, 1994), 34.

41. Chang, *Can't Stop Won't Stop*, 9.

42. Hager, *Hip Hop*, 10.

43. "'Taki 183' Spawns Pen Pals," *New York Times*, July 21, 1971.

44. Murray Forman and Mark Anthony Neal, eds. *That's the Joint! The Hip-Hop Studies Reader* (New York: Routledge, 2004), 23; Chang, *Can't Stop Won't Stop*, 122.

45. George J. Lankevich, *New York City: A Short History* (New York: New York University Press, 2002), 219.

46. Will Hermes, *Love Goes to Buildings on Fire: Five Years in New York That Changed Music Forever* (New York: Faber and Faber, 2011), 27.

47. Rose, *Black Noise*.

48. Clint Roswell, "Willis Reed Makes It Official," (NY) *Daily News*, September 20.1974.

49. Dave Hirshey, "Porter Eyes DeBusschere's Former Job," (NY) *Daily News*, May 29, 1974.

50. Sam Goldaper, "Gianelli Is Putting More Weight into Knicks' Lineup," *New York Times*, September 16, 1973.

51. Goldaper, "Gianelli Is Putting More Weight."

52. Red Holzman and Harvey Frommer, *Red on Red* (New York: Bantam Books, 1987), 128.

53. Kay Gilman, "The John Gianellis: He's 6–10, She's 5–4," (NY) *Daily News*, October 20, 1974.

54. "Nets Regain Top Spot; Kings Trounce Knicks," *New York Times*, January 18, 1975.

55. "NBA All Star Voting Results 1975–Phoenix," Just All Stars. Accessed May 1, 2020, https://www.justallstar.com/nba-all-star-game/voting/ballot-1975.

56. Keith Blauschild discussion with the author, March 2020.

57. Rick Telander, "He's Not Hot Stuff, He's My Brother," *Sports Illustrated*, March 2, 1981.

58. Larry Merchant, "Living Dangerously," *New York Post*, April 11, 1975.

59. "Barnett: Knicks' Leader in Punting and Prayer," *Sporting News*, March 1, 1975, 14.

60. Bill Verigan, "Barnett Produces in Knick of Time," (NY) *Daily News*, April 12, 1975.

61. Holzman and Frommer, *Red on Red*, 146.

62. Zachter, *Red Holzman*, 194.

63. Bob Ryan, "Knicks Gamble on Walk, Thin Question Mark," *Sporting News*, February 22, 1975, 21.

64. Ryan, "Knicks Gamble," 21.

65. Araton, *When the Garden Was Eden*, 30.

66. Dick Young, "Why Irish Wouldn't Fight Garden Ouster," (NY) *Daily News*, May 26, 1974.

67. Burke, *Outrageous Good Fortune,* 343, 362.

68. Joseph Durso, *Madison Square Garden: 100 Years of History* (New York: Simon and Schuster, 1979), 221.

69. Alan Hahn, *100 Things Knicks Fans Should Know and Do before They Die* (Chicago: Triumph Books, 2012), 2–3; Durso, *Madison Square Garden,* 247.

70. Thomas P. Oates, "Selling Streetball: Racialized Space, Commercialized Spectacle, and Playground Basketball," *Critical Studies in Media Communication,* 34, Issue 1 (2017), 94–100; Kalinsky and Hamill, *Garden of Dreams,* 23.

71. Sam Goldaper, "Knicks to Divest Holzman of Either Coach or Manager Role," *New York Times,* February 18, 1975.

72. Sam Goldaper, "Donovan Resigns: Hearing Set on Charges Knicks Tampered," *New York Times,* March 22, 1975.

73. Peter Vecsey, "Champagne at Clyde's Pad Greets Kings' Victory," (NY) *Daily News,* April 7, 1975; Judy Klemesrud, "Clyde," *New York Times,* February 16, 1975.

74. Vecsey, "Champagne at Clyde's."

75. Leonard Lewin, "Clyde Has a Block Party," *New York Post,* April 7, 1975.

76. Bill Verigan, "It's Win or No Tomorrow for Knicks," *New York Times,* April 10, 1975.

77. Holzman and Frommer, *Red on Red,* 145.

78. Holzman and Frommer, *Red on Red,* 146.

79. Mel Lowell discussion with the author, March 2020.

80. The Association for Professional Basketball Research, Accessed May 1, 2020, http://www.apbr.org/attendance.html; Bill Verigan, "Knicks Make the Playoffs," *New York Times,* April 7, 1975.

81. Mal Florence, "The Big Men: A Look at Dominant Figures in the Game: Wilt, Abdul-Jabbar, Thurmond," *Basketball Digest,* November 1973, 48.

82. Sam Goldaper, "Burke Is Retiring from Garden Posts," *New York Times,* September 20, 1981.

83. The draft picks netted Milwaukee Dave Meyers and Junior Bridgeman; the young players were center Elmore Smith and guard Brian Winters.

84. Sam Goldaper, "Knicks Pursuing M'Ginnis," *New York Times,* August 20, 1974.

85. Sam Goldaper, "McGinnis Sues to Be a Knick," *New York Times,* May 24, 1975.

86. Bill Verrigan, "76ers Call M'Ginnis Signing Piracy," (NY) *Daily News,* May 31, 1975.

87. Pete Croatto, *From Hang Time to Prime Time: Business, Entertainment, and the Birth of the Modern-Day NBA* (New York: Atria Books, 2020), 10.

88. Lawrence F. O'Brien, *No Final Victories: A Life in Politics—from John F. Kennedy to Watergate* (New York: Doubleday, 1974), 1.

89. Croatto, *From Hang Time to Prime Time,* 10.

90. Croatto, *From Hang Time to Prime Time,* 16.

91. Norm Miller, "Hawks Draft Thompson, Webster," (NY) *Daily News,* May 30, 1975.

92. Croatto, *From Hang Time to Prime Time,* 18.

93. *Welcome Back Kotter,* "Basket Case," episode 2, directed by Bob LaHendro.

94. Sam Goldaper, "Knicks Ask Lakers: Can We Open Talks with Wilt?" *New York Times,* September 27, 1975.

95. Pat Putnam, "The Fortune Cookie Smiled," *Sports Illustrated,* November 3, 1975.

96. Bill Verigan, "Knicks Hope to Land Wilt; Seek Permission for Talks," (NY) *Daily News,* September 29, 1975.

97. Bill Verigan, "Knicks Off to See Wilt; Compensation for LA," (NY) *Daily News,* October 16, 1975.

98. Verigan, "Knicks Off to See Wilt."

99. Putnam, "The Fortune Cookie Smiled."

100. Jim O'Brien, "The Wilt Chamberlain Impasse," *New York Post*, October 23, 1975.

101. Lee, *Best Seat*, 15.

102. Judy Klemesrud, "Donald Trump, Real Estate Promoter, Builds Image as He Buys Buildings," *New York Times*, November 1, 1976.

103. Themis Chronopoulos and Jonathan Soffer, "After the Urban Crisis: New York and the Rise of Inequality," *Journal of Urban History* 43, no. 6 (2017): 856.

104. Jonathan Soffer, *Ed Koch and the Rebuilding of New York City* (New York: Columbia University Press, 2010), 115; Oliver Allen, *New York, New York: A History of the World's Most Exhilarating and Challenging City* (New York: Atheneum, 1990), 308.

105. Kevin Baker, "'Welcome to Fear City'—The Inside Story of New York's Civil War, 40 Years On," *Guardian*, May 18, 2015.

106. Jeff Nussbaum, "The Night New York Saved Itself from Bankruptcy," *New Yorker*, October 16, 2015.

107. Lankevich, *New York City*, 219; Baker, "'Welcome to Fear City.'"

108. Nussbaum, "The Night New York Saved Itself from Bankruptcy;" Kim Phillips-Fein, *Fear City: New York's Fiscal Crisis and the Rise of Austerity Politics* (New York: Metropolitan Books, 2017), 2.

109. Frank Van Riper, "Ford to City: Drop Dead," (NY) *Daily News*, October 30, 1975.

2. "You Don't Get to Rebuild If You Are the New York Knicks"

1. Gavin Newsham, "When Pele and Cosmos Were Kings," *Guardian*, June 9, 2005, https://www.theguardian.com/football/2005/jun/10/sport.comment.

2. Spencer Haywood with Scott Ostler, *Spencer Haywood: The Rise, the Fall, the Recovery* (New York: Amistad, 1992), 92; Marc J. Spears and Gary Washburn, *The Spencer Haywood Rule: Battles, Basketball, and the Making of an American Iconoclast* (Chicago: Triumph Books, 2020).

3. Haywood and Ostler, *Spencer Haywood*, 94.

4. Kareem Abdul-Jabbar, *Coach Wooden and Me: Our 50-Year Friendship on and off the Court* (New York: Grand Central Publishing, 2017), 140.

5. Spears and Washburn, *The Spencer Haywood Rule*, 58.

6. Sean Deveney, "Spencer Haywood's Hall of Fame Eyes Opened by Fiery Jesse Owens Speech at 1968 Olympics," *Sporting News*, September 10, 2015.

7. Spears and Washburn, *The Spencer Haywood Rule*, 57.

8. Pat Putnam, "The Fortune Cookie Smiled," *Sports Illustrated*, November 3, 1975.

9. Harvey Araton, *When the Garden Was Eden: Clyde, the Captain, Dollar Bill, and the Glory Days of the New York Knicks* (New York: Harper, 2011), 259.

10. Harthorne Wingo discussion with the author, October 2016.

11. Red Holzman and Harvey Frommer, *Red on Red* (New York: Bantam Books, 1987), 15.

12. Marc Tracy, "Magic Number," *Tablet*, June 3, 2010.

13. Mort Zachter, *Red Holzman: The Life and Legacy of a Hall of Fame Basketball Coach* (New York: Sports Publishing, 2019), x.

14. Zachter, *Red Holzman*.

15. Haywood and Ostler, *Spencer Haywood*, 170.

16. Based on points allowed per one hundred possessions, the Knicks finished fourteenth in the eighteen-team league.

17. Michael K. Herbert, "How to Win? A Big Center and Defense," *Basketball Digest*, March 1976, 4.

18. Sam Goldaper, "Knicks out of Playoffs after Defeat," *New York Times*, March 31, 1976; Mike Lupica, "Knicks Glad to Go Home," *New York Post*, April 12, 1976.

19. Sam Goldaper, "Donovan Gives Views on Why Knicks Folded," *New York Times*, April 1, 1976.

20. Bill Libby and Spencer Haywood, *Stand Up for Something: The Spencer Haywood Story* (New York: Grosset & Dunlap, 1972); Haywood and Ostler, *Spencer Haywood*.

21. Haywood and Ostler, *Spencer Haywood*, 173.

22. Will Hermes, *Love Goes to Buildings on Fire: Five Years in New York That Changed Music Forever* (New York: Faber and Faber, 2011), 117.

23. Al Harvin, "Haywood, as Disc Jockey, Plays for New Audience," *New York Times*, September 15, 1976.

24. Haywood and Ostler, *Spencer Haywood*, 174.

25. Spears and Washburn, *The Spencer Haywood Rule*, 112.

26. Haywood and Ostler, *Spencer Haywood*, 177.

27. Spears and Washburn, *The Spencer Haywood Rule*, 133.

28. Haywood and Ostler, *Spencer Haywood*, 177.

29. Pat Putnam, "The Fortune Cookie Smiled," *Sports Illustrated*, November 3, 1975.

30. Jason Belzer, "NBA Renaissance Man: Earl Monroe Building a Business Empire off the Hardwood," *Forbes*, May 7, 2013, https://www.forbes.com/sites/jasonbelzer/2013/05/07/nba-renaissance-man-earl-monroe-building-a-business-empire-off-the-hardwood.

31. For the best explanation of the merger from the perspective of the ABA, see Terry Pluto, *Loose Balls: The Short, Wild Life of the American Basketball Association* (New York: Simon & Schuster, 1990).

32. Bill Verigan, "Knicks Only Challenge to 76ers in Atlantic," (NY) *Daily News*, October 18, 1977.

33. Jeffrey O. G. Ogbar, *Hip-Hop Revolution: The Culture and Politics of Rap* (Lawrence: University Press of Kansas, 2007), 3.

34. Miguelina Rodriguez, "Burn, Baby, Burn: The 1977 Blackout and Riots," in Neil Smith and Don Mitchell, eds., *Revolting New York: How 400 Years of Riot, Rebellion, Uprising, and Revolution Shaped a City* (Athens: University of Georgia Press, 2018), 221.

35. Quoted in Jonathan Abrams, *The Come Up: An Oral History of the Rise of Hip-Hop* (New York: Random House, 2022), 4.

36. Imani Kai Johnson, "Battling in the Bronx: Social Choreography and Outlaw Culture among Early Hip-Hop Streetdancers in New York City," *Dance Research Journal* 5, no. 2 (August 2018): 67.

37. "Experienced Vandals," *The Cyber Bench: Documenting New York City Graffiti*, accessed July 28, 2020, @149st, https://www.at149st.com/xvandals.html; Jaap de Jong, "The Fifth Element? A Study on the Common Ground Where Hip-Hop Meets Basketball," MA thesis, Utrecht University, 2019.

38. Steve Hager, *Hip Hop: The Illustrated History of Break Dancing, Rap Music, and Graffiti* (New York: St. Martin's Press, 1984), 31.

39. Onaje X. O. Woodbine, *Black Gods of the Asphalt: Religion: Hip-Hop, and Street Basketball* (New York: Columbia University Press, 2016), 42.

40. Jeff Chang, *Can't Stop Won't Stop: A History of the Hip-Hop Generation* (New York: St. Martin's Press, 2005), 77.

41. Quoted in Abrams, *The Come Up*, 4.

42. Jim Fricke and Charlie Ahearn, *Yes Yes Y'all: The Experience Music Project Oral History of Hip-Hop's First Decade* (Boston: Da Capo Press, 2002), 26, 41.

43. Israel, dir., *The Freshest Kids* (Los Angeles: QD3 Entertainment, 2002).

44. Fricke and Ahearn, *Yes Yes Y'all*, 65; Hager, *Hip Hop*, 33.

45. Chang, *Can't Stop Won't Stop*, 92, 96. In 2016, Bambaataa was accused of sexual assault on minors and, although he denied the allegations, resigned as head of Zulu Nation. See Kiersten Willis, "Afrika Bambaataa Steps Down as Zulu Nation Leader amid Reports of Child Sexual Assault," *Atlanta Black Star*, May 9, 2016.

46. Fricke and Ahearn, *Yes Yes Y'all*, 3; Abrams, *The Come Up*.

47. Chang, *Can't Stop Won't Stop*, 97.

48. Joseph G. Schloss, "'Like Old Folk Songs Handed Down from Generation to Generation': History, Canon, and Community in B-Boy Culture," *Ethnomusicology* 50, no. 3 (Fall 2006): 413.

49. Pete Croatto, *From Hang Time to Prime Time: Business, Entertainment, and the Birth of the Modern-Day NBA* (New York: Atria Books, 2020), 157.

50. Ivan Sanchez and Luis "DJ Disco Wiz" Cedeño, *It's Just Begun: The Epic Journey of DJ Disco Wiz, Hip Hop's First Latino DJ* (Brooklyn: PowerHouse books, 2009), 41.

51. Fricke and Ahearn, *Yes Yes Y'all*, 131.

52. Leonard Koppett, "Knicks Down Lakers, 102–97, in Opener," *New York Times*, October 22, 1976; Bill Verigan, "Knicks Nip Lakers, 102–97 in Garden Opener," (NY) *Daily News*, October 22, 1976.

53. Sam Goldaper, "Knicks Lose to Kings at the Buzzer," *New York Times*, November 24, 1976.

54. Anthony Paige, "Ticky Burden Unhappy but Still a Knick," *New York Amsterdam News*, December 18, 1976.

55. Sam Goldaper, "M'Adoo Deal Seems Near; Knicks Bid," *New York Times*, December 7, 1976

56. Goldaper, "M'Adoo Deal."

57. Charley Rosen, *God, Man, and Basketball Jones: The Thinking Fan's Guide to Professional Basketball* (New York: Holt, Rinehart and Winston, 1979), 133.

58. Curry Kirkpatrick, "Shoot if You Must . . . I Must, Says McAdoo," *Sports Illustrated*, March 8, 1976.

59. Shawn Fury, *Rise and Fire: The Origins, Science, and Evolution of the Jump Shot—and How It Transformed Basketball Forever* (New York: Flatiron Books, 2016), 206.

60. Jim Baker, "Buffalo's Bob McAdoo: The NBA's Top Scoring Machine," *Basketball Digest*, November 1975, 42.

61. Dave Cowens discussion with the author, October 2016.

62. Steve Hershey, "The NBA's 10 Most Valuable Players," *Basketball Digest*, December 1977, 49; Michael DelNagro, "McAdoo about Something Boffo in Buffalo," *Sports Illustrated*, March 18, 1974.

63. "Vindication," in *Pro Basketball '75–'76* (New York: Pocket Books, 1975), 148.

64. Steve Cady, "A New Gunner for the Knicks," *New York Times*, December 11, 1976.

65. Bill Verigan, "Burke Got McAdoo for N.Y. as well as for Knicks," (NY) *Daily News*, December 11, 1976.

66. Jim O'Brien, "Fans Go Wild Again over Knicks," *Sporting News*, January 22, 1977, 5.

67. Paige, "Ticky Burden Unhappy."

68. Joe O'Day, "Groin Pull Delays M'Adoo's Knick Debut," (NY) *Daily News*, December 11, 1976.

69. Pete Axthelm, *The City Game: Basketball in New York from the World Champion Knicks to the World of the Playgrounds* (New York: Harper's Magazine Press, 1970), 95–96, 100.

70. Walt Frazier with Neil Offen, *Walt Frazier: One Magic Season and a Basketball Life* (New York: Crown, 1988), 146.

71. Ernestine Bradley, *The Way Home: A German Childhood, an American Life* (New York: Pantheon Books, 2005), 172, 187.

72. Sam Goldaper, "Pistons Routed as Forward Gets 34 in 3 Periods," *New York Times*, December 27, 1976.

73. Sam Goldaper, "76ers Down Knicks on McGinnis Shot," *New York Times*, December 26, 1976.

74. Mel Davis discussion with the author, February 2017.

75. Dennis D'Agostino, *Garden Glory: An Oral History of the New York Knicks* (Chicago: Triumph Books, 2003), 157.

76. Butch Beard discussion with the author, October 2016.

77. Dave Anderson, "Defining What the Knicks Are Not," *New York Times*, January 25, 1977.

78. Joseph G. Schloss, " 'Like Old Folk Songs Handed Down from Generation to Generation': History, Canon, and Community in B-Boy Culture," *Ethnomusicology* 50, no. 3 (Fall 2006): 416.

79. Shea Serrano, *The Rap Year Book: The Most Important Rap Song from Every Year since 1979* (New York: Abrams Image, 2015).

80. Robert Ford Jr., "B-Beats Bombarding Bronx: Mobile DJ Starts Something with Oldie R&B Disks," *Billboard*, July 1, 1978, 65; Kembrew McLeod and Peter DiCola, *Creative License: The Law and Culture of Digital Sampling* (Durham: Duke University Press, 2011), 55.

81. Quoted in Abrams, *The Come Up*, 19.

82. Schloss, " 'Like Old Folk Songs," 420.

83. Joseph G. Schloss, *Foundation: B-Boys, B-Girls, and Hip-Hop Culture in New York* (New York: Oxford University Press, 2009), 61. As one B-boy explained, "A breakdancer is someone who has learned the dance for mercenary reasons while a B-boy has learned it through a commitment to the culture."

84. Israel, *The Freshest Kids*. Toprock is footwork done while standing; downrock is done with hands and feet on the floor.

85. Hager, *Hip Hop*, 32.

86. Schloss, *Foundation*, 29.

87. Murray Forman and Mark Anthony Neal, eds., *That's the Joint! The Hip-Hop Studies Reader* (New York: Routledge, 2004), 18.

88. Chang, *Can't Stop Won't Stop*, 116.

89. Forman and Neal, *That's the Joint!*, 37.

90. Imani Kai Johnson, "Battling in the Bronx: Social Choreography and Outlaw Culture among Early Hip-Hop Streetdancers in New York City," *Dance Research Journal* 5, no. 2 (August 2018): 64.

91. Sam Goldaper, "Kings Conquer Knicks, 112–105 on 36–19 Edge in Last Period," *New York Times*, January 30, 1977.

92. Anderson, "Defining What the Knicks Are Not."

93. Mike Lupica, "Earl Monroe: The Magic Show Is Back," *Basketball Digest*, March 1977, 18–23.

94. David Halberstam, *Breaks of the Game* (New York: Alfred A. Knopf, 1981), 245.

95. Spike Lee with Ralph Wiley, *Best Seat in the House: A Basketball Memoir* (New York: Crown Publishers, 1997), 70.

96. Lupica, "Earl Monroe," 20.

97. Jeff Duncan, "Remembering the Night Pistol Pete Scored 68 points," *Times-Picayune*, February 25, 2017, https://www.nola.com/sports/pelicans/article_2a81c7aa-908c-5809-a469-6494ba4688bd.html.

98. "Maravich: 68 in Rout of the Knicks," *New York Times*, February 26, 1977.

99. Spears and Washburn, *The Spencer Haywood Rule*, 134.

100. Holzman and Frommer, *Red on Red*, 159.

101. Zachter, *Red Holzman*, 228.

102. Bill Verigan, "Knicks Win, But Phil Calls 'em Losers," (NY) *Daily News*, April 11, 1977.

103. Jim O'Brien, "Jerry West and Willis Reed: 'Why the Game was Better in Our Day,'" *Basketball Digest*, May 1977, 35.

104. Alex Ogg with David Upshal, *The Hip Hop Years: A History of Rap* (New York: Fromm International, 2001), 41.

105. Hager, *Hip Hop*, 45.

106. David Toop, *Rap Attack 3: African Rap to Global Hip Hop* (London: Serpent's Tail, 2000), 29.

107. Sam Goldaper, "Nets Seeking to Move to Jersey, Sue Knicks Over Effort to Block It," *New York Times*, July 7, 1977.

108. "O'Brien Backs Knicks' Stand on Nets' Move," *New York Times*, July 9, 1977.

109. Bill Verigan, "Nets Draft Bernard King," (NY) *Daily News*, June 11, 1977.

110. Mike Glenn discussion with the author, October 2016; Sam Goldaper, "Knicks Pick Williams and Nets King in First Round," *New York Times*, June 11, 1977.

111. Mike Saunders discussion with the author, March 2020.

112. Glenn discussion, October 2016; A. J. Woodson, "BW History: Ray Williams," *Black Westchester Magazine*, November 2, 2016.

113. James Goodman, *Blackout* (New York: North Point Press, 2003), 23, 47; Abrams, *The Come Up*.

114. Rodriguez, "Burn, Baby, Burn," 223.

115. Goodman, *Blackout*, 83, 93.

116. Rodriguez, "Burn, Baby, Burn," 218–19.

117. Kevin Baker, "'Welcome to Fear City'—the Inside Story of New York's Civil War, 40 Years On," *Guardian*, May 18, 2015.

118. Quoted in Rodriguez, "Burn, Baby, Burn," 219.

119. Martin Gottlieb and James Glanz, "The Blackout of 2003: The Past; The Blackouts of '65 and '77 Became Defining Moments in the City's History," *New York Times*, August 15, 2003.

120. James Goodman, *Blackout* (New York: North Point Press, 2003), 192.

121. Lee Dembart, "Carter Takes 'Sobering' Trip to South Bronx," *New York Times*, October 6, 1977. The boundaries of the South Bronx have changed over time. Initially "South Bronx" referred just to the Mott Haven neighborhood, below 149th; now it encompasses everything south of Fordham Road.

122. Joanne Reitano, *The Restless City: A Short History of New York from Colonial Times to the Present* (New York: Routledge, 2010), 191.

123. Quoted in Ivor L. Miller, *Aerosol Kingdom: Subway Painters of New York City* (Jackson: University Press of Mississippi, 2012), 187.

124. Quoted in Abrams, *The Come Up*, 26.

125. Joe Flood, "Why the Bronx burned," *New York Post*, May 16, 2010.

126. Jonathan Soffer, *Ed Koch and the Rebuilding of New York City* (New York: Columbia University Press, 2010), 2.

127. Rodriguez, "Burn, Baby, Burn," 224.

128. Peter L'Official, *Urban Legends: The South Bronx in Representation and Ruin* (Cambridge, MA: Harvard University Press, 2020), 2.

3. "The Flashiest Losers in the League"

1. "Ed Koch Funeral: Former Mayor's Coffin Exits to 'New York, New York,'" Associated Press, February 4, 2013.

2. Robert D. McFadden, "Suspect in 'Son of Sam' Murders Arrested in Yonkers," *New York Times*, August 11, 1977.

3. Allan Tannenbaum, *New York in the 70s* (New York: Overlook Duckworth, 2011), 9.

4. Jonathan Soffer, *Ed Koch and the Rebuilding of New York City* (New York: Columbia University Press, 2010), 2.

5. Tom Robbins, "The Other New York Awaits Its Leader," in *New York Calling: From Blackout to Bloomberg*, ed. Marshall Berman and Brian Berger (New York: Reaktion Books, 2007), 152–65.

6. Soffer, *Ed Koch*, 146.

7. Sam Goldaper, "Reed Begins His Task of Rebuilding Knicks," *New York Times*, September 21, 1977.

8. Sam Goldaper, "Old Knicks Show New Tricks in Victory over Bucks," *New York Times*, October 2, 1977.

9. Steve Hershey, "Clyde Is Slower, but He Can Still Boost Cavs," *Sporting News*, October 29, 1977, 40.

10. Walt Frazier with Dan Markowitz, *The Game within the Game* (New York: Hyperion, 2006), 71.

11. John Papanek, "Clyde, Laughing Cavalier," *Sports Illustrated*, November 7, 1977.

12. Bill Verigan, "Frazier Considers Retirement or Cavs," (NY) *Daily News*, October 9, 1977.

13. Tony Kornheiser, "The Gospel according to Willis," *New York Times*, October 16, 1977.

14. Kornheiser, "The Gospel according to Willis."

15. Jim O'Brien, "Knicks' Big Mac Really Big Bust on Defense," *Sporting News*, April 8, 1978.

16. Phil Jackson and Charley Rosen, *More than a Game* (New York: Seven Stories Press, 2001), 50.

17. Sam Goldaper, "Reed's Debut Is Successful as Knicks Win," *New York Times*, October 19, 1977.

18. Bill Verigan, "The Knicks' New Clyde," (NY) *Daily News*, October 20, 1977.

19. George Kalinsky, Phil Berger, and Dennis D'Agostino, *The New York Knicks: The Official Fiftieth Anniversary Celebration* (New York: IDG, 1996), 149.

20. Papanek, "Clyde, Laughing Cavalier."

21. Bryan Miller, "Maxwell's Plum, a 60's Symbol, Closes," *New York Times*, July 11, 1988.

22. Frazier, *The Game within the Game*, 83.

23. Doug Smith, "Knicks Will Stand Pat," *New York Post*, December 6, 1977.

24. Mike Saunders discussion with the author, March 2020.

25. John Papanek, "Big Men the Knicks Got, but a Team They Ain't," *Sports Illustrated*, December 12, 1977.

26. Mike Lupica, "Things Shaping Up for Haywood?," (NY) *Daily News*, December 24, 1977.

27. Doug Smith, "Haywood Seethes on Bench as Knicks Bow," *New York Post*, December 21, 1977.

28. Bill Verigan, "Spencer: I'm Treated Like Plague," (NY) *Daily News*, December 22, 1977.

29. Doug Smith, "Talking with Willis Cools Off Spencer," *New York Post*, December 21, 1977; "Knicks Go Cold at End and Bow to Cavs," *New York Times*, December 23, 1977.

30. Jim O'Brien, "When Reed Shakes His Fist, Knicks Listen," *Sporting News*, December 24, 1977.

31. Kalinsky, Berger, and D'Agostino, *The New York Knicks*, 261.

32. Mel Lowell discussion with the author, March 2020.

33. Stan Fischler, "Werblin to Try His Green Thumb on Garden," *Sporting News*, January 7, 1978, 17.

34. Robert McGill Thomas Jr., "Sonny Werblin, an Impresario of New York's Sports Extravaganza, Is Dead at 81," *New York Times*, November 23, 1991.

35. Lowell discussion with author.

36. Phil Berger, "Making It Happen at the Garden," *New York Times*, September 30, 1979.

37. Hubie Brown discussion with the author, February 2020.

38. Lowell discussion with author.

39. Berger, "Making It Happen at the Garden."

40. Fred Ferretti, "Youths Roaming through Midtown Terrorize and Attack Passers-By," *New York Times*, September 27, 1976.

41. George Kalinsky and Pete Hamill, *Garden of Dreams: Madison Square Garden 125 Years* (New York: Stewart, Tabori & Chang, 2004), 168.

42. Tom Werblin discussion with the author, February 2020.

43. Lowell discussion with author.

44. Harvey Araton, *When the Garden Was Eden: Clyde, the Captain, Dollar Bill, and the Glory Days of the New York Knicks* (New York: Harper, 2011), 16.

45. Kalinsky, Berger, and D'Agostino, *The New York Knicks*, 130.

46. Saunders discussion with author.

47. Sam Goldaper, "Knicks Need a Breath of Fresh Air: A Victory," *New York Times*, January 22, 1978.

48. Jim Cleamons discussion with the author, November 2016.

49. Tony Kornheiser, "Knicks: Behind Big Mac Attack," *New York Times*, January 30, 1978.

50. Kornheiser, "Knicks: Behind Big Mac Attack."

51. Bob McAdoo discussion with the author, October 2016.

52. Kornheiser, "Knicks: Behind Big Mac Attack."

53. Alice Echols, *Hot Stuff: Disco and the Remaking of American Culture* (New York: W. W. Norton, 2010).

54. Judy Klemesrud, "Discotheque Fanatics Mob Latest Addition to Scene: Rating the Discos 'Playpen' Area," *New York Times*, June 9, 1978.

55. Klemesrud, "Discotheque Fanatics."

56. McAdoo discussion with author.

57. Butch Beard discussion with the author, October 2016.

58. Bernard King and Jerome Preisler, *Game Face: A Lifetime of Hard-Earned Lessons on and off the Basketball Court* (Cambridge, MA: DeCapo Press, 2017), 153.

59. Michael Weinreb, *Bigger than the Game: Bo, Boz, the Punky QB, and How the '80s Created the Modern Athlete* (New York: Gotham Books, 2010), 75.

60. Dennis D'Agostino, *Garden Glory: An Oral History of the New York Knicks* (Chicago: Triumph Books, 2003), 160.

61. Sam Goldaper, "Knicks Top Pacers; Haywood Scores 37," *New York Times*, February 10, 1978.

62. "Notes, Quotes & Comments," *Basketball Digest*, June 1978, 16.

63. Peter Maas, "A Long Way from Carolina," *New York Times*, March 6, 1978.

64. Jackson and Rosen, *More than a Game*, 51.

65. Bill Verigan, "Knick MD Backs Frazier's Claim," (NY) *Daily News*, April 16, 1978.

66. Bill Verigan, "Here Come 'Bump-and-Bang' 76ers," (NY) *Daily News*, April 16, 1978.

67. Dave Anderson, "Spencer Haywood's Strange Vibes," *New York Times*, April 16, 1978.

68. As of 2023, it remains the worst loss in Knicks playoff history.

69. Bill Verigan, "Knicks Humiliated by Philly, 130–90," (NY) *Daily News*, April 17, 1978.

70. Harvey Araton, "Knicks Suffer through Rerun of Horror Show," *New York Post*, April 19, 1978.

71. Bill Verigan, "76ers Enjoy Bullying Mild-Acting Knicks," (NY) *Daily News*, April 20, 1978.

72. Harvey Araton, "Knicks Teeter on the Brink of Extinction," *New York Post*, April 21, 1978.

73. Paul Zimmerman, "Knicks' Checkbook Style of Play Just Didn't Work," *New York Post*, April 21, 1978.

74. Mark Ribowsky, "This Big Mac's Got a Lotta Beefs," *Sport*, August 1978, 43.

75. Cleamons discussion with author.

76. Peter Braunstein, "'Adults Only': The Construction of an Erotic City in New York during the 1970s," in *America in the Seventies*, ed. Beth Bailey and David Farber (Lawrence: University Press of Kansas, 2004), 129–30; Jonathan Mahler, *The Bronx Is Burning: 1977, Baseball, Politics, and the Battle for the Soul of the City* (New York: Picador, 2005), 124.

77. Samuel R. Delany, *Times Square Red, Times Square Blue* (New York: New York University Press, 1999), 91.

4. "Meminger's Law"

1. Shea Serrano, *The Rap Year Book: The Most Important Rap Song from Every Year since 1979* (New York: Abrams Image, 2015), 8.

2. Jim Fricke and Charlie Ahearn, *Yes Yes Y'all: The Experience Music Project Oral History of Hip-Hop's First Decade* (Boston: Da Capo Press, 2002), 184, 189.

3. Fricke and Ahearn, *Yes Yes Y'all*, 196.

4. Jeff Chang, *Can't Stop Won't Stop: A History of the Hip-Hop Generation* (New York: St. Martin's Press, 2005), 130.

5. Quoted in Jonathan Abrams, *The Come Up: An Oral History of the Rise of Hip-Hop* (New York: Random House, 2022), 49.

6. Chuck Wielgus Jr. and Alexander Wolff, *The In-Your-Face Basketball Book* (New York: Everest House, 1980), 38.

7. Bakari Kitwana, *Why White Kids Love Hip Hop: Wanksta, Wiggers, Wannabes, and the New Reality of Race in America* (New York: Civitas Books, 2006).

8. Wielgus and Wolff, *The In-Your-Face Basketball Book*, 54, 41, 47.

9. Onaje X. O. Woodbine, *Black Gods of the Asphalt: Religion: Hip-Hop, and Street Basketball* (New York: Columbia University Press, 2016), 4, 9.

10. Wielgus and Wolff, *The In-Your-Face Basketball Book*, 59; Thomas P. Oates, "Selling Streetball: Racialized Space, Commercialized Spectacle, and Playground Basketball," *Critical Studies in Media Communication* 34, no. 1 (2017): 94–100.

11. Woodbine, *Black Gods of the Asphalt*, 42.

12. There were other basketball hotbeds at this time, to be sure. Philadelphia, and its famed Baker League where Earl Monroe earned the nickname "Pearl," and Boston, where the Celtics won more than a dozen titles in the sixties and seventies and with a rich playground heritage that Onaje X.O. Woodbine brings to life in *Black Gods of the Asphalt*, merit consideration. But New York City stood head and shoulders above them then.

13. "Power Memorial Academy: A Brief Chronology," https://www.powermemorial academy.com/files/Design/PowerStory.pdf.

14. Pete Axthelm, *The City Game: Basketball in New York from the World Champion Knicks to the World of the Playgrounds* (New York: Harper's Magazine Press, 1970), viii.

15. Sam Goldaper, "Will Knicks Bid for Thompson if He's Free?," *New York Times*, February 20, 1978.

16. Sam Goldaper, "A Trade for Abdul-Jabbar? Whisper Becomes a Rumor," *New York Times*, May 9, 1978.

17. Harvey Araton, "Nets Give Jackson Reprieve," *New York Post*, June 9, 1978; Sam Goldaper, "Nets Get Phil Jackson as Part of a Settlement with Knicks," *New York Times*, June 9, 1978.

18. Harvey Araton, "Knicks Pick an Unknown," *New York Post*, June 9, 1978.

19. Sam Goldaper, "Knicks Lose Again: Settle for a Guard," *New York Times*, June 10, 1978.

20. Goldaper, "Knicks Lose Again."

21. Araton, "Knicks Pick an Unknown.".

22. Harvey Araton, "Knicks' Draft Choices Cram Backcourt," *New York Post*, June 10, 1978.

23. Goldaper, "Knicks Lose Again."

24. Sam Goldaper, "Walton Asks for Trade and Blazers Agree to It," *New York Times*, August 5, 1978.

25. "Walton, Knicks to Meet," *New York Times*, August 6, 1978.

26. Curry Kirkpatrick, "Heavens, What a Year Ahead!" *Sports Illustrated*, October 16, 1978.

27. Kirkpatrick, "Heavens, What a Year Ahead!"

28. Kirkpatrick, "Heavens, What a Year Ahead!"

29. Quoted in Charley Rosen, *Sugar: Micheal Ray Richardson, Eighties Excess, and the NBA* (Lincoln: University of Nebraska Press, 2018), 16.

30. "Richardson Is Older, Wiser and Better," *New York Times*, November 6, 1980; Rosen, *Sugar*, 17; Armen Keteyian, Harvey Araton, and Martin F. Dardis, *Money Players: Days and Nights inside the New NBA* (New York: Pocket Books, 1997), 88.

31. Quoted in Rosen, *Sugar*, 12.

32. Michael Shapiro, "I'm at the Edge of a Cliff," *Sport*, April 1984, 102.

33. Rosen, *Sugar*, 18.

34. Mike Glenn discussion with the author, October 2016.

35. Mike Saunders discussion with the author, March 2020.

36. Dennis D'Agostino, *Garden Glory: An Oral History of the New York Knicks* (Chicago: Triumph Books, 2003), 160

37. Glenn discussion with author.

38. Bob McAdoo discussion with the author, October 2016.

39. Vincent M. Mallozzi, *Asphalt Gods: An Oral History of the Rucker Tournament* (New York: Doubleday, 2003), 2.

40. Wielgus and Wolff, *The In-Your-Face Basketball Book*, 136.

41. Nelson George, *Elevating the Game: Black Men and Basketball* (New York: Harper Collins, 1992), 75.

42. Quoted in Woodbine, *Black Gods of the Asphalt*, 45.

43. Mallozzi, *Asphalt Gods*, 153.

44. Harthorne Wingo discussion with the author, October 2016.

45. Axthelm, *The City Game*, 141.

46. Rick Telander, *Heaven Is a Playground*, 4th ed. (New York: Sports Publishing, 2013), 23.

47. Woodbine, *Black Gods of the Asphalt*, 17.

48. Telander, *Heaven Is a Playground*, 42.

49. Dick Young, "Rose's Case before Public," *Sporting News*, October 28, 1978, 14.

50. Harvey Araton, "Willis Sick of the Rumors," *New York Post*, November 7, 1978.

51. Journalist Harvey Araton used the phrase "vote of confidence" and blamed himself, at least in part, for the reaction of Knicks management to Reed's request for team support. Araton discussion with the author, September 2016.

52. Gene Ward, "No Support for Willis; Promises to Talk," (NY) *Daily News*, November 8, 1978.

53. Phil Pepe, "Holzman Replaces Reed," (NY) *Daily News*, November 11, 1978.

54. McAdoo discussion with author.

55. Glenn discussion with author.

56. Harvey Araton, "Holzman Must Pick," *New York Post*, November 12, 1978; Pepe, "Holzman Replaces Reed."

57. Red Holzman and Harvey Frommer, *Red on Red* (New York: Bantam Books, 1987), 163.

58. Holzman and Frommer, *Red on Red*, 163, 165.

59. Spencer Haywood with Scott Ostler, *Spencer Haywood: The Rise, The Fall, The Recovery.* (New York: Amistad, 1992), 182.

60. Harvey Araton, "Same Old Problems Taint Knicks' Opener," *New York Post*, October 13, 1978.

61. Holzman and Frommer, *Red on Red*, 166.

62. Glenn discussion with author.

63. Holzman and Frommer, *Red on Red*, 165.

64. Mike Lupica, "New Knicks Need Monroe's Class," (NY) *Daily News*, November 7, 1978.

65. Sam Goldaper, "Knicks and Holzman Are Changing Styles," *New York Times*, November 14, 1978; Jim Cleamons discussion with the author, November 2016.

66. "Notes, Quotes and Comments," *Basketball Digest*, March 1979, 14.

67. Sam Goldaper, "Knicks Rolling On; Nets Routed, 140–118," *New York Times*, November 22, 1978.

68. Tony Kornheiser, "Knicks: A Team Seeking Teamwork," *New York Times*, December 27, 1978.

69. Mort Zachter, *Red Holzman: The Life and Legacy of a Hall of Fame Basketball Coach* (New York: Sports Publishing, 2019), 218.

70. Holzman and Frommer, *Red on Red*, 169

71. Rosen, *Sugar*, 22.

72. Harvey Araton, "Knicks' Top Pick Demands Trade," *New York Post*, January 5, 1979.

73. Rosen, *Sugar*, 21, 22.

74. Bill Verigan, "Haywood to Jazz," (NY) *Daily News*, January 6, 1979.

75. Marc J. Spears, *The Spencer Haywood Rule: Battles, Basketball, and the Making of an American Iconoclast* (Chicago: Triumph Books, 2020), 138.

76. Harvey Araton, "Knicks Trade Haywood to New Orleans," *New York Post*, January 6, 1979.

77. Jeff Pearlman, *Showtime: Magic, Kareem, Riley, and the Los Angeles Lakers Dynasty of the 1980s* (New York: Gotham Books, 2014), 48.

78. Spears, *The Spencer Haywood Rule*, 146.

79. Haywood, *Spencer Haywood: The Rise, The Fall, The Recovery*, 192–093.

80. Pearlman, *Showtime*, 82.

81. Pearlman, *Showtime*, 90.

82. Sam Goldaper, "Knicks Drop Fifth in a Row, 122–105," *New York Times*, January 29, 1979; "Knicks' Holzman Finds Silver Lining," *New York Times*, January 26, 1979.

83. Sam Goldaper, "Knicks Lose, 107–104; Streak Is Now at Six," *New York Times*, January 30, 1979.

84. Harvey Araton and Mike Marley, "McAdoo Traded to Celtics," *New York Post*, February 12, 1979.

85. D'Agostino, *Garden Glory*, 164.

86. Harvey Araton, "Sonny: We've Got Nothing to Lose," *New York Post*, February 12, 1979; Sam Goldaper, "Werblin Recalls McAdoo Deal: The Start of Knicks' Road Back," *New York Times*, February 10, 1980.

87. Randy Harvey, "When It Came to Building a Championship Team, Boston's Red Auerbach and a Supporting Case Had All the Answers and, Eventually, the Top Players: The Making of the Celtics," *Los Angeles Times*, June 9, 1985.

88. Malcolm Moran, "McAdoo Frets over Family, Back Pay," *New York Times*, February 13, 1979; McAdoo discussion with author; Bill Verigan, "Mac: Thought I Had Found a Home," (NY) *Daily News*, February 13, 1979.

89. Verigan, "Mac."

90. Verigan, "Mac."

91. Jeffrey Lane, *Under the Boards: the Cultural Revolution in Basketball* (Lincoln: University of Nebraska Press, 2007), 128.

92. Goldaper, "Werblin Recalls McAdoo Deal.".

93. Boston sent McAdoo to Detroit as compensation for signing free agent M. L. Carr and received two first-round picks as well. One of those choices was the first pick of the 1980 NBA draft, which they flipped to the Golden State Warriors for McHale and Parish.

94. Sam Goldaper, "McAdoo Gone, Knicks Set to Rebuild," *New York Times*, February 13, 1979.

95. "What the Hell Happened to . . . Tom Barker?," *Celtics Life*, accessed December 4, 2020, http://www.celticslife.com/2014/09/wthht-tom-barker.html.

96. D'Agostino, *Garden Glory*, 165; Glenn discussion with author.

97. Harvey Araton, "Knicks Pitiful Season Closes on Sour Note," *New York Post*, April 6, 1979.

98. D'Agostino, *Garden Glory*, 167.

99. Araton, "Knicks Pitiful Season."

100. "Notes, Quotes and Comments," *Basketball Digest*, June 1979, 18.

101. Sam Goldaper, "Dear Knicks: Fans Offer Suggestions on Draft Picks," *New York Times*, June 5, 1979. In 1986, Garland went on tour with his half-sister as a background vocalist, having lasted just one season in the NBA.

102. Dave Sims, "Magic, Greenwood 1–2 in Draft," (NY) *Daily News*, June 26, 1979.

103. Harvey Araton, "Cartwright Gunning for No-Trade Contract," *New York Post*, June 26, 1979.

104. Harvey Araton and Leonard Lewin, "Knicks Pick Bill Cartwright," *New York Post*, June 25, 1979.

105. Jerry Izenberg, "Character Reference," *New York Post*, June 26, 1979.

106. Roy S. Johnson, "Were It Any Other Year . . . Bill Cartwright Would Be the NBA's No. 1 Rookie, Not Just the Knick MVP," *Sport*, March 17, 1980.

107. Bill Cartwright discussion with the author, October 2016.

108. Araton, "Cartwright Gunning for No-Trade Contract."

109. Bill Verigan, "Knick Fans Like Choice of Cartwright," (NY) *Daily News*, June 26, 1979.

110. Harvey Araton, "Webster: I'm the Center," *New York Post*, June 27, 1979.

5. "Black, White, Green, or Red"

1. David Halberstam, *Breaks of the Game* (New York: Alfred A. Knopf, 1981), 30.

2. Walt Frazier with Neil Offen, *Walt Frazier: One Magic Season and a Basketball Life* (New York: Crown, 1988), 23, 24.

3. Dave Anderson, "About the All-Black Knicks," *New York Times*, October 25, 1979.

4. Harvey Araton, "Garden Priority: Build a Winner," *New York Post*, October 23, 1979.

5. Jack Krumpe discussion with the author, March 2020.

6. Mike Saunders discussion with the author, March 2020.

7. Krumpe discussion with author.

8. "Over All Black N.Y. Knicks," *Jet*, December 27, 1979.

9. Araton, "Garden Priority."

10. Peter Vecsey, "Fan Views Differ on Color Scheme," *New York Post*, October 23, 1979.

11. Mort Zachter, *Red Holzman: The Life and Legacy of a Hall of Fame Basketball Coach* (New York: Sports Publishing, 2019), 218.

12. Barbara Barker, "Black History Month: Red Holzman's Knicks Were First NBA Team to Have All-Black Roster," *Newsday*, February 15, 2020, https://www.newsday.com/sports/basketball/knicks/knicks-black-history-month-red-holzman-g18781.

13. Ray Weedon, "Knicks . . . Nets: An Analysis," *New York Amsterdam News*, October 6, 1979.

14. "Some N.Y. Knicks' Fans Dislike All Black Team," *Jet*, November 29, 1979.

15. Mel Lowell discussion with the author, March 2020.

16. Marv Fishman with Tracy Dodds, *Bucking the Odds: The Birth of the Milwaukee Bucks* (Milwaukee: Raintree, 1978), 82.

17. Quoted in Bob Ryan, "One of Pro Basketball's Problems Is as Simple as Black and White," *Philadelphia Inquirer*, May 1982.

18. Pete Alfano, "Talking Basketball with . . . Larry O'Brien," *Basketball Digest*, June 1980, 61–62.

19. Ryan, "One of Pro Basketball's Problems Is as Simple as Black and White."

20. Dennis Tredy, "Reflecting the Changing Face of American Society: How 1970's Sitcoms and Spin-Offs Helped Redefine American Identity," *TV/Series*, no. 4 (2013), http://journals.openedition.org/tvseries/735.

21. Quoted in Jonathan Abrams, *The Come Up: An Oral History of the Rise of Hip-Hop* (New York: Random House, 2022), 15, 31.

22. Abrams, *The Come Up*, 30.

23. Tim Lawrence, *Life and Death on the New York Dance Floor, 1980–1983* (Durham: Duke University Press, 2016), 271.

24. Marty Bell, *The Legend of Dr. J* (Coward, McCann and Geoghegan, 1975), 15, 58; Julius Erving and Karl Taro Greenfield, *Dr. J: The Autobiography* (New York: Harper, 2013), 82.

25. Vincent M. Mallozzi, *Asphalt Gods: An Oral History of the Rucker Tournament* (New York: Doubleday, 2003), 103.

26. Chuck Wielgus Jr. and Alexander Wolff, *The In-Your-Face Basketball Book* (New York: Everest House, 1980), 127, 129.

27. Chuck Wielgus and Alexander Wolff, *The Back-In-Your-Face Guide to Pick-Up Basketball: A Have-Jump-Shot, Will-Travel Tour of America's Hoops Hotspots* (New York: Dodd Mead, 1987), 133, 139.

28. Wielgus and Wolff, *The Back-In-Your-Face Guide to Pick-Up Basketball*, xx.

29. Derrick P. Alridge and James B. Stewart, "Introduction: Hip Hop in History: Past, Present, and Future," *Journal of African American History* 90, no. 3 (Summer 2005): 190–95.

30. Thomas Turner, "German Sports Shoes, Basketball, and Hip Hop: The Consumption and Cultural Significance of the Adidas 'Superstar', 1966–1988," *Sport in History*, 35, no. 1 (2015): 127–55.

31. Gabe Filippa, "Sneakers That Defined 1980s Hip Hop," *Sneaker Freaker*, February 14, 2019, https://www.sneakerfreaker.com/features/sneakers-that-defined-1980s-hip-hop; Pete Croatto, *From Hang Time to Prime Time: Business, Entertainment, and the Birth of the Modern-Day NBA* (New York: Atria Books, 2020), 206.

32. Croatto, *From Hang Time to Prime Time*, 224.

33. Harvey Araton, *Crashing the Borders: How Basketball Won the World and Lost Its Soul at Home* (New York: Free Press, 2005), 26.

34. Quoted in Peter L'Official, *Urban Legends: The South Bronx in Representation and Ruin* (Cambridge, MA: Harvard University Press, 2020), 22.

35. Kyle Longley, "Why Donald Trump Is Just Following in Ronald Reagan's Footsteps on Race," *Washington Post*, August 4, 2019.

36. Peter Vecsey, "Fan Views Differ on Color Scheme," *New York Post*, October 23, 1979.

37. Vecsey, "Fan Views Differ on Color Scheme."

38. Dennis D'Agostino, *Garden Glory: An Oral History of the New York Knicks* (Chicago: Triumph Books, 2003), 167–69.

39. Barker, "Black History Month."

40. Rory Sparrow discussion with the author, February 2020. Sparrow was in his senior season at Villanova in 1979/80 and would go on to play for the Knicks from midway through the 1982/83 season through the very beginning of the 1987/88 season.

41. Barker, "Black History Month."

42. Dan Shaughnessy, "Recalling All-Black Knicks," *Philadelphia Inquirer*, May 3, 1982.

43. Spike Lee and Ralph Wiley, *Best Seat in the House: A Basketball Memoir* (New York: Crown Publishers, 1997), 94.

44. Howie Evans, "The Knicks: Color Them Black," *New York Amsterdam News*, October 20, 1979.

45. Frank T. Bannister Jr., "Search for 'White Hopes' Threatens Black Athletes," *Ebony*, February 1980, 130–34.

46. Richard Lapchick and David Zimmerman, "The 2020 Racial and Gender Report Card: National Basketball Association," July 23, 2020, tidesport.org/.

47. Jonathan Rieder, *Canarsie: The Jews and Italians of Brooklyn against Liberalism* (Cambridge, MA: Harvard University Press, 1985), 1, 41, 61, 121–22.

48. Saunders discussion with the author.

49. Sam Goldaper, "Can Williams Lead the Knicks?," *New York Times*, September 16, 1979.

50. Bill Cartwright discussion with the author, October 2016.

51. Sam Goldaper, "Only 7,911 at Garden Watch Knicks Rout Pacers by 136–112," *New York Times*, October 24, 1979.

52. Red Holzman and Harvey Frommer, *Red on Red* (New York: Bantam Books, 1987), 175.

53. Jim Cleamons discussion with the author, November 2016.

54. Sam Goldaper, "Knicks Defeat Bullets, 107–104, as Richardson Scores at the Buzzer," *New York Times*, December 6, 1979.

55. Jane Gross, "Earl Monroe: His Magic Act Isn't Over Yet," *Basketball Digest*, January 1980, 52.

56. Saunders discussion with author.

57. George Kalinsky and Pete Hamill, *Garden of Dreams: Madison Square Garden, 125 Years* (New York: Stewart, Tabori & Chang, 2004), 67.

58. Don Markus, "Four Decades Later, Baltimore Has Fond, Bittersweet Memories for Monroe," *Baltimore Sun*, March 21, 2012; "Earl Monroe," *Reverse Spin Entertainment*, accessed May 10, 2023, https://web.archive.org/web/20120312081656/http://reverse spinentertainment.com/earl-the-pearl-monroe.

59. William Jelani Cobb, *To the Break of Dawn: A Freestyle on the Hip Hop Aesthetic* (New York: New York University Press, 2007), 45.

60. Lawrence, *Life and Death on the New York Dance Floor*, 100.

61. Ken McLeod, " 'We Are the Champions': Masculinities, Sports and Popular Music," *Popular Music and Society* 29, no. 5 (December 2006): 531–47.

62. Todd Boyd, *Young, Black, Rich, and Famous: The Rise of the NBA, the Hip Hop Invasion and the Transformation of American Culture* (New York: Doubleday, 2003), 12, 15.

63. Quoted in Croatto, *From Hang Time to Prime Time*, 150, 155, 156.

64. Croatto, *From Hang Time to Prime Time*, 159.

65. David Toop, *Rap Attack 3: African Rap to Global Hip Hop* (London: Serpent's Tail, 2000), 161.

66. Ronin Ro, *Raising Hell: The Reign, Ruin, and Redemption of Run-D.M.C. and Jam Master Jay* (New York: Amistad, 2005).

67. Roy S. Johnson, "Were It Any Other Year . . . Bill Cartwright Would Be the NBA's No. 1 Rookie, Not Just the Knick MVP," *Sport*, March 17, 1980.

68. Johnson, "Were It Any Other Year."

69. Johnson, "Were It Any Other Year."

70. Cartwright discussion with author.

71. Barker, "Black History Month."

72. Al Harvin, "Knicks Raise Hopes for Playoff, Beating Cavaliers by 128–115," *New York Times*, March 26, 1980.

73. Joe O'Day, "Red Hollers Foul after Dr. J's Play," (NY) *Daily News*, March 28, 1980.

74. Harvey Araton, "Dr. J's Steal Puts Knicks' Playoff Hopes on Thin Ice," *New York Post*, March 28, 1980.

75. Holzman and Frommer, *Red on Red*, 177.

76. Sam Goldaper, "Knicks Root Hard in Vain," *New York Times*, March 31, 1980.

77. David Sims, "Richardson Watches Season End," (NY) *Daily News*, March 31, 1980.

78. Mike Lupica, " 'No Practice Today' Sign Goes Up at Garden," (NY) *Daily News*, March 31, 1980.

79. Harvey Araton, "Knicks Quietly Head Home," *New York Post*, April 1, 1980.

80. "Notes, Quotes and Comments," *Basketball Digest*, May 1980, 16.

6. "Colorful yet Colorless"

1. Jim Fricke and Charlie Ahearn, *Yes Yes Y'all: The Experience Music Project Oral History of Hip-Hop's First Decade* (Boston: Da Capo Press, 2002), 309.

2. Ronin Ro, *Raising Hell: The Reign, Ruin, and Redemption of Run-D.M.C. and Jam Master Jay* (New York: Amistad, 2005).

3. Quoted in Jonathan Abrams, *The Come Up: An Oral History of the Rise of Hip-Hop* (New York: Random House, 2022), 69.

4. Kevin Armstrong, "The Price of Being Pearl," (NY) *Daily News*, January 7, 2017.

5. Jack Wilkinson, "Draft crowd roars as Kiki goes Dallas," (NY) *Daily News*, June 11, 1980.

6. Wilkinson, "Draft crowd roars."

7. Harvey Araton, "Knicks: Woodson, Scales," *New York Post*, June 10, 1980.

8. Mimi Sheraton, "Restaurants," *New York Times*, April 14, 1978.

9. Michael Burke, *Outrageous Good Fortune* (Boston: Little, Brown, 1984), 407.

10. Mike Glenn discussion with the author, October 2016.

11. Glenn discussion with author. As of 2023, the only other Knick to win the award was Rory Sparrow in 1986, who was named co-recipient with Lakers guard Michael Cooper.

12. Sam Goldaper, "Knicks Showing Pep," *New York Times*, September 13, 1980.

13. Bill Cartwright discussion with the author, October 2016.

14. Sam Goldaper, "Knicks Fret over Knight," *New York Times*, September 25, 1980.

15. Campy Russell discussion with the author, January 2017; Sam Goldaper, "Knicks Get Russell, Lose Ailing Knight," *New York Times*, September 26, 1980.

16. Sam Goldaper, "New Season Brings New Faces and Inspires New Hope," *New York Times*, October 5, 1980.

17. Peter Vecsey, "Knick Backcourt Taking Command," *New York Post*, October 14, 1980.

18. Sam Goldaper, "Knicks Overwhelm 76ers, 113–93," *New York Times*, October 15, 1980.

19. Steve Hershey, "Campy What Knicks Needed to Trigger Fast Getaway," *Sporting News*, November 8, 1980, 33.

20. Carrie Seidman, "Knicks Triumph; Webster Ejected," *New York Times*, November 8, 1980.

21. Harvey Araton, "Knicks Seeking Back-up Forward," *New York Post*, November 10, 1980.

22. "Society World," *Jet*, December 4, 1980.

23. Russell discussion with author.

24. The 1980–81 Knicks finished fourth in the NBA in turnovers created and sixth in turnovers.

25. Sam Goldaper, "Knicks Extend Richardson Pact," *New York Times*, November 11, 1980.

26. Peter Vecsey, "Richardson Signs New Contract," *New York Post*, November 11, 1980.

27. George Vecsey, "As New Knicks Move Forward, They Must Deal with the Past," *New York Times*, February 2, 1981; Nat Gottlieb, "New Knicks Haunted by Old Halo," *Sporting News*, December 20, 1980, 31.

28. Vecsey, "As New Knicks Move Forward".

29. Gerald Eskenazi, "With Its New Arena, Meadowlands Influence Is Still Growing," *New York Times*, March 15, 1981.

30. "World Series Television Ratings," *Baseball Almanac*, accessed March 12, 202, 1https://www.baseball-almanac.com/ws/wstv.shtml.

31. Sam Goldaper, "Fan Loss Worries N.B.A.," *New York Times*, November 4, 1980.

32. Goldaper, "Fan Loss Worries N.B.A."

33. Allan Tannenbaum, *New York in the 70s* (New York: Overlook Duckworth, 2011), 6.

34. Sam Goldaper, "Knicks Win, Gain Home-Court Advantage," *New York Times*, March 21, 1981.

35. Sam Goldaper, "Knicks' Richardson: 27 Points, 19 Assists," *New York Times*, March 22, 1981.

36. Mike Shalin, "Gilmore Swats Away 'Flies' in the Middle," *New York Post*, April 1, 1981.

37. Rory Sparrow discussion with the author, February 2020.

38. Frank Litsky, "Gilmore Helps Slow Fast-Starting Knicks," *New York Times*, April 1, 1981.

39. Harvey Araton, "Bulls Back Knicks against Playoff Wall," *New York Post*, April 1, 1981.

40. Harvey Araton, "Bulls oust Knicks in OT, 115–114," *New York Post*, April 4, 1981.

41. Gary Myers, "Gilmore Plays Sluggo to Knicks' Mr. Bill," (NY) *Daily News*, April 1, 1981.

42. Gary Myers, "Confusion Reigns as Knick Season Ends," (NY) *Daily News*, April 4, 1981.

43. Sam Goldaper, "Knicks Facing Several Problems," *New York Times*, April 5, 1981.

44. Peter Vecsey, "Point Finger at Management," *New York Post*, April 6, 1981.

45. Red Holzman and Harvey Frommer, *Red on Red* (New York: Bantam Books, 1987), 183.

46. Campy Russell discussion with author.

47. John Papanek, "Now Randy Is a Dandy," *Sports Illustrated*, March 31, 1975, 56–59.

48. Sam Goldaper, "Knicks Get Cavs' Smith," *New York Times*, May 21, 1981.

49. Gary Myers, "Knicks Send No. 1 to Cavs for Smith," (NY) *Daily News*, May 21, 1981.

50. Harvey Araton, "Knicks' Newlin Deal Clouds Ray's Future," *New York Post*, June 9, 1981.

51. Sam Goldaper, "Financial Difficulties in Sight for N.B.A.," *New York Times*, June 14, 1981.

52. Araton, "Knicks' Newlin Deal Clouds Ray's Future."

53. Joshua Mendelsohn, *The Cap: How Larry Fleisher and David Stern Built the Modern NBA* (Lincoln: University of Nebraska Press, 2020), 25.

54. Peter Richmond, "The NBA Financial Picture: Cloudy, Fuzzy and Fading Fast?," *Basketball Digest*, March 1982, 54–61.

55. Kevin Kernan, "NBA Searches for Solution to Financial Woes," *New York Post*, January 30, 1982.

56. Bruce Newman, "Can the NBA Save Itself?" *Sports Illustrated*, November 1, 1982.

57. Mendelsohn, *The Cap*, 193.

58. Nelson George, "The New Bidding Game in Sports," *Black Enterprise*, January 1983, 31, 32.

59. Araton, "Knicks' Newlin Deal Clouds Ray's Future."

60. George Vecsey, "Knicks, Williams Do a Disco Dance," *New York Times*, August 10, 1981.

7. "The Ship Be Sinking"

1. "MTV Launches," *This Day in History*, HISTORY Network, accessed May 12, 2023, https://www.history.com/this-day-in-history/mtv-launches.

2. J. Pablo, "Ralph McDaniels Keeps Hip-Hop Culture Moving Forward," *Village Voice*, November 16, 2011, https://www.villagevoice.com/2011/11/16/ralph-mcdaniels-keeps-hip-hop-culture-moving-forward; Nas, dir., *You're Watching Video Music Box* (Showtime, 2022).

3. Pablo, "Ralph McDaniels."

4. Dave Sims, "Nets' Williams Isn't Just Heavy in the Wallet," *New York Daily News*, October 27, 1981.

5. Red Holzman and Harvey Frommer, *Red on Red* (New York: Bantam Books, 1987), 182.

6. Mike Glenn discussion with the author, October 2016.

7. Campy Russell discussion with the author, January 2017.

8. Neil Best, "New 'Beginnings' for Micheal Ray Richardson," *Newsday*, November 12, 2014.

9. Charley Rosen, *Sugar: Micheal Ray Richardson, Eighties Excess, and the NBA* (Lincoln: University of Nebraska Press, 2018), 35.

10. Holzman and Frommer, *Red on Red*, 182.

11. Russell discussion with author.

12. David Halberstam, *Breaks of the Game* (New York: Alfred A. Knopf, 1981), 55.

13. Sam Goldaper, "Lucas Shows Class in Debut for Knicks," *New York Times*, October 27, 1981.

14. Harvey Araton, "Lucas Finds Home under Knicks' Boards," *New York Post*, October 27, 1981.

15. Thom Greer, "New Lease on Life for Eager Lucas," *New York Daily News*, October 27, 1981.

16. Roy S. Johnson, "Lucas Keeps the House in Order," *New York Times*, December 6, 1981.

17. Jonathan Soffer, *Ed Koch and the Rebuilding of New York City* (New York: Columbia University Press, 2010), 262.

18. Themis Chronopoulos, *Spatial Regulation in New York City: From Urban Renewal to Zero Tolerance* (New York: Routledge, 2011), 83; Themis Chronopoulos and Jonathan Soffer, "After the Urban Crisis: New York and the Rise of Inequality," *Journal of Urban History* 43, no. 6 (2017): 855–63.

19. Chronopoulos, *Spatial Regulation*.

20. Quoted in Jonathan Abrams, *The Come Up: An Oral History of the Rise of Hip-Hop* (New York: Random House, 2022), 7.

21. Quoted in Chronopoulos, *Spatial Regulation*, 108.

22. Soffer, *Ed Koch*, 255.

23. Peter Bailey, "Can Harlem Be Saved?" *Ebony*, January 1983, 83.

24. Soffer, *Ed Koch*, 244.

25. Sam Goldaper, "Burke Is Retiring from Garden Posts," *New York Times*, September 20, 1981.

26. George Kalinsky and Pete Hamill, *Garden of Dreams: Madison Square Garden 125 Years* (New York: Stewart, Tabori & Chang, 2004), 92, 96, 98.

27. Disco Demolition Night in Chicago was July 12, 1979; punk transitioned to post-punk about two years earlier.

28. Jeff Chang, *Can't Stop Won't Stop: A History of the Hip-Hop Generation* (New York: St. Martin's Press, 2005), 128.

29. Murray Forman and Mark Anthony Neal, eds. *That's the Joint! The Hip-Hop Studies Reader* (New York: Routledge, 2004), 147.

30. Tricia Rose, *Black Noise: Rap Music and Black Culture in Contemporary America* (Hanover, NH: Wesleyan University Press, 1994), 5.

31. Chang, *Can't Stop Won't Stop*, 194. In 1986, Run-DMC performed "My Adidas" and the connection to hip-hop was complete.

32. Louie Robinson, "The Blackening of White America," *Ebony*, May 1980, 160.

33. Bakari Kitwana, *Why White Kids Love Hip-Hop: Wankstas, Wiggers, Wannabes, and the New Reality of Race in America* (New York: Basic Books, 2005), 24.

34. Quoted in Kitwana, *Why White Kids Love Hip-Hop*, 26–27.

35. Rhonda E. McKinney, "What's Behind the Rise of Rap?" *Ebony*, January 1989.

36. Kitwana, *Why White Kids Love Hip-Hop*, 71.

37. Charles Whitaker, "The Real Story behind the Rap Revolution," *Ebony*, June 1990, 34.

38. Chang, *Can't Stop Won't Stop*, 137.

39. Quoted in Abrams, *The Come Up*, 88.

40. Andrew Gee, "Beastie Boys' Mike D Recalls a 'F*cking Clown' Move That Taught the Crew to Be Themselves as White MCs," *Uproxx*, https://uproxx.com/music/mike-d-beastie-boys-white-rappers.

41. Thom Greer, "Lucas: Inside Story of Knicks' Success," *New York Daily News*, October 31, 1981.

42. Sam Goldaper, "Knicks Lose 4th Straight," *New York Times*, November 20, 1981.

43. Sam Goldaper, "Knicks' Latest Loss Follows a Pattern," *New York Times*, November 16, 1981.

44. Sam Goldaper, "Knicks Routed by Bullets, 114–88: Werblin Angered," *New York Times*, December 4, 1981.

45. Sam Goldaper, "A Mature Cartwright Becomes More Physical on Rebounding," *New York Times*, December 20, 1981.

46. Sam Goldaper, "'Sugar' Key to Knicks," *New York Times*, January 4, 1982.

47. Rosen, *Sugar*, 37; Ed Marks, "Nets Beat Knicks; Ax over Holzman," *Daily Record* (Morristown, NJ), December 26, 1981; Mort Zachter, *Red Holzman: The Life and Legacy of a Hall of Fame Basketball Coach* (New York: Sports Publishing, 2019), 223.

48. Rosen, *Sugar*, 36; Gary Buiso, "Knicks Fixed Games for Drug Dealers: FBI Probe," *New York Post*, September 14, 2013.

49. Brian Tuohy, *Larceny Games: Sports Gambling, Game Fixing and the FBI* (Port Townsend, WA: Feral House, 2013), 201.

50. Sam Goldaper, "Knicks Toppled in Overtime," *New York Times*, January 11, 1982.

51. "Knicks Set Back Hawks, 104–101," *New York Times*, January 23, 1982.

52. Sam Goldaper, "Questions Remain for Knicks," *New York Times*, January 29, 1982.

53. Steve Hershey, "Forward Problems Continue in 'As the Knicks Turn,'" *Sporting News*, January 23, 1982.

54. Sam Goldaper, "Williams of Knicks Draws Suspension," *New York Times*, January 31, 1982.

55. Harvey Araton, "Sly: I Was Shocked by the Suspension," *New York Post*, February 2, 1982; Roy S. Johnson, "Knicks Triumph; Williams Returns," *New York Times*, February 4, 1982.

56. Thom Greer, "Red's Task: Reinstate Discipline," *New York Daily News*, January 29, 1982.

57. Sam Goldaper, "Sonics Trounce Knicks," *New York Times*, January 26, 1982.

58. Chris Mitchell, "The Killing of Murder," *New York Magazine*, January 4, 2008.

59. Quoted in Herbert London, *The Broken Apple: New York City in the 1980s* (New Brunswick, NJ: Transaction Publishers, 1989), 203.

60. London, *The Broken Apple*, 193.

61. u/GaryTheJerk, "When turned over & placed side-by-side, these singles form a piece by graffiti pioneer/The Clash collaborator Futura 2000 (1982)," *Reddit*, January 8, 2020. https://www.reddit.com/r/vinyl/comments/em2p8e/when_turned_over_placed_sideby side_these_singles.

62. David Gonzalez, "Graffiti Is Back in Virus-Worn New York," *New York Times*, July 8, 2020.

63. Steve Hershey, "Bring on Wilt? Sixers Desperate," *Sporting News*, February 6, 1982.

64. Spike Lee and Ralph Wiley, *Best Seat in the House: A Basketball Memoir* (New York: Crown Publishers, Inc., 1997), 87.

65. Rosen, *Sugar*, 36.

66. Rosen, *Sugar*, 36.

67. London, *The Broken Apple*, 145.

68. Quoted in Chris Herring, *Blood in the Garden: The Flagrant History of the 1990s New York Knicks* (New York: Atria Books, 2022), 11.

69. Spencer Haywood with Scott Ostler, *Spencer Haywood: The Rise, the Fall, the Recovery* (New York: Amistad, 1992), 182.

70. Haywood and Ostler, *Spencer Haywood*, 33, 190, 192–93; Matthew Schneider-Mayerson, " 'Too Black': Race in the "Dark Ages" of the National Basketball Association," *The International Journal of Sport and Society*, 230.

71. Will Hermes, *Love Goes to Buildings on Fire: Five Years in New York That Changed Music Forever* (New York: Faber and Faber, 2011), 186, 193.

72. Michael Weinreb, *Bigger than the Game: Bo, Boz, The Punky QB, and How the '80s Created the Modern Athlete* (New York: Gotham Books, 2010), 63.

73. Associated Press, "Porter Yielded to Pressure" *Daily Union* (Junction City, KS), February 26, 1981.

74. Carol Anderson, *White Rage: The Unspoken Truth of Our Racial Divide* (New York: Bloomsbury, 2016), 124.

75. Todd Boyd, *Young, Black, Rich, and Famous: The Rise of the NBA, the Hip Hop Invasion and the Transformation of American Culture* (New York: Doubleday, 2003), 35, 39.

76. Sam Goldaper, "N.B.A. Will Ban Drug Users," *New York Times*, September 29, 1983.

77. Anderson, *White Rage*, 130.

78. Jamel Shabazz, *A Time before Crack* (Brooklyn: PowerHouse Books, 2005), 144–45.

79. "Former NBA All Star Micheal Ray Richardson Reportedly Has . . .," United Press International, May 5, 1987.

80. "Sonics Lose on Westphal," *New York Daily News*, March 7, 1982.

81. "Schulman Says No to Knicks," *New York Times*, February 25, 1982; Harvey Araton, "Knicks, Sonics battle for Westphal," *New York Post*, February 25, 1982.

82. Thom Greer, " 'Secret' Pact Worth Extra 700G to Westphal," *New York Daily News*, March 12, 1982.

83. Holzman and Frommer, *Red on Red*, 42.

84. John Hewig discussion with the author, October 2016.

85. Hewig discussion with the author.

86. Hewig discussion with the author.

87. Sam Goldaper, "Knicks Defeat Cavaliers," *New York Times*, March 24, 1982.

88. Sam Goldaper, "Bulls Beat Knicks," *New York Times*, April 15, 1982.

89. Harvey Araton, "All-Time Low Crowd at Garden Watches Bulls Trample Knicks," *New York Post*, April 15, 1982.

90. Andrew Bagnato, "As a Teen Paul Westphal Spurned National Power UCLA to Play at Rival USC. Now He Has Left the NBA Grind for a Low-Key Pepperdine Program," *Chicago Tribune*, February 15, 2002.

91. Bob Ryan, *Celtic Pride: The Rebuilding of Boston's World Championship Basketball Team* (Boston: Little, Brown, 1975), 157.

92. "'JJ' Sore over Westphal's Style of Pro Basketball," *Jet*, October 5, 1978, 13.

93. Sam Goldaper, "Bullets Defeat Knicks," *New York Times*, March 14, 1982; Sam Goldaper, "Knicks Suspend Absent Williams for the Season," *New York Times*, March 31, 1982.

94. Roy S. Johnson, "Knicks Eliminated as Playoff Contender," *New York Times*, April 9, 1982.

95. Quoted in Herring, *Blood in the Garden*, 11.

96. Johnson, "Knicks Eliminated."

97. Russell discussion with author.

98. "Statistical Minimums to Qualify for NBA League Leaders," https://www.nba.com/stats/help/statminimums.

8. "A Policy of Patience"

1. "The Presence of the Past: Turning Points in NYC," Philip Napoli, Macaulay Honors College, City University of New York, 2008, https://macaulay.cuny.edu/seminars/napoli08/articles/t/h/e/The_Tumultuous_80s_and_Bensonhurst_709c.html.

2. "Manslaughter Conviction in Racial Mob Slaying," United Press International, March 9, 1983, https://www.upi.com/Archives/1983/03/09/Manslaughter-conviction-in-racial-mob-slaying/9070416034000.

3. Jason Sokol, *All Eyes Are upon Us: Race and Politics from Boston to Brooklyn: The Conflicted Soul of the Northeast* (New York: Basic Books, 2014), 259.

4. John Hewig discussion with the author, October 2016.

5. Harvey Araton and Leonard Lewin, "It's Finally Official," *New York Post*, May 20, 1982.

6. Richard O'Connor, "Life in a Game Situation," *Sport*, February 1978, 45–48.

7. Steve Oney, "'It's Okay If You're a Machine': Inside Hubie Brown's Brutal Philosophy," *Atlanta Journal and Constitution*, December 9, 1979.

8. Richard O'Connor, "Rating the NBA Coaches," *Sport*, March 1979, 92.

9. Bruce Newman, "The Gospel According to Hubie," *Sports Illustrated*, October 31, 1983.

10. David DuPree, "Hubie Brown: Basketball's Sideline Showman Psyches Up for the Toughest Job in the NBA," *Sport*, November 1982, 25–30.

11. The boxing magazine was *The Ring*, the Boston restaurant was Clarke's, and the restaurant in Manhattan was the George Martin.

12. Leonard Sloane, "Dave DeBusschere Finds Business Is a Pleasure," *New York Times*, June 4, 1981.

13. Peter Alfano, "DeBusschere, Brown Try to Lift Knicks Out of Past," *New York Times*, October 24, 1982.

14. Hewig discussion with author. Hewig also tells a story about the introductory press conference during which DeBusschere and Brown barely acknowledged each other's presence.

15. Dave Sims, "DeBusschere Claims Brown Was His Pick," (NY)*Daily News*, May 21, 1982.

16. Sam Goldaper, "Knicks to Build by Draft: Aim for 2 High Picks," *New York Times*, June 16, 1982.

17. Harvey Araton, "Hubie: I Answer to DeBusschere," *New York Post*, May 21, 1982.

18. Eric Compton, "Knicks Regime Faces Initial Test of Draft Smarts," (NY) *Daily News*, June 29, 1982.

19. Harvey Araton, "Knicks Are Hot on the Trail of Suns' Truck," *New York Post*, June 28, 1982.

20. Sam Goldaper, "Knicks' Top Choice Is 6–5 Trent Tucker," *New York Times*, June 30, 1982; Maurey Allen and Harvey Araton, "Knicks Pick Gopher Guard Trent Tucker," *New York Post*, June 30, 1982.

21. Trent Tucker discussion with the author, November 2016.

22. Harvey Araton, "Knicks Deal Lucas to Suns for Truck Robinson," *New York Post*, July 8, 1982; Sam Goldaper, "Lucas Is Traded to Suns," *New York Times*, July 8, 1982.

23. John Feinstein, "As Camps Add Up, the Followers Are Divided," *Washington Post*, July 25, 1984.

24. Sam Goldaper, "Knicks See Grunfeld as 3-Position Player," *New York Times*, October 4, 1982.

25. Hubie Brown discussion with the author, February 2020.

26. Goldaper, "Knicks See Grunfeld."

27. Paul Knepper, *The Knicks of the Nineties: Ewing, Oakley, Starks and the Brawlers That Almost Won It All* (Jefferson, NC: McFarland, 2020), 51.

28. Jeff Chang, *Can't Stop Won't Stop: A History of the Hip-Hop Generation* (New York: St. Martin's Press, 2005), 18.

29. Sam Goldaper, "Brown Works Knicks Hard," *New York Times*, October 3, 1982.

30. Mike Douchant, "Hoop Scoop," *Sporting News*, October 4, 1982.

31. Kevin Kernan, "Knicks Ship Sugar," *New York Post*, October 23, 1982.

32. Sam Goldaper, "Warriors Match Offer to King," *New York Times*, October 14, 1982.

33. Harvey Araton, "Warrior Owner Foils King deal," *New York Post*, October 14, 1982.

34. Sam Goldaper, "Warriors Match Offer to King," *New York Times*, October 14, 1982.

35. Kernan, "Knicks Ship Sugar."

36. Goldaper, "Warriors Match Offer to King."

37. Harvey Araton, "Knicks Are Still Missing Point at Guard," *New York Post*, October 25, 1982.

38. Bernard King and Jerome Preisler, *Game Face: A Lifetime of Hard-Earned Lessons on and off the Basketball Court* (Cambridge, MA: DeCapo Press, 2017), 201.

39. Paul Needell, "Knicks' New King Anxious to Please," (NY) *Daily News*, October 26, 1982.

40. King and Preisler, *Game Face*, 201.

41. King and Preisler, *Game Face*, 206.

42. Sam Goldaper, "Knicks Beaten in Opener," *New York Times*, October 30, 1982; Paul Needell, "Nets Win Opener; 76ers Rip Knicks," (NY) *Daily News*, October 30, 1982.

43. Needell, "Nets Win Opener."

44. Harvey Araton, "Warriors Sweet on Sugar," *Sporting News*, November 29, 1982, 54.

45. King and Preisler, *Game Face*, 207. Darrell Walker clashed with Brown on numerous occasions, he told me. "I wasn't going to be talked to like I was a dog and wasn't going to accept that treatment." Darrell Walker discussion with the author, December 2016.

46. King and Preisler, *Game Face*, 208, 209.

47. King and Preisler, *Game Face*, 209.

48. Sam Goldaper, "Brown Works Knicks Hard," *New York Times*, October 3, 1982.

49. Sam Goldaper, "Knicks Win First after Seven Losses," *New York Times*, November 13, 1982.

50. Sam Goldaper, "Knicks Hedge on Point Guard," *New York Times*, October 26, 1982.

51. Sam Goldaper, "King's 25 Bolster Knicks," *New York Times*, December 2, 1982.

52. Sam Goldaper, "Robinson Slump Hurts Knicks," *New York Times*, December 6, 1982.

53. Sam Goldaper, "Knicks Beaten by Suns," *New York Times*, January 5, 1983.

54. Sam Goldaper, "Knicks: A New Look, but Few Watch," *New York Times*, January 23, 1983.

55. Steve Hershey, "Knicks Sagging at Center," *Sporting News*, January 10, 1983.

56. Harvey Araton, "Cartwright Rebounds against Foes, Critics," (NY) *Daily News*, January 21, 1983.

57. Sam Goldaper, "Knicks' Robinson Is Finding His Role," *New York Times,* January 24, 1983.

58. Sam Goldaper, "Knicks Win by 33 before 6,514 at Garden," *New York Times*, January 24, 1983.

59. "Knicks Acquire Sparrow," *New York Times*, February 14, 1983; New York Knicks, "#NYK70 Presented by Chase: Remembering '84," YouTube, March 29, 2017, https://www.youtube.com/watch?v=ZMkTsNWmQhE&ab_channel=NewYorkKnicks;Rory Sparrow discussion with the author, February 2020.

60. Sam Goldaper, "Knicks Win; 32 for Cartwright," *New York Times*, February 26, 1983.

61. Michael Katz, "Knicks Defeated by 76ers, 106–94," *New York Times*, March 2, 1983.

62. Steve Hershey, "Knicks Get the Message, Learn Defense Pays Off," *Sporting News*, March 7, 1983.

63. Frank Litsky, "Knicks Close Their Trap on Pacers," *New York Times*, February 9, 1983.

64. Sam Goldaper, "Knicks Defeat Celtics, 122–110," *New York Times*, March 14, 1983.

65. Mel Lowell discussion with the author, March 2020.

66. Sam Goldaper, "Knicks Trounce Bucks for 7th Straight," *New York Times*, March 17, 1983.

67. King and Preisler, *Game Face*, 109; Russ Devault, "Troubled Bernard Is Now King of the Nets," *Basketball Digest*, March 1978, 88–92.

68. Bert Rosenthal, "The Knicks' One-Man Offense Bernard King," *Basketball Digest*, April 1983, 16–21.

69. Israel, dir., *The Freshest Kids* (Los Angeles: QD3 Entertainment, 2002).

70. Quoted in Jonathan Abrams, *The Come Up: An Oral History of the Rise of Hip-Hop* (New York: Random House, 2022), 73.

71. "Basketball Throwdown Lyrics," Genius, accessed March 10, 2021, https://genius.com/The-cold-crush-brothers-vs-fantastic-freaks-basketball-throwdown-lyrics.

72. Sparrow discussion with author.

73. George Vecsey, "The Big East," *New York Times*, March 13, 1983.

74. Vecsey, "The Big East."

75. "Knicks Will Pay to Keep Hubie," (NY) *Daily News*, April 18, 1983.

76. Harvey Araton, "Hubie Blasts Larry," (NY) *Daily News*, April 22, 1983.

77. Paul Needell, "Knicks, Nets Cannot Wait to Get Going," (NY)*Daily News*, April 19, 1983.

78. Len Elmore discussion with the author, October 2016.

79. Roy S. Johnson, "Knicks Win Playoff Opener," *New York Times*, April 21, 1983.

80. Mike Lupica, "Knicks' Fans Shout: 'We Want Philly,'" (NY)*Daily News*, April 22, 1983.

81. Ed Barkowitz, "How Andrew Toney Became the 'Boston Strangler,'" *Philadelphia Inquirer*, May 26, 2012.

82. Kevin Kernan, "Moses Mows 'Em Down," *New York Post*, April 25, 1983.

83. Kevin Kernan, "King's Ankle Pains Knicks," *New York Post*, April 25, 1983.

84. Harvey Araton, "Numbers Don't Lie: Cartwright's Days Are Numbered," (NY) *Daily News*, April 29, 1983.

85. Mike Lupica, "Knicks' Special April—May It Last Forever," (NY) *Daily News*, May 1, 1983.

86. Sam Goldaper, "76ers Beat Knicks by 107–105 in Last 0:02 for 3–0 Lead," *New York Times*, May 1, 1983.

87. Paul Needell and Harvey Araton, "Truck to Suns: I Have Proven I'm Not a Loser," (NY) *Daily News*, May 2, 1983.

88. Kevin Kernan, "Death-Row Knicks Eye a Stay of Execution," *New York Post*, April 30, 1983.

89. "McHale and Knicks to Meet," *New York Times*, June 22, 1983.

90. Phil Pepe, "Fans Love Knick Pick of Walker," (NY) *Daily News*, June 29, 1983; Walker discussion with author.

91. Pepe, "Fans Love Knick Pick."

92. Pete Croatto, *From Hang Time to Prime Time: Business, Entertainment, and the Birth of the Modern-Day NBA* (New York: Atria Books, 2020), 43.

93. Croatto, *From Hang Time to Prime Time*, 58.

94. Quoted in Croatto, *From Hang Time to Prime Time* 105.

95. Shawn Fury, "How NBA Entertainment Helped Save the League and Spread a Renaissance," *Vice*, June 15, 2016, accessed December 4, 2020, https://www.vice.com/en/article/mgzgg3/how-nba-entertainment-helped-save-the-league-and-spread-a-renaissance.

96. Croatto, *From Hang Time to Prime Time*, 105.

97. Joshua Mendelsohn, *The Cap: How Larry Fleisher and David Stern Built the Modern NBA* (Lincoln: University of Nebraska Press, 2020), 223.

98. Sam Goldaper, "Financial Difficulties in Sight for N.B.A.," *New York Times*, June 14, 1981.

99. Mendelsohn, *The Cap*, 233, 235.

100. Quoted in Mendelsohn, *The Cap*, 271.

101. Phil Elderkin, "Pro Basketball's 'Landmark' Decision and What It Means," *Christian Science Monitor*, April 11, 1983.

9. "To the Hoop, Y'All"

1. Kevin Kernan, "Cool-Hand Hubie Returns," *New York Post*, October 25, 1983.

2. Bruce Newman, "The Gospel According to Hubie," *Sports Illustrated*, October 31, 1983.

3. John Hewig discussion with the author, October 2016.

4. Kevin Kernan, "Knick Tough Guys Fighting to Revive the Glory Years," *New York Post*, October 21, 1983.

5. Robert D. McFadden, "Owner of Rangers and Knicks Repeats Pledge to Keep Them in the City," *New York Times*, January 9, 1984.

6. Sam Goldaper, "Knicks' Walker Is Impressive," *New York Times*, November 14, 1983.

7. Ira Berkow, "Williams Makes a New Start with Knicks," *New York Times*, October 28, 1983.

8. Harvey Araton, "Williams's Star Shined in Knicks Guard Tandem," *New York Times*, March 22, 2013.

9. Charley Rosen, *Sugar: Micheal Ray Richardson, Eighties Excess, and the NBA* (Lincoln: University of Nebraska Press, 2018), 58.

10. Rosen, *Sugar*, 71.

11. Rosen, *Sugar*, 71, 73, 132.

12. Frank Isola, "Clear Sailin' Sugar Finds Life and Hoops Sweet at Last," (NY) *Daily News*, February 14, 2000.

13. Harvey Araton, *Crashing the Borders: How Basketball Won the World and Lost Its Soul at Home* (New York: Free Press, 2005), 13; Rosen, *Sugar*, 172.

14. Joshua Mendelsohn, *The Cap: How Larry Fleisher and David Stern Built the Modern NBA* (Lincoln: University of Nebraska Press, 2020), 297.

15. Pete Croatto, *From Hang Time to Prime Time: Business, Entertainment, and the Birth of the Modern-Day NBA* (New York: Atria Books, 2020), 166.

16. Lawrence K. Altman, "Rare Cancer Seen in 41 Homosexuals," *New York Times*, July 3, 1981.

17. Tom Fitzsimmons, "LGBTQ History Month: The Early Days of America's AIDS Crisis," NBC News, October 15, 2018, https://www.nbcnews.com/feature/nbc-out/lgbtq-history-month-early-days-america-s-aids-crisis-n919701.

18. "Mayor Edward Koch Papers: Selected Documents: Volume I: AIDS," prepared by Steven A. Levine and Marcos Tejeda, LaGuardia Community College/CUNY, LaGuardia and Wagner Archives, http://www.laguardiawagnerarchive.lagcc.cuny.edu/FILES_DOC/Koch_FILES/HIGHLIGHTS/Koch_and_Aids.pdf.

19. David France, "Ed Koch and the AIDS Crisis: His Greatest Failure," *New York Intelligencer*, February 1, 2013.

20. Jonathan Soffer, *Ed Koch and the Rebuilding of New York City* (New York: Columbia University Press, 2010), 8.

21. *New York Knicks 1983–84 Official Guide and Record Book*, ed. John Hewig (New York: New York Knickerbockers, 1983), 34.

22. Sam Goldaper, "Robinson Maturity Is Helping Knicks," *New York Times*, October 31, 1981.

23. UPI, "Macklin Getting Hate Mail over Comment on Reagan," *New York Times*, April 18, 1981.

24. Rudy Macklin discussion with the author, November 2016.

25. Kevin Kernan, "Opening Night Raves!" *New York Post*, October 28, 1983.

26. Kevin Kernan, "Knicks: Never a Dull Moment," *New York Post*, October 31, 1983.

27. Roy S. Johnson, "Knicks' 2d Team in Slump," *New York Times*, December 11, 1983.

28. New York Knicks, "#NYK70 Presented by Chase: Remembering '84," YouTube, March 29, 2017, https://www.youtube.com/watch?v=ZMkTsNWmQhE&ab_channel=New YorkKnicks.

29. Harvey Araton, "Knicks Top Spurs as King Gets 50," (NY) *Daily News*, February 1, 1984.

30. Roy S. Johnson, "King's Scoring Defies Knicks' System," *New York Times*, February 3, 1984.

31. Kevin Kernan, "King of the Road," *New York Post*, February 1, 1984; Harvey Araton, "King's '50' Gems Are Crowd Pleasing," (NY) *Daily News*, February 3, 1984.

32. Roy S. Johnson, "King Gets 2d Straight 50–Point Game; Knicks Win," *New York Times*, February 2, 1984.

33. New York Knicks, "#NYK70 Presented by Chase: Remembering '84."

34. Kevin Kernan, "Fantastic 50's," *New York Post*, February 2, 1984.

35. Kernan, "Fantastic 50's."

36. Kevin Kernan, "Knicks Revel in King's 50–50," *New York Post*, February 3, 1984.

37. Kernan, "Fantastic 50's."

38. Bruce Newman, "It Was a 50–50 Proposition," *Sports Illustrated*, February 13, 1984.

39. Bert Rosenthal, "Bernard King: The Knicks' Magnificent Kingpin," *Basketball Digest*, January 1985, 17–21.

40. Phil Pepe, "King Inspiration on or off Court," (NY) *Daily News*, February 3, 1984.

41. David Davis, "Marvin, Marvin," in *Basketball in America: From the Playgrounds to Jordan's Game and Beyond*, ed. Bob Batchelor (New York: Haworth Press, 2005), 43.

42. Croatto, *From Hang Time to Prime Time*, 191.

43. Shea Serrano, *The Rap Year Book: The Most Important Rap Song from Every Year since 1979* (New York: Abrams Image, 2015), 18.

44. Reiland Rebaka, *The Hip Hop Movement: From R&B and the Civil Rights Movement to Rap and the Hip Hop Generation* (Lanham, MA: Lexington Books, 2013), 84.

45. Todd Boyd, *Young, Black, Rich, and Famous: The Rise of the NBA, the Hip Hop Invasion and the Transformation of American Culture* (New York: Doubleday, 2003), 97.

46. Sam Goldaper, "Knicks Defeat Jazz, 114–105," *New York Times*, March 11, 1984.

47. Bernard King and Jerome Preisler, *Game Face: A Lifetime of Hard-Earned Lessons on and off the Basketball Court* (Cambridge, MA: Da Capo Press, 2017), 239.

48. Harvey Araton, "Knicks Rally, 94–93," (NY) *Daily News*, April 18, 1984.

49. Dave Anderson, "An Easter Sermon in Sneakers," *New York Times*, April 22, 1984; Harvey Araton, "Knicks Stumble," (NY) *Daily News*, April 20, 1984.

50. Charlie Vincent, "Bernard King: He's a New Man, on the Playing Court, and Off," *Sporting News*, April 30, 1984.

51. Bruce Newman, "Hero of a Showdown in Motown," *Sports Illustrated*, May 7, 1984.

52. Newman, "Hero of a Showdown."

53. "Best moments in Joe Louis Arena History: No. 10," *Detroit Free Press*, March 29, 2017.

54. New York Knicks, "#NYK70 Presented by Chase: Remembering '84"; Rory Sparrow (retired player) in discussion with the author, February 2020.

55. King and Preisler, *Game Face*, 244; 191

56. "Best Moments in Joe Louis Arena History: No. 10."

57. Sally Barnes, "To the Beat, Y'All: Breaking Is Hard to Do," *Village Voice*, April 22, 1981.

58. Israel, dir., *The Freshest Kids* (Los Angeles: QD3 Entertainment, 2002).

59. Kevin Kernan, "Frontcourt Massacres Hubie's troops," *New York Post*, April 30, 1984; Harvey Araton, "Knicks Defeat Celts, 118–113," (NY) *Daily News*, May 7, 1984; Sam Goldaper, "Celtics Romp by 110–92," *New York Times*, April 30, 1984.

60. Kernan, "Frontcourt Massacres Hubie's Troops."

61. Goldaper, "Celtics Romp by 110–92."

62. Harvey Araton, "Knicks Trail 2–0, on 116–102 loss," (NY) *Daily News*, May 3, 1984.

63. Dennis D'Agostino, *Garden Glory: An Oral History of the New York Knicks* (Chicago: Triumph Books, 2003), 180.

64. Kevin Kernan, "Bird's 37 Powers Celts past Knicks," *New York Post*, May 3, 1984.

65. Sam Goldaper, "Knicks Must Reshuffle Lineup," *New York Times*, May 2, 1984.

66. King and Preisler, *Game Face*, 253.

67. Harvey Araton, "Knick-Celtic Battle of Words Hit Court," (NY) *Daily News*, May 9, 1984.

68. Alan Hahn, *100 Things Knicks Fans Should Know and Do before They Die* (Chicago: Triumph Books, 2012), 252.

69. Kevin Kernan, "King, Knicks Crown Celtics," *New York Post*, May 7, 1984.

70. Peter Vecsey, "Back from the Dead," *New York Post*, May 7, 1984.

71. Kevin Kernan, "Boston Massacre," *New York Post*, May 10, 1984; Harvey Araton, "Knicks Battered," (NY) *Daily News*, May 10, 1984.

72. Phil Pepe, "Ainge: I Wasn't Trying to Hurt Walker," (NY) *Daily News*, May 10, 1984.

73. Sam Goldaper, "Celtics Trounce Knicks and Lead Series by 3–2," *New York Times*, May 10, 1984.

74. Kernan, "Boston Massacre."

75. Harvey Araton, "It Could Be Last Stand for Knicks," (NY) *Daily News*, May 11, 1984.

76. "16 Knicks, Celtics Fined," *New York Times*, May 16, 1984.

77. Kevin Kernan, "Knicks Brace for Blood Bath in Do-or-Die Battle vs Celts," *New York Post*, May 11, 1984.

78. Harvey Araton, "Knicks Stay Alive," (NY) *Daily News*, May 12, 1984.

79. Larry Bird, *Drive: The Story of My Life* (New York: Bantam, 1990), 127.

80. Paul Weedell, "King Claims Burden in 7th Game on Celts," (NY) *Daily News*, May 12, 1984.

81. Hewig discussion with author.

82. Bird, *Drive*, 127.

83. Sam Goldaper, "39 Points by Bird Make Difference," *New York Times*, May 14, 1984.

84. Kevin Kernan, "Bird's Brilliant Show Leaves Knicks in Awe," *New York Post*, May 14, 1984.

10. The Frozen Envelope

1. Ronin Ro, *Raising Hell: The Reign, Ruin, and Redemption of Run-D.M.C. and Jam Master Jay* (New York: Amistad, 2005).

2. Jim Fricke and Charlie Ahearn, *Yes Yes Y'all: The Experience Music Project Oral History of Hip-Hop's First Decade* (Boston: Da Capo Press, 2002), 328.

3. Todd Boyd, *Young, Black, Rich, and Famous: The Rise of the NBA, the Hip Hop Invasion and the Transformation of American Culture* (New York: Doubleday, 2003), 97.

4. Bob Hohler, "Desperate Times," *Boston Globe*, July 2, 2010.

5. Kevin Kernan, "Knicks Bomb on Draft Day," *New York Post*, June 20, 1984.

6. Sam Goldaper, "Knicks Seek Help; Decisions Looming," *New York Times*, May 15, 1984.

7. Harvey Araton, "What Next, Knicks?" (NY) *Daily News*, May 15, 1984. Waiving a player resulted in 50 percent of that player's salary being applied to the salary cap.

8. Sam Goldaper, "Knicks Seek Help; Decisions Looming," *New York Times*, May 15, 1984.

9. Sam Goldaper, "Knicks Moving to Acquire Paxson," *New York Times*, October 12, 1984.

10. Mel Lowell discussion with the author, March 2020.

11. Eileen Putnam, "Refurbished Statue of Liberty Reopened to Public," APNews, July 5, 1986, accessed April 9, 2021, https://apnews.com/article/a4f6246fbae244778d89e45970aba9b1.

12. Frank Litsky, "Cartwright Injures Foot, May Miss Knick Opener," *New York Times*, September 26, 1984.

13. Armen Keteyian, Harvey Araton, and Martin F. Dardis, *Money Players: Days and Nights Inside the New NBA* (New York: Pocket Books, 1997), 10.

14. Sam Goldaper, "Knicks' Webster Hospitalized," *New York Times*, October 3, 1984.

15. Sam Goldaper, "King Gets 34 in Knicks Romp," *New York Times*, October 28, 1984.

16. Mike Weber, "Will Knicks Dump Truck?," *Sporting News*, November 19, 1984.

17. Filip Bondy, "Off and Running: The NBA Preview," *Basketball Digest*, November 1984, 46.

18. Sam Goldaper, "Record 52 by King Help Knicks Win," *New York Times*, November 25, 1984.

19. Kevin Kernan, "King of Kings," *New York Post*, December 26, 1984.

20. Kernan, "King of Kings."

21. Sam Goldaper, "Nets 120 Knicks 114: King Gets 60, but Knicks Lose," *New York Times*, December 26, 1984.

22. Kernan, "King of Kings."

23. "Hawks Romp; King Scores 36," *New York Times*, December 27, 1984.

24. Bert Rosenthal, "Bernard King: The Knicks' Magnificent Kingpin," *Basketball Digest*, January 1985, 19.

25. Sam Goldaper, "Knicks Lose 6th Straight: Pistons 105, Knicks 89," *New York Times*, January 18, 1985.

26. Bernard King and Jerome Preisler, *Game Face: A Lifetime of Hard-Earned Lessons on and off the Basketball Court* (Cambridge, MA: Da Capo Press, 2017), 262.

27. Dennis D'Agostino, *Garden Glory: An Oral History of the New York Knicks* (Chicago: Triumph Books, 2003), 184.

28. Hubie Brown discussion with the author, February 2020.

29. "King Injured as Knicks Lose," *New York Times*, March 24, 1985.

30. King and Preisler, *Game Face*, 269.

31. "King Season in Doubt," *New York Post*, March 25, 1985.

32. King and Preisler, *Game Face*, 265.

33. Tom Fitzgerald, "Klay Thompson Injury: How NBA Players Have Returned after Torn ACL," *San Francisco Chronicle*, June 15, 2019.

34. Bryan Burwell, "Knicks' Brown Suffers Another Long Knight," (NY) *Daily News*, April 14, 1985.

35. Sam Goldaper, "Knicks View Draft as Vital," *New York Times*, April 4, 1985.

36. Paul Knepper, *The Knicks of the Nineties: Ewing, Oakley, Starks and the Brawlers That Almost Won It All* (Jefferson, NC: McFarland, 2020), 15.

37. Lyle Spencer, "Lucky Knicks Hit the Jackpot," *New York Post*, May 13, 1985; Dave Anderson, "God Is a Knick Fan," *New York Times*, May 13, 1985.

38. Anderson, "God Is a Knick Fan."

39. Lyle Spencer, "Stern: We Took Every Precaution," *New York Post*, May 13, 1985.

40. Chris Ballard, "The Ewing Conspiracy," *Sports Illustrated*, May 2015, www.si.com/longform/2015/1985/ewing/index.html.

41. Basketball John, "The Fixed 1985 NBA Lottery," YouTube, https://www.youtube.com/watch?v=bX1kMlG8c7Y&ab_channel=BasketballJohn.

42. Ballard, "The Ewing Conspiracy."

43. Elliott Kalb, *The 25 Greatest Sports Conspiracy Theories of All-Time: Ranking Sports' Most Notorious Fixes, Cover-Ups, and Scandals* (Chicago: Skyhorse Publishing, 2007), 39.

44. Peter Vecsey, "Pat Will Need Plenty of Help," *New York Post*, May 13, 1985.

45. Kevin Kernan, "Celts Joke: 'It Was Rigged'," *New York Post*, May 13, 1985.

46. Lyle Spencer, "Lucky Knicks Hit the Jackpot," *New York Post*, May 13, 1985.

47. Thomas Rogers, "Knicks Fans Already Excited about Ewing," *New York Times*, May 13, 1985.

48. Spencer, "Lucky Knicks Hit the Jackpot."

49. Harvey Araton, "Fixed Ideas Come to Life," (NY) *Daily News*, May 15, 1985."

50. Rogers, "Knicks Fans Already Excited."

51. Jack McCallum, "The Year of Ewing," *Sports Illustrated*, October 28, 1985, 44–50.

52. Spike Lee and Ralph Wiley, *Best Seat in the House: A Basketball Memoir* (New York: Crown Publishers, 1997), 106.

53. Quoted in Chris Herring, *Blood in the Garden: The Flagrant History of the 1990s New York Knicks* (New York: Atria Books, 2022), 122.

54. Lee and Wiley, *Best Seat in the House*, 132.

55. Walter Leavy, "Patrick Ewing: Can This Man Save the Knicks?" *Ebony*, February 1986, 59–62.

Epilogue

1. Kevin Kernan, "Big Apple Welcomes Ewing," *New York Post*, June 18, 1985.

2. Filip Bondy, "Mullin's Stock Up with Golden State," *New York Daily News*, June 18, 1985.

3. Sam Goldaper, "Ewing Signs Pact Worth Up to $30 Million," *New York Times*, September 19, 1985.

4. Sam Goldaper, "King Camp Scores . . . with Youngsters," *New York Times*, August 13, 1985.

5. George Vecsey, "King Is off Board," *New York Times*, September 29, 1985.

6. Roy S. Johnson, "Knicks Sign Cartwright to 6-Year Pact," *New York Times*, October 1, 1985.

7. Roy S. Johnson, "Two Knicks Hurt, Ewing Fouls Out in Loss to Rockets," *New York Times*, October 13, 1985.

8. Johnson, "Two Knicks Hurt."

9. Kevin Kernan, "Ewing Burning over $1500 fine," *New York Post*, October 24, 1985.

10. Kevin Kernan, "Knicks Defend Embattled Ewing," *New York Post*, October 21, 1985.

11. Kevin Kernan, "Ewing the Best of Bumper Rookie Crop," *Sporting News*, October 21, 1985.

12. Charley Rosen, *Sugar: Micheal Ray Richardson, Eighties Excess, and the NBA* (Lincoln: University of Nebraska Press, 2018), 36.

13. Sam Goldaper, "Knick Fans Show Their Impatience," *New York Times*, December 14, 1985.

14. George Vecsey, "King Vows Return: 'I'm a Fighter,'" *New York Times*, December 17, 1985.

15. Quoted in Chris Herring, *Blood in the Garden: The Flagrant History of the 1990s New York Knicks* (New York: Atria Books, 2022), 11.

16. Brendan Malone discussion with the author, December 2016.

17. Dennis D'Agostino, *Garden Glory: An Oral History of the New York Knicks* (Chicago: Triumph Books, 2003), 188.

18. Malone discussion with author.

19. Darrell Walker discussion with the author, December 2016.

20. Herring, *Blood in the Garden*, 11.

21. Harvey Araton, *Our Last Season: A Writer, a Fan, a Friendship* (New York: Penguin Press, 2020), 88.

22. George J. Lankevich, *New York City: A Short History* (New York: New York University Press, 2002), 234–35.

23. Jonathan Soffer, *Ed Koch and the Rebuilding of New York City* (New York: Columbia University Press, 2010), 388–89.

24. Soffer, *Ed Koch and the Rebuilding of New York City*, 403.

25. Araton, *Our Last Season*, 87.

26. Bernard King and Jerome Preisler, *Game Face: A Lifetime of Hard-Earned Lessons On and Off the Basketball Court* (Cambridge, MA: Da Capo Press, 2017), 281.

27. King and Preisler, *Game Face*, 283.

28. Ira Berkow, "Bernard King of the Bullets," *New York Times*, November 3, 1987.

29. Paul Knepper, *The Knicks of the Nineties: Ewing, Oakley, Starks and the Brawlers That Almost Won It All* (Jefferson, NC: McFarland, 2020), 13.

30. Torsten Ingvaldsen, "For Run-D.M.C., Authenticity Is Everything," *Hypebeast*, October 29, 2019, https://hypebeast.com/2019/10/run-dmc-darryl-mcdaniels-jbl-fest-interview.

31. Zac Dubasik, "This History of Run-D.M.C. and Adidas as Told by D.M.C.," *Sole Collector*, March 11, 2014, https://solecollector.com/news/2014/03/this-history-of-run-d-m-c-and-adidas-as-told-by-d-m-c.

32. Richard Sandomir, "Harthorne Wingo, 1970s Knick with Much-Chanted Name, Dies at 73," *New York Times*, January 26, 2021.

33. Knepper, *The Knicks of the Nineties*, 43.

BIBLIOGRAPHY

Abdul-Jabbar, Kareem. *Coach Wooden and Me: Our 50-Year Friendship On and Off the Court*. New York: Grand Central Publishing, 2017.

Abrams, Jonathan. *The Come Up: An Oral History of the Rise of Hip-Hop*. New York: Random House, 2022.

Allen, Oliver. *New York, New York: A History of the World's Most Exhilarating and Challenging City*. New York: Atheneum, 1990.

Anderson, Carol. *White Rage: The Unspoken Truth of Our Racial Divide*. New York: Bloomsbury, 2016.

Araton, Harvey. *Crashing the Borders: How Basketball Won the World and Lost Its Soul at Home*. New York: Free Press, 2005.

Araton, Harvey. *Our Last Season: A Writer, a Fan, a Friendship*. New York: Penguin Press, 2020.

Araton, Harvey. *When the Garden Was Eden: Clyde, the Captain, Dollar Bill, and the Glory Days of the New York Knicks*. New York: Harper, 2011.

Axthelm, Pete. *The City Game: Basketball in New York from the World Champion Knicks to the World of the Playgrounds*. New York: Harper's Magazine Press, 1970.

Bailey, Beth, and David Farber, eds. *America in the Seventies*. Lawrence: University Press of Kansas, 2004.

Batchelor, Bob, ed. *Basketball in America: From the Playgrounds to Jordan's Game and Beyond*. New York: Haworth Press, 2005.

Bell, Marty. *The Legend of Dr. J*. New York: Coward, McCann and Geoghegan, 1975.

Berman, Marshall, and Brian Berger, eds. *New York Calling: From Blackout to Bloomberg*. New York: Reaktion Books, 2007.

Bird, Larry. *Drive: The Story of My Life*. New York: Bantam, 1990.

Boyd, Todd. *Young, Black, Rich, and Famous: The Rise of the NBA, the Hip Hop Invasion and the Transformation of American Culture*. New York: Doubleday, 2003.

Bradley, Ernestine. *The Way Home: A German Childhood, an American Life*. New York: Pantheon Books, 2005.

Burke, Michael. *Outrageous Good Fortune*. Boston: Little, Brown, 1984.

Chang, Jeff. *Can't Stop Won't Stop: A History of the Hip-Hop Generation*. New York: St. Martin's Press, 2005.

Chronopoulos, Themis. *Spatial Regulation in New York City: From Urban Renewal to Zero Tolerance*. New York: Routledge, 2011.

Cobb, William Jelani. *To the Break of Dawn: A Freestyle on the Hip Hop Aesthetic*. New York: New York University Press, 2007.

Croatto, Pete. *From Hang Time to Prime Time: Business, Entertainment, and the Birth of the Modern-Day NBA*. New York: Atria Books, 2020.

D'Agostino, Dennis. *Garden Glory: An Oral History of the New York Knicks*. Chicago: Triumph Books, 2003.

Delany, Samuel R. *Times Square Red, Times Square Blue*. New York: New York University Press, 1999.

Durso, Joseph. *Madison Square Garden: 100 Years of History*. New York: Simon and Schuster, 1979.

Echols, Alice. *Hot Stuff: Disco and the Remaking of American Culture*. New York: W.W. Norton, 2010.

Erving, Julius, and Karl Taro Greenfeld. *Dr. J: The Autobiography*. New York: Harper, 2013.

Fishman, Marv, with Tracy Dodds. *Bucking the Odds: The Birth of the Milwaukee Bucks*. Milwaukee: Raintree, 1978.

Forman, Murray, and Mark Anthony Neal, eds. *That's the Joint! The Hip-Hop Studies Reader*. New York: Routledge, 2004.

Frazier, Walt, and Ira Berkow. *Rockin' Steady: A Guide to Basketball and Cool*. New York: Warner Paperback Library, 1974.

Frazier, Walt, with Dan Markowitz. *The Game within the Game*. New York: Hyperion, 2006.

Frazier, Walt, with Neil Offen. *Walt Frazier: One Magic Season and a Basketball Life*. New York: Crown, 1988.

Fricke, Jim, and Charlie Ahearn. *Yes Yes Y'all: The Experience Music Project Oral History of Hip-Hop's First Decade*. Boston: Da Capo Press, 2002.

Fury, Shawn. *Rise and Fire: The Origins, Science, and Evolution of the Jump Shot—and How It Transformed Basketball Forever*. New York: Flatiron Books, 2016.

George, Nelson. *Elevating the Game: Black Men and Basketball*. New York: Harper Collins, 1992.

Goodman, James. *Blackout*. New York: North Point Press, 2003.

Hager, Steve. *Hip Hop: The Illustrated History of Break Dancing, Rap Music, and Graffiti*. New York: St. Martin's Press, 1984.

Hahn, Alan. *100 Things Knicks Fans Should Know and Do before They Die*. Chicago: Triumph Books, 2012.

Halberstam, David. *Breaks of the Game*. New York: Alfred A. Knopf, 1981.

Haywood, Spencer, with Scott Ostler. *Spencer Haywood: The Rise, the Fall, the Recovery*. New York: Amistad, 1992.

Hermes, Will. *Love Goes to Buildings on Fire: Five Years in New York That Changed Music Forever*. New York: Faber and Faber, 2011.

Herring, Chris. *Blood in the Garden: The Flagrant History of the 1990s New York Knicks*. New York: Atria Books, 2022.

Hewig, John, ed. *New York Knicks 1983–84 Official Guide and Record Book*. New York: New York Knickerbockers, 1983.

Holzman, Red, and Harvey Frommer. *Red on Red*. New York: Bantam Books, 1987.

Israel, dir. *The Freshest Kids*. DVD. Los Angeles: QD3 Entertainment, 2002.

Jackson, Phil, and Hugh Delehanty. *Eleven Rings: The Soul of Success*. New York: Penguin Press, 2013.

Jackson, Phil, and Charley Rosen. *More than a Game*. New York: Seven Stories Press, 2001.

Kalb, Elliott. *The 25 Greatest Sports Conspiracy Theories of All-Time: Ranking Sports' Most Notorious Fixes, Cover-Ups, and Scandals*. Chicago: Skyhorse Publishing, 2007.

Kalinsky, George, Phil Berger, and Dennis D'Agostino. *The New York Knicks: The Official Fiftieth Anniversary Celebration*. New York: IDG, 1996.

Kalinsky, George, and Pete Hamill. *Garden of Dreams: Madison Square Garden, 125 Years*. New York: Stewart, Tabori & Chang, 2004.

Keteyian, Armen, Harvey Araton, and Martin F. Dardis. *Money Players: Days and Nights inside the New NBA*. New York: Pocket Books, 1997.

King, Bernard, and Jerome Preisler. *Game Face: A Lifetime of Hard-Earned Lessons on and off the Basketball Court*. Cambridge, MA: Da Capo Press, 2017.

Kitwana, Bakari. *Why White Kids Love Hip Hop: Wankstas, Wiggers, Wannabes, and the New Reality of Race in America*. New York: Civitas Books, 2006.

Knepper, Paul. *The Knicks of the Nineties: Ewing, Oakley, Starks and the Brawlers That Almost Won It All*. Jefferson, NC: McFarland, 2020.

Lader, Martin, and Joe Carnicelli, eds. *Pro Basketball Guide 1973*. New York: Cord Sportfacts, 1972.

Lane, Jeffrey. *Under the Boards: The Cultural Revolution in Basketball*. Lincoln: University of Nebraska Press, 2007.

Lankevich, George J. *New York City: A Short History*. New York: New York University Press, 2002.

Lawrence, Tim. *Life and Death on the New York Dance Floor, 1980–1983*. Durham: Duke University Press, 2016.

Lee, Spike, and Ralph Wiley. *Best Seat in the House: A Basketball Memoir*. New York: Crown, 1997.

Libby, Bill, and Spencer Haywood. *Stand Up for Something: The Spencer Haywood Story*. New York: Grosset & Dunlap, 1972.

L'Official, Peter. *Urban Legends: The South Bronx in Representation and Ruin*. Cambridge, MA: Harvard University Press, 2020.

London, Herbert. *The Broken Apple: New York City in the 1980s*. New Brunswick, NJ: Transaction Publishers, 1989.

Mahler, Jonathan. *The Bronx Is Burning: 1977, Baseball, Politics, and the Battle for the Soul of the City*. New York: Picador, 2005.

Mallozzi, Vincent M. *Asphalt Gods: An Oral History of the Rucker Tournament*. New York: Doubleday, 2003.

McLeod, Kembrew, and Peter DiCola. *Creative License: The Law and Culture of Digital Sampling*. Durham: Duke University Press, 2011.

Mendelsohn, Joshua. *The Cap: How Larry Fleisher and David Stern Built the Modern NBA*. Lincoln: University of Nebraska Press, 2020.

Miller, Ivor L. *Aerosol Kingdom: Subway Painters of New York City*. Jackson: University Press of Mississippi, 2012.

Monroe, Earl, with Quincy Troupe. *Earl the Pearl: My Story*. New York: Rodale, 2013.

O'Brien, Lawrence F. *No Final Victories: A Life in Politics—from John F. Kennedy to Watergate*. New York: Doubleday, 1974.

Ogbar, Jeffrey O. G. *Hip-Hop Revolution: The Culture and Politics of Rap*. Lawrence: University Press of Kansas, 2007.

Ogg, Alex, with David Upshal. *The Hip Hop Years: A History of Rap*. New York: Fromm International, 2001.

Pearlman, Jeff. *Showtime: Magic, Kareem, Riley, and the Los Angeles Lakers Dynasty of the 1980s*. New York: Gotham Books, 2014.

Phillips-Fein, Kim. *Fear City: New York's Fiscal Crisis and the Rise of Austerity Politics*. New York: Metropolitan Books, 2017.

Rebaka, Reiland. *The Hip Hop Movement: From R&B and the Civil Rights Movement to Rap and the Hip Hop Generation*. Lanham, MA: Lexington Books, 2013.

Reed, Willis, with Phil Pepe. *A View from the Rim: Willis Reed on Basketball*. Philadelphia: J. B. Lippincott, 1971.

Reitano, Joanne. *The Restless City: A Short History of New York from Colonial Times to the Present*. New York: Routledge, 2010.

Rieder, Jonathan. *Canarsie: The Jews and Italians of Brooklyn against Liberalism*. Cambridge, MA: Harvard University Press, 1985.

Ro, Ronin. *Raising Hell: The Reign, Ruin, and Redemption of Run-D.M.C. and Jam Master Jay*. New York: Amistad, 2005.

Rose, Tricia. *Black Noise: Rap Music and Black Culture in Contemporary America*. Hanover, NH: Wesleyan University Press, 1994.

Rosen, Charley. *God, Man, and Basketball Jones: The Thinking Fan's Guide to Professional Basketball*. New York: Holt, Rinehart and Winston, 1979.

Rosen, Charley. *Sugar: Micheal Ray Richardson, Eighties Excess, and the NBA*. Lincoln: University of Nebraska Press, 2018.

Ryan, Bob. *Celtic Pride: The Rebuilding of Boston's World Championship Basketball Team*. Boston: Little, Brown, 1975.

Sanchez, Ivan, and Luis "DJ Disco Wiz" Cedeño. *It's Just Begun: The Epic Journey of DJ Disco Wiz, Hip Hop's First Latino DJ*. Brooklyn: PowerHouse books, 2009.

Schloss, Joseph G. *Foundation: B-Boys, B-Girls, and Hip-Hop Culture in New York*. New York: Oxford University Press, 2009.

Serrano, Shea. *The Rap Year Book: The Most Important Rap Song from Every Year since 1979*. New York: Abrams Image, 2015.

Smith, Neil, and Don Mitchell, eds. *Revolting New York: How 400 Years of Riot, Rebellion, Uprising, and Revolution Shaped a City*. Athens: University of Georgia Press, 2018.

Soffer, Jonathan. *Ed Koch and the Rebuilding of New York City*. New York: Columbia University Press, 2010.

Sokol, Jason. *All Eyes Are upon Us: Race and Politics from Boston to Brooklyn: The Conflicted Soul of the Northeast*. New York: Basic Books, 2014.

Spears, Marc J., and Gary Washburn. *The Spencer Haywood Rule: Battles, Basketball, and the Making of an American Iconoclast*. Chicago: Triumph Books, 2020.

Tannenbaum, Allan. *New York in the 70s*. New York: Overlook Duckworth, 2011.

Telander, Rick. *Heaven Is a Playground*. 4th ed. New York: Sports Publishing, 2013.

Toop, David. *Rap Attack 3: African Rap to Global Hip Hop*. London: Serpent's Tail, 2000.

Tuohy, Brian. *Larceny Games: Sports Gambling, Game Fixing and the FBI*. Port Townsend, WA: Feral House, 2013.

Weinreb, Michael. *Bigger than the Game: Bo, Boz, the Punky QB, and How the '80s Created the Modern Athlete*. New York: Gotham Books, 2010.

Wielgus, Chuck, and Alexander Wolff. *The Back-In-Your-Face Guide to Pick-Up Basketball: A Have-Jump-Shot, Will-Travel Tour of America's Hoops Hotspots*. New York: Dodd Mead, 1986.

Wielgus, Chuck, and Alexander Wolff. *The In-Your-Face Basketball Book*. New York: Everest House, 1980.

Woodbine, Onaje X. O. *Black Gods of the Asphalt: Religion: Hip-Hop, and Street Basketball*. New York: Columbia University Press, 2016.

Zachter, Mort. *Red Holzman: The Life and Legacy of a Hall of Fame Basketball Coach*. New York: Sports Publishing, 2019.

INDEX

Page numbers in *italics* refer to illustrations.

Henderson, Gerald, 209
heroin, 96, 157–58
Hewig, John, 160–61, 166, 168, 192, 210–11, 264n14
high school basketball, 24, 82, 180–81. *See also* playground basketball
Hill, Bob, 235
Hillman, Darnell, 200
hip-hop, 6, 48–50, 56–57, 72, 79–81, 89, 105–8, 117, 123, 147, 149, 151–52, 155–56, 170–72, 200–201, 238; breaking and (*see* B-boy/B-girl dancing; dance battles); connections between basketball and, 3–4, 6, 42–43, 81–82, 106–8, 116–18, 179–80, *180*, 200–201, 237–40; emergence of, 4, 40–43, *56–57*, 239; mainstream consumption of, 6, 79–81, 116–17, 123–25, 149–52, 239; origin of term, 106; sneaker culture and, 108 (*see also* sneakers); white consumption of, 123–25, 150–52; youth culture and, 117, 150–51. *See also* deejays; rap music
Hollywood, DJ, 106
Holman, Nat, 37, 82
Holzman, Red: as Knicks coach (1967–77), 6, 12–13, 18, 20, 22–24, 33, 37, *44*, 48, 50–52, 58, 61, 64, 71; as Knicks coach (1978–82), 92–96, 101, 103–4, 114, 120–21, 127, 131, 134, 137–39, 141, 144–45, 149, 152–53, 155, 157, 160–61, 163, 166, 175, 185
Hosket, Bill, 12, 104
Houston Rockets, 19, 22, 24, *30*, 32, 89–91, 114, 129, 134, 157, 187, 199, 214, 217, 221, 224, 231
Howard, Ken, 136
Hunts Point-Crotona Park East, 57
Huston, Geoff, 112

Ice-T, 205
Iman (Zara Mohamed Abdulmajid), 38–39, 95, 157

Incredible Bongo Band, "Apache," 49, 80
Indiana Pacers, 9, 25, 40, 83, 114, 140, 176–77, 187, 217–19, 221–22, 226, 228, 233–34
In-Your-Face Basketball Book, 81, 88, 107–8
Irish, Ned, 21, 24, 160, 173, 181
Irvine, George, 219
Iverson, Allen, 238

Jackson, Mark, 236
Jackson, Phil, 83, 92, 185; coaching career, 5, 131, 166; as Knicks player, 9, 15, 28–29, 37, 39, 52, 63–65, 74
Jackson, Reggie, 61, 127, 147
James TOP, 56–57
jazz, 38, 95, 117
Jazzy Jay, 42
The Jeffersons, 105
Johnson, Dennis, 135, 162, 206
Johnson, George, 220
Johnson, Magic, 51, 82, 96, 99, 109, 115, 118, 130–31, 134–35, 150, 168, 176, 187, 195, 224, 230
Johnson, Vinnie, 214
Jones, Dwight, *30*
Jones, Sam, 162
Jordan, Michael, 159, 204, 217, 219, 225, 230
Judkins, Jeff, 119
Justine's (club), 130

Kansas City Kings (formerly, Kansas City–Omaha Kings), 23, 65, 83, 128, 138, 140, 142, 222, 226
Kasten, Stan, 226–27
Kauffman, Bob, 46
Kennedy, John F., 26, 132
Kennedy, Kevin, 127
Kennedy, Walter, 26, 45–46
Kenon, Larry, 135
Kentucky Colonels, 25, 166
King, Albert, 89, 182–83

New York Giants, 109, 136, 192
New York Jets, 5, 69, 192
New York Knicks: all-Black squad, 3, 6, 102–5, 109–12, 114, 119, 121, 126, 129, 145, 239; city life and, 72–73, 85–86; coaches, 5–6, 12, 89–93, 202 (*see also* Brown, Hubie; Holzman, Red; Reed, Willis); defense, 61, 177, 197; draft picks (*see* NBA draft); executives, 5–6, 103 (*see also* Burke, Mike; Cohen, Alan; DeBusschere, Dave; Donovan, Eddie; Werblin, Sonny); fans of (*see* fans); Knickerbocker logo, 112; NBA title wins (championships), 2, 9–11, 29, 41, 65, 82; ownership of, 68–70; practice schedules and locations, 66–67, 163, 174; season ticket sales, 28, 35, 43, 228; team colors, 112; training camps, 54, 64, 85, 128, 234–35; travel conditions, 70–71. *See also* Madison Square Garden; *individual players*
New York Nets, 11, 39–40, 53, 82, 167. *See also* New Jersey Nets
New York Rangers, 68–70, 89, 136, 192
New York Yankees, 6, 21, 57, 61, 127, 147
NFL (National Football League), 71, 187–88
Nichols, James, 74
NIT (National Invitational Tournament), 82, 84, 181
Nixon, Richard, 11, 13, 26
North American Soccer League (NASL), 34
Nuriddin, Jalal, 53

O'Brien, Larry, 26–28, 39, 53, 82, 105, 140, 169, 187–89; replaced as NBA commissioner, 194, 199
O'Brien, Pat, 226–27
Olajuwon, Akeem (later, Hakeem), 159, 214, 217, 224, 231
Old Timers' Game, 200
Olympic Games, 35, 204
Orr, Louis, 169–70, 177, 201, 220, 222–23

Pace University, 66–67
Parish, Robert, 98, 119, 126–27, 186, 206, 234, 255n93
Paulk, Charlie, 104
Paxson, John, 215
Pelé, 34–35, 143
Perkins, Sam, 159, 214, 219
PHASE 2 (graffiti artist), 17, 155
Philadelphia 76ers (Sixers), 22, 25, 27, 36, 48, 50, 68, 74–76, 91, 94, 103, 109, 120, 133–34, 141, 173–74, 177, 183–85, 189, 201, 215, 219, 221, 224
Philadelphia Eagles, 5, 133
Phoenix Suns, 18, 67, 161–62, 169, 175, 189–90, 193, 200, 206, 224
Pippen, Scottie, 235
Pitino, Rick, 169, 198, 202, 207, 214, 216, 222, 235–36
Plato's Retreat (club), 73
playground basketball, 43, 81, 87–89, *107, 180*, 181, 253n12; courts, 4, 107–8; hip-hop and, 42–43, 81–82, 106–8, 179 (*see also* dance battles; hip-hop). *See also* Rucker Park
Pollak, Bill, 173, 222
Porter, Howard, 18, 32
Portland Trail Blazers, 18, 52, 83, 139, 145, 174, 181, 214, 224
Power Memorial Academy, 24, 82, 181
Pretty Pearl Records, 116
Pryor, Richard, 158
Public Enemy, 80, 239
Public Schools Athletic League (PSAL), 181
Puma, 62–63, 108

Queens, 117–18, 123, 152, 238
Queensbridge, 149

race: cross-racial interaction, 123–25, 150–52; NBA and, 117, 150–51 (*see also* racial makeup of NBA). *See also* Black culture